Between Je

MARTIN HENGEL

Between Jesus and Paul

*Studies in the Earliest History
of Christianity*

Wipf and Stock Publishers
EUGENE, OREGON

Translated by John Bowden. The original articles appeared as follows:

1. 'Between Jesus and Paul' = 'Zwischen Jesus und Paulus'. *Zeitschrift für Theologie und Kirche* 72, 1975, pp. 151-206
2. 'Christology and New Testament Chronology' = 'Christologie und neutestamentliche Chronologie', in *Geschichte und Urchristentum. Festschrift O. Cullmann zum 70. Geburtstag*, Zurich and Tübingen 1972, pp. 43-67
3. 'The Origins of the Christian Mission' = 'Die Ursprünge der Christlichen Mission', *New Testament Studies* 18, 1971, pp. 15-38
4. ' "Christos" in Paul' = 'Erwägungen zum Sprachgebrauch von Χριστός bei Paulus und in der "vorpaulinischen" Überlieferung', in *Paul and Paulinism. Essays in Honour of C. K. Barrett*, edited by M. D. Hooker and S. G Wilson, SPCK 1982, English translation by kind permission of the publishers
5. 'Hymn and Christology', = 'Hymnus und Christologie', in *Wort in der Zeit. Festgabe für Karl Heinrich Rengstorf zum 75. Geburtstag*, Leiden 1980
6. 'Luke as Geographer and Historian' = 'Der Historiker Lukas und die Geographie Palästinas in der Apostelgeschichte', *ZDPV* 98, 1983

Wipf and Stock Publishers
199 West 8th Avenue, Suite 3
Eugene, Oregon 97401

Between Jesus and Paul
Studies in the Earliest History of Christianity
By Hengel, Martin
Copyright© January, 1983 by Hengel, Martin
ISBN: 1-59244-189-0
Publication date: March, 2003
Previously published by Fortress Press, January, 1983

VENERANDO ORDINI THEOLOGORUM
UNIVERSITATIS UPSALENSIS
ATQUE
VENERANDO ORDINI THEOLOGORUM
UNIVERSITATIS SANCTI ANDREAE
APUD SCOTOS
MAGNO THEOLOGIAE DOCTORIS HONORE ACCEPTO
HOC OPUSCULUM
GRATO ANIMO
DEDICAT
M. H.

Contents

Preface

The six studies in this volume translated into English by John Bowden come from the last twelve years. All of them – each in its own way and from a different perspective – deal with the theme which gives the title to the first of the articles: the decisive period of the primitive church 'Between Jesus and Paul'. Hence, too, the title of this book. It is concerned with the development of the Christian church from the earliest post-Easter community in Jerusalem to the world-wide mission of Paul the apostle. These fundamental first thirty years of earliest Christian history – fundamental in the deepest sense of the word – have been the special focal point of my research from about 1970. In them I have been able to draw on some of the results of earlier investigations into the historical and religious background in my books *Die Zeloten* and *Judaism and Hellenism*. Behind all these individual studies, connected by their one basic theme, is a wider plan to write a history of earliest Christianity and its christology. The collection made here does of course consist only of preliminary studies, fragments, which offer no more a partial and fragmentary view of the whole.

Whether I shall have the opportunity to carry out my plan is uncertain, since present-day pressures on teaching theology here in Germany hardly allow any time for real continuous research (which above all means reading source material). Nevertheless, I think that I have come some degree closer towards fulfilling my aim, and am reluctant to give up hope of that altogether. In these days such a goal has to be approached step by step.

The six studies here supplement my rather longer works which have appeared in book form: *The Son of God, The Atonement, Crucifixion* and *Acts and the History of Earliest Christianity*. Perhaps the attentive reader will also trace the inner – even theological – link which holds together these books the arguments of which are predominantly historical and philological.

Details of the articles included here, which I have worked over again before publication in English, appear on the copyright page.

The first article, 'Between Jesus and Paul', which sets out my programme, aims to shed as much light as possible on Luke's comments on the first Greek-speaking Jewish-Christian community in Jerusalem which proved to be of such decisive significance for the further course of the new 'messianic sect' of followers of Jesus. This was a tiny group, but it had a world-shaking effect because it was there for the first time that the new message was translated into Greek, the *lingua franca*.

The last article, 'Luke the Historian and the Geography of Palestine in the Acts of the Apostles', is a similar work, characterized by the same 'monograph' character and going into considerable philological and historical detail. It takes up a problem which has been much neglected in current scholarship and investigates the geographical details provided by the *auctor ad Theophilum* in his second book (cf. Acts 1.1). Was Luke really as completely ignorant of the geography of Palestine as 'radical-critical' scholars make out, or should we not make much more precise distinctions in his account – one might say, in a true historical critical fashion – if we are to understand Luke's work, which is far superior to that of most New Testament writers, as that of the first Christian historian? If we approach things in this way we can gain important insights into Luke's way of working which at the same time illuminate the history of earliest Christianity between 30 and 60 and compel us to revise some of our favourite presumptions.

The article 'Christology and New Testament Chronology' shows the difficulties which arise for the predominant way of approaching the history of the Christian tradition when the decisive developments in the early period 'between Jesus and Paul' are compressed into an amazingly short space of time, so that the usual chronological distinctions (early, late, very late tradition, and so on) and attributions to different contrasting communities often become questionable. Early historical research here has neglected the special importance of the Greek-speaking Jewish-Christian community which began in Jerusalem itself, and given too much weight to allegedly pagan 'Hellenistic syncretistic influences'.

'The Origins of the Christian Mission' begins with the secular non-Christian evidence for the amazing success of Christian propaganda and then turns to the phenomenon of the Pauline mission, which is unique in the history of ancient religion and can only be understood against the background of the eschatological self-understanding of the apostle. It goes on to consider the question of the Hellenist mission and the earliest community in Jerusalem and attempts to show that the ultimate stimulus for the earliest Christian mission came from Jesus himself, as the 'primal missionary'.

'Christos in Paul' argues that the fact that Paul already uses the word Christ, his most frequent 'christological term', only as a proper name and no longer as a title is not a case of thoughtless assimilation to a pre-Pauline 'Gentile Christian' terminology, but is a sign that this title had become indissolubly fused with the name Jesus, a fusion in which Paul never forgot the saving significance of the name in connection with the cross of Christ. The transformation of the title 'messiah' into a name goes back to the pre-Pauline community in Jerusalem and expressed among other things the offensive fact that the eschatological bringer of salvation was none other than the crucified Jesus of Nazareth.

'Hymns and Christology' is a condensation of a longer study which sadly has yet to be finished, about the intrinsic connection between the development of christology and the singing of hymns which in earliest Christian worship was regarded as a particularly important testimony to the work of the Spirit and which was already influential in the earliest community as a medium of developing christological conceptions. The starting point here was provided by the 'messianic' psalms of the Old Testament psalter like Pss. 110; 2; 22; 118, etc. Thus from the beginning eschatological enthusiasm and christological hymns were inseparably connected.

For all the multiplicity brought about by the work of the Spirit, I would still see earliest Christianity as an intrinsically connected and in essentials quite amazingly coherent movement which developed out of the activity of Jesus and the 'saving event' of his crucifixion and resurrection. A link with the earthly and exalted Lord and the eschatological gift of the Spirit remained the bond which held together all the Christian groups which we find within the New Testament (cf. e.g. I Cor. 15.11), though in individual cases the accents may have been placed differently. Anyone who wants to reduce earliest Christianity to often quite different and indeed unconnected 'lines of development' can no longer explain why the church in the second century remained a unity despite all the deviations and how the New Testament canon could come into being. In their view the church should have fallen apart into countless groups.

The disciples who had seen the risen Jesus and believed themselves to possess the promised spirit of the end time believed – to some degree like Jesus himself – that the kingdom of God had already dawned and that the end-event had been inaugurated by the death and resurrection of Jesus. This assurance produced something like a 'spiritual explosion' and at the same time brought about a profound transformation in every aspect of the lives of those whom it affected. One of the most obvious and momentous consequences of this was the active mission first in Judaism and then soon beyond its bounds, something that in this form is quite unparalleled in the ancient world. So we can fully endorse Wellhausen's remark 'Enthusiasm gave birth to Christianity' (*Einleitung in die ersten drei Evangelien*, ²1911,150). However, I would differ from him in that I would not limit this enthusiasm to the disciples but would connect it with Jesus' proclamation of the kingdom of God, which was also without analogy, which first laid the foundation for the Jesus movement. The beatitudes praising the poor, the hungry and those who weep; the commands not to be anxious and to love one's enemies, the saying about 'faith which moves mountains' and indeed Luke 10.18, 'I saw Satan fallen from heaven like lightning', or the saying about revelation in Luke 10.21f. (Matt. 11.25–27) can only be explained on the basis of the eschatological 'enthusiasm' of Jesus, i.e. his unique messianic assurance of God, his awareness that with his activity the kingdom of God was itself dawning. It is a coincidence that the Synoptic Gospels describe Jesus, the 'Son of God' and 'Messiah', as the exemplary eschatological 'bearer of the Spirit'. This is the same Spirit which after Easter makes the disciples the Messiah's heralds and whose work we find twenty years later in the first literary evidence from earliest Christianity, the letters of Paul, 'the apostle of Jesus Christ'. From the beginning this spirit could express itself in ecstatic phenomena and 'miracles' which today we might even find offensive. That was already the case with Jesus himself, and was still so for the Pauline community. Looking back, Luke sees them as a sign of the apostolic past, whereas Matthew has something of a critical view and in an authoritarian way accords a central place to the ethical teaching of Jesus. In this way it is Matthew, the rabbinically trained scribe, who becomes the leading evangelist in the 'post-apostolic' church which comes into being. However, this takes us beyond the period discussed in these six articles.

Of course the 'ecstatic' aspect of earliest Christian enthusiasm is only of limited significance and should not be overestimated. Nor can it simply be compared with the bacchanalian intoxication of the Dionysian mystery groups in the Hellenistic period. Furthermore by the time of the early empire these *thiasoi* had long become respectable. The Pauline mission communities took eschatological spiritual enthusiasm as a matter of course. In Corinth what Paul fought against were exaggerations and not the matter itself; these exaggerations went back to a 'Dionysian' misunderstanding of earliest Christian spiritual enthusiasm of a kind that was very natural for a Greek. The influence of this enthusiasm is much older and more extensive than what we are told about events in Corinth. In essence it affected the whole life and work of the earliest Christian communities: their christological message, their faith which is active through love (Gal. 5.6), the interpretation of the prophetic writings of the old covenant, their lively worship and the sharing which arose out of it, their mutual praise of God and his messiah in hymns and the hope of the *parousia* which shape their present. All theological thought, including 'ethical' paraenesis, is permeated by it – and we should not separate ethics and the message of faith, as people are so ready to do nowadays. The Spirit also provided a final stimulus for the *nous*, the reason given by the Creator and renewed by Christ. That intensive theological thinking which found expression in the writings of the New Testament canon as the earliest 'apostolic' testimony, from the letters of Paul to the Johannine corpus, is a fruit of this Spirit. It manifests itself in the development of christology and soteriology which also imply radical grace and a new anthropology. The important thing here is that all these writings including the Gospels grew out of worship, the focal point of the earliest church, and were written to be used in worship (I Thess 15.22). They have come down to us only because they were read in worship.

In the following articles I have tried to investigate the working of this Spirit in quite specific areas. It is manifested in worship, which in some way anticipates the praise of the community as perfected in the kingdom of God; in the stormy development of christology and soteriology, which gives believers a new being, i.e. a new self-understanding and new forms of life; and in the no less active mission which symbolically took possession of the provinces of the Roman empire for the Kyrios. Nevertheless, it would be misleading to suppose that in their spirit-led enthusiasm the earliest Christian communities simply transposed future heavenly glory to their earthly existence. They lived under severe external pressure, persecuted both by their own compatriots, who saw them only as dangerous messianic enthusiasts, and soon enough also by the Roman state authorities. Their message was offensive beyond all measure, for the Lord exalted to the right hand of God was identical with the crucified and accursed false teacher Jesus of Nazareth, and joining the new community brought disgrace and persecution along with a break with all familiar customs and patterns of life. For us enlightened, comfortable and bourgeois Christians of the twentieth century the world of earliest Christianity is in many ways strange and offensive, and I have tried to make clear in each connection the alien features which estrange us.

In terms of method I have been concerned to take seriously all the ancient sources – Christian, Jewish and Graeco-Roman. I have tried to avoid the pernicious specialization, so popular today, which works only in one narrow sphere and because of its self-chosen narrowness is no longer in a position to understand its particular area against a wider historical context. One cannot specialize in Mark or John without a good knowledge of ancient Judaism and the world of Gnosticism and the Hermetic literature, and one cannot be a 'specialist' in Luke without a thorough study of Hellenistic Judaism and ancient history writing. Nor have I been able to go on accepting the false and obsolete alternatives of a 'Jewish' or 'Hellenistic' origin for Christianity. Certain as it is that earliest Christianity grew completely out of ancient Judaism and that it is difficult to demonstrate direct 'pagan' influences in it which have not been communicated through the intermediary of Judaism, so it is certain that ancient Judaism before 70 was extremely pluralist – even in Palestine itself – and in turn was influenced in many ways by its 'Hellenistic' environment. The ancient world presents a relatively unified picture. Only if we keep the whole of it in mind can we also evaluate the unique and special features in the religion which had newly come into being. Moreover, while we must certainly introduce into our work the perspectives of sociology and social history which have long been neglected – particularly in Germany – we cannot simply concentrate on them in a one-sided way. In the first place the basis given by our source material is usually too narrow for fundamental conclusions, and secondly we have to keep the whole of the primitive Christian community in view. That includes in particular the ways in which its faith was thought about, the forms of its worship and – last but not least – the authoritative teachers and personalities who shaped it, and whose voices we hear in the earliest Christian literature. The Spirit works in and on individuals and only through individuals on the whole body of Christ.

The destructive scepticism, a particular feature of the modern world, which works in a predominantly analytical way, often ultimately ends up, not by furthering real historical understanding but by making it impossible. It is striking here that in particular those authors who apply radical criticism to early Christian narrators like Mark or Luke and who shred up the two letters to the Corinthians into ten or more parts often invent facts of their own which have no basis whatever in the sources and indeed go directly against them. Despite the anxiety of fundamentalists we cannot and should not refrain from the consistent application of historical methods (using German jargon one can also call them 'historical-critical' methods), but the widespread combination of radical critical attitudes and extravagant(-critical) methods. A few months ago my American publisher asked me, 'Why are you so conservative?' At that time I simply replied, 'Why not?' Perhaps I should have added: these distinctions between 'conservative' and 'liberal' or even 'progressive' (and what is progress in theology if not a new and reflective return to the testimony of the apostles and a concern for that to which they bore witness?) are ultimately meaningless. We are concerned only with the *truth*, theological and historical. The truth is our sole obligation; we have to seek and to present it. and in the end it will prevail against all our conjectures, all our desires to be right, our imaginative constructions and our anxiety. II Cor. 13.8: οὐ γὰρ δυνάμεθά τι κατὰ τῆς ἀληθείας ἀλλὰ ὑπὲρ τῆς ἀληθείας.

The six articles in this volume are therefore meant simply as attempts to come nearer to this truth – theologically and historically.

Tübingen, Easter 1983

A

Abbreviations

AAG	Abhandlungen der Akademie der Wissenschaften in Göttingen
AB	Anchor Bible
AGAJU	Arbeiten zur Geschichte des antiken Judentums und des Urchristentums
AGG	Abhandlungen der Gesellschaft der Wissenschaften, Göttingen
AGSU	Arbeiten zur Geschichte des Spätjudentums und Urchristentums
ALGH	Arbeiten zur Religion und Geschichte des hellenistischen Judentums
ALW	Archiv für Liturgiewissenschaft
AnBib	Analecta Biblica
ANRW	*Aufstieg und Niedergang der römischen Welt*, ed. H. Temporini and W. Haase, Berlin and New York
ASTI	Annual of the Swedish Theological Institute in Jerusalem
ATANT	Abhandlungen zur Theologie des Alten und Neuen Testaments
ATR	*Anglican Theological Review*
BENT	Beiträge zur Einleitung in das Neue Testament
BETL	Bibliotheca ephemeridum theologicarum Lovaniensium
BEvTh	Beiheft zur *Evangelische Theologie*
BHHW	*Biblisch-Historisches Handwörterbuch* ed. B. Reicke and L. Rost
BHT	Beiträge zur historischen Theologie
Bibl	*Biblica*
BJRL	*Bulletin of the John Rylands Library*
BWANT	Beiträge zur Wissenschaft vom Alten (und Neuen) Testament
BZ	*Biblische Zeitschrift*

BZAW	Beihefte zur *Zeitschrift für die alttestamentliche Wissenschaft*
BZNW	Beihefte zur *Zeitschrift für die neutestamentliche Wissenschaft*
CBQ	*Catholic Biblical Quarterly*
Chr d'Ég	*Chronique d'Égypte*
CIJ	*Corpus Inscriptionum Judaicarum*
CIL	*Corpus Inscriptionum Latinarum*
CPJ	*Corpus Papyrorum Judaicarum*
CSEL	Corpus Scriptorum Ecclesiasticorum Latinorum
DJD	Discoveries in the Judaean Desert
EJ	Encyclopedia Judaica
EKK	Evangelisch-Kritischer Kommentar
EQ	*Evangelical Quarterly*
ET	English translation
EvKomm	Evangelischer Kommentar
EvTh	*Evangelische Theologie*
ExpT	*Expository Times*
FF	Forschungen und Fortschritte
FGr	Hist Fragmente der Griechischen Historiker
FRLANT	Forschungen zur Religion und Literatur des Alten und Neuen Testaments
GCS	Die Griechischen Christlichen Schriftsteller der ersten drei Jahrhunderte
HAW	Handbuch der Altertumswissenschaft
HNT	Handbuch zum Neuen Testament
HTK	Herders theologischeer Kommentar zum Neuen Testament
HTR	*Harvard Theological Review*
HZ	*Historische Zeitschrift*
IEJ	*Israel Exploration Journal*
JAC	Jahrbuch der Antike und Christentum
JBL (MS)	*Journal of Biblical Literature* (Monograph series)
JJS	*Journal of Jewish Studies*
JR	*Journal of Religion*
JSHRZ	Jüdische Schriften aus hellenistisch-römischer Zeit
JSJ	*Journal of the Study of Judaism*
JTS	*Journal of Theological Studies*
KEK	Kritisch-exegetisches Kommentar über das Neue Testament
KNT	Kommentar zum Neuen Testament
KuD	*Kerygma und Dogma*

LXX	Septuagint
MTS	Münchener Theologische Studien
MusHelv	*Museum Helveticum*
NF	Neue Folge
NKZ	*Neue Kirchliche Zeitschrift*
NovTest (Suppl)	*Novum Testamentum* (Supplement)
NTD	Das Neue Testament Deutsch
NTS	*New Testament Studies*
OGIS	W. Dittenberger, *Orientis Graeci Inscriptiones Selectae*
PG	J. P. Migne, Patrologia Graeca
PW	Paulys Realencyclopa*die der classischen Altertumswissenschaft*
QuaestDisp	*Quaestiones Disputatae*
RB	*Revue Biblique*
RE	*Realencyclopädie für protestantische Theologie und Kirche*
REAug	*Revue des Etudes Augustiniennes*
REG	*Revue des Etudes Grecques*
RevQum	*Revue de Qumrân*
RGG	*Die Religion in Geschichte und Gegenwart*
RheinMus	*Rheinisches Museum für Philologie*
RNT	Regensburger Neue Testament
RP	*Revue de Philologie, de litterature et d'histoire anciennes*
RV	Religionsgeschichtliche Volksbücher, Tübingen
RVV	Religionsgeschichtliche Versuche und Vorarbeiten
SAH	Sitzungsberichtte der Heidelberger Akademie der Wissenschaften zu Berlin
SANT	Studien zum Alten und Neuen Testament
SB	Sammelbuch griechischer Urkunden aus Agypten, ed. F. Preisigke, F. Bilabel and E. Kiessling
SBS	Stuttgarter Bibelstudien
SBT	Studies in Biblical Theology
SJ	Studia Judaica
SNT	Studien zum Neuen Testament
SNTS	Studiorum Novi Testamenti Societas
SUNT	Studien zur Umwelt des Neuen Testaments
TB	Theologisches Bûcherei
TDNT	*Theological Dictionary of the New Testament*, ed. G. Kittel

TF	Theologische Forschungen
TLZ	*Theologische Literaturzeitung*
TR	*Theologische Rundschau*
TRE	*Theologische Realencyclopädie*
TS(B)	Theologische Studien (Basel)
TU	Texte und Untersuchungen
TZ	*Theologische Zeitschrift*
UNT	Untersuchungen zum Neuen Testament
VC	*Vigiliae Christianae*
VF	*Verkündigung und Forschung*
WF	Wege der Forschung
WMANT	Wissenschaftliche Monographien zum Alten und Neuen Testament
WUNT	Wissenschaftliche Untersuchungen zum Neuen Testament
WZ	Wissenschaftliche Zeitschrift
ZAW	*Zeitschrift fur die alttestamentliche Wissenschaft*
ZDPV	*Zeitschrift des Deutschen Palästinavereins*
ZDMG	*Zeitschrift des Deutschen Morgenländischen Gesellschaft*
ZKG	*Zeitschrift für Kirchengeschichte*
ZNW	*Zeitschrift für die neutestamentliche Wissenschaft*
ZPapEp	*Zeitschrift für Papyrologie und Epigraphie*
ZRGG	*Zeitschrift für Religion und Geistesgeschichte*
ZTK	*Zeitschrift für Theologie und Kirche*

1

Between Jesus and Paul
The 'Hellenists', the 'Seven' and Stephen
(Acts 6.1-15; 7.54-8.3)

In recent years New Testament scholars have been particularly interested in that Hellenistic Jewish Christianity before and contemporary with Paul in which the earliest Christian kerygma was first articulated in the Greek language and in which Paul – despite his assertions to the contrary in Gal. 1.11-24 – was introduced into the tradition of a community which was still very young. This was a tradition which he, outstanding scholar that he was, was a little later to play a prominent part in shaping. In the first flush of their joy in discovery, some scholars have wanted to make this Hellenistic Jewish Christianity – supposedly with exclusively apocalyptic colouring – the real nucleus of primitive Christianity and in practice to allot to it above all the whole production of the Jesus tradition.[1] We might ask whether this is not to turn the obscurity of early Christian history even more into complete Stygian darkness; it will be more meaningful to look intensively at those few points where this early Hellenistic Jewish Christianity appears in our sources and shed what light we can on it with the help of the philological and historical methods at our disposal.

The reader of Acts must be struck by the abrupt break which brings the description of the ideal conditions in the Jerusalem community (chs.1-5) to an end with 'the murmuring of the Hellenists against the Hebrews' in 6.1. F. C. Baur, who provided the basic stimulus for the critical interpretation of Acts 6 and 7, conjectured that behind the discontent of the Hellenists towards their fellow believers there was 'a deeper ground for the disagreement between the two parties . . . in the light of which such errors as followed proved to be important'. He also saw that with this sudden new beginning on the part of the *auctor ad Theophilum* 'all at once we come down from the ideal conditions of the harmony in the primitive community to the sphere

of the common reality of life'.[2] For him the Hellenists, and here again
Stephen in particular, were 'forerunners of the apostle Paul'.[3] Only
with them do we stand 'on firmer historical ground'.[4] It may therefore
be rewarding to begin our soundings there.

Today's widespread fashion of seeing Luke as a largely 'creative'
didactic writer whose work is less that of a 'historian' than in the style
of the later apocryphal acts of apostles,[5] counsels caution. The
boldness with which the most significant historian of the pre-World
War II period alongside M. Rostovtzeff, namely Eduard Meyer,
ventured to compare the author of Luke-Acts with Polybius and
Livy,[6] will seem mad to some 'historical-critical' commentators – if
only, perhaps, because they are so unfamiliar with ancient history
writing and its problems. No ancient historian wrote *sine ira et studio*,[7]
and antiquity was still spared the problem of a historical positivism.[8]
They were all tendentious writers, and Luke must have been so to a
special degree precisely because he was a 'theological historian'
through and through, and – in his own individual way – wanted to
take further the great tradition of biblical historiography, or better, to
bring it to completion. This deliberate 'tendency' leads to the almost
offensively strict way in which the author limits the material that he
uses and which gives his work the character of a 'historical monograph',[9] of the kind that we also find in Hellenistic Jewish historiography (Jason of Cyrene, Eupolemus, Ps. Hecataeus, I Maccabees,
Philo's *In Flaccum* and *Legatio ad Gaium*, Josephus' *Bellum Judaicum*
and Justus of Tiberias).

For that very reason the construction of his work is of unprecedented consistency. Conzelmann[10] rightly speaks of a 'straight-line
programme'. For Luke is even more a master of limitation and
omission than he is of the art of elaboration. The title 'Acts of the
Apostles' has always led the reader of his work astray. It should really
be called 'From Jesus to Paul', with the sub-title 'From Jerusalem to
Rome', and describes very strictly the straight line followed by the
gospel from unbelieving Israel to the Gentiles. The apostles – including Peter – essentially have the function only of preparing for the
appearance and activity of Paul, of providing a bridge between Jesus
and Paul. Once they have done their duty, they can disappear. To
serve Paul's greater glory they have to leave the stage one after the
other: he alone remains behind. The reason for such a 'one-dimen-
sional' account does not lie simply in the theme of divine guidance –
this could also have been worked out in a multiform way – but in the
central and positive interest in the person and missionary work of
Paul. He is the real goal of the work.

The 'murmuring of the Hellenists against the Hebrews' introduces a new direction in this literary one-way street, the second section of the tripartite work which comes to an end with the Apostolic Council and prepares for the real climax, Paul's great mission. It is striking here that this third and last great section also begins with a conflict: with the separation of the one true missionary to the Gentiles, Paul, from the more conservative Barnabas (15.36ff.). The conflict, which is only hinted at or at least considerably watered down, and which does not disturb the harmony and consistency of the overall development miraculously guided by God, is of decisive importance to Luke. It takes events – *confusione hominum Dei providentia* – in the new direction willed by God.[11]

The first division, between the two groups of the Hellenists and the Hebrews, and its resolution by the choice of the 'Seven' (6.1-6), at the same time forms the common introduction to the two narrative complexes which follow: the account of Stephen which ends with his martyrdom and Philip's successful mission, which for the first time goes beyond the bounds of Judaism. One might almost say that the fate of both these figures, the martyr and the evangelist (21.8), prefigures in advance the career of the 'thirteenth witness', whom his unique missionary testimony before Jews and Gentiles finally brings to prison. From there no retreat is possible since – as Luke knows, but does not tell us – it ends with the condemnation and martyrdom of the greatest of all missionaries (20.22ff.). Thus the group of the 'Hellenists' appears unexpectedly in 6.1: some indication of its existence has already been given, since in 2.5ff. Luke already had the 'mighty acts of God' proclaimed to the foreigners in Jerusalem in their own language.

Now of course we could completely dispense with an investigation of the historical background in view of Luke's strict literary concern and the fact that the whole account of the 'Seven', like that of Stephen, 'bears clear traces of revision by the author',[12] and be content with an account of Luke's theological tendencies, especially as in Bihler's view, at least in the account of Stephen, the earlier tradition – if there ever was one – 'has been completely submerged in Luke's composition'.[13] But precisely at this point theologians who are not particularly interested in historical questions and to whom for example the problem of the earthly Jesus seems to be 'theologically irrelevant' become particularly active and indeed imaginative; here, too, by way of an exception under a thin covering, the bedrock of a source clearly emerges. Thus in 6.1 we not only have for the first time the puzzling terms Ἑλληνισταί and Ἑβραῖοι, but also the word μαθηταί (6.1,2,7), which does not occur in chs.1-5. γογγυσμός and παραθεωρεῖν are similarly un-Lucan. Furthermore, καθημερινός appears only here in the New Testament, and Harnack already stressed that the 'daily provision' for the widows went against the ideal communism of possessions mentioned in 2.45, just as the vague and restrained information about the size of the community in 6.1,5 goes against the large numbers of chs.2-5 (cf. the three and five thousand in 2.41;4.4).[14]Similarly, the mention of the 'Twelve' in 6.2 is striking, since elsewhere Luke speaks only of the 'apostles'.[15] So here, above all since Harnack's investigations, people have conjectured the beginning of an 'Antiochene (Jerusalem) source'. [16] The existence of such a source, for which there is some justification, cannot be ruled out by the argument that it can no longer be reconstructed in any satisfactory way. The ancient historian took pride in so reshaping his sources that his model could no longer be recognized, and the mark of his own individual style emerged all the more clearly. This basic rule in the ancient use of sources is often too little noted by the sophisticated analysts who very neatly set tradition off against redaction.[17] Luke, the extremely able stylist (which at the same time means imitator of style),[18] is no exception here. We are confronted with a very similar problem in contemporary writers like Livy and Dionysius of Halicarnassus,[19] Plutarch and Josephus. In the case of the latter one can very easily monitor the transformation of style by a comparison with his sources – the Septuagint, I Ezra, the Letter of Aristeas or I Maccabees – because of the considerable identity of content.[20] In addition there is the problem of abbreviation to an extreme degree or the contamination of sources or their expansion, say by the insertion of speeches and dialogues. One should therefore reckon with the possibility that in the first half of Acts Luke above all had two sources or complexes of tradition at his disposal: 1. a collection of stories about Peter and 2. the so-called Antiochene source which clearly emerges with 6.1, but perhaps already began with the miracle of languages in 2.5ff., and among other things also contained the note about Barnabas in 4.36f. In particular the catalogues of persons and ethnic groups in 6.5,9; 2.9ff.; 13.l (cf. also 1.13f.) probably go back to written lists and were already available to Luke along with their wider context.[21]

There has long been dispute over the meaning of the designations Ἑβραῖοι and Ἑλληνισταί in 6.1. There seems to be endless talk above all over the term Ἑλληνισταί. Thus G. P. Wetter conjectured that these should be seen – at least predominantly – as Gentile Christians. He argued that there was already a mention of proclamation to non-Jews in the account of the apostles' speaking in foreign tongues in 2.5ff. and that the Ἰουδαῖοι in 2.5 attested by the majority of manuscripts was a secondary insertion.[22] On the basis of a thoroughgoing investigation H. J. Cadbury arrived at a similar result: 'we need not be surprised if in chapter vi the author refers casually to Gentile Christians already in Jerusalem.'[23] In his article in *TDNT* H.Windisch allowed the views of (Wetter and) Cadbury to stand on an equal footing alongside the traditional interpretation.[24] By contrast, in agreement with an old tradition of interpretation, E. Schwartz,[25] E. C. Blackman[26] and Bo Reicke[27] suggested Hellenistic proselytes, i.e. Gentiles who had gone over to Judaism.[28] The Gentile-Christian theory was developed further by scholars like W.Grundmann[29] and Walter Bauer. The latter saw them as 'certainly Gentiles who had become believers and Jews . . . who had no positive attitude towards the law . . .' and in the main 'probably came from Galilee and the adjacent Gentile regions'.[30] This truly bold conjecture by the great New Testament philologist has been taken up enthusiastically by W.Schmithals and combined with his theory of a pre-Christian gnostic mission. The starting point of the Christian mission is said to be ' "Galilee of the Gentiles" permeated by syncretism'.[31] Having moved directly from there into the area of Antioch in North Syria, young Christianity is said to have become infected with the active mission carried on by gnostic antinomianism. In that case, the Hellenists would be only the representatives in Jerusalem itself 'of the Christian antinomianism which had long been active outside the borders of Judaea'.[32] G. Schille goes one step further. In his view the seven Hellenists originally had nothing to do with Jerusalem. They are a *'group of collaborators from a city of Judaea outside Jerusalem'* who 'made an abortive attempt to get a footing there, in the process of which . . . one of them lost his life'.[33] It is only a small step from a supposedly historical-critical, radical dialysis of Acts to a completely new Acts of the Apostles – one might almost call it a Romance of the Apostles.

Cullmann's conjectures take quite another direction. For him Hebrews and Hellenists come predominantly from Palestinian Judaism. The latter are 'a group of former Jews . . . who split off from official Judaism and pursued more or less esoteric tendencies with a syncretistic stamp'. The fact that there were also some Diaspora Jews among them was 'a common characteristic'.[34] Here the expression 'Hellenists' is to be seen as an expedient of Luke's born out of desperation. Because of the *'syncretistic features* which were typical of them and the alien elements of non-Jewish origin . . . he called them "Hellenists" for want of a better name'. Cullmann found the reasons for his surprising thesis in Stephen's speech and its close connections with traditions from Qumran and the Johannine writings.[35] By contrast A.Spiro attempted to prove from the speech that Stephen was a Samaritan and as such belonged to the Hebrews, who were similarly Samaritans; they were in turn allied to the Hellenists, who had a syncretistic colouring.[36]

However, even where people accepted Chrysostom's old, clear information, Ἑλληνιστὰς τοὺς Ἑλληνιστὶ φθεγγομένους λέγει, 'He (Luke) uses Hellenists for those who speak Greek',[37] they were often not content with this information, which was thought to be too simple, and sought to read even more out of the mysterious designation. Thus it was M.Simon's view that while the Hellenists were indeed Greek-speaking Jews, the term had derogatory connotations, and indicated the influence of 'Greek' i.e. pagan thought; it had been used by Jewish-Palestinian and later Christian orthodoxy in the sense of paganizing. He also conjectured that this group was under suspicion even before it went over to the Christian community. To support his theory he refers to the catalogue of Jewish heresies in Justin's *Trypho* 80.4, where, among others, the quite mysterious Ἑλληνιανοί appear. He connects both these and the 'Hellenists' in Acts with Jews 'who followed or were suspected of following the ways of the Greeks, i.e. of the heathen'.[39]

J. Bihler criticizes the 'syncretizing' interpretation put forward by Cullmann (and Simon) with the remark that nothing can be inferred from the context of Luke's account which indicates a 'view of life' that distinguished the Hellenists from the Hebrews. For him they are Greek-speaking Jews who in Luke's view were interested in a 'mission to their Hellenistic environment'.[40]

This wide spectrum of opinions may be a reasonable indication. One could continue the enumeration even longer. Who do the 'Hellenists' and 'Hebrews' really represent?

The traditional answer which was already given by Chrysostom is linguistically the only one possible from the context: the 'Hellenists' are men who spoke Greek as their mother tongue. Presumably the simplicity of this solution led to increasingly complicated new hypotheses. The term appears before the fourth century AD only twice in Greek, in Luke. In 6.1 the context indicates that Jewish Christians must be meant. In the list of seven, which like most lists in the New Testament is in order of seniority[41] and in which, as the almost exclusively Greek names indicate, representatives of the Hellenists are introduced, the proselyte Nicolaus of Antioch appears only at the end – to some degree as a Jew of lower rank.[42] For Luke, Stephen (7.2) and Philip are obviously Jewish Christians. Before AD 70 Jerusalem had been fairly unattractive for non-Jews as a permanent place of residence; a mission apart from the law was as unthinkable there as missionary activity by Samaritans and Gentile Christians. The unique significance of the Holy City as a cultural centre of Judaism severely restricted freedom of movement for non-Jews.[43] Furthermore, a persecution of non-Jews by the Jewish authorities would hardly have been legally possible, as at all events they came under the jurisdiction of the prefect. It is highly improbable, too, that the 'Hellenists' came from Galilee, in connection with a mission to the Gentiles apart from the law. Our sources do not refer to that anywhere. Between Herod and the Jewish revolt – with the exception of the inhabitants of the two cities of Tiberias and Sepphoris, which significantly play no role in the New Testament [44] – the Galileans were predominantly nationalistic Jews who were faithful to the law, even if the Pharisees did not have the same influence there as they did in Jerusalem and Judaea. Because of the frontier situation their relationship with their neighbours, the Hellenized Syrians and Phoenicians, was relatively tense: the account of the situation there by Walter Bauer is one-sided and misleading.[45] Since the conquest of Jerusalem by Pompey the Galileans were for the most part embittered opponents of the Romans and their satellites. Outside Jerusalem, the most vigorous resistance in the Jewish War came from Galilee.[46] The saying which is often quoted, 'Galilee, Galilee, you hated (or you hate) the law; your end is to fall victim to the oppressors', is first assigned to Johanan ben Zakkai by Ulla, an Amoraean at the end of the third century, and is presumably apocryphal. To read out of this that the Galileans were relatively free with the law is as rash as to transfer the 'Galilee of the Gentiles' (Isa.8.23) from the time of the Assyrian king Tiglath-pileser III, about 733/32 BC, to Jewish Galilee of the first century AD.[47] Furthermore, the archaeological evidence for the period before 70 shows that Jewish Galilee was not more but less Hellenized than Jerusalem. For the people of Jerusalem it was a region of 'backwoodsmen'. That is also the reason for the low esteem in which it was held. Therefore the Galileans have as little to do with the 'Hellenists' in Acts 6 as the Qumran Essenes or the Samaritans.[48]

In Acts 9.29 there is a report of how on his return to Jerusalem Paul discussed with the 'Hellenists' there; thereupon they wanted to kill him, so that he had to flee to Caesarea. These people are clearly Jews, presumably Greek-speaking Jews, with whom Paul shared a mother tongue. That is, Luke connects the newly-converted Christian Paul with precisely those Jewish circles in which he had appeared as a persecutor of the Christians and with whom Stephen had already disputed (6.9). The variant reading Ἕλληνας of the Alexandrinus (9.29) is just an indication of the failure of a copyist to understand. Whereas the Syriac translation in 6.1 misunderstands and translates the term 'Greek disciples' (*yaunāyē' talmīdē'*), in 9.29 it paraphrases it quite rightly as 'Jews who knew Greek' (*yihūdāyē 'alyēn dyād'in* (h)*wau yaunā'ī̆t*). That the Latin manuscripts translate the term *Graeci* in both passages is connected with the fact that like the oriental languages they had no real equivalent to Ἑλληνισταί.[49]

There is considerable dispute as to whether in Acts 11.20 we should not also read Ἑλληνιστάς along with B, the second corrector of D and the Byzantine imperial text, as a third example of the Lucan terminology. For Cadbury the reading was one of his main arguments for the meaning 'Greeks' as early as 6.1. He and his followers regarded the Ἕλληνας in p[74](seventh century), A, the original of D, the third corrector of Sin, Eusebius and some of the Greek commentators (see n.37 above) as the easier, harmonizing form of the text.[50] However, it is presumably an early copyist's mistake. A copyist had got used to this term used by Luke in 6.1; 9.29, so that when Ἕλληνες first appeared he introduced the already familiar word. At all events the context calls for Ἕλληνας as a contrast to Ἰουδαίοις (11.19), just as in describing the mission outside Palestine Luke uses only Ἕλληνες – almost always as a contrast to the Jews (14.1; 18.4; 19.10,17; 20.21). The charge against Paul in 21.28 shows that Luke also uses Ἕλληνες and not Ἑλληνισταί for Gentile Greeks in Jerusalem: Ἕλληνας εἰσήγαγεν εἰς τὸ ἱερόν. This mistake was made easier by the fact that Ἑλληνιστής, which after Luke only appears again for the first time in the fourth century with Julian the Apostate, had in the meantime become synonymous with Ἕλλην in the sense of Gentile, non-Christian. Only in the later Testament of Solomon does Ἑλληνιστής appear in the linguistic sense as the opposite of Ἑβραῖος.[51] The conjecture by Warfield that Luke means Acts 11.20 'in the broad sense of "Graecizers" . . . the total mixed population of Antioch', is improbable, as it goes against Luke's terminology elsewhere.[52] By contrast, for the later Byzantine reader the term could have the meaning Gentile. However, this was certainly not yet the case for Luke and his source.

Now that means that the Ἑλληνισταί in 6.1, as in 9.29, are a phenomenon limited to Jerusalem, a city the majority of whose population spoke Aramaic as its mother tongue and which had only a limited minority within its walls who were Greek speakers from birth. On the other hand, for the Greek-speaking Diaspora the use of Ἑλληνιστής would be meaningless, as here the use of Greek as a mother tongue was taken for granted. By contrast the opposition between Ἕλληνες and Ἰουδαῖοι was very much in evidence as an indication of belonging to a people and to a religion.

The etymology of Ἑλληνιστής also exclusively supports the meaning 'Greek-speaking' without any syncretistic or even derogatory religious connotations.[53] 'Hellenistic syncretism' is a modern discovery, and the ancient world did not have any appropriate term for it. For the Jews there were only Gentiles, apostates or fellow-countrymen who did not observe the law. The word Ἑλληνιστής is derived from ἑλληνίζειν, just as βαπτιστής is from βαπτίζειν, ὑβριστής from ὑβρίζειν, λῃστής from λῃίζειν, ἐξορκιστής from ἐξορκίζειν or εὐαγγελιστής (Acts 21.8 = Philip; Eph. 4.11; II Tim. 4.5) from εὐαγγελίζεσθαι. However, in complete contrast to the intransitive meaning 'live in accordance with Greek custom', 'adopt' or – in the transitive sense – 'disseminate Greek customs and morality',[54] from Thucydides and Plato to Plutarch, Sextus Empiricus, Lucian and Dio Cassius the verb ἑλληνίζειν means almost exclusively 'speak Greek (perfectly)' and in some cases also 'translate into Greek'. Thus it has a concentrated linguistic sense. It is also used quite often in connection with barbarians who had learnt Greek. For the later grammarians it is partly identical with Attic Greek as the only correct use of the Greek language.[55] The few examples with a wider significance are relatively late. They appear as rare isolated instances first in Plutarch (c. 50-120),[56] Diogenes Laertius (second/third century AD),[57] Eusebius[58] and Libanius (314 to about 393).[59] Here – in the spiritual struggle of late antiquity dominated by Platonism – the conception of a 'Greek cultural mission' had come to the fore in a way which we do not find in the early Hellenistic period.[60] In Christian terminology, from the time of Eusebius, in addition to having the meaning 'to speak Greek', the word then also came to signify practising pagan faith.[61] One special instance is the intensified and very rare ἀφελληνίζειν, which in one passage in Philo corresponds to our transitive 'Hellenize' (viz. the barbarians) and in Dio Chrysostom characterizes the complete transformation of a Roman into a Greek.[62] The best equivalent to Ἑλληνιστής would therefore be the participle Ἑλληνίζων, 'one who speaks Greek'.[63] The opposite term is therefore not Ἰουδαΐζειν, as is so often claimed, but βαρβαρίζειν, or, when related to Judaism, Ἑβραΐζειν, a word which in Josephus once means 'speak Hebrew (or better, Aramaic)', or 'translate into Hebrew (Aramaic)'.[64]

The Ἑβραῖοι in Acts 6.1 are therefore also Aramaic-speaking Jews, just as in Acts 21.40; 22.2; 26.14 τῇ Ἑβραΐδι διαλέκτῳ or in John 5.2; 19.13,17,20 Ἑβραϊστί means 'in Aramaic'. It is very questionable whether Hebrew was still a widely spoken vernacular in Jerusalem; possibly Mishnaic Hebrew, with its strong Aramaic colouring, was still used in the villages of the hill-country of Judaea as well as by scholars and as the language of worship; but significantly all the Jerusalem place-names mentioned in the New Testament and in Josephus have been Aramaized. Therefore the language of Jesus the Galilean and the earliest community was also Aramaic.[65] For the

Greeks, and indeed for Diaspora Jews, there was virtually no difference between Hebrew and Aramaic. The objection that Ἐβραῖος in
Jewish-Hellenistic literature is an exact equivalent of Ἰουδαῖος is
wrong. Ἐβραῖος is a much rarer term;[66] 1. it is used as a deliberate
archaizing name for a people in the account of the biblical history;
2. we find the word in exalted poetic and literary language; 3. it
means the Jews who come from Palestine – i.e. the Holy Land – or
who have special connections with Palestine (this from the perspective of the Diaspora, but also in individual passages in non-Jewish
literature).[67] This is the case both with Jewish inscriptions (see nn. 99,
102 below) and with Paul's own remark that he is a Ἐβραῖος ἐξ
Ἐβραίων (Phil. 3.5; cf. II Cor. 11.22).[68] Now whereas Ἐβραῖος in the
Diaspora often means geographical origin from Palestine, in the
mother country, and above all in bilingual Jerusalem, the linguistic
interpretation would seem more likely, especially if the word is used
as a complementary term to Ἑλληνιστής. It simply means Jews
speaking Aramaic (or Hebrew) as their mother tongue. The particular
characteristic of the Jews coming from Palestine was usually their
command of Aramaic. Also in favour of this is the fact that in rabbinic
literature the use of ʿibrī is almost exclusively limited to the meaning
'Hebrew language (or writing)', and virtually ceases to mean 'Jew'.
In individual instances ʿibrī even seems directly to indicate Aramaic-
speaking Jews. Thus M. Gittin 9.8: 'A letter of separation . . . in
which one witness is ʿibrī (i.e. an Aramaic-speaking Jew) and one
witness is yᵉwānī (i.e. a Greek-speaking Jew) is valid.'[69] ʿibrīt probably
also means Aramaic in the Baraita Meg.18a (cf. Shab.115a) about the
reading of the Esther scroll in various languages: 'If he has read it in
Egyptian (gīpṭīt = Coptic), ʿibrīt (i.e. Aramaic), Elamitic, Median or
Greek, he has not done his duty . . . If it was Egyptian for Egyptians,
ʿibrīt for ʿibrīm, (i.e. Aramaic for Aramaic speakers), Elamite for
Elamites, Median for Medes, Greek for Greeks, he has done his
duty.'[70] For the Palestinian Josephus the linguistic element is similarly
stressed in the case of Ἐβραῖος. However, at the same time he extends
the adjective Ἐβραῖος/Ἐβραϊκός to the distinctive characteristics of
the Palestinian Jew. It is also striking that Philo makes a distinction
between the 'language of the Hebrews' and 'the language of the
Greeks' by explicitly dissociating himself as a Greek speaker from the
'Hebrews'.[71] ἔστι δὲ ὡς μὲν Ἐβραῖοι λέγουσι Φανουήλ, ὡς δὲ ἡμεῖς(!)
ἀποστροφὴ θεοῦ. The translators whom Ptolemy II Philadelphus
brings from Palestine to translate the Torah are Ἐβραῖοι, though of
course they also have the necessary Greek education for the translation. This last feature, which Philo takes over from the Letter of
Aristeas, indicates that in the case of the Ἐβραῖοι in Acts 6.1 we may

presuppose at least a partial knowledge of Greek.[72] Here, among others, we might think of men like Silas-Silvanus or John Mark. The later journeys of Peter are also inconceivable unless he had a basic knowledge of Greek, even if he used an interpreter. These bilingual 'Palestinian Greeks' are of decisive significance for the development of early Christianity.[73] Two famous Aramaic-speaking Palestinian Jews who had an excellent Greek education are the priest Flavius Josephus and Justus (Zadok) from Tiberias.[74]

It is much less likely that we could expect Diaspora Jews who returned to Jerusalem to have learned Aramaic. Anyone who had a command of the Greek *lingua franca* would hardly have troubled to learn a 'barbarian' language.[75] The best example is the well-educated Philo, who never put himself to the trouble of learning Hebrew, the sacred language, or Aramaic. He hardly seems to have distinguished the two. He visited Jerusalem as a pilgrim only once in his life.[76] Whether the Jewish inhabitants of the Hellenistic cities of the coastal plain knew their semitic mother tongue is already questionable. In the third century AD even the Shema was prayed in Greek in the synagogue in Caesarea.[77] The learned proselyte Aquila-Onkelos may have been a rare exception. C. F. D. Moule's conjecture that the Ἑβραῖοι at least knew some Greek and that the Ἑλληνισταί on the other hand will have understood little or no Aramaic will therefore be correct.[78]

So if in Acts 6.1; 9.29 we have different linguistic groups which were nevertheless bound together by their bilingual members, we can now go on to enquire into the conflict indicated in 6.1ff., its supposed resolution and the connection with the Stephen account in 6.8ff.

First of all a word about chronology. At all events the persecution of Stephen is to be put shortly before the conversion of Paul, which, if we begin from the year of the passover at which Jesus was killed, AD 30, took place somewhere between 32 and 34.[79] Paul's confession that he not only 'persecuted the community of God to excess' but also 'destroyed' it (ἐπόρθουν αὐτήν, Gal. 1.13; cf.1.23; Acts 9.21) is most likely to refer to the expulsion of the group around Stephen. Here a specific community was 'destroyed'.[80] Now that means that the happenings of which Luke gives so fragmentary a description must have taken place a relatively short time after the resurrection event which brought the community into being, and the origin of the group of the 'Hellenists' could very well go back to the beginnings of this 'foundation period', say to the Feast of Weeks following the passover at which Jesus died, when the disciples evidently appeared in public in Jerusalem for the first time. We should assume that some of these

'Hellenists' already belonged to those five hundred brethren or 'all the apostles' to whom, according to Paul, the Risen Christ appeared and some of whom he must have known.[81] We do not know whether in individual instances the group goes back to the activity of Jesus himself. The later, legendary catalogues of disciples naturally included the seven of Acts 6.5 among the Seventy who were sent out according to Luke 10.1.[82] Whereas we may assume that all or the majority of the Twelve chosen by Jesus and confirmed by the resurrection appearances[83] came from Galilee, in the case of the 'Hellenists' we may assume that the majority came from the 'Diaspora', which began as near as Gaza, Caesarea, Ptolemais/Acco or Tyre, and extended as far as Spain. 'Hellenistic' Judaism was even less a clearly definable, unitary entity than Palestinian Judaism, which at the time of Jesus was many-sided. The only link was the Greek language, the Greek Bible and Greek synagogue worship. The Theodotus inscription (see p. 17 below), various family tombs in Jerusalem or even the high-priestly family of Boethus summoned from Alexandria by Herod,[84] show that individuals who returned from the Diaspora settled firmly again in Jerusalem and that their descendants remained there. About thirty-three per cent of the 205 inscriptions from Jerusalem and its immediate surroundings in Frey's *Corpus* are in Greek, and a further nine per cent are bilingual.[85] Stephen (Acts 6.9) and later Paul (9.29) had discussions with the native synagogue communities of these people who had returned. That after the resurrection of Jesus the young community concentrated its activity above all on Jerusalem is not an invention of Luke's; the significance of the holy city is clearly stressed already by Paul. Here was the place at which at the great feasts not only almost all the Jews of Palestine but also many pilgrims from the Diaspora came together.[86] Only here could the whole people be called to repentance and to believe in God's Christ and coming Son of Man. The disciples were tnus simply continuing that intent which had already brought Jesus to Jerusalem, to die at the Passover. They also hoped for his eschatological revelation in the city of his death. Here Israel had to be made to decide. In particular the conversion of the 'Hellenists' in the holy city was a sign of missionary success.[87] The manifest contradictions in Luke's account have long been recognized.[88] Without exception, all the newly-chosen seven who 'care for the poor' have Greek names, whereas in the case of the 'Twelve' only two names, Philip and Andrew, are Greek. The 'Seven' are apparently all 'Hellenists'. Nothing is said about their work of looking after the poor; rather, Stephen and later Philip do precisely what the 'Twelve' have reserved for themselves: as missionaries they proclaim the new message. It is not the signs of Stephen, inserted in 6.8 to disguise this situation, which cause offence; it is his teaching which provokes his martyrdom. Philip is called 'the evangelist' because of his missionary proclamation of the word (21.8); at the same time he is called one 'of the Seven', i.e. he belongs to a quite independent group. In the persecution which breaks out after the martyrdom of Stephen all are 'scattered throughout the region of Judaea and Samaria, except the apostles'. Those who are thus 'scattered' (8.1 διεσπάρησαν; 8.4; 11.19 οἱ μὲν οὖν διασπαρέντες) travel around preaching and finally come to Antioch. Some Cypriots and Cyrenians among them 'also spoke to the Greeks and proclaimed Jesus as Kyrios' (11.20). In other words, only the 'Hellenists' were active missionaries outside Jerusalem and Judaea. By contrast Luke says nothing of a return of the fugitives to Jerusalem. According to Gal. 2.1, relations between Jerusalem and Antioch were evidently not particularly lively. Paul had not been there for fourteen years. Rather, according to Acts 9.31, the communities in Judaea, Galilee and Samaria were living in deep peace and building themselves up. Finally, there is also no explanation of precisely why it is only the 'Hellenist' widows who are looked after in the 'daily provision'.

There is also relatively widespread unanimity over the resolution of these contradictions, which were already pointed out by F. C. Baur. The 'Seven' are in reality not men who care for the poor, subordinate to the 'Twelve', but the leading group of an independent community, the 'Hellenists'. It is striking that their names include neither typically Jewish names like Dositheus, Theodorus, Jason, Sabbataeus, etc., nor pagan theophoric names. A comparison with the Jewish names in papyri and inscriptions and in Josephus shows that only Philip occurs with any frequency. A proselyte is also mentioned often in Jerusalem epitaphs.[89] According to Luke, Nicolaus of Antioch is basically the first former Gentile to become a Christian by way of Judaism. Thus Luke has carefully 'graded' the way towards the mission to the Gentiles. The conjecture that the Seven were composed of both 'Hebrews' and 'Hellenists'[90] is as improbable as Gaechter's assertion that the Hebrews also chose their own group of seven.[91] The difficulties in providing for the poor were less the occasion for these groups than a consequence of their formation. The persecution after the death of Stephen evidently affected only the Hellenists; the Hebrews were hardly touched by it. Like the Twelve (cf. 8.1), they remained in Jerusalem. The Hellenists who were expelled thus became the real founders of the mission to the Gentiles, in which circumcision and observation of the ritual law were no longer required. [92]

What were the reasons for the division of the community into two groups, Aramaic- and Greek-speaking, which finally led to tensions? What I see as fundamentally uncritical criticism – because of its 'radical' attitude – would see syncretism, paganism and antinomianism at work here, while conservative apologetic denies any division at all and opts for the continuation of the 'one heart and one soul' of 4.32. However, we should begin from the situation in Jerusalem at the time, and take the problem of language more seriously. The difference in the languages spoken by the community would necessarily and quickly have led to separate worship, since at least a considerable number of the 'Hellenists' could only have followed Aramaic worship partially, if at all. The 'Hellenists' may have been converted by the preaching of bilingual disciples and conversation with them; however, in the long run 'edification' in a service held in a foreign language would not have come up to the standard which Paul at a later date regarded as a *sine qua non* in Corinth for a proper service, and which lay at the root of his rejection of glossolalia.[93] Prayer, prophetic discourse, the interpretation of scripture and the remembrance of the words of Jesus had to be understandable to everyone – despite the lack of form in the service that was a result of its enthusiasm. However, as practical fellowship in worship and not external organization held the Christian community together in its earliest days,[94] the necessary and consistent holding of services in Greek led to the formation of a new, 'second' community in Jerusalem. The members chose the leading group of the Seven from among themselves, though we cannot exclude the possibility that, say, Philip was originally one of the 'Twelve' and now went over to the 'Seven'.[95] The growth of the community in Jerusalem will also have prompted such a 'division'. For Judaism, the formation of new liturgical communities of this kind was nothing special. A group of ten men eligible to join in worship was enough (Meg. 4.3 = T. Meg. 4.14). In all the great cities with a strong Jewish element there was therefore a majority of freely constituted and usually only loosely associated synagogue communities. Philo provides evidence for Alexandria,[96] the inscriptions of the Jewish catacombs for Rome, and Luke and the Talmud for Jerusalem. The instance of Rome is the most illuminating. Here we have indications from the Jewish catacombs between the first and the third centuries AD of eleven different synagogue communities, and there may well have been more. The names of the synagogue communities indicate distinctions of geographical area, nationality and profession. Loyalty to Augustus and Agrippa, whether on the part of a friend of the emperor or one of the two Jewish kings, gave names to two communities.[97] In the Monteverde catacomb in Trastevere, the old *transtiberina regio*, which according to Philo had been settled by the Jews brought to Rome by Pompey after the capture of Jerusalem in 63 BC who had then been gradually released,[98] two inscriptions were found from a synagogue community of the 'Hebrews'; a further one, which probably comes from there, was discovered in Porto near Rome, and a fourth one comes from an unknown location. Of the four inscriptions, three are in Greek and one is bilingual, in Greek and Aramaic.[99] It seems very likely that this was a gathering point for Jews coming from Palestine. In their strange environment they quickly gave up speaking Aramaic, but kept the name 'Synagogue of the Hebrews' as an indication of their homeland. Also from the catacomb of Monteverde we have four inscriptions by members of a synagogue of the 'Vernaculi', i.e. the 'natives'.[100] As it is evident from Cicero's *Pro Flacco* (59 BC) that even at that time, shortly after the triumph of Pompey, the first conqueror of Jerusalem (61 BC), there was a large and influential Jewish community in Rome,[101] we may assume that these 'Vernaculi' split off from the 'Hebrews' who arrived from Palestine and formed a community of their own, probably for linguistic reasons. This separation will then have continued long after the 'Hebrews' had come to speak Greek.[102] As Paul in Romans does not speak of a *community* in Rome, one could assume that at that time there were several Christian house churches in the great city just as there were various Jewish synagogues.[103] It is also striking that Paul never speaks of one ἐκκλησία in Jerusalem, but does twice mention 'communities in Judaea' (Gal. 1.22; I Thess. 2.14). By contrast the Pseudo-Clementine romance later reports that James the brother of the Lord was entrusted with the leadership of the community of the Hebrews in Jerusalem (πεπιστευ-μένῳ ἐν Ἰερουσαλὴμ τὴν Ἑβραίων διέπειν ἐκκλησίαν).[104]

The holding of separate worship in Greek and with it the formation of a new community, need not *a priori* have led to tension with the Aramaic-speaking mother community. Perhaps the leaders numbered seven instead of twelve because the group was substantially smaller; at the same time, however, this perhaps indicates a degree of subordination of the Seven to the Twelve, who probably claimed jurisdiction over all the communities in Judaea and Galilee. Perhaps the initiative for the foundation of the new group even came from the Twelve, and this is indicated in Acts 6.2ff. Luke further stresses this point by the act of laying on hands (6.6; cf. 8.17ff.; 9.12,17, etc.). As the group of leaders in the Jewish synagogue communites tended to be formed on analogy with that of the civic authorities, in Palestine by a presbytery and in the Diaspora often, as in Rome, by a select group of *archontes*,[105] seven overseers were appointed in analogy to the local Jewish leadership, the 'seven of a city'.[106] When in AD 66 Josephus organized the defence of Galilee, according to *BJ* 2,570f., he gave each city seven judges. In *Antt.* 4,214 he accordingly makes the command in Deut.16.18 quite specific: 'Seven men shall rule in each city, proved in *arete* and in zeal for righteousness.'[107] That the independence given by separate worship and the choice of the Seven did not mean the severing of all ties with the Aramaic-speaking mother community follows first from the fact that even the later Pauline mission communities retained Aramaic cries of prayer like 'Abba' and 'Marantha' in their services,[108] and secondly from the dispute over the daily provision for the widows which is reported by Luke. It is striking that among the Greek ossuary inscriptions in Jerusalem there are many women's names in particular.[109] It was the aim of many of those who returned to spend the evening of their life in the Holy City and to be buried there. The most famous widow from the Diaspora before AD 70 was Helena, the proselyte queen of Adiabene, who was buried in Jerusalem.[110]

With the enthusiastic expectation of the imminent coming of the Son of man and the concern for the common good which it inspired, the Christians, in contrast to the Essenes of Qumran, attached no importance to organized production and the economic exploitation of the possessions at the disposal of the community. So shortages must soon have arisen.[111] Whereas the native Christians could earn their living as day labourers or craftsmen, and often belonged to a larger family, single older women from the Diaspora often relied entirely on the support of the community, especially if they had generously given away their possessions. As a rule, eschatological enthusiasm and economic common sense, which includes rational organization, contradict each other. It is not surprising that the alien 'Hellenists' quickly ran into difficulties and complaints. The '*daily* provision' coped with the lack of any more long-term welfare. People deliberately lived from hand to mouth, as Jesus had commanded them in the Lord's Prayer (Luke 11.3 = Matt. 6.11) and in the prohibition against 'concern for the morrow' (Matt. 6.34). The well organized weekly care for the poor in the Jewish communities should not be used as a parallel here.[112]

By contrast, the formation of the new community had a positive influence on missionary activity. Now that newly-converted Christians from the Greek-speaking synagogues in Jerusalem could be invited to liturgical assemblies in their own mother tongue, concern for others who spoke Greek was intensified. In Acts 6.9, Luke speaks vaguely of a 'so-called synagogue (community) of the Libertines, the Cyrenians and the Alexandrians' and Jews from (τινές . . . τῶν ἀπό)

Cilicia and Asia Minor.[113] In reality there were certainly several Greek-speaking synagogue communities in Jerusalem (Acts 24.12). In Jewish Palestine the synagogue – mentioned for the first time by the New Testament and Josephus and clearly attested by the excavations in Herodeion, Masada and Gamala – was presumably definitively introduced by the Pharisees; the Temple hierarchy had no interest in encouraging liturgical competition inside and outside Jerusalem. There is evidence of synagogues in Egypt, however, as early as the third century BC; they are probably connected with the liturgical use of the LXX. The pre-Christian synagogue inscriptions from Ptolemaic Egypt and the island of Delos are exclusively Greek, and the designation of the synagogue building as 'proseuche' also sheds light on the form of the new form of prayer and worship without sacrifices, which was a revolutionary innovation.[114] Tosephta Megilla 3, 6 (Zuckermandel, p. 224) reports that R. Eleazar b.Sadoq bought the synagogue of the Alexandrians in Jerusalem and used it for profane purposes. According to the Mishnah (Meg. 3.1), such a sale was prohibited. In the discussion in the Gemara of the Palestinian Talmud the action is justified on the grounds that this was only the synagogue of a private group. The Gemara of Babli speaks of the sale of the synagogue of the 'Tarsians' or the (Alexandrians) 'metal workers' (*twrsyym*) to R. Eliezer (b. Hyrcanus).[115] Behind the whole account there is a clear denigration by the rabbinic scholars of these alien private synagogues. The synagogue of the *Libertines* is probably that of the Romans, in which according to Philo and Tacitus the freed Jewish prisoners of war played a decisive role.[116]

In view of the great Jewish Diaspora in Alexandria, Cyrenaica and Asia Minor it is understandable that the groups which came from those regions also had synagogues of their own in Jerualem. A cemetery found in the Kidron valley which contains eight un-Jewish Greek names out of twelve, also mentions an Alexander son of Simon with the Hebrew addition: *qrnyt*, i.e., possibly 'from Cyrene' (cf. Mark 15.21).[117] A further inscription from 'Dominus Flevit' mentions a Φίλων Κυρηναῖος.[118] Most interesting of all is the unique Theodotus inscription discovered shortly before the First World War on the Ophel, which certainly belongs to the period before AD 66:

Theodotus, Son of Vettenus, priest and archisynagogos, son of an archisynagogos, grandson of an archisynagogos, built the synagogue *for the reading of the law and instruction in the commandments*; also the lodging, the guest room and the water system to provide for those in need coming from abroad. The foundation stone was laid by his fathers, the elders and Simonides.[119]

The builder comes from a family which has already had three synagogue presidents in Jerusalem, which means that the synagogue community must have been founded in the time of Herod. The foundation stone for the synagogue which he completed was laid by his father and grandfather along with the leaders of the community and a further founder. It contains a lodging place[120] for the pilgrims from the Diaspora including bathing arrangements for ritual washings; it also provided for reading the law in worship and served as a school for teaching the law. The paternal name Vettenus could indicate Roman origin. Perhaps he was a freedman who owed his citizenship to a member of the *gens Vettena*.[121] We may take it for granted that worship and teaching the law were carried on in Greek. If we begin from the fact that the introduction of the synagogue to Palestine was encouraged by the Pharisees and moreover note the stress that is laid here not only on worship but also on 'instruction in the commandments'[122] and ritual bathing, we may assume that the founder was associated with the Pharisaic programme of 'educating the people in the law'. The Jews who returned to Jerusalem from the Diaspora had primarily religious reasons for their homecoming; as a rule they were certainly not 'liberal' and were probably closer to the attitude which Paul says he had when he was a Pharisee and before he became a Christian.[123] As returnees they felt a very deep tie to the Temple and the Torah; otherwise they would not have returned to Judaea, the culture and economy of which was hardly attractive, and would have chosen somewhere other than Jerusalem to live. This was the atmosphere in which the Hellenists tried to carry on their mission.

Of course Luke puts all the emphasis on Stephen, because he wants to concentrate on his martyrdom; however, the subsequent persecution of the group would be inconceivable if only one of its members had caused offence. As in accordance with Luke's view of history the proclamation of the word is restricted to the 'twelve apostles', at least to begin with (6.4), Luke only reports the great miracles of his hero (6.8); in his view the verbal controversy is introduced by the members of the Greek-speaking synagogue communities in Jerusalem who begin a discussion with Stephen and cannot cope with his spirit-given wisdom. Luke is right to emphasize Stephen in that – like Peter, John or James[124] – he must have been the spiritual leader of the new community. Even if the numerous occasions on which it is stressed that he was a charismatic filled with the spirit are a feature of Luke's style (6.5,8,10), this must be a feature which he took over from his source. Another indication of this could be that the key word σοφία occurs in Acts only in 6.10 in the case of

Stephen and in 6.3 with the appointing of the Seven, on each occasioned coupled with πνεῦμα. Apart from this it occurs only in Stephen's speech (7.10,22), in connection with Moses. The 'Hellenistic' missionaries evidently understood themselves as the bearers of special 'wisdom', through the eschatological inspiration of the Spirit.[125] This new freedom of the spirit and the wisdom revealed by God is the only explanation for the offence caused by Stephen and his colleagues. So here we are confronted with the question of the theological views of the community of the 'Hellenists' and their spokesman Stephen.

There is one course, often taken, which we cannot adopt in search of a closer definition of them. Stephen's speeech can be used only with considerable qualifications as the main evidence for the 'theology' of the Hellenists. Granted, it is not simply a literary composition from Luke's pen. He certainly made use of old and distinctive traditions in it. But it remains extremely dubious whether we should connect it directly with Stephen and the Hellenists.[126] Even if we assume that Luke, as elsewhere, has carefully provided a theological characterization of his protagonist through his speech in the framework of what is known about him,[127] we cannot infer more from the speech than what we also know from the accusations against Stephen. The speech simply accentuates these accusations. So we have to look above all at the accusation and the trial.

Stephen's worsted opponents incite men to accuse him of calumny against Moses the lawgiver and of blasphemy. 6.11 is at least in part un-Lucan in style, and could come from the source. It is also striking that in contrast to Acts 4; 5, the people and the elders and the scribes – who are distinct from the Sanhedrin – are stirred up. There is no further mention of the high priests and Sadducees, who hitherto have been behind the persecution;[128] only in 7.1 does the high priest for once put in a direct appearance. This looks like an alien element. Moreover, the time when the young community 'found favour with all the people' (2.47) since the people praised them and the leaders of the people were afraid of being stoned by the people (5.13,26) seems to have been forgotten. Might this originally have been a different λαός? The milieu has changed substantially. As the mention of the scribes shows, it has a Pharisaic rather than a Sadduceean colouring, even if Luke does not give such open expression to it with an eye to Gamaliel's counsel in 5.34ff. At the beginning of the persecution we find the people, the elders and the scribes, and at the end Saul – the Pharisee.[129] By contrast, surprisingly, the priestly hierarchy fades into the background.

Since F. C. Baur it has also been recognized that Luke's account fluctuates between an orderly trial before the Sanhedrin and a stormy example of lynch-law.[130] Quite apart from the fact that under the Roman prefects and later the procurators the Jews did not have the right to inflict capital punishment,[131] the meeting of the Sanhedrin seems artificial. The term 'Sanhedrin' appears only in 6.12,15; it does not appear at all in the account of the martyrdom; the venerable and for the most part aged members of the Sanhedrin here seem to turn into a raging mob. Luke uses the Sanhedrin to give an effective framework for the speech. Here is the beginning of the reckoning with official Judaism, which comes to an end in 28.26f.(= Isa. 6.9f.). However, we may conclude from 7.55 that the whole scene took place in the open air. Now even if we assume a case of lynch law, we must ask: was all the people of Jerusalem involved, or only a certain group? But which group could have had an interest in the execution of Stephen? With all these questions we keep coming up against that Greek-speaking minority of Diaspora Jews who had returned to Jerusalem for the sake of the Temple, the Law and the holiness of the land. They are the ones who, according to 9.29, also cross swords with their former compatriot Saul/Paul and similarly seek to kill him. We also find 'elders' and 'scribes', and the λαός (6.12), in the synagogue communities; by contrast we can rule out the involvement of the Sanhedrin as the supreme Jewish authority, especially as in some contexts 'Sanhedrin' can simply mean 'assembly'.[132] Was this originally a dispute with members of these Greek-speaking syn-agogue communities in Jerusalem, in which Stephen so provoked his opponents that they lynched him, quickly taking the law into their own hands? In that case the stoning was that of a blasphemer and false teacher caught in the act, and was evidently carried out by the members of the Greek-speaking synagogue communities who had been thus provoked. All the discussions will have taken place in Greek, and can hardly have been understood by the city mob of Jerusalem. These ethnic synagogue associations in Jerusalem cer-tainly had the possibility of exercising discipline within the com-munity – extending in some instances as far as the flogging mentioned in Deut. 25.3. By his own confession, Paul had been flogged five times by the synagogue authorities (II Cor. 11.24). Mark 13.9 says that the disciples will be handed over to the συνέδρια (plural) and be scourged in the synagogues.[133] It seems to me that the martyrdom of Stephen was connected with a synagogue assembly of this kind. No wonder that the Roman authorities did not intervene. Where there is no prosecutor, there is also no judge. The supporters of Jesus, who had been crucified as a rebel, will have been careful not to appear at a hearing in the city tribunals or before Pilate, who spent most of his time in Caesarea. The supreme Jewish authority, the Sanhedrin, which was dominated by the Sadducees, would if anything have been delighted over the affair. At a later stage, when he was attacked by Jews from Asia Minor, Paul only got away with his life because he exploited the tumult in the temple courtyard, which was under constant guard, and because he was a Roman citizen. After the stoning of James by Annas son of Annas, the Sadducean high priest, on the pretext of 'breaking the law', Annas was denounced by his Pharisaic opponents to Agrippa II and the new governor Albinus, who had just arrived, and was deposed (*Antt.* 20, 200ff.). In the two instances the situation was essentially different. In the case of James the Just the Pharisees were at least partially on the side of the Christians. In the case of Stephen, Greek-speaking Pharisees seem to have been the real opponents.

There remains the question of the basis for the accusation and the uproar which led to the spontaneous lynching. In 6.13f., false witnesses again make the charge of blasphemy quite precise: '. . . we have heard him say that this Jesus the Nazorean will destroy this (holy) place and will change the laws which Moses delivered to us.' It has rightly been stressed that in part Luke has modelled the martyrdom of Stephen on the passion narrative. Elements include the trial before the Sanhedrin, the false witnesses, the high priest's question, the reference to the Son of man (7.56), Stephen's dying prayer and the petition for the forgiveness of his murderers (7.59f.). In connection with the accusation by the false witnesses in 6.13f. it is supposed that Luke deliberately omitted the theme of the Temple from the trial of Jesus as contained in his Marcan model (14.58) and introduced it here in his account of Stephen as a false accusation. If the author only wanted to reproduce the passion narrative in the martyrdom of Stephen, however, his account would be of no historical value and we could not discover anything more about the accusation.[134] The other extreme is to see this latter as being influenced by the trial of Paul, against whom according to Acts 21.28 pilgrims from Asia Minor make the accusation: 'This is the man who is teaching men everywhere against the people (of God), the law and this (holy) place.' In this case Stephen had already anticipated Paul's quite radical criticism of the law.[135] However, despite Luke's concern to achieve a consistent style, we should particularly note the *differences* between the accusation against Stephen, the passion narrative and Paul's persecution.

The charges of the radical Jewish Christians against Paul in 21.21 are that he teaches Jews to apostatize from the law of Moses and become Gentiles and that he denies that Jews need to be circumcised.

The more pointed accusation of the Jews from Asia Minor in 21.28 declares that he is an enemy of the Jewish people who everywhere attacks Israel and the holy things entrusted to it, and has deliberately desecrated the temple with his Gentile companions. In 24.5 there is the additional charge of pestilentially causing an uproar.[136] The accusation against Stephen by no means has this comprehensive character; the 'words of blasphemy' in 6.11, like 6.13f., indicate individual, specific points of teaching. The Jesus who 'will change the laws which Moses has handed down to us' (καὶ ἀλλάξαι τὰ ἔθη ἃ παρέδωκεν ἡμῖν Μωϋσῆς) seems to be a new legislator rather than 'the end of the law' (Rom. 10.4).[137] In addition we should not overlook the christological basis. Jesus is the subject, the eschatological subject of this change which points towards the future. All this does not correspond either to Paul's doctrine of the Law or to Luke's picture of Paul.

There are also considerable differences from the passion narrative: in contrast to Mark 14.58, 6.14 says only that Jesus will destroy the temple; the χειροποίητος theme first appears in the charge in 7.48, where by contrast there is no mention of destruction. Similarly, nothing is said of any rebuilding.[138] The accusation stresses that Stephen claims that Christ will bring the end of the temple and its worship. However, the theme of changing the law is absent from the trial of Jesus before the Supreme Council, and the best parallel to the 'blasphemous words against Moses and God' (Acts 6.11) would be the spontaneous 'You have heard blasphemy' (Mark 14.64), which was not, however, the point of an accusation. Luke tones this down and omits the blasphemy in 22.71. The author takes it for granted that in both instances the accusation is made by false witnesses;[139] in his view the Christians represent the true will of God manifest in the law and the prophets (Acts 24.14; 26.22), to which the Jews are disobedient. That is what Stephen's speech is meant to prove. Mark already put what is presumably an authentic saying of Jesus in the mouth of 'false witnesses'.

As far as the accusation is concerned, Stephen's speech does not take us much further. The positive picture of Moses which makes Moses the type of Christ seems to contradict 6.11. After a relatively mild criticism of Solomon's temple built by human hands, the speech ends by turning the accusation upside down. The Jews themselves never kept 'the law received at the hands of angels'. Most serious is the charge that in their utter hardness of heart they have always resisted the holy spirit of God (7.47-53).

Here in my view we get to the decisive point. Stephen appears as *the* paradigmatic bearer of the spirit, marked out by miracles (6.8) and by the power and wisdom of his speech, inspired as it is by the Spirit (6.10).[140] He appears before his accusers like the epiphany of an angel: at the end of his speech the heavens open, and 'filled with the holy spirit' he sees the 'glory of God', the heavenly sanctuary and the Son of man, standing at the right hand of God.[141] This is the spirit of God being made manifest in him, which challenges his opponents to reply (6.9) and then, when they succumb, goes over to the attack (6.10f.). His spirit-inspired speech makes them extremely bitter (7.54); the heavenly vision provokes satanic hate which results in his murder. In my view Luke must already have found this theme of the intensifying contrast between the spirit of God manifest in Stephen and the satanic hostility of his adversary in his source; Stephen the martyr presumably appeared in it as a paradigm of the earliest Christian spirit-inspired enthusiasm.[142] This escalation of the theme of the spirit, which is unique in the New Testament, cannot be explained either by individual 'hagiographical' parallels from martyrdoms[143] as a purely Lucan invention.

The charge of blaspheming Moses and God (6.11), which is specified in 6.13f. as the announcement of the destruction of the temple and the changing of the law of Moses by Jesus, is basically a consequence of Stephen's spirit-inspired preaching (6.10). In Luke's redaction this feature is toned down by the insertion of the speech, and the connection between 6.15 and 7.55 is interrupted. Here we probably have a historical foundation. The criticism of law and temple is connected with the eschatological 'enthusiasm' of the Hellenists, inspired by the spirit.

As the gift of eschatological fulfilment (2.17) the Spirit shaped the present as a unique time of revelation. Through it the message and action of Jesus were now present as the work of the Risen Lord. That meant that the traditional Jewish 'saving event' of the exodus and revelation on Sinai were basically devalued in the light of the time of salvation which had now dawned with Jesus. In Jesus there is an expression of something not only more than Jonah and Solomon, but also more than Moses.[144] The law of Moses and its interpretation by the prophets extend only as far as John the Baptist. Then begins the new stage (cf. Luke 16.16) which Jesus himself introduces and which may no longer be poured into the old wineskins. In specific, individual instances his commandments break even the law of Moses. God's will is not fulfilled in a multiplicity of commandments standing on an equal footing; God's will is fulfilled in the commandment to love. The important thing is not ritual purity but a pure heart (Mark 7.15). The temple has lost its function as a place of expiation, for in the death of Jesus a truly valid sacrifice has taken place once and for all. It is significant in the future only as a house of prayer for all people (Mark 11.17). The 'blasphemy against Moses and God' is to be interpreted in this direction. Its starting point is in the proclamation of Jesus and it was later expressed in the synoptic tradition – which was handed down in Greek. That means that we need not introduce hypothetical Essene, Gnostic or any other kind of 'Hellenistic syncretism' to explain the Hellenists and Stephen; the decisive factor is the spirit-inspired interpretation of *the message of Jesus in the new medium of the Greek language.* Here Jesus' eschatological and critical interpretation of the Torah of Moses and the temple took on new contours, and we can understand how the Greek-speaking synagogue communities in Jerusalem – which presumably had a Pharisaic tone – regarded the new message as an intolerable blasphemy of their most sacred possessions, because of which in fact most of their members had come to Jerusalem. At a meeting called to impose community discipline, the provocation by the accused led to spontaneous lynching of the one who blasphemed against the lawgiver, his Torah and the sanctuary. It is no coincidence that the fundamental Jewish collection of sayings, the *Pirqe Aboth*, begins with the sentence, 'Moses received the Torah from Sinai' (i.e. from the God who revealed himself there). There follow the requirement for the 'hedge around the Torah' and the enumeration of the three things on which the world stands: 'the Torah, temple worship and good works'. All this seemed to be put in question by the crucified Jesus, who had led the people astray.

An understandable consequence of the martyrdom of Stephen was the persecution and expulsion of the Jewish-Christian 'Hellenists' from the Holy City (Acts 8.1,4; 11.19). They might regard the embittered reaction of their own kind from the Diaspora, which could express itself not only in the murder of Stephen but also in defamation, boycott, the implementation of community discipline and other acts of violence,[145] as a divine instruction to leave the Holy City in which the blood of Jesus and his witness Stephen had been shed (cf. Matt. 23.37; Luke 13.34), especially as they did not have ties to the Holy Land like those who had long been settled in Judaea and Galilee.[146] Possibly this sudden expulsion from Jerusalem – as a sign of the rejection of the majority of Israel - was a first stimulus to direct their mission towards the despised in Palestine, the 'marginal settlers' of Israel, the heretical Samaritans and the pagan godfearers. Here some of Jesus' instructions when he sent out his disciples could have had an effect (cf. Luke 10.10-15). Of course this development did not take place suddenly and all over the place; it will have happened in individual places and by stages. The direction of the spirit was probably essential. At the time when Paul was called, which cannot have been very long after the murder of Stephen, the mission to the Gentiles apart from the law was evidently still completely new. It was carried on a short time later in a really systematic way and on a large scale only by the community in the great city of Antioch (Acts 11.19ff.). This community therefore also carried on negotiations in Jerusalem at a later stage through its emissaries Paul and Barnabas (Gal. 2.1ff.; Acts 15.1ff.).

On the other hand, the violent 'purge' within the Hellenistic synagogue communities in Jerusalem may have had only a marginal effect on the Aramaic-speaking majority of the population of Jerusalem. The local Jewish Christians were only indirectly affected by the catastrophe which descended upon the sister community of the Hellenists. They saw that the storm had passed them by and only affected those whose spiritual freedom towards the temple and the ritual law they could not completely share. The later difficulties in making contact with the community in Antioch up to the time of the apostolic council could have their basis here.[147]

Palestinian Judaism had a particular fixation on the law and the temple – basically since the days of the Hellenistic reform attempt under Antiochus IV and the Maccabean revolt to which it led.[148] The sharp protests against Pilate, who had Roman standards with the imperial medallions introduced into the Antonia and later had dedicatory shields – presumably with inscriptions which were found offensive – put up for the emperor before the praetorium, i.e. the palace of Herod, and who further ventured to take money from the temple treasury for the building of an aqueduct for Jerusalem, speak for themselves, as do the serious disturbances which prompted Caligula's attempt in AD 39 to have his divine image set up in the Temple. 'Zeal for the law and sanctuary' was a regular feature of Jewish piety in Palestine between Herod and AD 70. Within Palestinian Judaism there was no freedom for open criticism of the Torah and the sanctuary which related to Moses himself.[149] Of course the earliest Aramaic-speaking community, following the preaching of Jesus, still did not have that strict attitude towards the law which at a later stage, under the leadership of James the brother of the Lord and after the withdrawal of Peter in about AD 43/44, marked it out;[150] however, if it was to survive in Judaea, it was far less able to escape the pressure of popular opinion than the Jewish-Christian 'Hellenists' who, under the unique, dynamic and creative impulse of the Spirit,[151] developed further the eschatologically motivated trend of the message of Jesus, which was critical of the Torah. The words of Jesus, newly interpreted through the experience of the Spirit and the certainty of the dawn of the end-time, provided the strength to break through the strong traditional link with Torah and cult. As a result, the holy scriptures were no longer interpreted primarily from the perspective of the law and its 613 commands and prohibitions, but as a prophetic promise focussed on Jesus.

In the context of this revolution we can hardly attach enough importance to the special significance of the new medium of the Greek language. Gerhard Ebeling, Ernst Fuchs and Eberhard Jüngel have recently drawn attention, quite rightly, to the fundamental significance of language for theology. Translated into Greek, the message of this new Jewish eschatological 'sect' took on a universal form in which the words of Jesus could first develop their complete, world-wide influence. This is evident not least from the fact that the 'Hellenists' expelled from Jerusalem also proclaimed the new message step by step in Greek to non-Jews, without making it dependent on acceptance of the Jewish law, albeit with the intrinsic consistency they had already employed in Jerusalem.

Thus at the same time earliest Christianity was changed from a basically rural and rustic sect whose founders were Galilean 'backwoodsmen' into an active and successful city religion. We cannot stress too much the difference between city and country in antiquity. The Jewish-Christian 'Hellenists', who themselves as a rule came from the cities of the Diaspora, transferred the mission to centres in the great cities.[152] This contrast between city and country is still clearly reflected in the distinction between the synoptic tradition and the arguments of Paul. Jerusalem was a decisive intermediate stage in this move from the countryside of Galilee to the cities of the Hellenistic world.

With the translation of the new message into the Greek *koine*, which in contrast to Aramaic was open to much greater variation and had a great power of expression – I need point only to the greater possibility of the modulation of verbs, the numerous particles, the participial constructions and the comparative – a series of theological terms came into the foreground which were to be determinative for early Christian theology. Here one might recall e.g. ἀπόστολος = *šali*ᵃ*h*,[153] εὐαγγελίζεσθαι = Aramaic *básser*, εὐαγγέλιον = *bᵉsorā*[154] 'in' or 'through the name of Jesus' =*bᵉ*– or *lᵉšūm yešuᵃ'*,[155] βασιλεία τοῦ θεοῦ (τῶν οὐρανῶν) = *malkūtā de'-lahā (dišmayyā)*, and also basic words like πίστις, πιστεύειν, ἀγάπη, ἐλπίς, ἀποκάλυψις and χάρις, which took on a new meaning in Christianity; further instances are παρρησία, παρουσία, and κοινωνία.[156] Like the translation of the Pentateuch in the third century BC in Egypt, now the translation of the new message had a creative effect on religious language. That is, the beginnings of a new theological language were created. At the same time the traditional terms of the Greek-speaking synagogue took on partially new content. We might perhaps begin to find a solution to the old dispute as to whether certain 'confessional formulae' like I Cor. 15.3f. or Rom. 1.3f. first arose in Antioch or go back to Aramaic originals by looking for their real point of origin in the 'Hellenist' community in Jerusalem. Although this community was active only for a very short time, its influence is unmistakable. It was the 'needle's eye' through which the earliest Christian kerygma and the message of Jesus, which was still indissolubly connected with it, found a way into the Graeco-Roman world. Thus we must reckon with the possibility that they also contributed the designation ἐκκλησία (τοῦ θεοῦ) – presumably already to distinguish themselves from the Jewish συναγωγαί in Jerusalem and to stress their eschatological claim.[157]

One remnant of their christology may be contained in the ancient confession in Rom.1.3f.,which Paul quotes as a sign of his christological agreement with the Roman community. Jesus the son of David (and Messiah designate) is appointed Son of God by his resurrection and at the same time has his messianic status confirmed by God.[158]

However, the term 'Son of David' at the same time points to the earthly Jesus, who was certainly much closer to the Hellenists than later to Paul. For in this community, too, the first attempt must have been made to translate the Jesus tradition into Greek. The activity of Jesus, and his death and resurrection which laid the foundation for the community, lay only a short while in the past, and remembrance of them was still vivid. The recently crucified Jesus could not have been proclaimed as Messiah to the Diaspora Jews in Jerusalem had not his sayings and activity been expressed in the new language. The Palestinian local colouring of large parts of the synoptic tradition has been·preserved so well because the translation into Greek did not begin in Antioch, Ephesus or Rome, but at a very early stage in Palestine itself. Even if the conjecture by T. Boman, that the translation and collection of the Q tradition ultimately goes back to Stephen and his circle, cannot be proved,[159] in that first Greek-speaking community a basic part of the gospel tradition, including the tradition of the passion, must have been translated, since without this basic part the missionary proclamation that the crucified Jesus who was though to have led the people astray was the Christ of God would have been impossible. The relative agreement between the Markan and Pauline accounts of the eucharist must point to a common origin which is to be sought here. A further indication for a fixed place for the translation of the Jesus tradition is provided by the rendering of *bar* ^ᵓ*nāš(ā)* (or *b^ereh de^ᵓnāšā*?) by ὁ υἱὸς τοῦ ἀνθρώπου with a clear messianic meaning, a rendering on which the New Testament is completely agreed. It must have happened at one particular place, since only in this way could it have come about that other possibilities of translation like the more obvious ἄνθρωπος or υἱὸς ἀνθρώπου could no longer appear. A definite christological conception must underly this unusual translation; perhaps it has found expression in the Son of man of Stephen's vision (7.56).[160] The translation of the Lord's Prayer, which begins with the address *'abbā*, also seems to me to go back to this early period, for the community of Jesus must have had it from the beginning.[161]

Finally, one could ask why the message of Jesus had such an effect in particular on the Greek-speaking Diaspora Jews in Jerusalem. As a rule they had religious reasons for staying in the 'Holy City'. However, in some circumstances the realities there could have a negative effect on those who had returned; they could be as ambivalent and indeed disappointing as was the 'Holy City', Rome, of Martin Luther's time when he went there on pilgrimage. The intellectual arrogance of the Pharisaic sages and the necessary casuistry of their interpretation of the Torah could be as offensive as the exploitation of the pilgrims in the temple by the Sadducean priestly nobility. World-famous places of pilgrimage always have both their dark and their bright sides. The focal point of attention in Jerusalem was certainly not in those features which were so dear to the heart of Hellenistic Jewish apologetics, the universality of Jewish belief in God and the prophetic ethos, stress on the ten commandments and philanthropy in contrast to esteem for the ritual law, in short the 'ethical monotheism' which must have been essential precisely to the educated Jew from the dispersion in his struggle for religious self-affirmation in the face of Hellenistic syncretism. Here conflict was possible in individual cases, and we can understand how the new eschatological-prophetic preaching of the earliest community, which combined the message of Jesus with the dynamism of the receiving of the spirit, could find a hearing among individual critics from among those who had returned to Jerusalem, since here they discovered decisive features which they had looked for in vain elsewhere there. The eschatological gift of the spirit freed them from their tie to the letter of the law and from the casuistic arguments of scholars, for knowledge of the true will of God in the commandment to love. The preaching of Jesus in fact also contained critical features of the kind that we can see to some degree in Greek gnomic wisdom or in Cynicism. Here there were points of contact which made it easier for the gospel to be translated into the quite different world of Greek language and Greek thought.[162] Even more effective was probably the experience of eschatological κοινωνία brought about by the spirit, in which the assurance of the forgiveness of sins and imminent reunion with the returning Lord took shape and found specific realization in the enthusiastic fellowship of the messianic community.

Precisely through the activity of the early Greek-speaking community, more of the proclamation of Jesus is present in the synoptic gospels than basically anti-historical modern hyper-criticism is willing to concede. Twenty years after Stephen, the earliest Christian kerygma shone out in all its glory in Paul's 'mission theology'. We owe the real bridge between Jesus and Paul to those almost unknown Jewish-Christian 'Hellenists' of the group around Stephen and the first Greek-speaking community in Jerusalem which they founded; this was the first to translate the Jesus tradition into Greek and at the same time prepared the way for Paul's preaching of freedom by its criticism of the ritual law and the cult. Only this community can be called the 'pre-Pauline Hellenistic community' in the full sense of the word.

2

Christology and New Testament Chronology
A Problem in the History of Earliest
Christianity

One of the most important New Testament monographs published since the Second World War is O. Cullmann's *Christology of the New Testament*.[1] As is evident from the constant flow of studies in christology which have appeared since, it is still influential today, even if later authors have thought it necessary to adopt different approaches.[2] Investigation of the earliest Christian confessional formulae is indissolubly connected with christology. Here too Cullmann did basic work which has been taken up by many scholars since.[3] I, too, am particularly indebted to his christological writings, and would like here to raise a few critical questions and make some suggestions in connection with contemporary discussion.

Although in recent decades Acts has been caught in the cross-fire of radical criticism – which sadly is not always self-critical enough – the few pieces of historical and chronological information in the book which can be assessed have proved to be largely reliable. This is true, for example, of the two notes about the expulsion of the Jews from Rome under Claudius and the governorship of Gallio in Achaea,[4] which give us a basis for Pauline chronology from which we can 'make further calculations with a tolerable degree of uncertainty amounting to about two years'.[5] The most recent investigations into the Gallio inscription by A. Plassart[6] conclude that the Twenty-Sixth Acclamation of Claudius took place in spring 52 and that a short time later Claudius' letter about the settling of new citizens in Delphi was already addressed to Gallio's successor. Furthermore, Gallio's report underlying the letter may date from the later period of his proconsulate. That would put the proconsulate between the beginning of May 51 and the beginning of May 52, and Paul's stay in Corinth (Acts 18.11ff.) between the end of 49 and the summer of 51 AD, a period of about eighteen months. Beginning from this, we can put the Apostolic

Council round about AD 48,[7] and date Paul's conversion, with the help of Gal. 1.18; 2.1 to the time between AD 32 and 34. A variety of indications suggests that the death of Jesus is to be dated to Friday, 14 Nisan (7 April) AD 30.[8]

There is a broad consensus over these familiar dates, and differences do not amount to more than a year or so; however, they do not touch on the probllem which we have to consider. The time between the death of Jesus and the fully developed christology which we find in the earliest Christian documents, the letters of Paul is so short that the development which takes place within it can only be called amazing.

On closer inspection the time available for the christological development leading up to Paul becomes even shorter. The earliest letter to the community in Thessalonica was written probably at the beginning of AD 50, at the start of Paul's activity in Corinth. The last letter, to the Romans, was presumably written in the winter of AD 56/57, again from Corinth. However, as we cannot detect any development in the basic christological views in his letters and furthermore he presupposes that the christological titles, formulae and conceptions which he uses are known in the communities to which he is writing, so that they go back to the content of his mission preaching when he founded these communities, we must assume that all the essential features of Paul's christology were already fully developed towards the end of the 40s, before the beginning of his great missionary journeys in the West. That means that there are less than twenty years available for the development of primitive Christian christology up to time of its earliest representative accessible to us, namely Paul.[9] This 'shortage of time' for the development of the christological tradition within the earliest community becomes yet more acute if on the basis of Gal. 1 and 2 we look back another fourteen to sixteen years, to the conversion of Paul between AD 32 and 34: now only between two and four years separate us from the death and resurrection of Jesus, the events which brought the Christian community into being.[10] Anyone concerned to clarify the beginnings of christology must answer two questions at this point. 1. What kind of picture of Christ might the newly-converted Pharisee have had, as it developed in his theological reflection immediately after his vision of the Risen Christ before Damascus, so as to become the foundation of his gospel apart from the law and his first attempts at missionary preaching? 2. Do we have any reason to suppose that Paul's christology changed in essential points during his activity in Syria and Cilicia in the years which now follewed? That leads immediately to a further question. Which Christians, or which communities, took the newly-converted Paul into their midst, influenced his theological thinking and shaped his christological ideas?

Scholars have no doubt that in his letters Paul uses an abundance of traditional, *'pre-Pauline'* formulae. A major part of contemporary exegetical concern is to trace formulae of this kind and to work out as far as possible their original form.[11] Of course, the term 'pre-Pauline' is itself again ambiguous and therefore open to misunderstanding. Strictly speaking, it would mean that 'pre-Pauline' formulae of this kind were already shaped in the few years before Paul's conversion. This would shift the focal point of the origin of christology to the short space of the earliest period of all, so that it would become virtually impossible to make any closer chronological and geographical distinctions. If we use the term 'pre-Pauline' in a wider sense, say to mean that such formulae could also have developed in the period between his conversion and the Apostolic Council, it remains obscure whether and to what extent Paul was himself actively involved as a theological authority in working out such formulae in the obscure fourteen to sixteen years before the Apostolic Council or how far he was taking over material which was really quite independent of him. A demonstration that individual christological and soteriological formulations also appear in a non-Pauline context – which is always later – is not enough to identify them *eo ipso* as 'pre-Pauline', i.e. as material which was originally quite independent of the apostle. In other words, how far was the authority of the apostle himself a factor in the christological development of the young mission communities in Syria and Cilicia, before he began his missionary onslaught on the West, to which we owe the account of his theology in his letters?[12] This keyword 'community' introduces a further concept which may perhaps do something to help us out of our difficulty.

It was a real step forward in scholarship when W. Heitmüller, in his article 'Paul and Jesus',[13], attempted to make more precise the old and somewhat crude contrast, going back to F.C.Baur, between the earliest community and Paul, by introducing a third factor, 'Hellenistic Christianity'. With acute perception, Heitmüller also recognized that this 'Hellenistic Christianity' had its roots in Jerusalem itself, among the Greek-speaking Jews of the circle around Stephen. They began 'to understand the universalist forces in the preaching of Jesus and to break through the particularist and nationalistic limitations connected with it'.[14] Accordingly, even before Paul, namely after their expulsion from Jerusalem, they laid the foundation for the mission to the Gentiles. Unfortunately, Heitmüller failed to reflect on the minimal distance of these Hellenists in time and place from the fundamental event which gave rise to the Christian community.

In the case of the Hellenists, the span of between two and four years which separates Paul's conversion from this event is reduced to an even shorter interval of perhaps only a few months; indeed we have to ask whether there were not some bilingual disciples among the followers of Jesus whose origin and education brought them much closer to Greek-speaking Judaism. But that would mean that the roots of this 'Helllenistic Christianity' perhaps lie in the 'original event', or that it was at least a result of the mission to the Jews which was sparked off by it.[15] Heitmüller could not see these connections, because his concerns took a quite different direction. He sought to explain the gulf between Paul and Jesus, and between Paul and Jerusalem by that event, and therefore in interpreting this unknown period he took a course which has been followed down to the present.

According to Heitmüller, the 'Hellenistic Christianity existing before and alongside Paul'[16] was radically removed from the historical Jesus, though it above all developed the universalist implications of Jesus' preaching. His place was taken by the 'Christ idea': 'christology comes into the foreground'[17] Of course this unbridgeable gulf between the earthly Jesus and 'christology' is really compelling only for those who want to recognize the modern dogma of the completely unmessianic Jesus. That this leads to a dead end is evident from the fact that Bultmann had to resort to the expedient of an 'implicit christology' to explain it.[18] Furthermore, this approach does not take enough account of the christological consequences of the resurrection event: would it not be possible that the greater part of the roots of later christological development lie in this revolutionary event which radically changed not only Paul's life but also that of Jesus' disciples, that is, in so far as it was not already rooted in the activity and proclamation of Jesus himself? By contrast Heitmüller – and even more markedly W.Bousset – sought to solve the riddle by positing a strong influence from 'Hellenistic syncretism'. 'As soon as it moved into Hellenistic territory, the preaching of the death and resurrection of Jesus . . . could and indeed had to become involved, in pagan minds, with apparently similar stories of the violent death and exaltation of gods.'[19] This 'amalgamation' is said to have included the adoption of the title Kyrios for the exalted Christ, veneration of him in the cult, the sacramental understanding of this in terms of Hellenistic mystery religions, and 'the beginnings of Christ-mysticism'. Paul is said already to have come up against this approach and adopted it in Damascus, where he became a Christian, or at the latest in Antioch. By a one-sided reference to Gal. 1.22 which still has an influence today, the statements in Acts 7.58-8.3; 9.1ff. were pushed on one side as unhistorical and Paul, the Pharisee with scribal

training, was transformed into a pure 'Hellenistic Diaspora Jew' who
to begin with did not have any connection with Jerusalem at all.[20]
Quite apart from the fact that it is very questionable whether we may
suppose that a Judaism influenced by syncretism and accordingly a
'progressive' syncretistic Christian community can be found in Damascus, which geographically is close to Palestine, here again we
come up against the problem of chronology. Is such a development
conceivable in the few years before Paul's conversion? Since in
addition we must assume that the founders of the community in
Damascus themselves came from Palestine to Syria a short time
before this event, the whole problem of the origin of the Hellenistic
community is necessarily shifted back to Palestine.[21] But how can we
imagine a massive 'syncretistic' influence there? That leaves only
Antioch, where according to Acts 11.19ff. there was an active mission
to the Gentiles in the second half of the 30s. W. Bousset makes this
community his focal point, rightly stressing that 'the universalist
religious community of Antioch, consisting of Jews and Hellenes,
came into being without Paul'. Where Paul 'refers to tradition, this is
not the tradition of Jerusalem but primarily that of the Gentile
Christian community in Antioch'.[22] This may readily be conceded,
though it is striking that Paul never speaks of his links with the
community in Antioch and seems much more strongly oriented on
Jerusalem – though at times polemically. We almost get the impression that he had written off his Antiochene past.[23] What causes
offence is something rather different, namely that to some degree
under-handedly and without justification W. Bousset transforms the
community in Antioch 'made up of Jews and Hellenes' into a
Gentile-Christian community. The term 'Gentile Christian' is vague
and open to misunderstanding simply because of the unmistakable
group of proselytes and godfearers who were a particularly favourable audience for the earliest Christian mission.[24] We should restrict
mention of the 'Gentile-Christian community' to situations where
the spiritual leaders of a community and therefore also its theology
had a 'Gentile-Christian' stamp. But that was certainly not the case in
Antioch between about AD 35 and 48.

Nevertheless, 'critical' scholarship did not shrink from radical
consequences in order to 'underpin' its postulate of a massive
syncretistic pagan influence on pre-Pauline christology. Thus R. Bultmann, following R. Reitzenstein, postulated the existence of gnostic
communities in which 'the Redeemer was identified with the god of
the Phrygian mysteries. In such a manner the (gnostic) movement
also made its way into the Christian community.'[25] Such a 'combination' of 'mystery ideas and gnostic myth' is said to appear as early

as Paul.[26] So it was quite consistent for Bultmann in part to follow W.Bousset in describing the 'cult religion' of 'Hellenistic Christianity' as 'a completely new religion compared with earliest Palestinian Christianity, which belongs in the context of the mystery religions and gnosticism'. Here christology appeared as 'the exponent of cultic piety'.[27] Unfortunately this does not answer the question when, where and how such a 'penetration' and foundation of a new religion might have taken place. Paul, Barnabas and the other 'prophets' in Antioch (Acts 13.1f.; cf. 11.20) would thus become people who on their encounter with the risen Christ were at the same time led astray into unbridled syncretistic speculation. Is it not historically more appropriate here to explain the christological development up to the Apostolic Council intrinsically on Jewish presuppositions, which of course are richer and more varied than the fathers of the history-of-religions school could have supposed? Thus the old theme of 'the history of religion and earliest Christianity' turns into the question of 'the history of religion and ancient Judaism', which in the New Testament period already had a history reaching back over many centuries and for a long time – even in Palestine – had been influenced by Hellenistic thought.[28]

It was therefore a real step forward when F.Hahn broke with this obscure picture of a pre-Pauline Hellenistic Christianity and consistently attempted to work out the contours of the 'Jewish-Christian and Hellenistic community' before and alongside Paul. As a result he produced a four-stage scheme: 1. Jesus; 2. Palestinian Jewish Christianity (= the earliest community); 3. Hellenistic Jewish Christianity; 4. Hellenistic Gentile Christianity. The second and third stages were equally decisive for christological development; Hellenistic Gentile Christianity, the boundaries of which are said to be 'fluid', rightly fades well into the background.[29] In my view this can be seen clearly in the Pauline missionary communities; we can say that they had real, independent theological significance only in the period after AD 70. For this reason I would in principle hesitate to attribute the hymn in Phil. 2.6-11 to 'the Hellenistic-Gentile Christian community', especially as for Hahn himself, 2.9-11 'seems to be almost still on the threshold of Hellenistic Judaism'. This only goes to show how difficult distinctions of this kind are.[30] Therefore even for Hahn the real problem is the early period 'before Paul'. With the help of a method which works consistently in terms of tradition criticism he attempts to demonstrate christological development step by step, starting with individual honorific titles, which means that he must constantly make chronological judgments. Of course here he works with relative indications of time, like 'earliest tradition'. 'old', 'late', 'recent' and so

on, and avoids more exact chronological indications, though sometimes he also speaks of the 'old' or 'early Palestinian community' or
'early Hellenistic community';[31] given the largely hypothetical character of this approach there cannot be really exact indications of time.
In this approach, there had to be bold conjectures; sometimes they
were energetically rejected by Hahn's critics, for example above all
the distinction in principle between the assumption and the exaltation
of Jesus. The earliest community immediately after the resurrection
is said only to have expected the parousia of its Lord who had been
taken up into heaven and not to have developed any concept of
exaltation; this was only the product of the Jewish Hellenistic community.[32] Hahn's affirmation of the chronological priority of the Son
of Man christology over against the title Messiah has met with similar
repudiation. It fails to note not only that in the few Jewish references
to the 'Son of Man' he can always be identified with the Messiah,[33]
but also that the fact that Jesus was crucified as 'king of the Jews' -
which Hahn also accepts – immediately raised the christological
problem of the crucified Messiah.[34] In general Hahn does not deal
enough with the fundamental problem, already formulated clearly
by Cullmann, that 'the whole development of Christological perception progressed parallel to the missionary work of early Christianity',[35] and hardly notes the fact that the 'Hellenistic' community itself
had its origin in Palestine.[36]

Hahn's work was supplemented by W. Kramer's dissertation,
which appeared somewhat later, devoted to the analysis of the
christological titles and formulae in Paul. In the first part he discusses
the 'pre-Pauline material' in detail. He seems hardly aware of the
problem that the Paul of the letters already has a 'Christian past' of
between sixteen and eighteen years, in which he himself probably
had a share in shaping this 'pre-Pauline' development. The notion of
a tradition running alongside Paul appears only quite marginally, in
connection with later post-Pauline formulae.[37] Like Hahn, he distinguishes three pre-Pauline communities: '1. the Hellenistic Gentile-
Christian community; 2. the Greek-speaking Jewish-Christian community = the "Hellenists" of Acts 6.1 = the "Stephen circle" in the
wider sense; 3. the Aramaic-speaking primitive community (in Jerusalem).' Some progress in approach is marked by the fact that in the
case of the second and third groups he suggests that the difference in
language is the real dividing factor and he connects the second group
closely with the 'Hellenists', who, like the Aramaic-speaking primitive community, had their roots in Jerusalem.[38] Of course there is a
chronological and historical problem which with both Hahn and
Kramer considerably limits the conclusiveness of this three-stage

pattern. The beginnings of the Greek-speaking breach in the primitive community in Jerusalem go back into its earliest period. The division forced on the community by the need for separate worship in Greek must have happened very soon, perhaps a year or two after the resurrection. Here the picture of a differentiated christological development in the earliest period comes under extreme chronological pressure. In addition, even in the Aramaic-speaking community we have to reckon with bilingual Palestinian Greeks like Barnabas; indeed, after the persecution by Agrippa I in AD 43/44 the head of the primitive community, Simon Cephas/Peter, went over to Greek-speaking Jewish-Christian territory and visited Christian communities in the Diaspora.[39] The Aramaic-speaking primitive community in Jerusalem and the Greek-speaking Jewish-Christian community in Jerusalem, Caesarea, Damascus, Antioch and Rome do not so much come one after another in time as stand side by side,[40] so that it would also be possible in theory that traditions from the Greek-speaking 'primitive community' were also taken over by the Aramaic-speaking community. For example, in wanting to assign only the statement 'God . . . raised up Jesus (or: the Messiah)(from the dead)' to the Aramaic-speaking community and claiming the formula 'Christ died for our sins' for Greek-speaking Jewish Christians on the grounds that this conception is absent from Q and the Lucan special material, Kramer says nothing about the time when the formula originated. There were Greek-speaking Jewish Christians from 30/31 up to the time of Paul – indeed he himself was one of them.[41] They were the real vehicles for the expansion of Christianity up to AD 70. When Kramer goes on, with reference to Acts 8.14, to assume an 'express approval (for the formula) of those who were closest to the original apostles', he is presenting more of an imaginary than a vivid picture.[42] We simply know too little about the development of the Aramaic community between 30 and 66 to be able to arrive at clear, exclusive verdicts. The much misused reference to Q is hardly of any more help here, for Q in no way contains the whole christology of the community, but only its collection of logia of Jesus. Indeed we also look in vain in Q for statements about the resurrection of Jesus, quite simply because Jesus himself said nothing about it. It would be nonsensical to want to conclude from this that the resurrection of Jesus had no significance for the Q community. Christology and the tradition about Jesus need not always have coincided.

Kramer gets into even more difficult over the 'Hellenistic Gentile Christian community'. He fails to define this vague term, and simply takes it for granted. What was said above in connection with Bousset may also be said of Kramer. Before the Apostolic Council one should not speak of 'Gentile-Christian communities', but more precisely of 'mixed communities'. The mix in any particular community could change, but at all events the Jewish Christians remained the spiritual and theological leaders. Above all in his discussion of the title Kyrios, Kramer arrives at a distorted account of christological development, as here he has succumbed to the views of S. Schulz about the fundamental division between a Hellenistic, cultic 'acclamation Kyrios' coming from pagan sources and a Jewish-Palestinian 'Mare Kyrios' connected with the parousia. Schulz's basic argument that 'Mara was an extremely insignificant concept from the viewpoint of religion', which Kramer takes over without examining it, rests on a completely one-sided and superficial choice of sources and is fundamentally wrong.[43] These artificial constructions are refuted by Kramer's own judgment that 'with only three exceptions it is the title Lord which is linked in the Pauline corpus with the parousia'. The tortured attempts to reconcile this situation with his hypothesis of a division themselves refute the hypothesis.[44] Here we can see a methodological limitation which affects the whole book: while we must recognize Kramer's concern to begin by treating individual titles, formulae and phrases in isolation, and he has done fundamental work here, the attempt to project back these 'atomized' statements on the tradition of the 'pre-Pauline communities' makes the christological development incomprehensible as a whole. Indeed the individual christological formula is always only an isolated cipher, underlying which in the earliest Christian communities there was a living, vivid understanding of the saving event in the sense of the eschatological revelation of God through his Christ. The ultimate aim of a meaningful account of the earliest Christian christology must be an overall view and not the isolated consideration of the individual christological ciphers.[45]

Furthermore, the putative pre-Pauline, christologically productive 'Gentile-Christian community' is a fiction. Granted, Kramer thinks he can find a criterion for its existence in the change of the title Christ into a proper name,[46] a development which is indicated for the first time by the transference of the designation *Christianoi* to the Christians in the second half of the thirties in Antioch. However, even this is as yet no proof that at that time the community in Antioch became 'Gentile-Christian' and borrowed from the mystery cults there. Such a transformation of a title into a name was easily possible in the Jewish-Christian milieu of the Diaspora, as the title 'Christos', while being easier to understand than 'Son of Man', was nevertheless very strange. Outside a number of passages in the LXX, it hardly occurs in Hellenistic-Jewish literature. The transformation of the confessional statement Ἰησοῦς Χριστός into a name made complete sense for the Jewish Christians, because as a result the designation of his status was very closely, indeed one might say indissolubly, connected with the name of Jesus. Even the Palestinian Jew Josephus talks of Jesus as ὁ λεγόμενος Χριστός (*Antt.* 20,200). The post-Pauline use, which extends to Luke, John and Justin, shows that people remained aware of this even in Gentile-Christian circles. Thus we can bring this critical consideration of Protestant German research to a close; more recent researches like those of Wengst and Kegel[47] hardly offer new perspectives on the question; they too remain within the framework of the three-communities pattern, which cannot clarify historical developments, because the decisive development took place in that Greek-speaking Jewish-Christian community which we can trace back into the earliest period of the primitive community in Jerusalem, a community to which Paul belonged for many years and with which even Peter came into close contact at a later date. There were certainly distinctions within this Hellenistic Jewish Christianity over the course of time, and the degree of Gentile-Christian involvement in the community could have had some effect here. However, we should not present it as being a completely disparate and quite separate phenomenon from Jerusalem.[48]

To sum up results so far and to assess their consequences:

1. In principle the New Testament scholar should never forget Overbeck's critical judgment: 'In earliest Christianity the veil which lies over every tradition becomes so dense as to be impenetrable.'[49] More than in other disciplines the New Testament scholar has to work with hypotheses. However, that should not prevent him from accounting for his hypotheses 'in space and time'. Now this means that in assigning them dates he also reflects on the chronological problem and does not simply content himself with assigning them to 'communities' which are often defined in a very vague way. If we look through some works on the history of earliest Christianity we might get the impression that people in them had declared war on chronology.[50]

2. Since the letters of Paul – including Romans, which is addressed to a 'pre-Pauline' community – demonstrate a stereotyped christology within which we cannot establish any real development, we must assume that even before Paul set off on his great missionary journeys in the West, that is, at the latest with the Apostolic Council about AD 48, his christology was largely complete. Thus the christological development from Jesus as far as Paul took place within about eighteen years, a short space of time for such an intellectual process. In essentials more happened in christology within these few years

than in the whole subsequent seven hundred years of church history. Philippians 2.6ff.; I Cor. 8.6; Gal. 4.4; Rom. 8.3 and I Cor. 2.7 already bear witness to the pre-existence and divine nature of Jesus and his mediation in creation. The subordination which is clear in I Cor. 15.23-28 does not tell against this; in its way it only demonstrates the unique connection between the Son and the Father which is quite unparalleled. By contrast, the new element in the later Logos christology and the development leading up to the formation of the doctrines of the early church was that there was a concern to bring the 'divine functions' of the Son of God into line with the conceptuality and thought patterns of the Greek metaphysics of being.[51]

3. The christological development during these brief twenty years took place above all in the Greek-speaking Jewish-Christian communities of Jerusalem, Caesarea, Damascus, Antioch and other places in Syria and Palestine, i.e. in an area which was limited both sociologically and geographically. The part in this played by the Aramaic-speaking community in Jerusalem (or Galilee) is not to be taken lightly, since the time during which the two 'communities' existed together and side by side is incomparably longer than the brief interval in which the Aramaic-speaking community in Jerusalem was the only one there. Moreover, we have no evidence that the two 'communities' were strictly separated; quite independently, the letters of Paul and Acts show that the opposite was the case.

The ultimate roots of the Greek-speaking Jewish-Christian community may already go back to the group of followers of Jesus himself. Of course this first took shape in Jerusalem. Presumably we must reckon almost as much with a mutual influence of one group on the other as with an adoption of the earliest conceptions by the Greek-speaking part of the community. Here, for example, we might ask how far originally 'Hellenistic' elements, say those connected with emancipation and enlightenment, were not at work in the proclamation of Jesus himself, just as we also find them in Cynic and Stoic diatribes. This would make his particular appeal to the Hellenists all the more understandable.[52] The bilingual Palestinian Greeks like Barnabas, Philip, John Mark, Silas-Silvanus and so on also played a major role. Peter and Paul must also be included among them. It is striking 1. that the Paul of the letters above all has in view the primitive community in Jerusalem and not, for example, Antioch; and 2. that his differences with Jerusalem become clear in soteriology and the doctrine of the law, and not, by contrast, in his statements about the person of Christ.[53] Did christology in Jerusalem too become 'more Hellenistic' after the expulsion of the group around Stephen than the later Ebionite reports suggest? Furthermore the community in Judaea was evidently no 'monolithic block' (Acts 15.1ff.; Gal. 2.2ff.) and in a situation of being oppressed by Judaism. Unfortunately we know almost nothing about the christological views of James, the Lord's brother. It is worth remembering that his influence only became effective at a later period. It is also striking that the christology of the Gospel of Matthew, which comes from the Jewish-Christian milieu of Syria, is closer to that of Paul than to the Ebionite view of Christ. It is extremely improbable that to begin with there was a multiplicity of mutually exclusive, rival 'christologies', as is continually claimed.[54] The earliest community made christological 'experiments', if one likes to put it that way, but not in sectarian exclusiveness; they had a readiness to accept new elements and thus 'enrich' the worth of Christ. The multiplicity of christological titles does not mean a multiplicity of exclusive 'christologies' but an accumulative glorification of Jesus. The titles must be considered from the perspective of a 'multiplicity of approaches' of the kind that is typical of mythical thought.[55] This is particularly true of the early phase of expansion.

4. It is wrong to talk of a christologically productive Gentile-Christian community before Paul. Even the Syrian missionary communities were at best 'mixed communities', in which the Jewish-Christian element was for a long time theologically dominant. Syria in fact had the strongest Jewish Diaspora. Virtually all the Gentile-Christian missionaries of the first twenty-five years were Jewish Christians; only from Paul do we know that Gentile Christians also joined them as auxiliary missionaries. The mission to the Gentiles apart from the law in the decisive early period is completely and utterly the work of Christian Jews. The consequence is that even in this early period one cannot assume any direct, massive pagan influences as was the view in the first joys of discovery among the history-of-religions school. The conception of the sending of the Son does not come from a pre-Christian gnostic myth – which in fact never existed – but has its roots in Jewish wisdom speculation; the confession κύριος Ἰησοῦς is not borrowed from the cult of Attis, Serapis or Isis, but is a necessary consequence of the exaltation christology in which Ps. 110.1 in particular played a part; the Jerusalem *maranatha* formula represented a preliminary stage in which the exalted Christ was called upon to return soon.

In my view, here we have an expression of what was still a completely personal relationship on the part of the earliest community to its now exalted Lord. Recollections of the Master were still very much alive in the early period. The same is the case with the formula 'the brothers of the Lord'. Thus the form of address '(our)

Lord' was already part of the basic material of earliest Christian christology, which was even taken over by the group around Stephen when they began to worship separately. Influences from the mysteries, say in the doctrine of the sacraments, were communicated through Greek-speaking Judaism; 'the language of the mysteries' was part of the religious *koine* of the time and was also accepted by Judaism, as is shown by Wisdom, Joseph and Asenath, and Philo. It even penetrated partially into Palestinian Judaism.[56]

5. Thus as the pattern of three communities is in no way adequate to explain the rise of christology before and alongside Paul, we should consider whether we do not have to indicate other historical and chronological stages in order to understand the enormously rapid christological development of the first years. These might include: 1. the separate worship of Aramaic- and Greek-speaking groups in Jerusalem, which must have already happened at a very early stage, say about AD 31 or 32. 2. The murder of Stephen and the break-up of the Greek-speaking part of the community took place a little later, about AD 32/33. 3. The conversion of Paul, about 32/34, forms a further stage. 4. Almost at the same time there begins the first 'Gentile mission' of the 'Hellenists' who have been driven out of Jerusalem, first of all among the 'semi-Jews' of Samaria and then also in the coastal region of Palestine and Phoenicia and beyond there as far as the Syrian cities of Damascus and Antioch, about 33/35.[57] These first four or five years are therefore characterized by a tremendously rapid sequence of events. This is the only time that we can call the 'pre-Pauline period' in the full sense of the word. The question then is: does this almost 'explosive' missionary expansion at the beginning of the earliest Christian history not also have a parallel in the development of christology? There is much to suggest that these first four or five years, up to the conversion of Paul and the beginning of the mixed community in Antioch composed of Jews and Gentiles, again takes on a quite special significance within the wider context of the roughly eighteen years before the Apostolic Council. There must already have been clear christological contours to the Messiah Jesus, who was so compelling to the former Pharisee trained by the scribes that for Paul he could take the place of the Law as the sole way of salvation for all men. The atoning saving significance of the death of Jesus will have been clearly formulated at the same time; furthermore, Gal. 1.15f. suggests that the title 'Son of God' was already taken for granted and that the claim that Christ Jesus was the mediator of salvation had a context which made it relevant to all men, that is, a cosmic context.[58] Only against this background can we understand how the Hellenists who were driven out of Jerusalem began with an

intensive Gentile mission – against the resistance not only of the Jewish synagogue communities but also of their conservative Jewish-Christian brothers in Palestine. It seems to me that against this background Joel 3.5 was already effective as a proof-text for the earliest universalist Christian mission, with an eschatological motivation, and driven by the Spirit. This was a saying which, according to Rom. 10.13, Paul presumed to be familiar to and acknowledged by the community in Rome, who were strangers to him: because according to the prophetic promise people are saved only by calling upon the name of the Kyrios Jesus, the Law can be disregarded as a way to salvation.

6. The second half of the 30s led to the development of the Gentile mission in Antioch, the formation of a mixed community, which, as the name *Christianoi* shows, was also understood by outsiders as a relatively independent group over against the synagogue.[59] After Paul's move to 'Syria and Cilicia' we have to see the theological weight of the Christian scholar and missionary to the Gentiles as being effective there. So we should ask whether the transference of features of pre-existent wisdom to the exalted Christ was not a necessary consequence of his theological approach, in which Christ had taken the place of the Torah/Hokmah understood in ontological terms. The theological significance of Paul in his Antiochene period also follows from the fact that along with Barnabas he carried on the negotiations in Jerusalem for the recognition of a mission to the Gentiles apart from the law. It is understandable that the earliest community in Palestine was very unwilling and hesitant to make concessions in this direction. The persecution of the group around Stephen and, a decade later, the persecution by Agrippa I in AD presented an unmistakable warning. Furthermore, precisely at this time the nationalistic zealot attitude of Palestinian Judaism towards the Torah hardened, as is evident for example from the sharp reaction to Caligula's attempt in AD 38/39 to set up his statue in the Jerusalem temple.[60] It is impossible for us nowadays to evaluate the boldness of the break with the ritual regulations of the Torah in the Greek-speaking Jewish-Christian communities. It becomes understandable if we recognize the 'christological consistency' underlying it; this was the same 'christological consistency' which led to the recognition of the mission to the Gentiles apart from the law by the earliest community in Jerusalem at the Apostolic Council. It is possible that a mediating role was played by Peter, who had left Palestine for a while in AD 43 or 44 because of Agrippa's persecution (see n. 39 above) and first of all worked as a missionary to the Jews in the territory of the Greek-speaking Diaspora. I have no doubt that at a

later date he similarly turned to the mission to the Gentiles. Only in this way can we understand the rise of a Cephas group and interest in Cephas in Paul's Gentile-Christian missionary community in Corinth.[61] It seems to me questionable whether there were fundamental christological differences between Peter and Paul. Paul's sharp attack in Antioch shows his disappointment over the unexpected conduct of Peter and Barnabas yet nevertheless still presupposes a common basis for argumentation (Gal. 2.11ff.).

7. The real problem for the origin of earliest Christian christology lies in the first four or five years which are 'pre-Pauline' in the full sense of the word. Here I can only attempt to sketch out the course of developments quite briefly and provisionally. This course becomes understandable only if we see the necessity of assuming a twofold starting point for the origin of earliest Christianity. (*a*) The activity of Jesus, which had a tremendous effect on the disciples and in addition on wide circles of the people in both Galilee and Judaea, to a degree that we find it hard to imagine. It can be described adequately only with the term 'messianic'.[62] (*b*) The immediate succession of the crucifixion of Jesus as a messianic rebel and the radical change brought about by the resurrection appearances. This complex event set off a unique dynamic and creative impulse which expressed itself in connection with the eschatological community of salvation, the experience of the Spirit, missionary sending by the risen Christ and not least in christological reflection. This spirit-directed development of christological conceptions came about not least through the singing and composition of messianic psalms in the earliest Christian worship (see below, pp. 86ff.). Different themes were at work in it simultaneously from the beginning:

1. The activity and the proclamation of Jesus contained the beginnings of an explicit christology which first makes it possible to understand the starting point for the christological thought of the earliest community. Jesus appeared claiming to be a messianic prophet, used the mysterious term 'Son of man', and was regarded by his followers, the people of Galilee and his opponents as a messianic pretender; it was as a pseudo-Messiah that he was crucified. For the resurrection event itself had no 'messianological' connotation from a background in the history of religion. Judaism did not know of a risen Messiah, nor did the confession of a risen 'rabbi or prophet' necessarily have christological consequences. Only the fact that Jesus had already spoken of the coming Son of Man and his connection with him (Luke 12.8f.) makes it possible to understand how the disciples could take up this particular christological title, known only

on the periphery of Judaism, in order to interpret the experience of the resurrection.[63]

2. In this way the resurrection came to be interpreted as the exaltation and enthronement of the Son of man. At the same time, by the gift of the spirit and the command to mission he showed himself to be the Lord of his community, whose imminent coming to judgment and redemption was expected, and who was called upon as 'Mar(e)' in the prayer for his parousia. The cries 'abba' and 'maranatha', uttered in prayer, were regarded as workings of the spirit, indicating the new feature which from the beginning distinguished the earliest community from Judaism.[64]

3. A whole series of designations were speedily transferred to the Son of man in accordance with his various 'functions'.[65] This is true in the first instance of the title Messiah. From the beginning its use was a matter of course, because (i) Jewish circles had already identified Son of Man and Messiah (see n. 33); (ii) Jesus had been handed over to the Romans and executed as a messianic pretender and therefore the community had to bear witness to him as the crucified Messiah; and (iii) the title Messiah was much more appropriate for missionary usage than the mysterious designation *bar ('e)nāšā*. Accordingly we often find 'Christos' in kerygmatic formulae, whereas the designation 'Son of Man' is handed down in the tradition almost exclusively as a term used by Jesus of himself.[66]

4. The command to missionize their own people represented a special stimulus towards christological reflection (see n.35 above). Clear statements were needed about the functions of the one who was proclaimed: about the Son of Man as the coming judge, the Messiah and son of David as the redeemer and ruler over the people of God, the servant of God who makes expiation through his suffering, the 'Lord' of the community and the Son of God. One could put Käsemann's emphatic statement that 'apocalyptic . . . is the mother of all Christian theology' even more precisely, to the effect that the eschatological mission of the earliest community prompted by the resurrection appearances became 'the mother of christological reflection' and thus of early Christian theology generally.[67]

5. Along with christological reflection, the missionary task set the argument from scripture in motion. Christology and the interpretation of scripture were indissolubly connected from the beginning. Messianic proof from scripture was an essential part of missionary argumentation in particular with Palestinian Judaism. The individual honorific titles and functions were always closely connected with the central proof-texts, the significance of which was clarified particularly in Palestine by the fact that the rabbis later were extremely restrained

towards them and reinterpreted them. II Samuel 7 and Ps. 2 were the basis for the designation 'Son of God'; Ps. 8 connected the conception of exaltation with the Son of Man, and Ps. 110 with the designation 'Lord'. It was particularly necessary to provide a basis in scripture for the saving significance of the death of Jesus. It was necessary, for example, to refute Jewish objections to the crucified Messiah (Deut. 21.23).[68] In addition to Jewish notions of sacrifice, Ps. 22 and Isa. 53 were used to interpret it. Among other elements, from the beginning the tradition of the Last Supper was the *Sitz im Leben* for this tradition. The messianic psalms of the Old Testament were not only used as proof texts but still more were sung in services as hymns in praise of the Messiah Jesus. Through the inspiration of the Spirit new hymns were created for this enthusiastic form of worship which preceded christological thought.

6. It is very difficult to demonstrate a differentiated chronological sequence in the development of these functions, honorific designations and confessional formulae, especially as only in individual cases – for example, the 'maranatha' formula – is it possible to assign them precisely to the Aramaic- or Greek-speaking community. The time available is simply too short and too easily leads to hypothetical criteria.

In terms of method, the most promising approach is still the attempt to work out individual kerygmatic 'primal formulae'. Of course there is also a danger in this method, because in applying it one can too easily forget that the beginning of a christological statement is not an abstract formula; rather, this formula always already presupposes a complex state of affairs of which it is the distillation – at a secondary stage. The 'saving event' proper inspired free praise of it in worship and its interpretation by scriptural proof always precede the fixed formula. Even from the beginning we must reckon with a plurality of formulae, for the consequences of the resurrection of the crucified Messiah cannot be expressed in a single statement (see n. 45).

7. Probably the basic element of so-called 'pre-Pauline' christology – with the exception of pre-existence christology and the conception of the sending of the Son – was already to be found in the time before the conversion of Paul. Thus in a very short time the 'dynamic and creative impulse' of the primal event which led to the founding of the community laid the foundations for the christology which predominates in the New Testament. In one way the last appearance of the risen Christ to the Diaspora Pharisee from Tarsus already brought to a close the first period of the history of earliest Christianity – which was decisive for the whole of later developments. A new period of

christological development then began which about fourteen to sixteen years later came to full development in the Pauline 'world mission' after the Apostolic Council and bore rich fruit.

3

The Origins of the Christian Mission

After Harnack's standard work,[1] for decades the beginnings of the Christian mission have ceased to occupy the main attention of scholars. Only very recently has a change become perceptible. Since Ferdinand Hahn's *Mission in the New Testament*, published in 1963, there has been a new monograph every year.[2] This newly-awakened zeal at the same time indicates a growing interest in the history of primitive Christianity generally.[3] The irresistible expansion of Christian faith in the Mediterranean world during the first 150 years[4] is the scarlet thread running through any history of primitive Christianity. One answer to the question of the 'continuity' of the message of the New Testament, a subject which is constantly raised today,[5] might be that whatever else, its *de facto* continuity – no matter in what way it is described – can be seen in the success of the earliest Christian mission, which was unique in the ancient world.

1. The evidence of the secular Roman historians

Here the secular Roman evidence is particularly illuminating. About eighty years after the crucifixion of Jesus, Pliny the Younger, then governor of the province of Pontus and Bithynia, complained bitterly about the aggressive expansion of the *superstitio prava, immodica* to which the crucifixion had given rise. People of every age and social standing were affected by it. The plague extended even into the villages and the countryside, with the result that the temples were deserted and there were no more sacrifices (*neque civitates tantum, sed vicos etiam atque agros superstitionis istius contagio pervagata est*).[6] Tacitus also stresses the danger of this *exitiabilis superstitio*: though checked for the moment by the execution of the *auctor*, 'it again broke out not only in Judaea, the first source of the evil, but also in Rome itself, where all things hideous and shameful from every part of the world meet and become popular'. In AD 64 a *multitudo ingens* there was affected by Nero's persecution.[7] Suetonius, who in his short note about this event speaks of a *genus hominum superstitionis novae ac maleficae*,[8], takes us back fifteen years in mentioning the expulsion of the Jews from Rome by Claudius: *Iudaeos impulsore Chresto assidue tumultuantis Roma expulit*.[9] In other words, only nineteen years after the execution of Jesus, his message caused such unrest among the Jews of the imperial capital that the emperor had to intervene. It is certainly no coincidence that the Roman writers described only two other ancient religions in a similar stereotyped way as *superstitio*: Judaism and Egyptian religion. These had their greatest missionary success about the beginning of the Christian era.[10]

2. The Pauline mission

The expulsion of the Jews from Rome by Claudius coincides with the first full-scale development of the earliest Christian mission. About AD 49, Paul began his so-called second missionary journey and arrived in Corinth probably by the end of the year. A little later he wrote from there the first of his letters that we have, to the church in Thessalonica.[11]

It is most likely that in the context of a history of primitive Christianity at this point we are still treading on firm ground.[12] According to Paul's own account, the Pauline mission is an unprecedented happening, in terms both of the history of religion in antiquity and of later church history. It was no longer concerned with gaining proselytes locally or setting up new places of worship in one place or another; rather, it extended throughout the then known world. Paul wanted to carry the message of the 'lordship of Christ' to the ends of that world; for him that would be the fulfilment of the 'prophetic' promise:

'their sound is gone out into all lands
and their words to the ends of the world'

εἰς πᾶσαν τὴν γῆν ἐξῆλθεν ὁ φθόγγος αὐτῶν,
καὶ εἰς τὰ πέρατα τῆς οἰκουμένης τὰ ῥήματα αὐτῶν.[13]

With Paul, for the first time we find the specific aim of engaging in missionary activity throughout the world. This governs his plans, so that he works within the framework of whole provinces: Syria and Cilicia, Asia, Macedonia, Achaea, Illyricum. His thoughts stray further afield after Rome, even as far as Spain.[14] In his case one can talk in terms of a real 'missionary strategy'. He concentrated his own personal work especially on provincial capitals: Thessalonica, Corinth and Ephesus: he spent about eighteen months in Corinth and two or three years in Ephesus.[15] He appointed assistant missionaries to maintain contact with the communities he had founded and in order to open up the hinterland; his letters were a further expedient to this end. In them Paul develops his theological ideas as a *missionary*; i.e., the *Sitz im Leben* of Pauline theology is the apostle's mission.

This gives rise to two questions.

Did Paul have this world-wide view of mission from the beginning, or did he develop it only at a later stage? Presumably the latter is the case. For about fourteen years his activity was limited to the Roman province of Syria and Cilicia,[16] to which according to Acts 13 and 14 we must add nearby Cyprus and the immediately adjacent areas of Asia Minor.[17] We can also assume Acts to be correct in showing that during this period Paul was working not primarily as a missionary on his own authority but – for at least part of the time – together with Barnabas and under the aegis of the church in Antioch. He also went to Jerusalem with Barnabas as a representative of that church.[18] From this we may conclude that a *development* took place in Paul's understanding and strategy of mission which was influenced above all by the positive outcome of the Apostolic Council (AD 48), his parting from Barnabas and his separation from Antioch. Paul the missionary was not the same man after the Apostolic Council and the incident in Antioch (Gal. 2.1lff.): only from this point on does his missionary activity take on its world-wide aspect and its forward impetus.

Closely connected with this is the question of the basic motives of his mission. Here we have to distinguish two elements, one connected with eschatology and salvation history and the other with christology and soteriology.

There is controversy, in particular, over the area of Pauline eschatology; at this particular point too often theological desires have prejudiced the comments of exegetes. Thus Conzelmann sought to play off Paul the wisdom teacher against Paul the apocalyptist, failing to notice that he was posing false alternatives, since wisdom and apocalyptic had long been closely connected in Judaism.[19] Furthermore, it can hardly be doubted that the imminent expectation of the parousia of Christ was of decisive significance for Pauline theology and that Paul understood the righteousness of God revealed to the believer and the gift of the Spirit as anticipations of eschatological salvation. Must not Paul's missionary commission and the parousia also have been connected here? Most recently, Ulrich Luz has disputed such a connection, but in so doing has paid too little attention to Rom. 11.25-27:[20]

Lest you be wise in your own conceits, I want you to understand this mystery, brethren: a hardening has come upon part of Israel, until the full number of the Gentiles come in (to faith), and so all Israel will (ultimately) be saved, as it is written, 'The Deliverer will come from Zion, he will banish ungodliness from Jacob.'

Here Paul is speaking in the style of an apocalyptic revelation (cf. I Cor. 15.51). The present period of the world-wide mission to the Gentiles is at the same time the period of the hardening of the Jews. Only when the 'full number' of Gentiles appointed by God has come to faith will the hour of deliverance for Israel also have struck. According to the quotation from Isa. 59.20, it coincides with the parousia. The ἥξει ἐκ Σιὼν ὁ ῥυόμενος is a periphrasis for the return of Christ.[21] This gives rise to far-reaching consequences for understanding Paul's mission.

It does not take place in the context of a future with an uncertain orientation; in principle it is related to the parousia. As the herald of the Kyrios, the apostle announces to the world his act of reconciliation and lordly rule and in so doing gives the nations a last chance to accede to the revelation of the righteousness of God in the person of the Kyrios through the obedience of faith, and in this way to escape the threat of judgment (I Thess. 1.9f.; Rom. 5.9f.; II Cor. 5.20f.; Rom. 1.17ff.).

In defining his missionary task as 'priestly service' and the winning of the Gentiles as a 'sacrifice' (Rom. 15.16), not only does Paul connect this with the praise to God offered by believing Gentiles (Rom. 15.9-13), but at the same time the Gentiles are brought to their 'full number' determined by God by this προσφορὰ τῶν ἐθνῶν. Indeed it is Paul's wish that this sacrifice should be accepted by God (ἵνα γένηται ἡ προσφορὰ τῶν ἐθνῶν εὐπρόσδεκτος, ἡγιασμένη ἐν πνεύματι ἁγίῳ).[22]

The imminent expectation of the parousia inevitably lost something of its pressing immediacy as a result of such a world-wide 'missionary programme'. The task of mission to the Gentiles intervened as a *conditio sine qua non* between the direct presence and the return of the exalted Christ. This is clear from a comparison between the traditional I Thess. 5.2, 'The Day of the Lord comes like a thief in the night' – here it is still quite impossible to calculate the end, though it is threateningly near – and Rom. 13.11: 'Now salvation is nearer than when we first believed (i.e. almost twenty-five years ago); the night is far spent, the day is at hand.' The final terminus has indeed come nearer, but first Paul must complete his missionary work in the West as he has already done so in the East.[23] According to I Cor. 7.29 there is still an interval: a short one. This 'interval' is itself the time of mission.

At the same time, there is a change in the prophetic prediction which had influenced earlier views of the primitive community, namely that the turning of the nations to the God of Israel was simply a consequence of the full dawn of the time of salvation. It is not the Gentiles who will turn to God through the parousia of the Messiah, but Israel, which apart from a small remnant has now been hardened.[24] For Paul this produces a paradoxical situation: at the present time the mission to the Jews is a virtually useless enterprise and the mission to the Gentiles has absolute priority. For the salvation of the Jews, too, will only be furthered by an intensive, world-wide mission to the Gentiles.[25] We can hardly assume that Paul had already presented this interpretation of his mission, oriented on salvation history and eschatology, to the three 'pillars' in Jerusalem; otherwise they would hardly have come to recognize his mission to the Gentiles without requiring them to observe the law and the amicably *laissez-faire* ἡμεῖς εἰς τὰ ἔθνη, αὐτοὶ δὲ εἰς τὴν περιτομήν (Gal. 2.9).[26] Presumably he developed this view only during the course of his independent 'world mission', from the second missionary journey onwards, polemically setting himself apart from other Jewish-Christian views.[27]

The amazing self-awareness of the ἐθνῶν ἀπόστολος (Rom. 11.13) accords with this. He 'laboured more' than all the other apostles;[28] his ambition is to work only where no one else has preached the gospel. After he has filled the whole area from Jerusalem and its surroundings to Illyricum with the gospel, he no longer finds it possible to work there and presses on further westwards.[29] It is striking that in the brilliant survey contained in Rom. 15.15-23 the activity of other missionaries to the Gentiles is passed over completely. Traugott Holtz[30] seems to me to be right in pointing to prophetic models, and above all to (Deutero-) Isaiah, for the 'unique position which Paul claims for his apostolate'. He too was aware 'that the coming of salvation for his people and for the world was bound up with his person'.[31]

So we know only the Paul of the letters, who is at the peak of his missionary activity. The Paul of the early period is largely unknown to us. The interpretation of his apostolate to the Gentiles, which is presented to us above all in Rom. 9-11, seems to have developed only with the full flowering of his mission from the end of the forties. It reached its final culmination in the last letter which he wrote in freedom. He came to Rome only as a prisoner. The missionary and theological work which he produced over a seven- to eight-year period (between about AD 49 and 57), when the church was barely twenty years old, has remained unparalleled over the subsequent 1900 years. In this sense his awareness of his mission as being truly 'apostolic' is legitimate, and cannot be repeated. If at all, it can only be compared with Jesus' awareness of his mission, the Jesus whom Paul almost certainly never knew as man but whom more than anyone else he confessed in word and deed as his Kyrios.[32]

Had the interpretation of the mission in terms of salvation history and eschatology developed in this way, we might ask whether this was not also the case with the gospel apart from the law. In other words, Did Paul only gradually become the missionary to the Gentiles? Strictly speaking, this supposition would go against his own testimony in Gal. 1.15f.; Phil. 3.4ff. and the accounts in Acts.[33] For the former Pharisee from the Greek-speaking section of the school of Hillel,[34] the appearance of the risen Christ before Damascus meant a radical break with the whole of his previous past. The place of the law as the way to salvation was taken by the crucified Messiah. However, this turning point in his life not only overthrew all his previous values but at the same time put him under an obligation: the risen Christ made the former persecutor his messenger: ἵνα εὐαγγελίζωμαι αὐτὸν ἐν τοῖς ἔθνεσιν (Gal. 1.16). Paul seems to have entered into this ministry without delay. Instead of speaking of Paul's conversion we would do better to describe it as his calling. This calling forms the basis of his whole theology:[35] Paul, the former scribe, becomes the first Christian 'theologian' because he is a missionary; that is, his theology is 'mission theology' in the comprehensive sense.[36]

This raises new questions which take us back into the time before Paul and therefore to the beginnings of the earliest Christian mission.

What was it that led the former Pharisee and persecutor of the Christians to turn to the mission to the Gentiles in particular? Would it not have been much more natural for him to preach the crucified Messiah to his own compatriots? Could he not have developed much further in this connection the education he had received as a scribe?

Here we must consider two points.

The Jewish mission reached its climax under the protection of Augustus' *pax romana*. Among the Jewish groups in Palestine the school of Hillel – who himself came from the Babylonian diaspora – had the most positive attitude towards mission. It was also relatively open to Hellenistic culture. We must therefore suppose that Paul the 'Hillelite', the citizen of Rome and Tarsus, was already familiar with the practice and problems of the Jewish mission before he became a Christian.[37]

Acts connects him with the persecution directed against Stephen and the 'Hellenists'. Here we come up against those circles which laid the foundations for the mission among the non-Jews. Its starting point was in the Greek-speaking Diaspora synagogues in Jerusalem.[38]

Paul, too, came from this milieu, and as a Pharisee who was faithful to the law will have persecuted these Christian dissidents in Jerusalem before he came to join them in Damascus.[39] His previous interest in the Jewish mission to the Gentiles was changed by his call into the ἀποστολὴ . . . εἰς τὰ ἔθνη.[40] A decisive feature here was that Paul came up against a Christian community which was itself in process of moving from mission to the Jews to mission to the Gentiles. It is of course improbable that Paul – and the Christian 'Hellenists' – already argued that the Gentile mission had priority in terms of salvation history and eschatology; first of all they had to wait for more than a decade until the mission to the Gentiles 'without obligations under the law' could be approved by the authorities in Jerusalem. Such a revolutionary innovation needed time to develop, and in addition before the Apostolic Council the Gentile Christian mission was evidently limited to Syria and Cilicia and the adjacent regions. The community in Rome (see n. 9 above) began as a Jewish Christian community.

The presupposition for Paul's mission is his doctrine of freedom from the law, which previously had separated Israel from the nations. It is a basic element of his gospel. He stresses passionately that this was not communicated to him by men, but from a revelation of Christ (Gal. 1.11-17). This will certainly be true of the revolutionary basic recognition that only the crucified Christ and not Moses can give salvation. But is it conceivable that he laid the foundations of his theology without the influence of those Hellenists whom he himself had persecuted - probably because of their criticism of the law and temple (see below)?

3. The Hellenists in Jerusalem and the beginnings of the Gentile mission

Luke and Acts

The scene of events shifts back more than fifteen years from the Apostolic Council to a time a few years after the death and resurrection of Jesus. As a source we are directed to Luke's Acts of the Apostles, the historical value of which is nowadays subjected to radical attack, as I believe, wrongly. Luke did not write the first novel about the apostles but a missionary history, for which – as for the Gospel – he used sources. For the first half he had two in particular: a collection of stories about Peter and a 'Hellenist source' from Antioch. Both were already attributing the foundation of the Gentile mission to their heroes.[41] Like other ancient writers, Luke fused together his sources: it is almost impossible to separate them by literary criticism. He did not lack source material, but was as skilled in the art of abbreviation and passing over events in silence as in elaborating narrative. Above all, however, he had one clear aim to which everything else was subordinated: to describe the ideal world mission, that is, Paul's mission. His work is a deliberate history of the Pauline mission 'with an extended introduction'. For example, the reports about the Hellenists – in harmonized form – had to serve to provide a bridge between the apostolic foundation, which was authoritative for Luke, and the real hero of his work. Whereas all the other figures involved disappear prematurely, Paul occupies the stage until the curtain falls. That Luke is to be taken seriously as a historian is evident, for example, from the fact that in contrast to his somewhat later contemporaries 'Matthew' and Clement of Rome he does not present the unhistorical construction that the twelve apostles were sent out all over the world by the risen Christ and worked as missionaries there. Rather, according to Luke, the mission outside Judaea is begun and ended by outsiders: by the Hellenists and by Paul, the model missionary to the Gentiles. We can hardly dispute that in this decisive respect Luke, generally speaking, provides a historically reliable report.[42] It is commonly said that Luke is the 'theologian of salvation history'; however, this phrase must be made more precise: he thinks in terms of the 'history of mission'. For him the history of salvation and the history of mission coincide – even in .the Gospel (see below, p. 179 n. 77). Over against this, and in contrast to his teacher Paul, the eschatological element fades into the background, though it too is not missing altogether (Acts 1.11; 2.17, against Joel 3.1 LXX).[43]

The Hellenists in Jerusalem

Acts 6.1ff. is the decisive break. Luke suddenly describes tension between two groups in the primitive community in Jerusalem, the Aramaic-speaking 'Hebraioi' and the Greek-speaking minority of 'Hellenistai'. Critical Acts scholarship has long since shown that Luke plays down this conflict. The separation of two groups in Jerusalem had become necessary because of the language of their liturgy. Difficulties in caring for the poor were an easily explainable consequence. Presumably, however, there were also differences in doctrine: we can of course only infer them hypothetically from the accusation against Stephen and the persecution, which was limited – contrary to Luke's account – to the Hellenists and drove them from the city, while the Aramaic-speaking part of the community was hardly affected. We can conclude from this that the charges against

Stephen which Luke mentions in Acts 6.11,13f., 'he does not cease to blaspheme against this holy place and the law', are not Luke's invention but repeat in abbreviated form the accusation of Pharisaic Jews against this Christian minority: they were persecuted because they dared to criticize the temple and the Torah, i.e. the two pillars on which Judaism rested.[44] In Jewish Palestine only a community which remained strictly faithful to the law could survive in the long run.[45]

Their attitude to law and mission

Evidently the decisive move towards a more critical attitude to the law had already come about in this Jewish-Christian Hellenistic group in Jerusalem. The beginnings of the mission among the hated Samaritans,[46] who were worse than Gentiles in the eyes of Jews with a national consciousness, and the first tentative attempts at a mission in the predominantly Gentile coastal region of Palestine, in Phoenicia and Syria as far as Antioch, where the Gentile mission then first developed to the full,[47] are the achievement of these Hellenists who were driven out of Jerusalem. There is no indication of a mission to the Gentiles directly from Galilee, a theory which is repeatedly put forward nowadays.[48] On the contrary, we must reckon with the fact that individuals, like Barnabas and John Mark, who first belonged among the 'Hebraioi' in Jerusalem, later moved over to join the Greek-speaking avant-garde.[49]

Of course, we can hardly expect that people in these circles would reflect on the problem of the law as the way to salvation to the profound extent that Paul did. It should be noted that Stephen's criticism was directed against both temple *and* law. This suggests that along with their questioning of the temple the Hellenists at the same time also questioned the cultic and ritual parts of the law, but not its ethical side.[50] There continued to be profound respect for the Decalogue; in addition one could ask whether the optimistic confidence in man's capacity to do God's will – say in the context of the doctrine of the two ways – which is so widespread later in the 'post-apostolic' writings does not go back to it.[51] One might also think of a more pragmatic basis for freedom from the law as expressed in Peter's speech in Acts 15.10: the (ceremonial) law is a yoke 'which neither we nor our fathers were able to bear'.[52] This would also explain why Paul did not remain permanently associated with this Jewish-Hellenistic Christianity but parted from it after the 'Apostolic Council', and indeed was forced to have a critical confrontation with its emissaries in Corinth (see n.26 above).

What were the reasons which led these Hellenists to attack the cult and the ritual law even in Jerusalem?

1. If a Jew returned to Jerusalem from the Diaspora to live there, to study there, or perhaps to spend the evening of his life there, he almost certainly did so partly for religious reasons. The return to Palestine was regarded as a meritorious work, performed only by a small 'religious elite'.[53] The realities of the 'holy city' might, however, bring as much disillusionment to someone returning there as Renaissance Rome did to Martin Luther as a pilgrim. In the temple the Sadducean priestly nobility were exploiting the pious visitors; as the predominant spiritual movement in Palestine, Phariseeism, with its subtle casuistry and its esoteric arrogance, was not especially attractive either. By contrast, the special concerns of the Diaspora Jews, ethical monotheism and the idea of universalist mission, met with only limited understanding.[54]

2. Against this background we can understand how the proclamation by the new eschatological movement of primitive Christianity found a ready hearing among those Jews who had returned from the Diaspora. In the preaching of Jesus they could detect features which were particularly dear to their hearts and which they could not find anywhere else in Jerusalem: that it was not food which made people unclean but what came forth from their hearts, or that the command for active love of neighbour was to be put above other commandments, even above the sabbath commandment.[55] Jesus' criticism of temple worship and the understanding of the death of Jesus as expiation for the forgiveness of sins made the temple and its worship superfluous,[56] and the interpretation of the resurrection of Jesus as the dawn of the end-time made it possible to replace the Torah of Moses with a new, purely ethical, 'messianic' Torah which could take up Jesus' criticism of the Law expressed in the antitheses of the Sermon on the Mount. Last and not least, the experience of the spirit of prophecy also brought freedom from ties to the letter and the scribal way of thought expressed in casuistic terms.

Ancient Judaism was not a monolithic block; in it we also find some beginnings of criticism of the law, above all in the Diaspora. Furthermore, the Jewish communities there were often divided by the progress of the Jewish mission. Around the nucleus of circumcised, full Jews, was a group of 'godfearers' who felt that they belonged to the Jewish synagogue community. The Hellenist mission to the Gentiles seems to have begun among this group of 'godfearers' and to have promised them full rights to salvation without demanding circumcision.[57] Here they could take up Jesus' open attitude to the ʿammē hā-āreṣ, whom the Pharisees regarded as second-rate Jews and semi-pagans.[58] It was similar with the Samaritans, who could be regarded as a schismatic splinter group from the people of God.[59] In the first place the Hellenists were presumably not concerned with an open, large-scale 'Gentile mission' but that the Samaritans and 'godfearing' Gentiles, the outsiders and those who had been deprived of their rights, should be incorporated on equal terms into the new people of God which was taking shape. The real mission to the Gentiles in the full sense of the word may only have begun in Antioch (Acts 11.19ff.). Whereas hitherto the universal restoration of the nations had been expected as the eschatological work of the Messiah on his return, the further step now was to gather together the people of God from both Jews and Gentiles. Its detachment from Judaism then led this early Hellenistic community, following the LXX, to give itself the name *ekklesia* and in this way to proclaim its eschatologically conditioned difference from the Jewish synagogue communities.[60] In the same way – in contrast, say, to the mission carried on by the school of Hillel, the proclamation of the εὐαγγέλιον took the place of the proclamation of the law.[61]

4. The beginnings of the primitive community in Jerusalem

Following Martin Dibelius, Ernst Haenchen has put forward the view that the earliest primitive community in Jerusalem did not do open missionary work but rather led a tranquil, 'pious' life, even in the Jewish sense. The spreading of the new faith took place only in the tranquil personal encounter of one individual with another, and this situation was only brought to an end by the dispute with the Hellenists.[62] This view can be refuted by the simple fact that at that time it proved possible in the relatively short space of perhaps one or two years in Jerusalem to win over so many Greek-speaking Jews that they had to found their own worshipping community. That hardly happened as a result of individual, quiet conversation, but was possible only by real missionary activity, even if we assume that Jesus himself had individual Greek-speaking followers.[63] The missionary zeal of this still young community is unmistakable. It was caused by the commission of the risen Lord, through the gift of the Spirit, which was no longer to serve to nurture pious souls, and through the sacred duty to proclaim to apostate Israel its last chance of repentance before the coming of the Son of man.

The significance of Jerusalem

One further point tells in favour of active mission in Israel: the return of the Galilean disciples to Jerusalem a short time after the first appearances. Paul (Gal. 1.17f.) and Luke testify quite independently that from the very beginning, for the primitive community Jerusalem and not say Galilee was the 'gateway to salvation'. There are different reasons for the unique significance of Jerusalem for the earliest community:

1. Jerusalem was the place of the last supper, the passion and resurrection of Jesus, i.e. the place where he accomplished his saving work.

2. According to widespread Jewish belief Jerusalem was the sacred centre of the world and the place where the Messiah would appear, to which in the messianic kingdom not only the Israelites of the dispersion but also the nations would stream in pilgrimage to pay homage to the true God of Zion.[64]

3. The disciples returned to Jerusalem, there to preach the risen Messiah to all Israel. Jerusalem was not only the 'gateway' to eschatological salvation but at the same time the centre of all missionary efforts in connection with Judaism. At the three great pilgrimage festivals not only virtually all the adult Jews of Palestine gathered together, but also large numbers from the Diaspora. Anyone who wanted to address all Israel had to do so in Jerusalem. In this respect the disciples followed their master, who had gone up to Jerusalem on the feast of the Passover for a similar reason. Presumably, therefore, they travelled back up to Jerusalem from Galilee fifty days later for the next feast, the Feast of Weeks:[65] the appearances of the risen Jesus had freed them from their fear. They would have been better able to live a quietist withdrawn life in expectation of an imminent parousia had they stayed in Galilee. However, unlike the Essenes by the Dead Sea they did not separate from the *massa perditionis* of Israel but sought to win their people for the Messiah Jesus (see n. 60 above).

The 'apostles'

A further indication of the activity of the earliest community is the office of apostle.[66] The strongly differentiated use of the term as a title is certainly pre-Pauline. Had the specific use of this title been an invention of Paul's it would remain incomprehensible why Paul had to defend it so bitterly against his opponents. In Gal. 1.17ff.; I Cor. 9.5; 15.7f., Paul presupposes that the ἀπόστολοι were a fixed, closed group which had its point of origin in Jerusalem or Palestine. The only proper philological derivation of the term is therefore still that from Jewish messenger law, as a translation of *šālūᵃh*. The ἀπόστολος Ἰησοῦ Χριστοῦ was of course fundamentally different from the Jewish *šᵉluhīm*. He had not been sent by men but by God and his Christ; the sending was not by a commissioning according to secular

law, with a limited character, but as a result of an appearance of the
risen Lord, who engaged until the parousia the one who was called
in his missionary service; in other words, the office was eschatological. The apostles had to announce to Israel the imminent rule of God
in his crucified messiah who was exalted and would return as judge.
The uniqueness and novelty of their message also determined the
uniqueness and novelty of their office. The circle of these primitive
Christian apostles was evidently wider than that of the Twelve: on
the basis of his vision of Christ Paul too included himself among them
– by way of an exception. It is quite mistaken to deny the Twelve
membership of the group of ἀπόστολοι because of their alleged
stabilitas loci in Jerusalem; this *stabilitas loci* is a feature of Luke's
schematic form of presentation; it is contradicted by Gal. 1.18f. Luke,
too, does not deny that the Twelve were engaged in the mission to
the Jews. However, the first apostles in Jerusalem did not have
mission outside Palestine and among the Gentiles within their
perspective; their task was first of all limited completely to Jerusalem.
The intensive expectation of an imminent end left no room for more
ambitious missionary plans. For that very reason the primitive
community in Jerusalem became the centre for mission.

Sending by the risen Lord

Thus the office of apostle is based on sending by the risen Lord, i.e.
it is as old as the primitive community itself.[67] This sending, which
lays the foundation for the church, is also confirmed for us – quite
apart from Paul – by all the Gospels.[68] Of course it is no longer
possible to make a reconstruction of the resurrection appearances;
the early community was not particularly interested in elaborating
them. What was decisive was the fact, attested by a great variety of
evidence, of the appearance of Jesus and the sending. The two are
connected, as Kasting and Conzelmann rightly stress, in the protophany to Peter.[69] The name 'Cephas' and the image of fisher of men,
both of which come from Jesus himself, now took on a new meaning.
Peter, who had already played a special part among the group of
disciples around Jesus, therefore also became the dominant figure in
the earliest community and the leading missionary to the Jews. Of
course it would be a misunderstanding to seek to see Peter as the
'primal missionary'[70] who, prompted by his protophany, first of all
by himself proclaimed the risen Christ, then with the help of a further
community vision created a group of twelve men – including himself
– and along with these called into life the community of the new
eschatological Israel. Taken to its logical conclusion this would lead
to the position that the visionary Simon Peter was the real founder of

Christianity, that he assumed the nickname 'the rock' and laid the foundation for the Christian community by his preaching. There is no support in the sources for the conjecture of such a Petrine 'primacy'. The 'Twelve' are not the work of Peter's first missionary efforts, but go back to an appointment by Jesus himself. Peter was able to recall this group after his resurrection vision because it had already been brought into being in the period before Easter.[71] The fact that the significance of this Galilean group quickly faded into the background in Jerusalem only shows that in the long run it could not cope with the new missionary situation there. Thus the sending of the disciples by the risen Christ was not an absolute new beginning without any antecedents. We can certainly say with Kasting: 'The cause of Jesus had a future only on the basis of Easter. Easter had a creative significance for the church';[72] but given the tendency which is so popular in Germany today to eliminate the earthly Jesus because it is said to be impossible to grasp him and that he has no theological significance, it is necessary to stress the obvious fact that without the activity of the earthly Jesus it becomes absurd to speak of 'Jesus' concern', and the church founded by Easter which, for whatever reason, no longer dares to ask after the earthly Jesus, is separated from its starting point. One can speak meaningfully of Easter only if one knows that here the *man Jesus of Nazareth is raised*, someone who in his human life, with its activity and suffering, is not just any interchangeable blank sheet.[73] We therefore have to look for the earthly Jesus if we want to elucidate 'the beginnings of the earliest Christian mission'.

5. Jesus as the 'primal missionary'

Jesus' proclamation of the imminent kingdom of God did not carry any endorsement of the Palestinian Jewish piety moulded by Phariseeism which put the traditional values of ancient Judaism in question at decisive points. In a particular way he turned to those who were outcast from Jewish society and proclaimed the possibility of a new life to them on the basis of the nearness of the love of God. At the same time he accentuated sharply the ethical demand of the law and concentrated it on the commandment to love: the coming judgment presupposes quite different standards from those of current piety in accordance with the law. In this sense the content of the preaching of Jesus had just as much 'missionary' character as that of his disciples after Easter.

This 'missionary' character was matched by its unconventional form. Jesus did not cherish the *stabilitas loci* of the rabbinic scribe who was tied to the house where he taught; he went about Galilee and the adjacent regions as a travelling teacher and popular preacher, without firm ties to family, profession or dwelling. It was in accord with his activity as a travelling teacher that unlike the rabbis he did not accept pupils to learn the Torah from him; rather, he called individuals from their occupations and families to 'follow' him, i.e. accompany him and share his uncertain destiny. This 'call to discipleship' was not an end in itself, but put the disciples at the service of the cause of the kingdom of God. This intention can be seen for example in the remarkable saying about 'fishers of men' uttered at the call of Peter and Andrew (Mark 1.17); it is realized in the sending out of the disciples.[74] An analysis of the tradition about such sending shows that the community was concerned to adapt the instructions of Jesus, no longer adequate for their missionary situation, to the new demands.[75] However, it is possible to extract a nucleus from the Q tradition the radical demands of which (*a*) contradict the later missionary situation and (*b*) were extremely offensive to Jewish sensibilities. The latter is above all true of the command 'eat what is set before you' (Luke 10.8), which has points of contact with Mark 7.15, to the effect that food cannot make a person unclean. This saying hardly fits the later Palestinian community, but in the light of its whole context it cannot derive from the mission of the Greek-speaking communities free of the demands of the law; it accords with Jesus' sovereign attitude towards the ritual law and his Pharisaic interpretation. That a nucleus of the tradition about the sending goes back to Jesus is also evident from the fact that it has no christological content; rather, the disciples sent out have the task of proclaiming Jesus' own message of the imminent rule of God and like him of working as exorcists and healers of the sick. Here we still cannot trace anything of the christological distance to be found after Easter. But at the same time that means that Jesus has the disciples whom he has called participating in his 'messianic task', which itself must be described essentially as a 'mission'.[76] Here we are confronted with the real starting point of the primitive Christian mission: it lies in the conduct of Jesus himself. If anyone is to be called 'the primal missionary', he must be.[77]

The question how Jesus viewed the mission to the Gentiles[78] is a secondary problem. We cannot demonstrate that Jesus himself engaged in a mission to the Gentiles nor is it probable that he forbade his disciples to engage in it on principle. It lay outside his field of vision, which was concentrated on Israel. Matthew 10.5f. comes from circles in Palestinian Jewish Christianity which rejected mission among the Gentiles. Here we can merely affirm two points:

(*a*) a degree of openness on the part of Jesus towards non-Jews – including the Samaritans – which was expressed in particular situations. This openness of Jesus to be seen as analogous to his attitude towards the *'am hā-āreṣ*, the publicans and sinners.

(*b*) It is also evident from the fact that Jesus could contrast Samaritans and Gentiles with the failure of Israel, to provide an opposite picture.[79] In some logia this positive reference to the Gentiles contains an eschatological element, as in Luke 11.30,32, where the people of Nineveh and the queen of Sheba will rise up as 'witnesses in the judgment against this generation'. Luke 13.28f. is also in this context. The rejection of the hardened Jewish hearers in the judgment is contrasted with the acceptance of many Gentiles.

6. Summary

We are approaching the end. Let me sum up what we have discovered in five points:

1. The first secular Roman witnesses to early Christianity give striking expression to the rapid expansion of this dangerous *superstitio*.

2. The *Sitz im Leben* of Pauline theology is the mission of the apostle among the 'nations'. He understands it as a world-wide eschatological proclamation of the rule of the Kyrios. The mission to the Gentiles has priority in the history of salvation since it forms the presupposition for the deliverance of Israel at the parousia. Paul's 'eschatological' understanding of mission presumably developed to the full only in the time between the Apostolic Council and the Letter to the Romans (*c.* AD 49-56).

3. The first impetus towards the mission among non-Jews came from the 'Hellenists' in Jerusalem. They were led in this direction by connecting Jesus' positive criticism of the law and his activity in helping all the outcasts with their own mission-oriented situation in the Diaspora and began to bring together the eschatological people of God from Jews and Gentiles.

4. The earliest community in Palestine was also a missionary community from the beginning: the foundation for this lies in the sending by the Risen Christ. Their proclamation of the crucified Messiah who had been exalted and would come again to judge the world was limited to Judaism. Therefore Jerusalem had to become the centre of the primitive community.

5. The ultimate basis for the earliest Christian mission lies in the messianic sending of Jesus. Jesus' activity as a travelling preacher, the call and sending out of the disciples and Jesus' openness in

helping all those who were outcast and despised – including the non-Jews – form the ultimate starting point for the later mission.

In short, the history and theology of earliest Christianity are 'mission history' and 'mission theology'. A church and theology which forgets or denies the missionary sending of believers as messengers of salvation in a world threatened by disaster surrenders its very foundation and in so doing surrenders itself.[80]

4

'Christos' in Paul

Among the titles and names which are used in the authentic letters of the apostle (Romans; I and II Corinthians; Galatians; Philippians; I Thessalonians; Philemon), Χριστός[1] comes second only to θεός in frequency of usage. According to the Concordance to the twenty-sixth edition of the Nestle-Aland Greek text it appears 270 times in all (as opposed to θεός, 430 times)[2]; that means we find more than half the 531 instances of Χριστός in the NT in the corpus of letters by the earliest Christian author. In the case of the other christological names and titles the relationship between Pauline terminology and that of the later New Testament writings is far from being so one-sided. In Paul Ἰησοῦς appears 143 times (as opposed to 919); κύριος 189 times (719)[3]; υἱὸς θεοῦ (or the absolute υἱός) only 15 times (105).[4] As there are quite a number of textual variants particularly in the christological titles and names in the Pauline corpus, the figures given may need to be adjusted up or down, as also emerges from a comparison with Morgenthaler's statistics[5], but this makes virtually no difference to the general impression. This predilection for the designation Χριστός also continues in the Deutero-Pauline letters – though to a much lesser degree – with the exception of the Letter to Titus, whose christology has a particular Hellenistic stamp, as is evident from the strikingly frequent use of σωτήρ.[6] By contrast, the Acts of the Apostles, the longest writing in the New Testament, has only 26 instances,[7] the Johannine corpus (Gospel and Epistles) 30.[8] In extent, both are only about twenty per cent shorter than all the authentic letters of Paul put together. With its seven instances, Revelation falls short of the eight in Philemon; Hebrews (12) and I Peter (22) have substantially fewer instances of Christ than the shorter Philippians (37).

This clear evidence is hardly a coincidence, and calls for some explanation. However, we should not be over-hasty in reading theological significance into this indisputable situation. Consequently I would hesitate to go along completely with Cerfaux's comment that ' "Christos" is the key term in the letters of Paul'.[9] That is certainly true of the *person* of Jesus Christ, but in that case the same thing can be said of virtually all the New Testament writings. In the case of the *name* Christ, we have to give some reasons. The strikingly frequent use of the term to denote Jesus in Paul seems to be more of a riddle than a 'key' to a better understanding of Pauline christology.

The mystery increases when we remember that according to the earliest gospel tradition, i.e. Mark and Q, Jesus never claimed the title Messiah directly for himself in so many words. It does not appear at all in Q, and in Mark – leaving aside 9.41, where we already have the typical Christian usage of it as a name – it is always applied by others to Jesus.[10] That immediately raises a question which is in fact the basic problem of earliest christology. How did Jesus become the Messiah, and how did it come about that within a relatively short time – for religious developments in antiquity – the title Messiah came to be so closely associated with the name Jesus that it could not only be added to Jesus as a *cognomen* but could even take its place, and therefore is used by the first Christian writer as the most frequent designation of Jesus?[11]

The earliest letter of Paul, to the Thessalonians, written about AD 50, already presupposes this terminology in the abundance that we find elsewhere in the authentic letters of Paul[12] and in stereotyped phraseology. i.e., it must have become established some time before. In Thessalonians we find the liturgical-sounding formula κύριος Ἰησοῦς Χριστός at the beginning of the letter,[13] and the more extended version ὁ κύριος ἡμῶν Ἰησοῦς Χριστός appears even more frequently, especially at the end of the letter (5.9,23,28; cf.1.3).[14] There is also the simple ἐν Χριστῷ (4.16) and the extended ἐν Χριστῷ Ἰησοῦ (2.14; 5.18)[15] and finally the similar εὐαγγέλιον τοῦ Χριστοῦ (3.2).[16] Here the christological terminology of the first extant letter of Paul makes an almost atypical impression in comparison with his other letters. For in this case we find Χριστός only 10 times, while κύριος appears 24 times and Ἰησοῦς 16. This may be connected with the fact that in this letter there is special focus on the theme of the parousia of Jesus, which from earliest times had been closely connected with the title κύριος. The formula *maranatha* in I Cor. 16.22 already points to this special connection. Therefore the designation 'Lord' occurs only in the two decisive eschatological chapters I Thess. 4; 5 (15 times). This should not suggest to us that Paul's christological terminology and thus his preaching changed fundamentally in the few years between I Thessalonians and Galatians or I Corinthians.

That Paul changes the order of the name of Jesus in the introductions to the later letters as compared with I Thess. 1.1; Gal. 1.1 and writes 'Christ Jesus' at the beginning of I Cor.; II Cor.; Phil.; Philemon; Rom. instead of the traditional 'Jesus Christ' is not a point of any importance; it is connected with the particular form of the introduction in each case.[17] Here the commentaries have often made unfounded conjectures in connection with Rom. 1.1.[18] The numerous uncertain textual variations over the order 'Jesus Christ' or 'Christ Jesus' should warn us against reading too much into things here.[19] We may accept in principle the judgment passed by E. von Dobschütz in his commentary on I Thessalonians: 'For Paul, Christ is as much a personal name as Jesus, which sometimes he uses indiscriminately and sometimes incorporates into a double name.' The reversed form Christ Jesus may originally have been a title, but this is no longer evident in Paul; there are usually clear linguistic reasons for his use of it.[20] Thus we have to limit Cerfaux's theory to the sentence, 'κύριος Ἰησοῦς and not Ἰησοῦς ὁ Χριστός is Paul's basic confession.'[21] The careful investigations made by N.A.Dahl and W.Kramer have endorsed von Dobschütz's theory and given it more precision. Dahl's four basic philological observations speak for themselves:[22]

(a) In Paul Χριστός is no longer just a title, but always simply the designation for one particular person, i.e. Jesus.

(b) Nowhere is Χριστός a predicate. In contrast to the account of his preaching in Acts, in the letters Paul no longer has to affirm 'Jesus is the Messiah' (see below).

(c) In contrast to pre-Christian Old Testament and Jewish tradition[23] it is never governed by a genitive (θεοῦ, κυρίου, etc.) or a possessive pronoun.

(d) One can also look in vain in Paul's letters for the appositional form Ἰησοῦς ὁ Χριστός.

One might also add that nowhere does Paul advance a proof that Jesus is the anointed one and bringer of salvation promised in the texts of the Old Testament. Of course he presupposes that Jesus is the Davidic Messiah and uses an earlier confessional formula,[24] but he never employs this in the course of his argument. The traditional messianic proof texts of the Old Testament do not play any direct or essential role in his letters, and that is also true of those instances which are significant for the Christian scriptural proof of the messiahship of Jesus. 'Of course the Jew and rabbi Paul knows that Χριστός means anointed = Messiah,'[25] but in his letters he has no occasion to give reasons for this obvious insight or to develop it. The few possible indications of this are fortuitous and atypical. Thus in II Cor. 1.21 he indicates this knowledge in a kind of word-play: ὁ δὲ βεβαιῶν ἡμᾶς σὺν ὑμῖν εἰς Χριστὸν καὶ χρίσας ἡμᾶς Θεός: 'The one who has founded and anointed us (together) with you on Christ is God (himself)'.[26] It is significant that in contrast to the terminology of the New Testament elsewhere, the apostle does not use the verb χρίειν in connection with the 'anointing' of Jesus but with that of believers,[27] which takes place through the Spirit (cf. I John 2.20). On this Schlatter comments: 'Anointing consecrates a person for royal action: I.4,8. It is implied in the identification of the community with Christ.'[28] Underlying the formulation is probably a similar notion to Rom. 8.14-17, 29, that God has made us his sons through the Spirit on the basis of the mediation of the one Son. But this is no more than an allusion for those who are already in the know. Even if here and in some other passages (von Dobschütz mentions Rom. 9.5; II Cor. 5.10; Phil. 1.15 and Dahl adds I Cor. 10.4; 15.22; II Cor. 11.2f.; Phil. 1.l7; 3.7)[29] the old significance as an honorific title still 'plays some part',[30] this makes no difference to the clear Pauline terminology in which, to understand the apostle, 'it is never necessary to know that "Christ" is a term filled with content and highly significant. All the statements in the letters make good sense even to those who only know that Christ is a surname for Jesus.'[31]

In respect of external form this fixed form for the name of Jesus has clear parallels in the Hellenistic and Roman world. The traditional form of the name, ὁ κύριος Ἰησοῦς Χριστός (see n. 13 above), which Paul is fond of using in ceremonial contexts, say at the beginning and end of letters, has a similar form to that of the Roman ruler:

Imperator Caesar Augustus
Ἀυτοκράτωρ Καῖσαρ Σέβαστος[32]

or Hellenistic kings:
Βασιλεὺς Πτολεμαῖος Σωτήρ
Βασιλεὺς Ἀντίοχος Ἐπιφανής.[33]

Jesus was the real proper name, 'Christos' the cognomen and 'Kyrios' the title.[34] Further honorific designations could be added, like 'Son of God' by itself (τοῦ υἱοῦ αὐτοῦ Ἰησοῦ Χριστοῦ τοῦ κυρίου ἡμῶν, I Cor. 1.9; cf. II Cor 1.19), or even 'Soter' (I Tim. 1.10; Titus 11.4; 2.13; 3.6; cf. Phil. 3.20). In an analogous way the names and titles of Hellenistic rulers and the Roman emperor were also variable and could be either abbreviated or expanded.

That despite all this Paul remained aware that 'Jesus' was the real proper name and Christ was originally a title is evident from the fact that the confession of the Pauline communities was κύριος Ἰησοῦς or κύριος Ἰησοῦς Χριστός,[35] whereas the formula κύριος Χριστός never occurs. Romans 16.18, which seems to be the only exception, can be explained from the context, which is about false service: οἱ γὰρ τοιοῦτοι τῷ κυρίῳ Χριστῷ οὐ δουλεύουσιν ἀλλὰ τῇ ἑαυτῶν κοιλίᾳ.[36] When the form of the name is 'Christ Jesus', the 'Kyrios' can never come first; it is always put afterwards.[37]

N. A. Dahl and W. Kramer have indicated the essential linguistic peculiarities. The simple 'Christ' appears most frequently, about 150 times in all, about 60 of them with the article. Like 'Kyrios', it has the position of subject in the sentence fairly often, above all in the formula about Jesus' death, frequent in Paul, which comes from the pre-Pauline tradition.[38] Against the views of H.Conzelmann, neither the form with the determinative nor the position as subject can be taken as indications that the term is used as a title.[39] When 'Christ' appears in a form governed by a genitive, it always has the article, even when the governing noun also has the article, as for example in the relatively frequent formula τὸ εὐαγγέλιον τοῦ Χριστοῦ, which also comes from pre-Pauline tradition.[40] There is usually no article after prepositions, as in the frequent formulae ἐν Χριστῷ,[41] ὑπὲρ Χριστοῦ[42] and εἰς Χριστόν,[43] but in the case of διά with the genitive and the accusative there are forms both with and without the article.[44] In other cases the use of the article may be a result of anaphoristic usage, as in the case of the proper name Jesus. Even where Christ with the article is in the nominative, 'in no case can we discover an appropriate reason for the determination'.[45]

In particular with texts where the use of Christ as a title may possibly still stand in the background, the article seems to be used essentially at random. We find it in Rom. 9.3,5 but not in 10.4.6f.; it appears in 15.3,7 but not in the important text 15.8, where Paul refers to Christ as the διάκονος περιτομῆς who fulfils the promises given to the fathers. This can only be a reference to the 'messianic service' of Jesus towards his people. He is 'the root of Jesse' (15.12: ἡ ῥιζὰ τοῦ Ἰεσσαι = Isa. 11.10) in which the Gentiles will hope. In other words, there is no demonstrable connection in principle between the use of the article and a rudimentary significance as a title.[46]

It is also hard to explain other subtle differentiations in terminology, for example why the simple 'Christ', with and without the article, appears most frequently in II Corinthians.[47] Is this connected with the fact that in this most personal of all letters all liturgical and formal talk of Christ retreats more markedly into the background? It is also mysterious why the proportions in usage between 'Christos' and 'Kyrios' in the individual letters vary relatively markedly except in the special instance of I Thessalonians, the main theme of which is the parousia (see p. 66 above). Only in I Corinthians are both designations used almost equally (64 : 66), whereas in II Corinthians

'Christos' is by far the more predominant, as it is in Romans (66 : 44); in Galatians the relationship is particularly striking (38 : 6). Here we could ask whether this 'disproportion' is connected with the stress on the kerygma of the crucified Christ in the controversy with the Judaists? However, one can hardly claim from the relationship in Philippians (37 : 15), apart from the striking connection of the name Christ with sayings about the parousia, that ' "Christ" is increasingly inserted into contexts in which originally the title Kyrios belonged'.[48] Far less can we use this variation in the number of occurrences as an argument for dating the letters.

The use of 'Christos' basically embraces the whole saving event; while the representative death and the resurrection of Jesus are certainly central here, in addition the title has a wide variety of connotations, so that individual focal points cannot be so clearly delineated as in, say, the use of Kyrios (parousia, Lord's Supper, the question of slavery and marriage in I Cor. 7, etc.), or in the case of the much rarer Son of God (sayings about his sending). We can best talk of a concentration of the name 'Christ' where it is firmly rooted in the earlier 'pre-Pauline' tradition, as in the case of nouns and verbs connected with proclamation and faith, in connection with the formula about Christ's death, the cross of Christ, and indeed in sayings about the passion and resurrection of Jesus generally. Finally, it also occurs in connection with the typically Pauline formula ἐν Χριστῷ (Ἰησοῦ),[49] and in the context of the duty of the individual.[50] Nevertheless, we have to say that because of the varieties of usage, generally speaking, of all the christological names and titles in Paul, 'Christos' has the least distinctive profile.

A further fundamental point is that for Paul, Χριστός, like βασιλεία τοῦ θεοῦ or the resurrection from the dead, remains an eschatological concept.[51] The end-event is ushered in by the death and resurrection of Christ. For Paul his death is the decisive 'eschatological' saving event. By virtue of that, at the same time he is the fulfiller of the Old Testament promise.[52] The missionary proclamation of the εὐαγγέλιον τοῦ θεοῦ governs Paul's present activity as ἀπόστολος Ἰησοῦ Χριστοῦ (I Cor. 1.1; II Cor. 1.1; cf. I Thess. 2.7; II Cor. 11.13)[53] up to the parousia, which in Rom.11.26 he describes on the basis of Isa. 59.20 as the coming of the 'redeemer from Zion'. The traditional connection of the title Kyrios with remarks about the parousia does not exclude Paul from also using the name Christ in this connection. The use of ἡμέρα Χριστοῦ as a formula in Phil. 1.10; 2.16 shows that this term had become virtually interchangeable with the ἡμέρα κυρίου already to be found in the Old Testament.[54] One should therefore be wary of the judgment that the change of the title 'Christos' into a proper name is at the same time a clear indication of the diminution of eschatological expectation at the time of the transition to the mission to the Gentiles.[55]

What conclusions are we to draw from this remarkable terminological usage? Let us attempt to answer, in order, a number of basic questions.

1. Why did Paul use 'Christos' in particular with such striking frequency as an individual word, but also in connection with other designations, in complete contrast to the rest of New Testament terminology? We must ask very carefully whether this is a matter of mere convention or chance, or whether 'Christ' did not possess and retain a clear decisive theological significance for Paul because it is the designation for Jesus which he uses most often.

2. If that is the case, we immediately come to the next question. Why does the original significance of the title fail to come out more clearly – one might even say, never come out clearly – in his letters, although he himself must of course have been quite familiar with it? One of the main reasons why the pupil of Pharisaic scholars became a persecutor of the earliest community was that he felt that the proclamation of the crucified Jesus as the Messiah of Israel was a blasphemy. This is still indicated by sayings like Gal. 3.13, to the effect that the crucified 'Christ' 'became a curse for us', on the basis of Deut. 21.23. The formulae σταυρὸς τοῦ Χριστοῦ[56] or Χριστὸς ἐσταυρωμένος[57] are an indication of this. As far as we know, the Pharisees looked for the one royal Messiah from the family of David as the central eschatological saving figure. The popular character of this expectation is demonstrated by later Jewish prayers and Targumim. For Paul the Pharisee and pupil of the scribes, the 'crucified Messiah' Jesus of Nazareth had evidently himself been the supreme 'scandal' (cf. I Cor. 1.23; Gal. 5.11), a source of deep religious offence which could be done away with only by the persecution of the blasphemers (cf. Gal. 6.12) and the destruction of their communities.[58] The appearance of the Risen One before Damascus made him certain that the crucified Jesus really was the promised Messiah and that his death was the decisive saving event.[59] The fact that in Gal. 1.15f. Paul says that at that time God had revealed his Son to him, indicates that according to early Christian understanding the title Son of God interpreted the title Messiah and made it more precise. First moves towards this were already to be found in contemporary Judaism.[60] The many-sided use of the name Christ in the later letters therefore presumably shows the continuing interest of the apostle in this designation and at the same time demonstrates that in the letters which were written to Christian communities the question of the messiahship of Jesus was no longer

a matter for discussion but was completely taken for granted. When Paul speaks of 'Christ', 'Jesus Christ' or 'Christ Jesus', he does not use the traditional Jewish *title* Messiah, but he does not simply use a new, *arbitrary* additional name for Jesus of Nazareth; he just establishes without the need for any further discussion that only this Jesus – and no other – is the redeemer promised[61] by the prophets of the old covenant. The astounding variation in the use of 'Christos' shows that it does not particularly matter whether one can discover traces of a possible or probable significance as a title in individual contexts or certain grammatical forms, but that it is precisely as a 'proper name' that 'Christos' expresses the uniqueness of Jesus as 'eschatological bringer of salvation'. [62]

3. Now of course according to a widespread view this close association of the original title 'Christos' with the proper name Jesus to form a double name is 'rigidification',[63] in which 'the eschatological and Messianic element in the conception of Jesus are falling more and more into the background'.[64] With a reference to Acts 11.26, this process is located in the early Antiochene community: here the disciples were called 'Christians' for the first time. The pagan population is said to have seen Christ as a kind of party leader, and accordingly to have given his followers a party name.[65] These events presuppose the firmly established use of 'Christos' as a 'proper name' over a fairly long period of time. Evidently the 'name' Χριστός, which sounded unusual to Greek ears, was misunderstood as Χρῆστος; this is indicated not only by the famous note in Suetonius,[66] but also by the original reading *Chrestiani* in Tacitus, *Annals* 15.44.2.[67] The use of the masculine verbal adjective χριστός as the designation for a person occurs as a linguistic innovation only in the Septuagint; Greek vernacular knew only the neuter, e.g. as the noun τὸ χριστόν, meaning 'ointment' or 'dressing'[68] for medicinal or magical use.

The conclusion drawn from the development in Antioch, that in the 'Gentile Christianity' there 'Christ' 'almost completely lost' its significance as a title and thus its eschatological connotations, and that Paul therefore found this use of 'Christos' as a proper name there, taking it over himself,[69] is extremely improbable for a number of reasons. Above all, the fabrication of an early and predominantly 'Gentile Christian' community in which the development of christology was decisively influenced by the misunderstandings of newly-converted non-Jews is an incredible fiction.[70] In the first place, as far as we can see, in these earliest 'Gentile Christian' communities theological thought was largely governed by their Jewish-Christian spokesmen, and only secondly by the so-called 'Gentiles' who were converted by the message of the new Messiah in Antioch or even later in Rome were to begin with predominantly godfearers and sympathizers attached to the synagogue, to whom the new Jewish sect granted complete equality of religious rights by abolishing the requirement for circumcision.[71] With the prospect of the speedy return of the crucified Messiah and Lord who had been exalted to God, the ritual law had lost its exclusive significance. In this limited sense, for the first, unknown Jewish-Christian missionaries from the group of the Hellenists mentioned in Acts 6 Christ was already 'the end of the Law'.[72] On his missionary journeys Paul visited the synagogue first of all, not least in order to reach these 'godfearers'. Therefore these first 'Gentile Christians' who came from the circle of non-Jewish sympathizers and synagogue-goers could not have been so unfamiliar with the term Christ (which they will have found in the Septuagint and Jewish messianic expectation) that they had ceased to understand it – even before the beginning of Paul's mission –[73] and had falsified it to such a degree that it had become a meaningless proper name.

Even in the places where the earliest mission to the Gentiles was carried on, the development of christology was largely associated with leaders of opinion who were Jewish-Christian or at least god-fearers.[74] It was certainly through them that the Jewish term 'Christos', which was so un-Greek, underwent an ongoing Christian interpretation, though we must ask whether this interpretation is not to be traced back to the first community in Jerusalem and perhaps even, as I am myself convinced, to Jesus himself, who in his 'messianic authority' gave the title Messiah a new interpretation which diverged markedly from the contemporary Jewish pictures of the Messiah. However, this question would take us beyond the bounds of our present considerations.

4. First of all let us simply remember that Pauline and 'pre-Pauline Gentile Christianity' were not uncomprehending or indifferent towards the eschatological significance of Christ as a title. There was no such thing as an independent, specifically 'Gentile-Christian' christology, which Paul is already said to presuppose in his letters. If the four evangelists, Luke in Acts, the author of I John and Revelation quite naturally presuppose awareness that Christ is a title,[75] this awareness must also have been present in the much older communities to which the letters of Paul are addressed. Luke reports – in my view quite accurately – that Paul preached as a missionary in the synagogues that Jesus was the Messiah and that he had to suffer.[76] The fact that this theme no longer plays a part in the letters of Paul

and is at best indicated by the formula Χριστὸς ἀπέθανεν ὑπέρ, 'Christ died for', merely shows that we know very little indeed about Paul's *mission* preaching. The letters of Paul do not cover all his proclamation and teaching. Still, Paul preached this nucleus of the new belief in the death of 'Christos' for us in Corinth (and certainly also in other communities) ἐν πρώτοις as the εὐαγγέλιον τοῦ Χριστοῦ, and we must assume that he explained to the Corinthians and all the other newly founded communities what the name 'Christos' meant.[77] For on the other hand the letters of Paul demonstrate impressively the thorough knowledge of the Old Testament and Jewish tradition which Paul presupposed among his 'Gentile-Christian' communities. Anyone who could understand so difficult a typological interpretation as I Cor. 10.1-11 will surely also have known the true meaning of the 'name' ὁ Χριστός, the bearer of which is identical with the 'spiritual rock' of the journey through the wilderness. It would be silly to assume that the Pauline communities did not know that 'Christos' was not the common name for a slave but a designation of unique eschatological status which pertained only to Jesus. We can safely suppose that only non-Christians, the real pagans, confused Χριστός with Χρῆστος.

5. In fact 'Christos' seems to be a word with a character all of its own. It was neither one name among many, like Jesus, nor was it a customary Greek title, an honorific designation like βασιλεύς, κύριος or δεσπότης. Even if there was a relatively varied 'messianic expectation' in contemporary Judaism, leaving aside the priestly and Davidic Messiah in Qumran, as a rule only one dominant 'messianic' figure was expected, though this figure could have very different features. Like the related κύριος, Χριστός expressed the 'inalienable uniqueness' of Jesus.[78] The name *Yešuᵃᶜ*, the shortened form of *Yᵉhošuᵃᶜ*,[79] the religious and national hero of the conquest, was extraordinarily popular at the time of Jesus. Like the popular Maccabaean names Judas, Simeon, Eleazar or Jonathan, it expressed the tense religious and nationalistic awareness of the time. By contrast, the name 'Christos' was singular and indeed unique. For this reason alone it had to be set alongside the common name Jesus to distinguish it further and indeed partially to replace it. The boundary between certain biblical titles and proper names is very blurred: 'θεός and κύριος (= *yhwh*, but also Χριστός) also denote a being of unique nature, and these words (above all κύριος) come very close to being proper names.'[80] For this reason (ὁ) Χριστός and ὁ κύριος and above all the formulae ἐν κυρίῳ and ἐν Χριστῷ can be used almost interchangeably. As G. Dalman,[81] K. H. Rengstorf[82] and above all J.

Jeremias[83] have shown, even in later rabbinic terminology *mašiªh* without the article can partially assume the significance of a proper name. The age of this linguistic form is still disputed; it could perhaps occur as early as the Damascus Document in the phrase *mšyh ma'hrwn wmyśr'l*[84]. It is striking in this context that particularly in the Semitic sphere the transformation of what were originally titles into proper names is not uncommon in religious terminology. We find the phenomenon in the case of *šāṭān*,[85] *bᵉliyyaʿal* and *maśṭemā*,[86] and also in the case of 'Marnas', the city god of Gaza, whose designation originally meant 'our Lord' (Aramaic *mr'* with the first person plural suffix) and who was identified in Hellenistic times with Zeus,[87] of the Syrian *Baʿal šamem*, who similarly became Zeus, the Phoenician Adonis and the divine designation *ʿelyon*-ὕψιστος.[88] Klaus Berger also points in this connection to the name *kephaʾ*-Πέτρος given to Simon.[89]

6. That 'Kyrios' retained its significance as a title more strongly in connection with the name Jesus and that as κύριος Ἰησοῦς it became an acclamatory confession by the Pauline mission communities is connected with the fact that in the earliest confession of the Palestinian community 'Jesus' and 'Messiah' had been indissoluby connected in the formula *yešuªʿ mᵉšīḥā* (or *(ham-)māšiªh*); thus from the beginning both stood closer together than Kyrios and Jesus. A further factor was that for the Greek-speaking synagogue 'Kyrios' had already long taken the place of the tetragrammaton; it was the *qᵉrę*, the liturgical name for God, in place of the name which was not to be pronounced. Thus through its liturgical usage Kyrios had the higher status. That this 'name which is above every name', used of God himself, was transferred to the crucified one and that the exalted Jesus was acclaimed by all creation as κύριος Ἰησοῦς Χριστός (Phil. 2.9,11), was an additional accentuation of the status of Jesus which went beyond the eschatological *maṣiªh*, Χριστός. It was already prepared for in the Palestinian community,[90] where the address *mārān* or the absolute *mare* in conjunction with Ps. 110.1 had suppressed the mysterious and unkerygmatic *barʾᵉnaṣā* but had not yet taken on that fundamentally – may one already say? – 'divine' significance that it had in the Pauline communities.[91] As long as the earliest Christian mission was addressed predominantly to a Jewish audience, the confession of Jesus as Messiah remained the focal point and made it certain that at the latest when the new message was transferred to the Greek language area the two 'names' would be combined in an indissoluble unity. Paul the Pharisee will already have come across the confessional double name Ἰησοῦς Χριστός among the Hellenists in Jerusalem; it took on the accent that was so scandalous to him through the

formula Χριστός ἀπέθανεν ὑπὲρ ἡμῶν.[92] For if we do not know for certain whether there was a fixed tradition of the suffering servant of God and Messiah in Judaism before the time of Jesus,[93] we can at least say with some certainty that because of Deut. 21.23 the message of the *crucified* Messiah Jesus must have been extremely offensive in those circles which were faithful to the Law. For Paul, what had previously been offensive became the central stay of that εὐαγγέλιον τοῦ Χριστοῦ which he received δι'ἀποκαλύψεως Ἰησοῦ Χριστοῦ.[94]

7. The historical basis for this towering central significance of the confession of Jesus as Messiah in the earliest community which continued for Paul in a different terminology, more particularly in the strikingly frequent use of 'Christos' as a unique 'proper name' for Jesus himself, lies in the one hand in the historical fact that Jesus had been executed as a messianic pretender by Pilate on the instigation of the leaders of the people. The trial of Jesus up to and including the *titulus* with the reason for the death penalty and the mocking of Jesus on the cross (Mark 15.26-32), revealed his 'messianic' claim publicly and finally.[95] It is no coincidence that this claim runs like a scarlet thread through the earliest account of the trial, in Mark. Those radical critics who seek to eliminate it at the same time destroy the possibility of any historical understanding of the beginnings of christology. The community knew that Jesus had gone to his death as Messiah on the basis of his 'good confession' (I Tim. 6.13) before Pilate and that God had recognized his messianic service and status through the resurrection. At the same time, as the sinless anointed one Jesus had made atonement for the sin of the people. The indissoluble combination of *yešuᵃᶜ mᵉšīḥā* Ἰησοῦς Χριστός both rejected all claims by other Jewish messianic pretenders – which were evidently quite frequent – and established that the 'nature' of the Messiah was not to be defined in the light of any traditional messianic expectations but was determined 'once for all' through Jesus, his atoning death on the cross, his resurrection by God, his exaltation to the right hand of God and his parousia as judge and redeemer. How effective this fusion was even where the eschatological status of Jesus was rejected is evident from Josephus, who in *Antt.* 20, 200 mentions 'James the brother of Jesus the so-called Christ' (τὸν ἀδελφὸν Ἰησοῦ τοῦ λεγομένου Χριστοῦ).[96]

To summarize these conclusions briefly: the amazingly many-sided use of 'Christos' in Paul, the most frequent name of Jesus in his letters, is no coincidence nor thoughtless convention, no mere assimilation to Gentile-Christian terminology. On the other hand, it makes little sense to seek to discover in Paul the use of the name as a title. 'Christos' is indissolubly fused with Jesus in such a way that the saving significance of the name is naturally present to the apostle in respect of the crucifixion of Christ. We may suppose that Christ had already become a name by the time that there were Christians in Antioch, but this usage goes back to the pre-Pauline Hellenistic community in Jerusalem and was taken over by Paul after his call before Damascus. It expressed the fact that the crucified Jesus and no other is the eschatological bringer of salvation. *yešū$^{a\,c}$ m^{c}šīḥā* was already the most important missionary confession in the earliest Palestinian community, which even in the Aramaic form demonstrated the tendency towards making this a double name. The historical basis for it can be found in the crucifixion of Jesus as a messianic pretender.

5

Hymns and Christology

The topic of hymns and christology first of all brings us up against the riddle of early Christian worship. 'Satisfactory answers have not yet been provided for the many questions that have been raised', remarked Hans Lietzmann on the subject,[1] and he was one of the best informed about this difficult material. He could also explain why this was the case. 'There is little or no information about the liturgy in the early writers; probably this was because such matters seemed too self-evident to need recording. Nor would Paul have discussed any of these if disorders had not arisen in Corinth, causing him to admonish the people and give them directions.'[2] Fortunately, we might add, for because of this disorder in Corinth at least we know a very little about what happened in the worship of the Pauline mission communities.

1. In I Cor. 14.26 the apostle writes about how things should be done in worship. 'What then, brethren? When you come together, each one has a hymn (ἕκαστος ψαλμὸν ἔχει), a lesson, a revelation, a tongue, or an interpretation. Let all things be done for edification.' This list indicates the multiplicity of gifts of the Spirit which are at work in worship. So it is all the more striking that Paul puts the hymn at the beginning. Schlatter believe that worship will have opened with a hymn.[3] It is also striking that Paul here uses the work ψαλμός, which the Greek reader might misunderstand, and not, say, ὕμνος or even παιάν. For the Greeks ψαλμός meant playing on a stringed instrument; in the Septuagint headings to the Psalms, however, the word is a virtually stereotyped rendering of the Hebrew *mizmor*, so that in Hellenistic Judaism it took on the special meaning of 'religious hymn'. This choice of a new word by the Septuagint translators was certainly not unintentional, since the Jewish ψαλμός was fundamentally different from the traditional Greek hymn to the gods with its strict metre, dependent on the variation between stressed and unstressed syllables. By so naturally presupposing the use of the word

ψαλμός in its un-Greek Jewish meaning, Paul could be referring to the tradition from which the composition of religious songs in his community, prompted by the Spirit, derived.

It further emerges from the context that the ψαλμός sung at the beginning will hardly have been an Old Testament 'psalm' learnt off by heart; it will have been a new composition, inspired by the Spirit. It is obvious that this song was rendered in a way which everyone could understand; in some circumstances it could have been learnt off by heart so that everyone could join in the singing. Thus it served to 'build up' the community and was not a song sung 'with tongues', though Paul and the community at Corinth will also have been familiar with that.[4] Alongside the teaching and the word of revelation,then, the song was evidently a basic ingredient in the spirit-inspired worship of the Pauline missionary communities.

2. This picture is also confirmed by two deutero-Pauline instances:

(*a*) Let the word of Christ (ὁ λόγος τοῦ Χριστοῦ) dwell in you richly in all wisdom,
teach and admonish one another
with psalms inspired by the spirit, and hymns and songs in a state of grace,
sing in your hearts to God.
And whatever you do in word or deed,
do everything in the name of the Lord Jesus,
giving thanks to God the Father through him (Col. 3.16f.).

(*b*) . . . but be filled with the Spirit,
addressing one another in spiritual psalms and hymns and songs,
singing and making psalmody to the Lord with all your heart,
always and for everything giving thanks to God the Father,
in the name of our Lord Jesus Christ (Eph 5. 18c-20).

The text of Ephesians is dependent on that of Colossians and is the first commentary on it. Against the punctuation of the Nestle text but following Clement of Alexandria, Westcott and Hort, Lightfoot, Lohmeyer and others, the ψαλμοῖς ὕμνοις ᾠδαῖς πνευματικαῖς is presumably to be connected with the preceding participles διδά-σκοντες and νουθετοῦντες. The text was already understood in this way by the author of the Letter to the Ephesians, who summed up both these participles in a single λαλοῦντες. We often find hymnic passages in the New Testament which have a didactic character and partly also serve as paraenesis. Therefore the exegesis of the text of Colossians will have to begin with the λόγος τοῦ Χριστοῦ. What follows takes its content from that. The word of Christ and the word about Christ is to govern everything when the community meets for worship. It is striking that the formula λόγος τοῦ Χριστοῦ is used only here in the whole of the New Testament. Evidently the author wants it to emphasize the christological determination of the word proclaimed in worship. It is to 'be present' (ἐνοικεῖν) in the community πλουσίως ('in abundance' and at the same time in a constantly new way), but at the same time also ἐν πάσῃ σοφίᾳ ('in all wisdom in the power of the Spirit').

However, for the author the word of Christ in rich and constantly new forms, and as wisdom brought about by the Spirit, takes concrete form in worship through the multiplicity of songs which serve the mutual edification and admonition of the community. Its function is to build up the congregation by the collaboration of the various charismatic writers and singers of hymns. There are many examples of such songs as 'the word of Christ' in the New Testament letters, not least in Colossians and Ephesians.

The three successive terms ψαλμοί, ὕμνοι, ᾠδαί are an expression of this abundance; they do not indicate different genres of song, but refer to one and the same kind. Here the author is merely using the three most important Septuagint terms for the religious song.[5] However, it is not a coincidence that ψαλμός is used first, as the most important word. The adjective πνευματικός following the three nouns characterizes the song used in worship as inspired by the Spirit. As gifts of the Spirit the songs are not 'the teaching and commandment of men' (Col. 2.22), but the 'Word of Christ'.

The last phrase, 'sing in your hearts to God', designates the liturgical song described earlier as a song produced in the heart to the praise of God. That is to say that the spirit which gives this song moves not only the lips but above all and first of all the heart as the innermost part of a human being. The aim and the perfecting of the 'word of Christ' which produces the song in the heart through the spirit for the edification of the community, is the praise of God. In that the community makes the word of Christ 'dwell' in its midst by singing psalms to Christ, in order to instruct and admonish itself by the hymnic narration of the saving action of Christ, it gives glory to God, the Father of Jesus Christ. So it is a matter of inner consistency that the hymn to Christ in Philippians ends with the phrase 'to the glory of God the Father' (2.11).[6]

This attempt at interpretation is confirmed by the interpretation of Col. 3.16 in Eph. 5.19. Here the invitation 'Let the word of Christ dwell in you richly in all wisdom' is replaced by the simple imperative, 'Be filled with the spirit', a command which stresses that the hymn in

Christian worship is a gift of the Spirit.[7] The mutual teaching and admonition which follow are combined in an 'addressing one another' and the singing is supplemented by a 'making psalmody'. Here ψάλλειν does not mean playing on a stringed instrument, but the psalm singing which is typical of the Jewish tradition; there, as there was no fixed number of syllables in the verses of psalms, it was impossible to follow a consistent pattern of melodic composition; a melodious tonal movement was possible only at certain points, say at the beginning and end of each verse; for the other variable parts of the verse it was necessary to maintain the same note. The form of such a psalm allowed many possibilities, ranging from short acclamatory liturgies to extended hymnic texts.

However, it is most striking that in Eph. 5.19, at the end of the verse the τῷ θεῷ, 'to God', is replaced by τῷ κυρίῳ, to the Lord, which must certainly be given a christological interpretation. This change accords with Deichgräber's[8] observation that in the New Testament and probably also in early Christian worship there is much more evidence of hymns to Christ than of hymns to God. The hymn to Christ was not just a speciality of Christian liturgical celebration which distinguished it from synagogue worship; it gave expression in a central way to the fact that God has disclosed his eschatological salvation only through his Son.

Let me try to sum up what I have said so far.

1. Liturgical hymns had a special significance in the meetings for worship of the earliest Christian mission communities, and were an essential part of that worship.

2. These were not just traditional songs; they will just as often have been spontaneous compositions. They were not regarded as purely human creations, but as works of the Holy Spirit.

3. In content the liturgical hymn was primarily governed by the saving event which had been brought about in Christ, i.e. it was predominantly a hymn to Christ.

4. Despite the variety of possibilities, in form it will have been a 'psalm'; i.e. it will not have had the strict metre of the Greek religious hymn: in this respect it wil have been closer to the Old Testament and Jewish tradition, and in its musical presentation it will have been connected with the form of psalmody to be found there.

3. We also find a close connection between hymns to God and hymns to Christ in the most detailed description of a 'service' that we have in the New Testament, in Rev. 4; 5. However, this is not earthly worship but heavenly worship, before the throne of God. We cannot therefore simply assume that the liturgical texts which appear here

have been taken over from the liturgy of the community. Rather, they have been deliberately been composed by the seer with an eye to his own work. At the same time, however, we may assume that the apocalyptist is referring to the liturgical usage of his community.[9]

The description reaches its real climax with the appearance of Christ in ch. 5. As the '(sacrificial) Lamb who has been slain', he alone is worthy to receive from the hand of God the mysterious book of the eschatological judgment. As a result, he, the crucified Kyrios, is made God's eschatological plenipotentiary and entrusted with carrying out his plan of salvation and judgment. As a sign of the authority which has been bestowed on him the four creatures and the twenty-four elders pay homage to him and sing him 'a new song'. This context, the stress on the homage and the singing of the 'new song' gives the first hymn to Christ in Revelation which now follows its unique significance. It begins with an acclamatory 'Worthy art thou' (ἄξιος εἶ), which presents the new messianic ruler as the plenipotentiary of God:

> Worthy art thou to take the scroll
> and to open its seals,
> for thou wast slain
> and by thy blood didst ransom men for God
> from every tribe and tongue
> and people and nation,
> and hast made them a kingdom and priests
> to our God,
> and they shall reign on earth (5.9b,10).

To heighten the scene further, the choir of all the heavenly beings follows this hymn narrating the saving action of Christ with its *axios* doxology, giving the 'Lamb once slain' seven predicates which elsewhere are attributed only to God. That is, the veneration received by the Christ is not inferior to the praise and honour which are due to God himself.

The heavenly liturgy reaches its climax and conclusion in the last doxology. The previous framework is burst apart, for now all creatures 'in heaven and on earth and under the earth and in the sea and all that is in them' unite in one choir to praise God *and* his Christ:

> To him who sits upon the throne and to the lamb be blessing and honour and glory and might for ever (5.13).

In a special way, this scene emphasizes the fact that the apocalyptist, in contrast to all the other hymnic sections, introduces the first hymn to Christ in his work as ᾠδὴ καινή, new song, emphasizes this scene in a special way. The 'new song' is a stereotyped formula in the Psalms. Underlying it is the notion that the 'old song' has become inadequate because God has done new, wonderful things. In Deutero-Isaiah it appears as the eschatological praise which is occasioned by the new thing that God will proclaim:

And new things I now declare,
before they spring forth
I tell you of them.
Sing to the Lord a new song,
his praise from the end of the earth (Isa. 42.9b-10a).

Within the book of Revelation the theme appears elsewhere only in 14.3 as the song of the angelic host before the Lamb and the 144,000 redeemed on the heavenly Zion. This 'new song' can be understood only by the members of the redeemed community. In other words, the author of Revelation quite deliberately related the 'new song' only to Christ and to his perfected community. The christological hymn is a 'new song', because it is the foundation for the eschatological renewal of creation by the Messiah who has been appointed by God.

The theme of Rev. 5.9 here has common elements with most of the hymns to Christ in the New Testament. It is concerned first of all with the death of Jesus, including his meaning of universal salvation for the world; furthermore, if we take the whole of ch. 5 into account, it is concerned with the glorification or exaltation of Jesus, which leads to the homage of all the heavenly powers, indeed all creatures, and to his status as one who can share the divine throne.

4. We could describe the two chapters Rev. 4; 5 with their account of heavenly worship as a 'prologue in heaven' which is the necessary presupposition of the end event extending from ch. 6 onwards; in its closing doxology (5.13) this 'prologue' already anticipates the consummation brought about by the rule of God.

It is one of the peculiarities of the hymns to Christ in the New Testament that they often describe the very event which the seer depicts in his vision of the opening of the heavens, and that in so doing they are also a partial anticipation of the end. What the seer saw 'in the Spirit' as a real scene in heaven has been summed up in a few verses by unknown poets, inspired by the spirit. Here are some examples:

Therefore God has highly exalted him
and bestowed on him the name which is above every name,

that at the name of Jesus every knee should bow,
in heaven and on earth and under the earth,
and every tongue confess that Jesus Christ is Lord,
to the glory of God the Father (Phil. 2.9-11).

He was manifested in the flesh,
vindicated in the Spirit,
seen by angels,
preached among the nations,
believed on in the world,
taken up into glory (I Tim. 3.16).

He reflects the glory of God
and bears the very stamp of his nature,
upholding the universe by his word of power.
When he had made purification for sins,
he sat down at the right hand of the Majesty on high (Heb. 1.3).

This last hymn fragment has a further continuation on which we must spend rather more time. Verse 4, where the author of Hebrews clearly changes to 'prose', was still 'written under the influence of a hymn to Christ which had been composed before him'[10]: 'Christ is as much superior to the angels as the name he has obtained is more excellent than theirs' (Heb. 1.4). Now the unique thing about the Letter to the Hebrews is that it is not content to quote from one hymn to Christ, drawing from that the consequences for the status of the exalted one; in addition, it quotes further texts, all of which (with one exception) come from Old Testament 'hymns',[11] to demonstrate the unique status of Christ in the heavenly world and over against all creatures including the angels. Here it possibly goes back to an older collection of texts. Thus in Heb. 1 we find six further texts, one after another, which at a pinch we could also call 'hymn fragments', including the most important christological text in the Old Testament, Ps. 110.1, to which the author had already alluded in the hymn which he quoted and the first verse of which, as the earliest Christians understood it, gave expression to what was depicted in the 'prologue in heaven' in Rev. 4; 5. 'To what angel has God ever said, "Sit at my right hand, till I make thy enemies a stool for thy feet"?'

It is striking here in Heb. 1 how naturally various Old Testament psalms are interpreted to some extent as 'hymns to Christ', a procedure which is continued in Heb. 2. In 2.6f., there is a quotation from the wisdom psalm which primarily refers to human beings:

What is man that thou art mindful of him,

or the son of man, that thou carest for him?
Thou didst make him for a little while lower than the angels,
thou has crowned him with glory and honour,
putting everything in subjection under his feet (Ps. 8.5-7 LXX).

The christological interpretation which follows brings this psalm quotation, too, close to the 'prologue in heaven' of Rev. 5. For the 'all' refers to the whole of creation. There is nothing that is not subjected to him by God, even if we cannot yet see that (Heb. 2.8). But Jesus, who for a short time was humbled below the angels, was 'crowned with glory and honour because of the suffering of death' (Heb. 2.9). Leaving aside the pre-existence which the author of Hebrews reads into the text of Ps. 8, in the exegesis of this psalm in Heb. 2 we find a similar christological scheme to that in the hymns in Rev. 5. However, the parallels to the hymn in Phil. 2.9-11 are also unmistakable. There are three main points here.

1. The basis for the exaltation of Christ is his sacrificial death.

2. The crowning with 'glory' (δόξα) and 'honour' (τιμή) in Ps. 8.6 is exactly matched by the twofold 'honour' and 'glory' of the two doxologies Rev. 5.12,13 and by the receiving of the 'name above all names' in Phil. 2.9b.

3. The subjection of the whole creation in Ps. 8.7 has its parallel in the homage of all creatures before God and the Lamb (Rev. 5.13) and the no less universal *exhomologesis* of all created beings before the Kyrios (Phil. 2.11).

4. Here we evidently have an ancient christological basic pattern which could be developed in many ways: in an exegesis of Old Testament psalms, in the apocalyptic vision of the heavenly worship to glorify the slain Messiah and also in the form of a hymn to Christ, at different times and in different places and in different traditio-historical contexts.

5. It also becomes clear that the problem of understanding the hymn to Christ in earliest Christian worship and its significance for the development of christology cannot easily be understood unless alongside the so-called 'Christ-hymns' and 'hymn fragments' in the New Testament letters and Revelation we also take into account those Old Testament texts which as 'Christ psalms' gave decisive stimuli to christological thought. Three further fragments of hymns should demonstrate this:

Christ suffered for sins once for all,
the righteous for the unrighteous,
that he might bring us to God,
being put to death in (the) flesh

but made alive through (the) spirit

. . .

who has gone into heaven
and is *at the right hand of God*,
with angels, authorities and powers
subject to him (I Peter 3.18-22).

or:

. . . when he raised him from the dead
and made him sit *at his right hand*
. . . and *he has put all things under his feet*
and has made him the head over all things (Eph. 1.20-22).

or:

Christ Jesus who died,
yes, who was raised from the dead,
who is *at the right hand of God*,
who indeed intercedes for us (Rom. 8.34b).

Common to all three texts is the reference to the death or resurrection of Christ and his exaltation *to the right hand of God*, a theme which
goes back to Ps. 110, a christological psalm, since only there in the
Old Testament is there mention of an enthronement at the right hand
of God. Here it is striking that neither the fragment from Ephesians
nor that from I Peter is content with a reference to Ps. 110.1. Rather,
with the formula 'he has put all things under his feet', Eph. 1.22
quotes a second christological psalm, Ps. 8.7, a text which is already
familiar to us from Heb. 2.7. Here we may see a deliberate connection
of the two psalms which for the early Christian exegetes contained
two different 'titles', namely κύριος and υἱὸς (τοῦ) ἀνθρώπου.[12] This
fusion of psalms can also be found in the first fragment quoted, I
Peter 3.22, where after the reference to 'sitting at the right hand' from
Ps. 110.1, the formula 'with authorities and powers subject to him',
at the same time refers to Ps. 8.7, 'has subjected all things to him'. In
both instances the decisive verb is ὑποτάσσειν.[13]

In terms of the history of tradition the most interesting text of the
three quoted is the third, with the earliest mention of the enthronement theme in the New Testament (Rom. 8.34). That this is a formula
deriving from the fragment of a hymn is evident, *inter alia*, from the
fact that the Pauline formulation 'who is at the right hand of God'
occurs again in precisely the same words in I Peter 3.22, again in the
context of a hymn. The Pauline version seems to be secondary and

rounded off compared with the quotation from Ps. 110.1, already bearing witness to a longer development of that tradition. In the use of this expression by Paul it is striking that only here in Romans does the apostle refer to the sitting of the exalted one 'at the right hand of God' and that at the same time this takes place in a stereotyped liturgical form. Paul probably knows that this hymnic formula was highly esteemed in the community in Rome (cf. Hebrews; I Peter; I Clem. 36.5).

Yet another reference in Paul is illuminating. The enthronement 'at the right hand of God' is followed by a concluding line: 'who indeed intercedes for us' (ὅς καὶ ἐντυγχάνει ὑπὲρ ἡμῶν). We find the verb ἐντυγχάνειν in the special sense of intercession elsewhere only in Heb. 7.24f., where the eternal high priesthood of Christ is explained in accordance with Ps. 110.4: 'But he holds his priesthood permanently, because he continues for ever. Consequently he is able for all time to save those who draw near to God through him, since he always lives to make intercession for them' (εἰς τὸ ἐντυγχάνειν ὑπὲρ αὐτῶν). It is striking that Rom. 8.34 is akin to Heb. 7.25b, even down to its formulation. This prompts the conjecture that the tradition of the high-priestly service of the exalted Christ which is developed in an arbitrary way in Hebrews already underlay the fragment of a hymn which was used by Paul. In that case it is easy to trace the origin of this tradition. If in Rom. 8.34c the place of the exalted Christ 'at the right hand of God' goes back to Ps. 110.1, the high-priestly intercession of the exalted Christ in Rom. 8.34 is best explained on the basis of Ps. 110.4, which is so familiar to us from the Letter to the Hebrews: 'Thou art a priest for ever, after the order of Melchizedek'.[14] But that would mean that in Rom. 8.34 we have early evidence that Ps. 110 already influenced the formation of a relatively early hymn to Christ.

When the earliest community in Jerusalem, driven on by the power of the Spirit, was concerned to work out in theological terms the overwhelming experience of the resurrection of Jesus, it must very soon have come upon this psalm which is also unique in the Old Testament, and put it to its own use. Its early influence is already evident from the fact that it was also recorded in two forms in the synoptic tradition, in Mark, whereas in Paul it is also connected with Ps. 8.7.[15] The experience that Jesus was raised by God as the crucified Messiah and was even the expected Son of Man evidently led very soon to the certainty that God had now enthroned this Jesus, the erstwhile *rab* or *rabbūn*, i.e. the Lord and Master of the disciples, as *ʾadōn* or Kyrios at his right hand.[16] Through this Lord the community had access to the heavenly sanctuary in worship, with its spirit-inspired prayers and hymns as depicted in Rev. 5.8;[17] his sitting at the right hand of God created a constant correspondence between the worship before the divine throne and the earthly community under persecution, and they could pray for the early coming of their Lord in the plea *māran* *ᵘtā'*.[18] However, at the same time this call amounted to more than a prayer for the imminent parousia; it was also an expression of the close connection in the present between the disciples of Jesus and their Lord who had been exalted to share God's throne, an expression of the earliest spirit-filled enthusiasm of the primitive church.

6. It has emerged from what has been said so far that the hymn to Christ had a quite essential significance for earliest Christian worship as for the formation of christology. It contained a narration of the work of Christ, above all his death, the salvation that death achieved, his exaltation and, at a later stage of the tradition (which we cannot go into now because of the limitations of space), his pre-existence, mediation at creation and incarnation. The focal points of the content of the various hymns may differ, but despite the difference in the individual themes the majority of the fragments of hymns which we can still identify had one theme in common, binding them together: the contrast and at the same time the intrinsic connection between the death of Jesus and his exaltation as they are also depicted in the visionary 'prologue in heaven' (Rev. 5). The enthronement and authorization of the risen Lord and at the same time the homage of the divine and ungodly powers, indeed of all creatures, could belong to the complex of the exaltation.

Of course, it could be objected that the number of the hymns to Christ which can be demonstrated with any certainty is not large, and moreover that the attempts to demonstrate such fragments of hymns in the various letters in the New Testament have not always been convincing. The difference between hymnic prose and the early Christian psalm, the metre of which cannot be clearly established, has not always been easy to show.[19] One answer to this would be that the letters in the New Testament are explicitly prose writings and that it is of itself a striking fact that individual passages with a poetic form can be indicated within them. I cannot go into the formal criteria for them here; they have been known since Eduard Norden.[20]

It is not easy to distinguish the fragments of hymns from more extended acclamations, benedictions, doxologies and so-called confessional formulae, as these could in turn be parts or strophes of larger hymnic units. Furthermore a simple series of two or three lines could be sung as a hymn. Nevertheless, there is a relative consensus among scholars at this point. In the New Testament – including the prologue to the Gospel of John but excluding the Apocalypse – there are a good dozen christological texts from a period of about fifty or sixty years, between about AD 40 and AD 100, which are almost always of great significance for our knowledge of the earliest christology. That the composition of hymns continued we know not only from Pliny but also from the letters of Ignatius and the Odes of Solomon. Then, of course, it breaks off. The liturgical model of Justin (cf. *Apology* 1,67,3ff.) is no longer familiar with the singing of extempore hymns; in both scriptural reading and prayer it has become completely assimilated to the liturgy of the word in synagogue worship. The difference between this later ordering or worship and the free working of the spirit in the early period cannot be exaggerated. This may be connected with the fact that the Christian gnosticism of the second century appropriated the composition of hymns, indeed – if we are to take the Naassene Hymn (Hippolytus, *Philos.* 5,10,2) and the fragment of Valentinus (Hippolytus, *Philos.* 6,37,7) as examples – now in strict anapaests; furthermore, with Valentinus, Basilides and Marcion the authors are named, as claimants to possession of the Spirit. Thus one could see both metre and the indication of author as an indication of the 'acute Hellenization of Chistianity' by the Gnostics.[21]

By contrast, for the period of the Pauline mission and up to the time of Ignatius it is beyond question that the liturgical hymn to Christ was an essential influence on the development of christological thought. Here, however, we have to raise a series of questions which take us further:

(*a*) Could not the influence of the liturgical hymn to Christ also be effective in a whole series of christological statements where it is no longer possible to point to fragments of hymns? At one point we tried to investigate such an influence: in the influence of Ps. 110 and to a lesser degree of Ps. 8. Of course here it is not a question of a 'new song' but of Old Testament 'Christ psalms'.

(*b*) That raises the further question: are the Old Testament 'Christ psalms' which were a decisive influence on the development of christology directly connected with the origin of the Christ hymns in earliest Christian worship, or are these essentially new forms in contrast with the psalms to be found in the Old Testament and Judaism?

(*c*) Here we come up against the problem which really concerns us. Is it possible to pursue the origin of the Christ hymn behind the letters of Paul into the obscure period between AD 30 and AD 50, where the real decisive christological development took place?

(*d*) This is again at the same time a question of the history of religion. Is the earliest Christian hymn a product of the enthusiasm of the 'Hellenistic' mission communities which were under strong syncretistic influence, and therefore are its nearest parallels, if not in the hymns of the mystery associations, at least in the songs of philosophical gnostic circles, with their stronger 'oriental' influence, such as we find for example in the Hermetic Corpus?[22] Can we even assume, as has long been claimed in German scholarship, that what were originally gnostic hymns appear in primitive Christian writings with only relatively slight changes?

(*e*) One argument in favour of this theory might be that so-called 'official' Pharisaic Judaism did not have any singing of hymns in its synagogue services, leaving aside say the recitation of the hallel psalms on certain feast days. The religious hymn, the so-called *piyyut*, found its way into the synagogue only in the fifth and sixth centuries and had to overcome heavy resistance.[23]

7. This difference between the Palestinian synagogue worship of a Pharisaic stamp and reports which we have about the assemblies of the Pauline communities say in I Cor. 14 led so significant a scholar as Walter Bauer to conclude that the worship of the Gentile-Christian mission communities was at most peripherally dependent on synagogue celebrations and was organized very much more on the model of mystery celebrations or the Hermetic Gnostic conventicle. There is hardly adequate historical basis for this theory.[24] It may be true that the institutionalized singing of psalms in Palestine was primarily limited to the temple and its great choirs of levites and that Pharisaic synagogue worship knew only prayer, scriptural readings and preaching, but this Pharisaic ordering was by no means the only one, even in Palestine. Not only the hymns in the infancy narratives of the Gospel of Luke or the Psalms of Solomon but even more the Qumran discoveries are evidence that particularly in Jewish Palestine there was abundant composition of religious songs, which were perhaps sung even in worship at Qumran.[25] The rejection of the hymn in the rabbinic synagogue may therefore very well be connected with the elimination of heretics. The Jewish diaspora was even freer: here, above all according to the testimony of Philo, singing hymns was of great significance. What he says, e.g. about the celebrations of the Jewish therapeutae in Egypt, is so reminiscent of the earliest Christian worship that Eusebius interpreted them as Christian celebrations (HE 2,17,21ff.).

We can hardly doubt that the word ψαλμός in I Cor. 14.26; Col. 3.16 and Eph. 5.19 points back to the tradition of the Old Testament and Jewish psalms, for only there is it used to denote liturgical song. The objection that the conception that the earliest Christian hymns were inspired by the spirit and have their nearest parallel in the inspiration of Hellenistic mysticism is unconvincing. Certainly among the Greeks from the time of Homer and Hesiod the divine inspiration of the poet had become a commonplace. But we have analogous conceptions in Judaism as well. I shall recall only the well-known verse of the psalm, 'O Lord, open my lips, that my mouth may show forth thy praise!'[26] In the Testament of David (II Sam. 23.1-3), David himself confesses that the spirit of God is speaking through him:

> The oracle of David, the son of Jesse,
> the spirit of the Lord speaks by me,
> his word is upon my tongue.

For Judaism and earliest Christianity David was not only king but, as the writer of psalms, also a prophet endowed with the Spirit. Apart from the Pentateuch, Philo cites the psalms more than all other Old Testament writings, and for primitive Christianity, too, after Isaiah the Psalter was the work most quoted. This conception of David the prophet-poet has found expression in the well-known David text from the Psalm Scroll of 11Q:

> And Yahweh gave him a wise and enlightened spirit . . . And the sum (of his songs) was 4050. These he uttered through prophecy (*bnbw'h*), which had been given him by the most High.[27]

8. This inspiration through the Spirit is also determinative for earliest Christianity. We know that the first community in Jerusalem was stamped in a very elemental way by the primal event, the appearances of the risen Christ and the eschatological experience of the Spirit. Therefore the worship of the early community logically emerged as the work of the Spirit, who inspired the Christian prophets to admonitions, 'revelations', visions, but also glossolalia. This ecstatic-enthusiastic form of worship was not just a new development in the Gentile-Christian mission communities, but in my view goes back to the first beginnings. 'Enthusiasm engendered Christianity'.[28] That created a fundamental difference between earliest Christian worship and the ordering of synagogue worship. Through its risen and exalted Lord the community stood in a direct connection with the heavenly sanctuary, and through the Spirit the Lord himself was present in it. The kingdom of God no longer had to be expected in an uncertain future; it was already dawning. If Jesus was the 'firstfruits of those who have fallen asleep' (I Cor. 15.20), the spirit was his 'gift

of first fruits'(Rom. 8.23). This unique eschatological-messianic self-awareness in the first community inevitably burst apart the traditional forms and conventions of worship and created new things. The picture of the earliest community which Luke gives in Acts 2-5 is not exaggerated and too idealistic, but rather too bland and too conventional. This community had the assurance that the spirit of the prophets, which had disappeared from Israel since the time of Ezra, was alive in it more powerfully than ever before, and that the Spirit was not just leading it – as it had led the Teacher of Righteousness – 'to interpret all the words of his servants the prophets'(1QpHab 2,8f.),[29], but was making the very members of the Jesus community into prophets. And just as the effects of the Spirit in the Old Testament included not only prophetic sayings and visions but also the praise of God's acts in song, so now there was newly inspired composition of hymns. At the same time people read and sang the Old Testament songs in a new way. This was particularly the case with the 'messianic' psalms and those that could be interpreted in this way: Pss. 2; 8; 22, etc. – I need not list them all. After Ps. 110, Ps. 118, the Hallel psalm, is particularly interesting; this is the last psalm which Jesus sang with his disciples before the passion and which prefigured Jesus' fate with the image of the rejected stone which becomes the corner stone (v. 22) and the vision of the triumph of the one to come. The fact that the hosanna appears in the account of the entry to Jerusalem in all four Gospels, then again in the eucharistic liturgy of the Didache (10.6) and finally in Hegesippus' account of the martyrdom of James[30] shows that the liturgical use of Ps. 118.26 must go back to the earliest community.

Unfortunately Luke does not tell us anything about the hymn in worship. That hymns were sung can be assumed only from the praying and singing of Paul and Silas in prison in Philippi (Acts 16.25). However, we have a note from the earliest community in Acts 2.46f., which takes us further: 'Breaking bread in their homes, they partook of food with jubilation (ἐν ἀγαλλιάσει) and simplicity of heart, praising God and finding favour with all the people.' That means that the Lord' Supper took place ἐν ἀγαλλιάσει, i.e. in 'eschatological jubilation'.

In the LXX, both the verb ἀγαλλιᾶσθαι and the noun ἀγαλλίασις occur by far the most frequently in the Psalms. R.Bultmann remarks in connection with the New Testament terminology, 'God's help is always the theme of the ἀγαλλιᾶσθαι, which is a jubilant and thankful exultation . . . It is indeed the eschatological act of divine salvation which is supremely the theme of rejoicing.'[31] To some degree it appears as the anticipation of the joy of the redeemed in the kingdom of God, just as in Rev. 19.7 it is expressed in the last hymn on the dawn of the rule of God and the 'marriage feast of the lamb'. We also find the anticipation of this joy in I Peter 1.8: 'Though you do not now see him you believe in him and rejoice with unutterable and exalted joy.' Now how could this ἀγαλλίασις at the community meal in memory of the crucified Lord and in hope that he would soon come again be better expressed than as a hymn to Christ, whether in the form of the messianic psalms of the psalter which were now seen as being fulfilled, or as new songs inspired by the Spirit?

The important point is that these 'new songs' were songs of thanksgiving and praise; earliest Christianity no longer had psalms of lamentation (cf. James 5.13: εὐθυμεῖ τις ψαλλέτω). The remembrance of the death of Christ, too, does not end with lamentation but with celebration of victory, as is already the case in Ps. 22.[32] From the beginning, the 'remembrance' of the death of Jesus and its saving effect 'for us', along with contemplation of the exalted Christ and his coming, expected in the near future, were constitutive elements in the Christian celebration of the eucharist. Here, evidently, the cry of 'Maranatha' or 'Hosanna' also had a fixed place: these had quickly turned from cries of prayer into an acclamation of praise. Must one not expect that here too the new hymn on the death of Christ and his exaltation as a sign of the ἀγαλλίασις and as a remembrance of Christ's work and fate would have been sung?

We can sum up the conclusions of this investigation in four points:

(a) The hymn to Christ grew out of the early services of the community after Easter, i.e. it is as old as the community itself. The starting point was formed by the 'messianic psalms' which were discovered in a new way after Easter and to which new compositions were added. In the case of Pss. 110; 8, we can demonstrate influence on the new 'hymn to Christ'. It was regarded as an effect of the prophetic spirit of the end-time and had its independent function alongside the other manifestations of the spirit in worship: in prayer, in prophetic admonition, exegesis of scripture and the re-presentation of the tradition about Jesus. It was part of the community's general praise of God, but had its own special place within that, since in the 'hymn to Christ' the work, nature and destiny of the crucified and exalted Lord were presented. That is, in contrast to the hymn to God it took on a marked narrative character. Thus one could regard the hymn to God and to Christ as a fruit of the earliest post-Easter enthusiasm. Its external form came from Judaism and took up Jewish psalmody.

(b) The original setting of the 'hymn to Christ' was the eschatological joy of the Lord's supper, the ἀγαλλίασις of Acts 2.46. This joy can be understood as an anticipation of the expected consummation in the return of the Son of Man. However, we must remember that even at the beginning, after the resurrection appearances, the relationship of the community to its exalted Lord was never purely a future one, without reference to the present. In the first place, retrospective remembrance of the master, his person, still remained alive, and secondly there was the certainty that this 'our Lord (*maran*)', exalted to the right hand of God, was at the same time active among them in the Spirit. Precisely because it was believed that with the resurrection of Jesus the rule of God was now dawning, a direct relationship to the exalted Christ in the present was quite natural. The Risen Christ had not simply been 'transported' to heaven. People knew where they had to look for him. He had not become a *deus otiosus*. The Old Testament messianic psalms and the new songs opened up a view into God's heavenly sanctuary and of the glorified Son of Man. Here the earliest community stood directly within a Jewish apocalyptic exaltation tradition which had its parallels in the fragment 11QMelch, the Similitudes of Ethiopian Enoch and the Metatron speculation of the Sepher Hekhalot (III Enoch). The 'prologue in heaven' in the Book of Revelation presents an early Christian apocalyptic scheme which is of Palestinian origin. According to this, earthly worship was closely bound up with heavenly worship, and glossolalia was probably understood, as in the Testament of Job[33], as speaking in the tongues of angels (I Cor. 13.1). The high-priestly intercession of the exalted one at the right hand of God (Rom. 8.34) corresponded to the intercession of the spirit in glossolalia 'with sighs too deep to utter' in the assembly of the community (Rom. 8.26f.). At the same time the heavenly praise of God and his Christ as depicted in the Book of Revelation is matched by the 'sacrifice of praise' inspired by the spirit as a 'fruit of the lips' (Heb. 13.15) in the hymn to God and to Christ during earthly worship.

(c) More than earliest Christian prayer or the hymn to God, the hymn to Christ had a 'didactic' character and thus influenced the development of the 'doctrine of Christ', christology. In it the passion of Christ, his glorification and the subjection of the powers were at the same time both 'narrated' and 'proclaimed' with constantly new nuances. These two elements can in fact hardly be separated in earliest Christianity. At a rather later stage of development wider-reaching functions, like pre-existence before creation, mediation at creation and incarnation were transferred in the hymns to the exalted Christ – to some degree as a consequence of 'the name above every name' (Phil. 2.9) which was bestowed on him. This pattern of development was arrived at even before the beginning of the world-wide Pauline mission, i.e. at the latest in the middle of the forties (cf. above, p. 50). The consequence of this thinking was basically simple: by virtue of the dignity of the revelation which took place through him, the unrestricted eschatological plenipotentiary of God must at the same time also have been the protological 'plenipotentiary', since God's words and actions in the end-time and the beginning of time form a unity by virtue of God's truth.[34] This step was not a gnostic, syncretistic falsification but a necessary last consequence of primitive Christian thinking. Here the community moved, and could not do otherwise: from a historical and theological perspective it was quite right to do so. The effect of this historical model of thinking is evident from the fact that the rabbis later expressed themselves in the following way: 'And thus you find the way in which God acts: that everything that he loves is before (everything) other' (SiphDev 37). How could the 'beloved Son' not become the 'first begotten before all creatures'(Col. 1.15)? The wisdom tradition stemming from Prov. 8 and Sir. 24 played a considerable role in the transference of this conception.[35] To put it briefly, the hymn to Christ served as a living medium for the progressive development of christological thinking. It begins with the messianic psalms and ends in the prologue to John. We still find traces in Ignatius, and in a sense the Roman pagan Pliny forms a christological and liturgical conclusion with the extract from proceedings at a trial: *carmenque Christo quasi deo dicere secum invicem*.[36]

(d) We too have come to the end. If my remarks have seemed too bold, I would like to refer to an Old Testament scholar: 'There were, for Israel, perceptions which could be expressed, strangely enough to our ears, only in the form of the hymn.'[37] *Mutatis mutandis* this is even more the case with the earliest Christians. The Spirit urged them on beyond the content of preaching, the exegesis of scripture and indeed the content of confessional formulae expressed in prose to express new, bolder, greater things in 'the new song' of the hymn to Christ, because earthbound human language could not do justice to God. As in ancient Israel in the case of David and the prophets, and also as among the Greeks, the Spirit sought poetical form for the expression of hyberbolical things which were not yet ripe for expression in prose, which could be expressed only in the form of the narrative praise of the song, in divinely inspired singing. Why should this phenomenon not also have applied to earliest Christianity, that movement which more than any other in antiquity was filled with the enthusiastic spirit? And there is a second point. In contrast to learned exegesis or long-winded preaching the singing of a song quickly found a place; indeed it could be sung as a whole or in part as a refrain by the community, and thus created community in the union of ἀγαλλίασις in praise and spirit-filled διδασκαλία; indeed the unity of the earthly and heavenly communities became evident in the singing. Paul probably had this κοινωνία-forming power of the praise of God in mind when in his admonition at the end of the letter to the Romans he says: 'May the God of steadfastness and encouragement grant you to live in such harmony with one another, in accord with Christ Jesus, that together you may with one voice glorify the God and Father of our Lord Jesus Christ' (Rom. 15.5f.).

6

Luke the Historian and the Geography of Palestine in the Acts of the Apostles

(i) The Problem

One of the firm convictions of present-day 'critical' exegesis is that the author of the two-volume work dedicated to Theophilus was not at all well up in the geography of Palestine. Thus D.Gewalt attributes to him 'complete ignorance of geographical conditions in the area of Syria and Palestine'.[1] In H.Conzelmann's well-known monograph *The Theology of St Luke*, the mysterious verse Luke 17.11 is among the evidence which the author uses to support this judgment, and he draws far-reaching consequences from it.[2] In so doing he could refer to the eminent expert on Palestine, C.C. McCown, who some time before had characterized Luke as an 'armchair geographer with no practical experience'.[3]

Of course we make it too easy for ourselves if we compare our modern knowledge (also usually acquired at our desks) with that of ancient writers who had very much less help and far fewer sources of information than we take for granted today. Conzelmann[4] therefore tries to arrive indirectly at a fairer assessment of the 'Hellenistic historian' Luke by referring to the work of ancient 'armchair geographers', for example to Strabo's account of Palestine,[5] which has a great many errors in it, and to the confused remarks of Pliny the Elder,[6] who completely muddled up his sources. Tacitus, too, had only very inaccurate ideas of the geographical relationship of Samaria and Galilee within the province of Judaea.[7] Even Ptolemy, who sought to give exact locations of places in Palestine with indications of longitude and latitude, makes serious mistakes: his mention of Idumaea, 'which lies well to the west of the Jordan'(!), is an anachronism in the second century AD and his location of Sebaste and Gaza in Judaea, in contrast to Joppa, Ashkelon and Γαζαίων λιμήν, is also misleading.[8] That even educated Jews had little information about the geography of Palestine is clear from the imaginary description of Judaea and Jerusalem in the Letter of Aristeas[9] or that of the Holy City by Pseudo-Hecataeus;[10] we can presuppose that even Philo had only a vague knowledge of Jerusalem, the Temple and the Holy Land, though he did visit it once in his life.[11] To some extent the valuable geographical details given by an expert in political and military matters like Josephus contrast with this. The educated son of a Jerusalem priest, he was a military commander in Galilee in AD 66/67, and could provide very detailed geographical information which is of abiding and inestimable value for the historical geography of Palestine. However, even Josephus is not always reliable and free from error, and draws some of his precise information from Roman sources.[12] The same is true of the unknown author of I Maccabees or the five-volume work underlying II Maccabees, which was written by Jason of Cyrene, who must have known Palestine quite well.[13] Polybius, too, bases his account of the first conquest of Palestine by Antiochus III in 219/218 BC on a well-informed – military – source.[14] The relatively exact but unfortunately very scanty details of distances in Palestine in the *Itinerarium Antonini Augusti* and the *Itinerarium Burdigalense*, which were important for Christian pilgrims to Palestine, probably also go back to earlier official Roman military lists.[15] Exact geographical details and information presuppose either eyewitnesses or at least reliable sources which in turn are based on personal experience. In 2,5,10 Strabo refers to extended journeys of his own, e.g. from the Black Sea to Ethiopia, but like his predecessors and rivals he obtained most of his information at second hand (ἀκοῇ παραλαβόντες). His serious mistakes are evidence of this.

Even in the early period of the Principate, exact and detailed geographical knowledge on the basis of maps and accurate descriptions of places was limited to a very tiny elite of soldiers, politicians and scholars, and even with them, personal knowledge of a place was irreplaceable.[16] In addition, there were accounts of voyages and journeys, but by themselves they were hardly enough to provide a faithful geographical picture of a distant land. And as, for example, the Peutinger Tafel[17] and some other fragments of ancient maps indicate, by the standards of our modern cartographic material ancient maps were not particularly instructive. Furthermore, it is more than doubtful whether evangelists like Mark or Luke ever caught sight of a map of Palestine. The famous Madaba map from the end of the sixth century AD is a special exception. Ultimately it seems to go back to Eusebius' map for his *Onomasticon*. Maps and accounts of travels in Palestine only became more frequent when pilgrims began to flock to Palestine in the fourth century.[18] Although it may be said to be one of the best preserved maps from antiquity, even the Madaba map does not make it very easy for anyone who does not already know Palestine to get an accurate idea of the country. So in the last resort the only sure way of getting to know a place better was to go there and see for oneself.

As we cannot assume that the Greek Luke ever visited Galilee, Samaria or the Jordan valley, we cannot expect that he would have exact knowledge about the course of the frontiers of Samaria and Galilee or about the relationship of Galilee to the area of the Jordan or to Judaea. The same is also true of the much-criticized, deficient knowledge of Galilee and the adjacent regions in Mark. Given that the author of the second Gospel had presumably never been there, it is not as bad as all that.[19]

Luke poses a further special problem in that he does not always use the term Judaea in the same sense.[20] In one instance it can denote the Roman province along with Judaea and Samaria, which in contrast to Galilee was subject to the *imperium* of the Roman procurator,[21] but sometimes it can also denote the whole of Palestine.[22] However, it is most frequently used to refer to the part of Palestine inhabited by Jews, apart from Samaria and Galilee, and even excluding Caesarea.[23] Finally, Luke also sometimes makes a distinction between Judaea and Jerusalem.[24] The reason for this vagueness may be, first, that because of the numerous changes in political circumstances and in boundaries, official terminology was itself inconsistent, and secondly, that the old LXX phrase 'the land of Judah'[25] still influenced him.

Luke is much more concerned for a clear pattern than for geographical exactitude. He is strictly selective in writing his two-volume work as a 'monograph' with a purpose, and therefore in the Gospel he simplifies the geographical details in Mark, his model: there they are much richer. Anything that disturbs or distracts is eliminated. Luke is concerned not about the journeys and the places but about Jesus' teaching and activity. Furthermore, Jesus' proclamation is concentrated on· Israel, so for Luke it makes no sense that the messianic prophet Jesus should spend any time in Gentile territory. Consequently the excursionns into Gentile territory have to disappear, apart from an unsuccessful foray into the territory of the 'Gerasenes, which lies over against Galilee' (8.26-39). For the same reason, Luke avoids mentioning the Decapolis and the area 'beyond the Jordan'. Thus Jesus' activity is concentrated in two areas: Galilee, from which the whole movement begins, and Judaea – or more exactly Jerusalem, the place of the last struggle which takes place primarily in the Temple – and which thus represents a final focal point.[26] It is from Jerusalem that the apostolic proclamation goes out after the resurrection.

Samaria is only touched on in the Gospel,[27] a reference to the coming mission.

There has been much discussion as to how Luke imagined the geographical relationship of the three areas of Galilee, Samaria and Judaea, which were essential for him because he already found them in the Old Testament. It is no longer possible to give a simple answer. In Luke 17.11, the geographical information over which scholars have argued so much and which tends to be over-interpreted remains utterly obscure. We do not know what the author had in mind here. For 'Luke's only concern is to explain the presence of a Samaritan among the Jews' (17.16).[28] So there is no need to see the reference to the journey to Jerusalem διὰ μέσον Σαμαρείας καὶ Γαλιλίας as any more than a narrative slip of the kind that can also be found elsewhere in Luke.

None of this is new; indeed it should be stressed more than ever that, given conditions in antiquity, Luke *could* not have had any better knowledge of the places which Jesus frequented, as he had never seen Galilee, Samaria and the area of the Jordan with his own eyes. In his basically kerygmatic 'Jesus biography' he is barely interested in geographical details. That also has its good side. He does not have to improve the tradition by inventing geographical details to deck it out. Consequently he only makes a few stylistic improvements to Mark, his model, by making the 'sea' (θάλασσα) of Galilee – rightly, in fact – an 'inland lake' (λίμνη), while he accurately puts Tyre and Sidon on the sea coast (παράλιος). With the exception of some key passages like 2.1f.;3.1, he only gives geographical details where he found them in his sources (cf. 4.16, 31; 7.1,11; 9.10; 10.13); more often he leaves them out.

It is striking that in the Acts of the Apostles the situation is quite different, at least in part. Obviously one could not write the history of a 'mission' from Jerusalem to Rome with so few geographical details as are to be found in the Gospel. This, of course, raises the question where Luke puts the stress in his geographical comments. It is also striking that despite the flood of modern literature on Acts, the geographical detail in the Acts of the Apostles has attracted far less attention from scholars than the sparse notes in the Gospel. So far, this detail has been subjected only to partial investigation – much to the detriment of scholarship on Luke.[29] In what follows I shall make a few comments and raise some questions; it should be noted that it is impossible to separate the Gospel and Acts completely. It will emerge how geographical details, historical information and theological tendency can all hang together.

(ii) The Temple in Jerusalem[30]

The first seven chapters of Acts are exclusively limited to Jerusalem. This is in accordance with the strict pattern of salvation history which governs the whole of the two-volume work: Jesus' career leads from Galilee, where as the 'primal missionary'[31] he himself proclaimed the good news, via Judaea to the Holy City, whereas the preaching of the primitive church begins in Jerusalem, goes on to Judaea and Samaria, and finally even reaches the Gentiles in the wider world. So Luke does not need to go into Galilee again.[32] Acts 1.8, which has been much discussed, describes this development, so we can see it as the programme for the second volume. Of course the last phrase, ἕως ἐσχάτου τῆς γῆς, points beyond what Luke reports, and is essentially a description of the missionary programme of the church in the last decades of the first century, as it is also defined in the Gospels and in non-canonical texts.[33] What we have here is more than a mere table of contents for Acts.[34] For in contrast to his rather bombastic opening statement, Luke shapes the content of his work by a strict, indeed rigorous selection and limitation of the material. The content of his work is not the world-wide mission of the apostles. Once the frontiers of Judaea and Samaria have been crossed, Luke limits himself essentially to one man's, an outsider's, mission to the Gentiles, and his progress from Jerusalem to Rome as the 'thirteenth witness'.[35] Despite Ps. Sol.8.15, the distinctively Isaianic formula 'to the ends of the earth'[36] hardly envisages Rome[37] as the conclusion of Paul's activity and the centre of the then known world; the decisive factor is the way in which the Greek reader could understand this statement: 'For the people of antiquity the frontiers lay at the Atlantic, among the Germani, Scythians, Indians and Ethiopians.'[38] In other words, the fulfilment of Acts 1.8 is not described completely in the 'second volume', which contains, rather, what Luke thought to be the most significant events leading to this goal. Acts contains selected scenes, the decisive stages in the course of the message of salvation from the resurrection of Jesus to Paul's Gentile mission and his imprisonment in Rome. Thus we could say that the theme of Acts, indeed of the whole two-volume work, is 'From Jesus to Paul';[39] the secondary title ΠΡΑΞΕΙΣ ΑΠΟΣΤΟΛΩΝ is misleading.

To mention Jerusalem as the starting point is still not exact enough. In reality the proclamation of the crucified and risen Messiah begins at the holy place where according to the salvation history of the Old Testament God was present. Luke already has the Gospel beginning (1.5ff.) with an epiphany scene in the Temple. And just as Jesus, after coming down from the Mount of Olives (Luke 19.37), immediately appears in the Temple (19.35: without going through the city), to drive out the merchants and to teach there day by day,[40] so in Jerusalem the apostles preach primarily in the Temple. Originally the Temple might possibly have been supposed to be the scene even of the Pentecost story, though it is not mentioned there in so many words.[41]

The Temple, or more precisely the στοὰ τοῦ Σολομῶντος, 'the hall of Solomon' (3.11; 5.12, cf. John 10.23), is at the same time the place where the community meet every day (2.46; cf. 5.42). We can perhaps identify it from Josephus' description of the Temple. According to this the hall of pillars, with a single nave four hundred cubits long, was situated on the east side of the sanctuary of Solomon dropping steeply to the Kidron valley; that is, this part of the outer forecourt probably dated from before the time of Herod.[42] However, it remains doubtful whether Luke imagined its location in this way.

The second topographical detail about the Temple, the so-called 'Beautiful Gate' (πρὸς τὴν θύραν τοῦ ἱεροῦ τὴν λεγομένην Ὡραίαν 3.2; τῇ Ὡραίᾳ πύλῃ τοῦ ἱεροῦ, 3.10), is far more difficult to determine because this designation occurs only in Luke, who in 3.1-11 evidently supposes that the apostles go through the 'beautiful gate' in the Temple to the 'hall of Solomon'. Presumably this more specific reference had already been in the pre-Lucan legend of Peter, originally coming from Jerusalem. As the Temple had numerous gates,[43] the gate at which the miracle took place had to be described more precisely. Neither the Tractate Middoth nor Josephus speak of a 'beautiful gate'. It is usually identified with the Nicanor Gate, for which there is evidence in Talmudic literature; it was made of gleaming 'Corinthian bronze' and took its name from Nicanor of Alexandria, who had endowed it.[44] According to a note in Tos. Yoma 2.4, 'it was as beautiful as gold' (*hyh yph kzhb*).[45] By contrast Josephus speaks only of the 'bronze'[46] or 'Corinthian' gate.[47] This last piece of information suggests an identification with the Nicanor gate, but there is a difference in the location. According to Middoth, the Nicanor gate lay betwen the court of the men and the court of the women, whereas the eye-witness details in Josephus (some of which present serious textual problems) are more in favour of the eastern gate between the court of the women and the court of the Gentiles. Since E. Schürer's impressive investigation,[48], the majority of scholars follow the information given in Josephus, as (more recently) does A. Schalit;[49] on the other hand, O. Holtzmann and E. Stauffer, followed by J. Jeremias and H. Conzelmann, have emphatically argued that the account in the Mishnah is original.[50] It is hardly possible to arrive at a really satisfying conclusion. Even if we assume the identity of the Nicanor Gate and the bronze gate – because of the manufacture from precious Corinthian metal – and that the location given by Josephus is more reliable, identification with Luke's 'beautiful gate' remains doubtful. In the first place, we do not know when Nicanor endowed the gate – the only possible period is the time after Herod, between AD 6 and AD 60[51] – and secondly, the reference could be to other gates of the Temple – say, the outer forecourt – because the Mishnah names only some of them. In addition, it is also doubtful whether it would have been possible for a crippled beggar to beg at the main eastern gate of the Temple proper, within the holy precinct, as Levites and priests kept a guard on the gates.[52] Consequently, T. A. Busink, following F. de Saulcy and others, conjectures that the 'beautiful gate' is meant to be the eastern gate of the outer courtyard by the Kidron valley, mentioned only in Middoth 1.3, which was in the immediate vicinity of the hall of Solomon and above which 'the citadel of Susa' was depicted.[53] In about 570, the pilgrim of Piacenza found the *porta speciosa* in the immediate vicinity of the eastern gate of the city, i.e. by what is now Stephen's Gate. A little later, as a result of a misreading of the Greek ὡραῖα, Latin *(h)orea in aurea*, the east gate of the old Temple precinct was given the name 'Golden Gate' which is still current today.[54] Josephus knows of four gates without names on the west side of the outer forecourt, of which the two southern ones lead to the city – one of them over a bridge to the royal palace – and the two northern ones lead to the suburbs. By contrast, the tractate Middoth mentions only one gate in the west, the Qiponos (Coponius?) gate. On the basis of archaeological evidence, B. Mazar even assumes that there were five gates on the west side.[55] One of these western gates could also have been called 'beautiful', perhaps the southernmost gate, which according to Josephus was approached by an attractive flight of stairs, the foundations of which have been excavated very recently. This connected the Temple precinct with the real centre of the city on the south-west corner of Mount Zion, where the great routes from the north-west, north, east and south came together.[56] However, here we are in the realm of conjecture. The whole question is made more difficult by the fact that Luke – like the other New Testament writers – never makes a distinction between the inner sanctuary and the court of the Gentiles. They are all speaking only about the one ἱερόν, the real Temple. This is in some way in accordance with rabbinic terminology, which makes a sharp distinction between the sanctuary proper (*miqdāš, hab-bayit*, etc.) and the outer courtyard, the 'Temple mount' (*har hab-bayit*), which is not called sanctuary. It is also possible that Luke did not regard the outer courtyard - which would be the only place he would have been allowed to enter as a Gentile – as the ἱερόν, although of course he knew that godfearing non-Jews came to Jerusalem 'to worship' (8.27).[57]

The information given by Luke about the 'beautiful gate' in Acts 3.1-11 would correspond better with an identification with the Corinthian or Nicanor gate and its location at the eastern exit from the Courtyard of the Women if with Zahn, Clark and Lake we could follow the Western text (Cod.D, h and the Middle Egyptian translation).[58] Here, according to 3.11, the lame man, who had accompanied the two apostles as they went into the Temple (3.8), went out again with them (ἐκπορευομένου δὲ τοῦ Πέτρου καὶ Ἰοάνου συνεξεπορεύετο κρατῶν αὐτούς οἱ δὲ θαμβηθέντες ἔστησαν ἐπὶ τῇ στοᾷ τῇ καλουμένῃ Σολομῶντος ἔκθαμβοι). However, this was a way in which a later redactor sought to remove a difficulty in Luke's text, in a barbaric style and a way which could again be misunderstood.

Thus it is impossible to conclude from Luke's two topographical details about the Temple either that he was generally ignorant or that he had exact knowledge. Conzelmann's conclusion that 'Luke has no knowledge of locations'[59] can be challenged simply on the grounds that our own knowledge of the Temple of Herod is still too fragmentary for us to demonstrate that Luke has clearly made a mistake. He has taken over the 'beautiful gate' and the 'hall of Solomon' from the tradition and incorporated them in a text which he has fashioned himself, without bothering further about details.[60] In contrast to Josephus he does not attach any importance to a description of the Temple. He simply wants to provide *a* location for the first healing miracle to be performed by the two leading apostles and to give an indication of where the community met. We cannot yet trace in him anything of the 'topographical curiosity' about holy places which is characteristic of the later accounts by pilgrims. At most his interest is in making an effective preparation, by means of the miracle, and the local colouring which goes with it, for Peter's speech in the Temple which he himself has devised. Thus it may be a historical tradition that the earliest community met in the hall of Solomon in the outer forecourt and that Peter preached in public there.

The specific reference to the time of prayer at the ninth hour points to a precise knowledge of Jewish customs in the Temple. This was the time of the *tamid* sacrifice, in the afternoon, which was concluded with an incense offering and the priestly blessing.[61] Luke 1.8-11,21f. says that the people assembled for prayer in the Courtyard of the Men in front of the Temple building proper (ναός as opposed to ἱερόν).[62] In contrast to Luke 1.8, where in connection with Zachariah's temple service Luke even knows about the assignation of priestly duties by lot, which is attested only in the Mishnah,[63] in Acts he speaks only of the fixed hour of prayer[64](cf. also 10.3,30: the ninth; 10.9: the sixth). Might this be connected with the fact that Luke knew that for the primitive community in Jerusalem the Temple had changed from being a place of sacrifice to a place of prayer?[65]

So far the details have been isolated and fortuitous, and therefore do not allow of further conclusions. However, in my view Luke's account of Paul's arrest in the Temple (Acts 21.27-40) shows a more extensive knowledge of the location and the legal regulations associated with it: the author knows not only that for non-Jews to enter the sanctuary proper, which was marked off in a special way, was a crime punishable by death, because this would be to desecrate the holy places (cf. 24.6,13), but also that anyone who desecrated the Temple was immediately removed from the sanctuary to be executed – in some circumstances by lynch-law.[66] To have killed the criminal in the Temple itself would have defiled the holy place.[67] Luke also knows that the Roman commandant of the city, i.e. the commander of the city cohort in the Antonia, could survey the Temple and its surroundings and could intervene at any time (21.31f.), as the barracks (παρεμβολή: 21.34,37; 23.10), on a higher level, were connected by stairs (ἀναβαθμοί) with the Temple site (21.35, cf. 32; κατέδραμεν; 22.30; 23.10,20: κατάγειν; καταβαίνειν). The whole description of the event can be illustrated well from the account in Josephus:

> Whereas the tower standing on the south-east corner (of the Antonia) was seventy cubits high (the other towers were only fifty cubits high), so that the whole Temple area could be viewed from there. But at the place where the Antonia joined the two cloisters of the Temple it had stairs down both sides (i.e. to the south and to the east), by which the guard went down. For there was always a Roman division in the fortress, the soldiers from which were posted, fully armed, on feast days on the roof of the cloisters of the outer court in order to watch the people, so that no rebellions broke out. If the Temple was set over the city like a fortress, the Antonia formed a guard for the Temple, and the troops posted there watched over all three.[68]

According to 20.16, Paul had wanted to visit Jerusalem for the Feast of Weeks, which in contrast to the Feast of Unleavened Bread lasted for only one day. The accusation against him was made by Jewish pilgrims to the Feast from Asia Minor; however, it was then taken up by the supreme Jewish authorities and pursued further after he had been taken into custody by Roman troops. On several occasions Josephus reports unrest in Jerusalem or in the Temple court at the

great festivals, which forced the Roman troops to intervene: after the
death of Herod and also at a Feast of Weeks (*Antt.* 17,254ff.). There is
a report of a further occurrence some years before Paul's arrest, when
Cumanus was procurator: a soldier posted on the roof of one of the
cloisters had caused uproar among the crowd at Passover by an
obscene gesture (*BJ* 2,223ff. = 20,105f.,108ff.); thereupon Cumanus
sent his troops against the crowd.

Luke's account here presupposes some accurate information about
conditions, but as elsewhere, he does not reveal an 'archaeological',
scholarly interest extending as far as points of detail, which seeks to
reproduce events as exactly as possible. Rather, he is concerned to
give a vivid, dramatic and psychological account of the conflict. This
corresponds to his ideal of a 'solemn' historiography which he shares
with numerous historians of the Hellenistic period, not least the
author of II Maccabees.[69] As a result, scenes are depicted in a vivid
way for the sake of the effect this makes on the reader and to give a
dramatic impression of events; there are divergences from what
actually happened, as was allowed and indeed sometimes required
by contemporary rhetoric and historiography.[70] Thus, as usual, in
21.30ff. Luke does not make a distinction between the city of Jerusalem
and the outer courtyard. In so doing he demonstrates that all
Jerusalem and not just the crowd in the Temple had risen up against
Paul (ἐκινήθη τε ἡ πόλις ὅλη 21.30, cf. 31: ὅτι ὅλη συνχύννεται
Ἱερουσαλήμ), to some degree following the motto: the more enemies
the greater the glory. This lack of clarity, which can also be noted in
all the other Gospels, may seem justified by the fact that the outer
court of the Temple essentially replaced the Agora of the city and was
the scene of a good deal of very secular activity (see above, pp. 101f.).

The external circumstances of the speech which Luke has Paul
making from the steps leading to the barracks (21.40; 22.24) before a
crowd in uproar are required by the course of the narrative as a whole
and therefore certainly do not accord with historical reality in the
form in which they are recorded.[71] However, the event as a whole
and the setting for the scene correspond amazingly to what we know
from Josephus and must have a basis in history. In my view, at this
point Luke was not just working over an outside source, but may be
drawing on his own memories (see below, pp. 126f.).

(iii) Jerusalem and the Hill Country of Judah

Although Luke gives us few details about the sanctuary, he does
inform us about the topography of Jerusalem and its environs. He is
not concerned to praise the splendid Temple and the city in the way

we encounter in some Jewish Hellenistic writers (see above, p. 106) – that city which his contemporary Pliny the Elder called *longe clarissima urbium Orientis non Judaeae modo*.[72] However, he is able to use what he has taken over from tradition in a straightforward way, and probably also has some idea what he is talking about. He knows from Mark that one goes up to Jerusalem from neighbouring Jericho (Luke 19.1,11,28), that Bethphage and Bethany are near to the Mount of Olives and that on coming down from the mountain one can see the city and the Temple in all their grandeur and magnificence. That is reason enough for Jesus to weep over its coming fate, a point which Luke stresses more than any other New Testament author.[73] He also seems to presuppose that one could enter the Temple directly from the side of the Mount of Olives. For pilgrims who came from the East that was the most direct way into the sanctuary.[74]

The mention of two places in connection with the ascension poses a difficulty (which is heightened further by the difference in the time assigned to the event). The best explanation for the difference is that Luke wrote the second book some time after the πρῶτος λόγος had already been produced. The alternative, that 1.3-14, which gives rise to the discrepancy, is a later interpolation, breaking up what was originally one work, is highly improbable. There is no real support for it in the text.[75] According to Luke 24.50, Jesus takes the disciples to Bethany, while according to Acts 1.12, the Ascension takes place on the Mount of Olives, only a 'sabbath day's journey' from Jerusalem. The 2000 cubits (about 880 metres) which make up a sabbath day's journey are as vague as the two pieces of information provided by Josephus: five stadia (about 1000 metres, *Antt.* 20,169)or six stadia (about 1200 metres, *BJ* 5,70). The differences can easily be explained from the size of the mountain and a variety of possible points of reference. The term 'a sabbath day's journey' which appears only here in the New Testament presupposes an amazingly intimate knowledge – for a Greek – of Jewish customs. Evidently Luke wants to make a direct connection between the Ascension – and the Parousia (Acts 1.11) – and the Holy City. G. Lohfink rightly remarks in this connection that this observation, which goes beyond the bounds of what might be expected, is not therefore to be understood 'as the task of a historian interested in detail'. The Ascension took place in the neighbourhood of Jerusalem, 'for a sabbath day's journey according to Jewish legal fiction is in fact a negation of any real distance'.[76]

Apart from notes of this kind which have theological importance, Luke continues to be very restrained over details. One could also refer to the village (κώμη) of Emmaus, 60 stadia (about twelve kilometres) from Jerusalem (Luke 24.13), which the narrator seeks to

use to demonstrate the time spent walking with the risen Jesus and
the fatigue of the return by night to Jerusalem. This is a place which
it has so far proved difficult to identify, since here Luke has possibly
made a mistake about the distance. Some manuscripts therefore have
160 stadia (about thirty-two kilometres), which corresponds more
closely to the distance of a place called Emmaus of which there is
evidence in the books of Maccabees and often in Josephus. It lies
twenty-four kilometres west-north-west of Jerusalem as the crow
flies, but as the chief place in a toparchy was certainly not a village
(24.13,28). Furthermore, the distance from Jerusalem may be too great
for the situation presupposed in the story. Possibly a mistake was
made by Luke or the tradition which he took over: perhaps, though,
he also means Ἀμμαους, thirty stadia from Jerusalem, where according to *BJ* 7,217, Vespasian founded a military colony.[77]

The Aramaic designation Ακελδαμάχ for 'field of blood' has been
correctly handed down in Acts 1.19; this is a place name which is also
known by Matt. 27.8 (Aramaic *ḥªqeldᵉma'*, see H. P. Rüger, *TRE* 3,603).
Its exact phonetic transmission probably presupposes a written
source. The same is true of the note about the 'synagogue of
Libertines, Alexandrians and Cyrenians' (6.9). In the latter case it is
not clear whether there was one synagogue or more. Probably there
were various synagogues. Possibly the Theodotus inscription found
on the Ophel is a reference to this synagogue of Roman freedmen in
Jerusalem, mentioned by Luke.[78]The author does not give any further
details of place than he does in the case of the mysterious ὑπερῷον
(1.13), the 'house' (2.2), unless it is meant to be the Temple – and the
homes of some Jerusalem Christians, for example the splendid house
of Mary the mother of John Mark (Acts 12.12), distinguished by its
forecourt (πυλών), and the abode of James the brother of the Lord
(Acts 21.18) who receives Paul only on the day after his arrival like a
prince of the church with a court of elders, or the home of the 'old
disciple' Mnason from Cyprus, who gives a warm welcome to the
new arrival (21.16). We cannot even detect the beginnings in Luke of
an interest in 'holy places' in Jerusalem and its surroundings. The
'tomb of David', already mentioned in Neh.3.16 and Josephus, *Antt.*
7,392ff. (cf. 13,249; *BJ* 1,161), which is to be located 'on the southern
slope of the Ophel above the spring of Siloah near to the eastern wall
of the city'[79] is mentioned only in passing in the kerygmatic context
of Peter's sermon (2.29) as part of the argument. He merely repro-
duces tradition even in the case of the place of the Skull (Luke 23.33)
and the tomb[80] (23.53). This refutes modern hypotheses which
presuppose fixed 'journeys' to the tomb as early as the first century
and a special interest in 'local legends'. The eschatological mood of

the communities already tells against this. The note that the place 'Arimathaea' is 'a city of the Jews' is an explanation for the Greek reader and does not presuppose any further special knowledge on Luke's part (Luke 23.5l).[81]

There is no further account of the mission in Judaea, either. Leaving aside Jerusalem, with two exceptions, Lydda and Joppa, the communities in Judaea, which, according to the earliest Christian document, I Thess.2.14, were undergoing persecution, do not come into the picture. Nor is there mention of any sending out of the apostles on a mission; compare Gal. 2.8; I Cor. 9.5. Only the Hellenists who were driven out of Jerusalem make a missionary journey through Judaea and Samaria (8.1,4ff.), and then speedily leave Jewish territory behind (11.19ff.). Peter's journey into the coastal regions (9.32ff.) is not really a missionary journey but a tour of inspection, and the important note (12.17) which quite abruptly (indeed in a way open to misunderstanding, cf. 12.2) introduces James (the brother of the Lord) as the later leader of the community, ends with the cryptic comment that the previous head of the group of the Twelve went 'to another place'. In all this, at least on occasion, we may have a certain negligence in writing, though by and large Luke considers very carefully what he says – and what he does not say. At the latest, at this point we are led to wonder whether Luke's restraint is not just caused by deficient geographical or topographical tradition, but is in fact based on a fundamental indifference to geographical details of this kind *in Judaea*. On the one hand, especially if one follows the view popular today that he simply invented facts – he could easily have added such material as illustration and thus could have given colour and concrete detail to the mission in the Holy Land, and on the other hand this restraint is in strange contrast to the fluent information about Paul's mission from ch. 13 onwards, an abundance which when he reaches the 'we' sections increases to become a mass of geographical data which almost confuses the scholar.

All things considered, then, we might conclude from this that in Acts – in the Gospel the situation is different because of the concentration on the person of Jesus – Luke shows by the 'biographical' and the 'geographical' details where his real interest lies. Despite the ideal picture, this is not primarily in the primitive community in Jerusalem or in Judaea, over which he passes rapidly, nor in Peter, who has to leave the stage in an abrupt, enigmatic way in 12.17 and then again in 15.11 with praise for Paul's preaching of grace and faith, but with the 'thirteenth witness', through whom alone the promise of the Lord in 1.8 (put in geographical terms) really comes nearer to fulfilment. Everything else must serve the purpose of describing

Paul's mission as far as Rome and preparing for it. The primitive community in Jerusalem is only the connecting link – necessary and indispensable – between Jesus and Paul, between the 'messiah' and 'saviour' (Luke 2.11) and the mission to the Gentiles apart from the Law.

On this one point, the rigorous narrative organization of the whole work round the 'chosen instrument' (9.15), progressively suppressing and even misrepresenting everyone else, one could represent Luke as a 'radical Paulinist of a particular kind', even if today we believe that he did not understand much of Paul's theology and take offence that because of his eye-witness theory of salvation history he does not give Paul the title of apostle (except in 14.4,14). The 'thirteenth witness' 'worked more', indeed for Luke he is more important 'than all of them' (cf. I Cor. 15.10). Evidently people could be fascinated by Paul even without being able to follow him in all his theology. Perhaps this is connected with the fact that Luke knew Paul from a perspective that we can all too easily neglect for Paul the theologian: as the missionary, the charismatic and the founder of communities.

Luke ignores the communities in Judaea in an almost offensive way, not to mention those in Galilee, which are mentioned in 9.31 only in passing. For him Galilee is interesting only as the place where it all began (10.37; cf. 13.31). The mission there had already been carried out through Jesus, while according to Luke missionary work in Judaea took place predominantly in Jerusalem itself: 'the population from the cities round about Jerusalem' bring their sick, who are all healed (5.l).[82] In a similar way to the healing of the lame man (3.1ff.), Philip's mission in Samaria (8.5ff.) and the healing of Aeneas in Lydda by Peter (9.32-35), these miracles are to be understood as the signal for the successful missionary preaching which Luke stresses by a steady increase in numbers. Despite these successes, the future of the church lies neither in Galilee nor in Jerusalem and in Judaea. Therefore the author can leave these areas behind him without laying much stress on them.

(iv) The Cities of the Coastal Plain

The first movement in what is a static picture of the primitive community – at least in geographical terms – comes with the expulsion of the Hellenists. Those who are driven out of Jerusalem go through 'the districts of Judaea and Samaria' (8.1) – as 8.4 shows, as missionaries. Here Luke does not of course mean that all the churches other than the earliest community in Jerusalem were first founded by the

Hellenist mission. There were already Christians in Galilee, as there were 'throughout Judaea' (9.3l). Peter's 'tour of inspection' in Lydda and Joppa, which follows immediately afterwards, illustrates this situation. The author passes over the way in which the communities came into being and leaves it to the reader to recall that Jesus already had followers at the time of his ministry in places like Emmaus (Luke 24.13), Jericho (19.9) and perhaps also Arimathea (23.5l). He does not dwell on past matters, or on incidentals, but hurries his narrative on towards its preconceived goal. Therefore he does not spend further time on the missionizing of Judaea, but immediately has Peter appearing in Samaria (8.5ff.): the winning over of these 'heretics' or 'semi-Jews' is the first step towards the mission to the Gentiles.[83] This becomes completely clear through the second 'Philip legend', the conversion of the eunuch who is the Ethiopian finance minister. Here Luke deliberately leaves it open whether he was a real proselyte or only a godfearer. The detailed description of his high office and his origins, and the commandment in Deut. 23.2 which prohibits eunuchs from being members of the saving community, suggests that the author himself regarded him as a godfearer, even if he does not say as much. Perhaps he sometimes assumes that readers can read between the lines.

In this connection we are particuarly interested in the geographical details. O. Bauernfeind already stressed that Philip's activity 'in the city of Samaria' (κατελθὼν εἰς τὴν πόλιν τῆς Σαμαρείας) and the fact that he is sent 'on the way which leads from Jerusalem down to Gaza' (ἐπὶ τὴν ὁδὸν τὴν καταβαίνουσαν ἀπὸ Ἰερουσαλὴμ εἰς Γάζαν) is a direct contradiction of Jesus' instructions in Matt. 10.5:'Do not take the road to the Gentiles and do not enter into a city of the Samaritans' (εἰς ὁδὸν ἐθνῶν μὴ ἀπέλθητε καὶ εἰς πόλιν Σαμαριτῶν μὴ εἰσέλθετε).[84] The way which the Ethiopian took from Jerusalem to Gaza on the coast, which brought him via Egypt to his distant homeland at the end of the habitable earth,[85] was a way to the Gentiles. The earliest 'commentator' on this narrative, Irenaeus, stresses twice that the new convert became a missionary there.[86] This may also have been Luke's view, but he says nothing of it and leaves the reader to his own reflections. The κατὰ μεσημβρίαν indicates the unusual time of day and is not an indication of direction;[87] the mysterious αὕτη ἐστὶν ἔρημος is not a learned (and at the same time misleading) note copied from Strabo[88] about Gaza, which had once been destroyed by Alexander Jannaeus – the city had been rebuilt long since. Rather, it stresses the unusual nature of the command: there are no people on the road in the heat of the day. Later pilgrims were concerned with questions like which road to Gaza was meant, through the Shephelah in a south-westerly direction or over the hill-country of Judaea southwards in the direction of Hebron, or even in what water the Ethiopian was baptized, but they are unimportant to Luke.[89]

Still, this narrative confirms that Luke had a certain basic knowledge of Palestine. The way from Jerusalem to Egypt or Ethiopia runs through Gaza, the first Gentile city, which Luke mentions in Acts in connection with the progress of the mission even before the calling of Paul at Damascus. The mention of Azotus/Ashdod in this context, as the place to which Philip is carried off, also indicates geographical knowledge. It was just over thirty miles west of Jerusalem and about twenty miles north-east of Gaza and was once a Philistine city. Presumably Luke chose from a larger number of stories about Philip the two which contradicted Matt. 10.5. The brief notes in 8.39a, 40a suggest that here he has summed up a further story in two phrases. The story of Philip's transportation, which is unique for Luke and indeed unique in the New Testament, points to the stormy return of the prophetic spirit and the way in which there were ecstatic experiences of it in the primitive community and among the Hellenists, for whom the miraculous 'divine guidance' of the mission was also connected with the eschatological gift of the Spirit (cf. 13.2f.; Gal. 2.1; Acts 16.6; 10.19, etc.).[90] We might ask whether the original pre-Lucan story of the transportation of Philip to Azotus might not be meant to express a divine legitimation of the preaching of the missionaries from the 'Hellenist' circle in a semi-Gentile city (see below). Luke has allowed the theme of the transportation to stand as an archaic relic – which no longer accorded with his time – but left out the story which went with it.

It is worth our looking more closely at the two places Azotus and Caesarea by the sea, which are mentioned in connection with Philip's further activity. These were no longer Jewish cities in the strict sense of the word, but had a strong Gentile element in their population. There were certainly more 'Greek' citizens than Jews in Caesarea, a polis with a Hellenistic constitution and a considerable territory.[91] Conditions in Azotus are not so clear; it is possible that here there were equal numbers of Jews and Gentiles. Still, the Life of Jonah in the *Vita Prophetarum* says that Jonah came from Kariathmaou, πλησίον πόλεως Ἑλλήνων Ἀζώτου; in other words, the 'Greek' character of the city is deliberately stressed, despite the substantial Jewish element in the population. It is also striking that in contrast to neighbouring Jamnia, it plays no further role in the Talmudic tradition.[92] A look at both cities demonstrates the changed milieu of the missionary activity of Philip as against Jerusalem and Judaea, and at the same time makes it clear that here Luke has worked over traditions which he has also put in the right setting. In supposing that 'v. 40 seems to have been edited by Luke on the basis of accounts of Philip's stay in Caesarea (21.8)'[93], Conzelmann leaves unexplained the decisive introductory Φίλιππος δὲ εὑρέθη εἰς Ἄζωτον. It is also striking that Luke makes Philip, who for him is still the missionary to the Jews (cf. 11.19), preach in 'all the cities' as an individual travelling missionary, but mentions only the Hellenistic places Azotus and Caesarea as the beginning and end of his journey, whereas predominantly Jewish cities like Joppa and Lydda appear for the first time only on Peter's tour of inspection.

Azotus had been destroyed by Jonathan the Maccabee (I Macc. 10.84; 11.4) and restored as a polis by Pompey (or Gabinius). It came under the rule of Herod and thus lost its political independence. Presumably it was now just the main city of a taxation district. As Georgius Cyprius gives the city the epithet ἡ Ἵππινος in his *descriptio orbis Romani*, like Gaza it could have been a colony of Herodian cavalry.[94] In his will the king left the place along with Jewish Jamnia, about nine miles further to the north-east and equally mixed, but more strongly Jewish, to his sister Salome. Probably like Jamnia, after her death it came into the possession of the empress Livia and subsequently directly into that of Tiberius as *patrimonium Caesaris*. With bitter polemic, Philo says that in Jamnia 'there lived a mixed population, the majority of them Jews but the rest a number of foreigners who had nested there as vermin from neighbouring territories'.[95] In AD 39/40 they provoked the Jews by erecting an altar to the emperor Caligula. The Jews tore it down, an act of violence which led the megalomaniac emperor to command that his image should be set up in the temple in Jerusalem. The episode indicates the hatred between Jews and Gentiles in the mixed cities of the coastal plain, which equalled that between Jews and Samaritans.[96] In 67 Vespasian conquered both cities, introduced a garrison as protection and deported the Jewish part of the population, which at the beginning of the revolt had evidently begun to gain the upper hand in Azotus, too.[97]

That Hellenists like Philip carried on their missionary work particularly in this mixed area, marked out by hatred between Gentiles and Jews, could be connected with the 'pacifying' character of the gospel. We are better able also to understand traditional statements like Gal. 3.28 (cf. Col. 3.11; Eph. 2.11ff.) against this background.

The situation in Caesarea was very similar. The Phoenician foundation of Strato's Tower had been conquered by Alexander Jannaeus and regained its freedom from Pompey. Herod refounded it, provided it with a splenndid harbour, and to honour Augustus gave it the name Καισάρεια (Σεβαστή or ἡ πρὸς Σεβαστῷ λιμένι). In AD 6 it became the official capital of Judaea and the official seat of the prefect (from Claudius this official was a procurator). The tensions between Jews and 'Greeks', not least over equal political rights for the former, were intensified in the time of Nero to the point of street fighting and subsequent harsh pogroms, which in the spring of 66 led to the Jewish revolt. At the same time these disputes were of a religious character. Their ultimate cause lay above all in the ancient hatred of the Hellenistic Philistines/Phoenicians for the Jews because of Jewish expansion in the Maccabaean and Hasmonaean period.[98] So the situation is not without modern parallels.

For Luke, Caesarea, which he mentions fifteen times, is the second most important city in Palestine, as the residence and seat of the procurator and of a garrison (10.1; 12.19ff.; 23.23-27.1), and also as a harbour and gateway to the ecumene, i.e. to the 'world mission' (9.30; 18.22; 21.8ff.; cf. 27.1). It is striking that he no longer assigns it to Judaea in the strict sense, since in 12.19 he describes the journey of Herod Agrippa I from Jerusalem to Caesarea as κατελθὼν ἀπὸ τῆς Ἰουδαίας εἰς Καισάρειαν (cf. also Agabus, 21.10; 11.1; 10.37). This is an indication that as a 'city state' the predominantly pagan Caesarea had a degree of independence over against the other 'regions'. Judaea and Jerusalem, Samaria and Galilee. Agrippa I wanted to negotiate there with the delegations from the city states of Tyre and Sidon; these sought peace with him because they were economically dependent on the hinterland of Galilee and Samaria which was under his control (διὰ τὸ τρέφεσθαι αὐτῶν τὴν χώραν). The Gentile δῆμος of the city hailed him as God (12.22). In other words, for Luke too this was a predominantly pagan city; here he is describing the situation of Caesarea not simply from the perspective of an overseas visitor – who would probably have located the residence in Judaea – but rather from the Jewish standpoint,[99] showing his familiarity with the special characteristics of the πόλις.

The Hellenistic πόλις of Caesarea, open to the 'great wide world', becomes the permanent abode of the charismatic missionary Philip, who had been the second of the 'Seven' (6.5: τοῦ εὐαγγελιστοῦ, ὄντος ἐκ τῶν ἑπτά, 21.8). Through these precise details, with the title evangelist and the reference to the nucleus of the Seven, Luke puts the representative of the Christian community in Caesarea at a certain distance from that of Peter and the twelve apostles and then from Jerusalem represented by James and the elders, and from the communities in Judaea dominated by Jerusalem (cf. 11.1). His four prophetic daughters also give a very distinctive stamp to this 'travelling charismatic', who ultimately becomes firmly established. Presumably – despite Luke's silence on the matter – he carried on the mission to the Gentiles as well in mixed Jewish and Gentile cities like Azotus or Caesarea, i.e. *inter alia* he at least addressed the Gentile godfearers too; that is suggested by the episode with the distinguished Ethiopian. Luke leaves it to the reader to draw the further conclusions which the legends he used may have suggested even more clearly. Finally we should note that in the end Luke, the Greek city-dweller, transfers the activity of the first missionary to be depicted in detail to 'Hellenistic' cities. This accords with the course of the expansion of Christianity generally; originally, as Luke knows very well, it had been a Galilean country movement of uneducated people.[100]

Caesarea, which according to Pliny lay on what perhaps was originally Samaritan territory and in the east bordered on the Samaritan villages in the coastal plain, itself had a Samaritan minority.[101] Perhaps Philip had come up against the Samaritan problem there, so that his 'Samaritan mission' developed from the port. In that case it might be even more justified to assume that there was a degree of rivalry between it and the community in Jerusalem and in Judaea. At all events, Luke was concerned to deal with this and to integrate it into his harmonious overall picture of the earliest Christian mission by the sending of Peter and John (8.14ff.). Finally, the friendly reception of Paul and his companions when they arrive in Caesarea on the last journey, described in the 'we report' (21.8ff.), which is clearly contrasted with the more reserved account of the reception by James and the elders in James's 'residence', where the advice, or rather command, of James leads to the subsequent conflict in the Temple (21.18ff.), shows that Philip was also a missionary to the Gentiles. Luke wants to use this background account to demonstrate that in contrast to the threatening situation in Jerusalem, his hero was *persona grata* to Philip and the Christians in Caesarea who accompanied him on his difficult journey to Jerusalem (21.16). It is understandable that, as we can infer from later reports in Papias, Polycrates of Smyrna and so on, Philip or his daughters later left Palestine and settled in Hierapolis in Phrygia. Probably the situation had become impossible for them as a result of the intensification of the conflict between Jews and Gentiles in Caesarea before AD 66.[102]

In the light of all this, Luke's knowledge of the coastal plain seems to be substantially better than that of Galilee, Samaria, the hill-country of Judaea and the territory around Jerusalem. We need only compare with these sensible geographical details the confused geo-

graphical accounts in the apocryphal Acts of Philip.[103] This argument
can be substantiated by further indications.

(v) Peter's Journey (9.32 – 11.18): Lydda, Joppa and Caesarea

In connection with two miracle stories, Luke in Acts 9.32-43 depicts
Peter's tour of inspection round the communities in Lydda and Joppa.
Of the numerous 'cities' in Judaea, only these two are of interest to
him, as they are the most important almost purely Jewish places on
the coastal plain.[104] The geographical details connected with the story
are completely correct. If one goes down from Jerusalem into the
predominantly Jewish sector of the coastal plain one comes to Lydda,
the first large Jewish place in the plain, about twenty-five miles
north-west of Jerusalem as the crow flies (cf.Josephus,*BJ* 2,244).
Joppa, the only Jewish port of any significance, which lost much of its
influence as a result of the founding of Caesarea, lies another eleven
miles or so further on in the same direction; thus the two places are
'close together' (9.38: ἐγγὺς δὲ οὔσης Λύδδας τῇ Ἰόππῃ). According to
Eusebius of Caesarea, the plain of 'Sharon' (9.35), in which, according
to Luke's hyperbolic account, the healing of the paralysed Aeneas is
said to have had a tremendous effect on the mission, stretched from
Caesarea to Joppa; according to Jerome it also comprised the territory
of Lydda, Joppa and Jamnia.[105]

Lydda, at the foot of the Shephelah, which cannot always be clearly
distinguished from the plain of Sharon (cf. Josephus, *Antt.* 15.33,41),
had long been settled by Jews.[106] When Cestius Gallus advanced
against Jerusalem with his army in 66, he found the 'city' of Lydda
'abandoned by all its inhabitants' (κενὴν ἀνδρῶν τὴν πόλιν καταλαμ-
βάνει, *BJ* 2,515). Vespasian settled 'pacified' Jews there (and in Jamnia)
two years later (see n. 97 above). In *Antt.* 20.130, Josephus calls it a
village, though one 'which in size does not fall short of being a city'
(κώμην . . . Λύδδαν πόλεως τὸ μέγεθος οὐκ ἀποδέουσαν). He says this
because Lydda, like all other places in Judah, in contrast to the *poleis*
of Caesarea, Gaza, Ashkelon and so on, did not have any civic rights.
It was significant because, like Joppa, it was the chief centre of one of
the ten (or eleven) toparchies of Judaea.[107]

By contrast, Joppa, Hebrew Japho, had originally been a Hellenized
Canaanite-Phoenician city which – as the only good port on the coast
of Palestine before the foundation of Caesarea – had been developed
into a strong fortress by the Ptolemies and Seleucids. Even before the
time of Alexander the Great, Greek saga had connected it with the
myth of Andromeda. It was then conquered by Simon the Maccabee,
who drove out all the Gentile population (I Macc. 12.33; 13.11). In

this way the Jews gained a port on the Mediterranean, from which according to Strabo (16.2,28) they also engaged in piracy in the time of the Hasmonaeans. This may be one of the reasons why Pompey detached the city from Judaea (*BJ* 1,156; *Antt.* 14,26). However, in contrast to Azotus it was not re-Hellenized, but remained predominantly Jewish, so that Caesar restored it to the Jews. At the beginning of the war in AD 66, unlike Azotus and Jamnia it became a centre of the revolt against Rome and was therefore destroyed by Cestius Gallus (*BJ* 2,508); after his defeat at Beth-horon it was fortified once more and then captured again by Vespasian (*BJ* 3,4l4ff.).[108]

Thus Peter's activity as ' inspector' of the Jewish-Christian communities in the coastal plain[109] is primarily limited, in contrast to Philip, to expressly Jewish cities. This is hardly a coincidence. Thus to some degree there is confirmation here of the Petrine ἀποστολὴ τῆς περιτομῆς (Gal. 2.7) according to Luke's view. We cannot pursue further here a question which is ultimately insoluble, namely whether and how far in the stories about Peter Luke was working over tradition or shaping it editorially. Presumably, as elsewhere, he did both. If he himself were the one who connected the two miracle stories by the note in 9.38, which is geographically accurate, we would have to say that his knowledge of the coastal area was amazingly good for a Greek who was foreign to the country. Perhaps, however, he already had a whole 'cycle' of stories about Peter which will then of course have included the basic nucleus of the Cornelius story in 10.1-11.18 and which represents the narrative aim of the author in respect of the Philip and the Peter stories, both of which frame the account of the conversion of Saul before Damascus. After the call of the future great missionary to the Gentiles it is time for the conversion of the first Gentiles, by the leading member of the primitive community. Peter's journey to the coast and so to the boundary of the territory of Judah, i.e. Judaea according to Acts 1.8, is thus simply geographical preparation for the conversion of the first Gentile, the centurion Cornelius, in Caesarea. The two miracle stories in Lydda and Joppa see to it that this amazing story, to which Luke attaches particular importance, is not too isolated; he could have passed over the two miracles of the apostle in themselves, as over so much else that he had available in the tradition. Thus in connection with the note in 9.31 Luke has reached a clear boundary, both geographically and in the history of the mission. 'Jewish' Palestine – Galilee, Jerusalem, Judaea and Samaria – is missionized; the missionary of the future is called, the gospel is on the threshold of going out 'to the ends of the earth'. The eunuch who travels to Ethiopia; Philip, who works in Caesarea as an 'advance party'; the missionary success of Peter in the plain of Sharon, which extends as far as Caesarea,[110] and in the end the apostle by the sea at Joppa, mark out this threshold. From a geographical point of view as well, 'salvation history' is ready for the next stage.

Even the Cornelius story, which, in contrast to the usage of the *auctor ad Theophilum* elsewhere, is elaborated with a great many repetitions and indeed is almost too overloaded with detail, contains some remarkable geographical notes. The report of the angel that the house of Simon the host is 'by the sea' (10.5; cf. 9.43; 10.17) may be a novellistic feature prompted by the fact that there was little introduction to the occupation of the tanner; at all events, however, it indicates that from a geographical point of view Peter really had reached the ultimate border of Judaea. His name and the mention of the 'Italian cohort'[111] characterize the hero of the story as a foreigner, as a Roman. Nor is it a coincidence that he and even more the Ethiopian are members of the upper class. Luke stresses both figures in view of the prominent position of the person to whom his two-volume work is addressed, Theophilus, also a member of the upper class. The inclusion of the times of prayer characterizes the centurion as a godfearer,[112] who takes things seriously. Cornelius is praying at the ninth hour, about three o' clock in the afternoon; on the command of the angel, without delay he dispatches two slaves and a godfearing soldier to Joppa. They arrive the next day at the time of prayer, the sixth hour, that is, round about noon (10.3,7-9). The distance between Joppa and Caesarea is about thirty miles; in view of the importance of the mission this is quite a possible journey for a Roman soldier who is used to marching, and able-bodied slaves.[113] For the return journey the day after next Peter and the brothers who accompany him from Joppa are allowed a full day, and perhaps even more, as there is no indication of time; it is part of the coluring of the story that the centurion is already waiting impatiently for him. Even if Luke had made all this up – which I do not believe for a moment – it would have been a good idea: in this case geographically plausible.[114]

Luke gives an accurate description of yet another journey to Caesarea: in the 'we account' in 21.7ff. there is a journey by ship from Tyre to Ptolemais-Akko and from there, after the voyage, a further journey on foot to Caesarea, which again is a march of about thirty miles. Here, however, there are no details of time.

Finally, in 11.1f., we are told: 'Now the apostles and the brethren who were in Judaea (οἱ ὄντες κατὰ Ἰουδαίαν) heard that the Gentiles also had received the word of God. So when Peter went up to Jerusalem, the circumcision party criticized him.' Here there is confirmation that Luke no longer reckoned Caesarea in the strict sense as part of Judaea but as Gentile territory[115] and that with his excursion there Peter had crossed a frontier which had hitherto been forbidden. Furthermore, that the community in Jerusalem and in Judaea form a unity in Luke as they do for Paul. Although Luke sometimes differentiates the two, the Holy City cannot be detached from Judaea (see n. 109 below).

(vi) Antipatris and the Road from Jerusalem to Caesarea

One last paradigm can finally round off Luke's knowledge of the coastal region. We had already noted that the account of Paul's arrest in Acts 21 presupposes some knowledge of the connection between the Temple and the barracks in the fortress Antonia. It accords with this that from the beginning of the 'we report' from ch. 20 onwards the historical and geographical details increase in liveliness and content. This is also true of the account of the events which lead the Roman tribune Claudius Lysias to hand Paul over to the procurator Felix in Caesarea. He learns through the nephew of the missionary that religious zealots have made a conspiracy to murder Paul at the next hearing before the Sanhedrin. Thereupon without delay he has the threatened prisoner moved to Caesarea under the protection of two centuries of auxiliary troops, two centuries of lightly armed troops and seventy cavalrymen. In a march which also extends through the night the troops reach Antipatris,[116] about forty-five miles from Jerusalem, a smaller city founded by Herod, who named it after his father. At the same time it served as a military post, being just twelve miles north of Lydda on the border between the territory of Judaea and that of Samaria; its territory in the west ran parallel to that of the Hellenistic polis Apollonia, which lay on the coast, and to that of Joppa; in the north it bordered on the territory of Caesarea, in the east on that of Samaria and in the south on the westernmost toparchy of Judaea, Lydda. It was a place which Herod had deliberately sought out for strategic reasons. The next day Paul was brought by the cavalry to Caesarea, which was about twenty-five miles further on, while the infantry returned to their barracks in Jerusalem (23.23-32). We may take the number of troops mentioned by Luke and the capacity of the soldiers for marching to be rather exaggerated – the strong guard and the speed of the undertaking at the same time emphasize the importance of the person under arrest; by and large, however, this account fits admirably into the strange – one might almost say macabre – milieu in Judaea in the time of the last procurators: Felix, under whose long administration the political situation worsened to an acute degree, Festus, Albinus and after

them Gessius Florus. As events under Felix's predecessor Cumanus
already showed, the charge of defiling the temple was political
dynamite, as it could incense the people to the point of open
rebellion.[117] Regular events of the time included conspiracies, assas-
sinations by sicarii (21.38) and other manifestations of religious
fanaticism, further tumults, street battles, abductions and
ambushes.[118] Even before Felix, at the time of Ventidius Cumanus,
an imperial slave, perhaps belonging to the financial administration,
accompanying a consignment of money, was attacked and robbed on
the main route from Jerusalem to Caesarea – i.e. the same road along
which Paul was probably also taken – on the way up to Beth-horon
(*BJ* 2,228: κατὰ . . . τὴν Βαιθωρὼ δημοσίαν ἄνοδον, cf. *Antt.* 20,113, so
PA, Lat, Thackeray, cf. *Antt.* 20,113). In the later years of Felix, at the
time of Paul's arrest in say the year 57 or 58, the situation in Judaea
had become even more unsafe. Eight or nine years later, in October
66, at the same place, the ascent to Beth-horon, i.e. the road through
the pass which leads down to Lydda, the Governor of Syria, Cestius
Gallus, with his army of about 33,000 men was attacked by the
badly-equipped Jewish insurgents and only escaped annihilation by
withdrawing secretly overnight to the coastal plain, leaving behind
his heavier military equipment. The following morning he was
pursued by the Jews as far as Antipatris (*BJ* 2,540-555).[119] Against the
background of this situation we can understand the action of the
Roman commandant in the Antonia in removing as quickly as
possible from the danger zone the Jew under special arrest and the
Roman citizen who had stirred up resentment among the population
of Jerusalem by supposedly desecrating the Temple and leading the
people astray. Here the route of march was especially endangered in
the hill-country of Judah and the descent to the coastal plain, indeed
as far as the boundaries of Judaea, i.e. as far as Antipatris. Hence the
guard of a detachment of foot soldiers who on the completion of their
task returned from Antipatris to Jerusalem. Josephus could hardly
have depicted the event more apppropriately. In other words, in my
view the account must ultimately derive from an eye-witness. It
demonstrates the political uncertainty in Judaea towards the end of
Felix's period of office. We may forgive Luke for exaggerating some
things in the interests of his hero.

This last instance shows in an even more evocative way what we
were already able to note in connection with Paul's arrest, namely
that at particular points even in the context of Palestine itself the
geographical details and the event narrated can very readily be
brought together into a unity which needs to be taken seriously in
historical terms. In my view this is above all the case where the

author, Luke the physician, was close to events. According to Acts
21.15 he himself had gone up the road from Caesarea to Jerusalem.
His knowledge of conditions in Judaea during roughly the last fifteen
years before the outbreak of the Judaean war and his special concern
with the destruction of Jeruslem show how he was affected by these
events and stood relatively close to them; this makes it impossible to
date his work in the second century. His basic theological problem,
namely the rise of the Gentile mission apart from the law and the
separation of the church from the synagogue, was no longer acute in
this period.

It was also striking that – in complete contrast to the late
romance-like acts of apostles – Luke usually uses exact geogr-
information only when it is there in the tradition and is si-
the narrative or for his theology. He does not ne
provide novellistic elaboration, since he does not
specialist learned knowledge nor does he have the
pilgrims in satisfying curiosity by depicting 'holy plac
account in the first person plural gives his own views; in
is demonstrating that he was present at the time. A comp
Mark, his model for the Gospel, shows that he simply i
details which he finds superfluous or open to misunderstai
which will not fit into his approach. This is still more the ca   ...th
Acts, where he had to cope with a longer period and more material.
We can also note where he is reporting at second or third hand
without having more detailed knowledge, and where he has adopted
certain geographical notions on the basis of his own information.

To conclude with, I would like to make a kind of contrary demonstration by considering a complex which we have not looked at so far
and over which there is particular dispute among scholars.

(vii) Samaria in the Acts of the Apostles

Samaria is strikingly significant within the programme put forward
in Acts 1.8. There the mission stands to some degree as a connecting
link between the mission (to the Jews) in Jerusalem and Judaea on the
one hand and the world-wide mission (to the Gentiles) on the other.
This connecting link would not have been at all necessary in itself.
The communities in Samaria had no visible influence on the further
course of church history, and the only connection which Luke makes
between them and Paul (and Barnabas) in 15.3 seems somewhat
artificial. At best there remain the Samaritan heresiarchs Simon and
Menander. In their case the question is whether their significance
does not largely rest on the polemic (and scholarship) of later heresy

hunters from Justin[120] and Irenaeus onwards and the imagination of some apostolic romances like the Acts of Peter and the Pseudo-Clementines. In the case of Luke such an influence of the Samaritan church and the heretics on 'church history' cannot be seen at all. For him the 'Samaria' chapter already comes to an end with 9.31.

Basically, so far as Luke's terminology goes, we can say that he always uses the word Σαμαρεία to refer to the territory of the Samaritans, that ethnic religious group whose members are not proper Jews but even less can be counted among the Gentiles. In this sense, in 8.9 he can speak – quite properly in legal terms – of the ἔθνος τῆς Σαμαρείας[121]; this differs completely from his use of δῆμος, which means the civic assembly of a polis (12.22; 17.5; 19.30,33). The three texts about the Samaritans in the Gospel also show that he is aware of the deep division, indeed of the mutual contempt and hatred, existing between the two kindred religious groups, Samaritans and Jews (cf. 9.52ff.; 10.33; 17.16). We may probably understand the reason he gives for the rejection of Jesus and his disciples 'because he was on the way up to Jerusalem' (Luke 9.53) as an indication that he was also aware of the tensions or clashes between Galilean pilgrims going up for festivals and the Samaritans. Presumably he was also aware of the Samaritan rejection of the Jerusalem cult.[122] In contrast to John 4, however, at no point does he go into the religious peculiarities of the Samaritans. Well as he knew the political significance of the Sadducees and certain doctrinal differences between the Pharisees and Sadducees, with whom indeed the Samaritans are compared,[123] he will also have known of some of the peculiarities of the Samaritans, given that he is the non-Jew with by far the best knowledge of Judaism and the LXX down to the first century AD. However, he does not mention these peculiarities in any way, although by so doing he restricts the revolutionary act represented by the shift of the Hellenist mission towards the Samaritans. He is interested only in the 'geographically' visible progress of the mission as a development in 'salvation history', which pursues its divinely directed course despite and indeed because of the persecution of the community in Jerusalem. At the same time the contrast between the hardened inhabitants of Jerusalem and the Samaritans who gladly believe (8.8,12f.) is brought out in the bas-relief fashion of which Luke is so fond. This contrast in terms of geography and salvation history between Jerusalem and Samaria is probably the most important thing for Luke in his report in ch. 8. Since his narrative reaches a new stage with the conversion of the Ethiopian eunuch and the calling of Saul the persecutor, and since he already has in view the gaining of the first 'real' Gentile, in 9.31 he can close the chapter on

Samaria along with Judaea. For him it is only an episode which, if need be, he could have omitted (despite 1.8). The fact that he mentions it at all is connected with the special intermediary role which he has to accord the Hellenists, to do justice to historical truth and to provide a bridge to Paul.[124]

The fact that in 15.3 Luke makes Paul and Barnabas travel from Antioch to Jerusalem via the communities of Phoenicia and Samaria – and not through Galilee – is probably an indication that he sees a connection here: they are open to the story of 'the conversion of the Gentiles' and are delighted about it. Furthermore, this note demonstrates over against a widespread interpretation of Luke 17.11 that Luke knows that Samaria lies north of Jerusalem and can be reached directly from there; moreover, that one can travel directly from Samaria to Phoenicia, i.e. in the direction of Ptolemais and Tyre (21.7) and back again. The sequence 'all Judaea, Galilee and Samaria' (9.31) in no way means that in Luke's view Galilee lies nearer to Judaea; in accordance with his outline of missionary history he mentions first the Jewish areas and in pride of place among them 'all Judaea' (including Jerusalem), which is so decisive for him.[125]

The geographical details of the pericope, skilfully divided by Luke, yet disparate in its ingredients, in which he probably combined different and conflicting narratives, begin from a difficult and therefore disputed statement (8.5a): Φίλιππος δὲ κατελθὼν εἰς (τὴν) πόλιν τῆς Σαμαρείας. Against the omission of the article in some late majuscules and the *textus receptus*, reminiscent of Luke 1.39 εἰς πόλιν Ἰούδα or 9.52 εἰς κώμην Σαμαριτῶν, the article should be retained on the basis of the most important Egyptian evidence.[126] However, the sentence is not to be translated, 'He went down into the city (with the name) Samaria', as happens so often in the commentaries, but, 'He went down into the (capital) city of Samaria.' This is not, as in II Peter 2.6 (καὶ πόλεις Σοδόμων καὶ Γομόρρας τεφρώσας) an appositional genitive. A number of historical reasons tell against this interpretation. However, the other, better possibility of translation, 'into the (capital) city of Samaria', has its difficulties. In connection with them, here are some basic considerations:

1. Luke never uses Σαμάρεια elsewhere as the name of a city but always only as the designation of the area in which the people of the Σαμαριτεῖς (Luke 9.52; 10.33; 17.16; Acts 8.25) live. Thus Luke 17.11; Acts 1.8; 9.31; 15.3 and in the context 8.1,9,14, together with the reference to the many κώμαι τῶν Σαμαριτῶν between the anonymous πόλις and Jerusalem (8.25).

2. The old Macedonian fortress of Samaria,[127] a military settlement founded by Alexander or Perdiccas, no longer existed in Luke's time.

After a one-year siege in 108/7 BC, it was completely destroyed by the Jews under John Hyrcanus. In 63 BC Pompey again separated the city territory from Judaea, but the new foundation took place only under Gabinius. Possibly at that time the citizens of the new polis already designated themselves as Γαβινεῖς, after the new κτιστής; i.e. the city had been given the name Γαβίνια (or the like) rather than Σαμαρεία. It began to be really significant again only with the second new foundation by Herod in about 25 BC. He made it substantially larger, settled six thousand colonists there, some of them Gentile soldiers and some people from the neighbourhood (including Samaritans), and gave it the name Sebaste. Like Caesarea, it too was a predominantly Gentile city with an enormous temple to Augustus and a sanctuary to Persephone. It was not the religious and ethnic centre for the Samaritans. Scholars argue as to how far the central area of Samaritan settlement was part of the city territory of Sebaste. In all probability the territory of Sebaste was substantially smaller than the territory of the Samaritan *ethnos*. The strongly fortified city became a pillar of Herodian and later Roman rule and along with Caesarea provided an essential part of the auxiliary troops in the country, the so-called Σεβαστηνοί, who were Gentiles and not Samaritan 'semi-Jews'. Whereas in the Jewish War Sebaste was obviously on the Roman side (*BJ* 2,460, cf. *Antt.* 17,289), the Samaritans tried to rebel against the Romans but were overthrown by Vespasian (*BJ* 3,307-315). A consequence of this was the founding of the Roman veterans' colony Flavia Neapolis[128] right next to the ruins of old Shechem. Only now did the territory of the *ethnos* of the Samaritans become the city territory of the newly founded Roman colony, which rapidly surpassed Sebaste because of its considerable extent.[129] Thus we must make a distinction between the 'Sebastenes' amd the 'Samaritans'.

3. Another factor which tells against the identification of the Σαμάρεια in 8.5 with Sebaste is that the name Sebaste very rapidly suppressed the old city name. Josephus[130] uses Σαμάρεια for the time after Herod only in the sense of Σαμαρεῖτις, i.e., like Luke, for the district and no longer for the city. Strabo (64 BC – AD 23) already mentions the new name alongside the old.

4. The predilection of some scholars for Gentile Sebaste is not least connected with the mysterious figure of Simon Magus. That was thought to be the necessary 'syncretistic milieu' for his alleged identification with the supreme God, or Zeus, and scholars thought that they could demonstrate fantastic relationships between the Kore-Persephone worshipped in Sebaste and his πρώτη ἔννοια Helen.[131] But Luke only gives an account of a magician and wonder-

worker, and one should not want to be over-hasty in reading speculations from later Simonian gnosis into his simple report.[132] In addition, supposed Samaritan 'syncretism' is an invention of early Jewish polemic which already found expression in II Kings 17.24-41, but which has a weak historical basis. According to Samaritan sources, this group was no more 'syncretistic' than contemporary Palestinian Judaism. The Samaritans kept as unshakeably as their kindred in Judaea to faith in the 'one God' and his law despite all persecutions. Finally, and in conclusion, from a traditio-historical and narrative point of view the Simon Magus story is only loosely connected with Philip's mission among the Samaritans. It can be detached without difficulty. As Gitta, Simon's birthplace, is perhaps on the coastal plain and is part of the city territory of Caesarea (see n.141), we might ask whether Simon's activity is not to be located there.[133]

5. Anyone who wanted to address the Samaritans as a religious group had to seek them out at their religious centre on Mount Gerizim. Therefore since Wellhausen,[134] Shechem has regularly been mentioned in the commentaries as a second possibility for 'the city of Samaria'. However, that is even more improbable. For this centre, which the Samaritans had erected on the ruins of the old biblical Shechem after Alexander or Perdiccas had deprived them of Samaria, was also destroyed along with the temple on Gerizim in 128 BC, under John Hyrcanus, too, and as a city vanishes from history.[135] Flavia Neapolis, about a mile further to the north west and founded by Vespasian as late as AD 72, came to have some significance in the second century. But this cannot be meant, for chronological reasons.

6. For anyone in search of a particular Samaritan 'capital' the most likely place would be the Sychar of John 4.5, present-day 'Askar at the south-eastern foot of Ebal, about half a mile north east of Tell Balata, the ruins of old Shechem. Its significance is attested by Jewish and Samaritan sources,[136], and more recently by the discovery of an interesting tomb from the end of the second and beginning of the third century.[137] At the same time, however, it must be remembered that in the first century the real religious centre for the Samaritans was not a city but the holy mount Gerizim itself.[138] Even Sychar retained its significance after the destruction of Shechem only because it was the nearest substantial place to Gerizim.

7. The conjecture, which also appears in commentaries, that this was Gitta, the home village of Simon Magus, is completely wrong.[139] This Samaritan locality,[140] mentioned only in connection with the heresiarch in some old church sources after Justin, was at any rate completely insignificant. Its situation is disputed. A.Alt conjectures

that it was at Gett on the coastal plain about eleven miles south-west of Caesarea.[141] That would seem to be the most likely.

8. Linguistically, then, the εἰς τὴν πόλιν Σαμαρείας at any rate remains unusual. We must probably think of a Samaritan 'capital' the name of which Luke either no longer knew or left out as being unimportant.[142] Presumably he found it quite natural that Samaria should have a 'capital', as Judaea did in Jerusalem. However, whereas in Judaea Jerusalem was 'surrounded by cities' (5.16), apart from its anonymous 'capital' Samaria – and this information is by no means incorrect – had only 'villages' (8.25) to show. Gentile Sebaste can be left completely out of account.

The formulation 'the city of Samaria' is already striking because by contrast the LXX, which Luke so often follows, often speaks only in the plural of the 'cities of Samaria' and never of 'a' or 'the city of Samaria'.[143] The hypothesis of an Aramaic source in which – as in Luke 1.39 – a m^edinat šōm^eron was wrongly rendered by πόλις instead of χώρα (cf.8.1: κατὰ τὰς χώρας τῆς Ἰουδαίας καῖ Σαμαρείας) is not much help, since an Aramaic source is improbable and does not explain the disruptive article.[144]

Here we find that Luke is basically as free over geographical details as we find him in connection with Palestine – leaving aside the 'we narratives' and the coastal plain. There is confirmation of the conjecture that Luke had not visited Samaria any more than Galilee, the Jordan valley or the hinterland of Judaea. That means that those places where he gives exact and well differentiated information deserve special attention, i.e. in relation to some of the cities of the coastal region, the road from Jerusalem to Caesarea and the connection between the citadel and the Temple. H.Conzelmann characterized the geographical picture of Palestine as follows: 'The whole country seems to be viewed from abroad. Luke is familiar with the coastal region of Phoenicia, in Acts with the connection between Judaea and the coast. He appears to imagine Galilee as inland, but adjoining Judaea, and Samaria as being to the north of Judaea; this is suggested by the account of the mission in Samaria in Acts 8 and by the statement in Acts 15.3.'[145] Apart from the observation about Galilee, where the author over-interprets a carelessly formulated remark by Luke, one could happily agree with Conzelmann. But unfortunately he has not sufficiently gone into the more interesting information in Acts, and thus the striking difference in Luke's knowledge of the different parts of the country remains unexplained. I would therefore change Conzelmann's verdict somewhat and in so doing rely on what in this respect is the clear information in Acts.

'The whole country seems to be viewed' with the eyes of a man who comes 'from abroad', more precisely from the 'coastal region of Phoenicia' (Acts 21.3-7: Tyre, Ptolemais), who travelled up to Jerusalem from Caesarea with a party, could stay there for only a few days because of unfavourable conditions and then returned to Caesarea (21.15ff.; 24.11). Chapters 21-24, a vividly written continuous passage, indicates Luke's own view: together with the continuation in chs. 25-28 this is the climax of the whole work which Luke wants to attain in his two volumes and which he hints at a long time before, in the ἐν ἡμῖν of the prologue. Whether as a travelling companion of Paul he stayed in Caesarea for the whole of the two years that the apostle was imprisoned there is in my view improbable.[146] At all events he had no occasion to pay another visit to Judaea, which continued to be unfriendly, disturbed and, for a Gentile-Christian follower of Paul, positively dangerous. The accusation against Paul because of Trophimus (21.29) might well pose a threat to other Gentile-Christian travelling companions of Paul. After the death of Festus in AD 62, the Jewish priestly nobility led by the high priest Annas son of Annas even had James the Lord's brother, a strict observer of the law, and other leading Jewish Christians, put to death on the charge of transgressing the law.[147] In prison in Caesarea Paul's gaze will have been directed more towards the communities in the West than to those governed by James and his elders in Judaea. Luke then again accompanied the apostle on the journey to Rome (27.1ff.).[148] He may have written his two-volume work some twenty to twenty-five years later, perhaps referring back in the so-called 'source' to earlier notes which he had written himself. The gap in time can explain some obscurities and mistakes, and also his carelessness in narrative must be noted. He could not have been aware how almost two thousand years later his carelessness would have set the pens of critical scholars writing. He did not present his readers with free romance-like invention in the style of the later apostolic acts, and we should not attribute that to him.

In this way we can provide a plausible explanation for the two-level knowledge of Palestine in Luke. We should not require geographical knowledge at an academic level either of him or of the other evangelists; probably none of them had ever so much as seen a map of Palestine, nor did they possess any special geographical interests. Perhaps we New Testament scholars would be more careful if we tried to give an accurate description of the geography of the outer suburbs of our home towns or even to put on a blank map of Palestine those places the location of which Luke knew. Some years ago a graduate secretary in the faculty at Erlangen asked me, 'Tübingen ·

is that in Hessen?'; since then I have ceased to be surprised about geographical knowledge.

Bibliography to 'Between Jesus and Paul'

B. W. Bacon, *The Gospel of the Hellenists*, New York 1935, 74ff.

L. W. Barnard, 'Saint Stephen and Early Alexandrian Christianity', *NTS* 7, 1960/61, 31-45

C. K. Barrett, 'Stephen and the Son of Man', in *Apophoreta. Festschrift Ernst Haenchen*, BZNW 30, 1964, 32-8

W. Bauer, 'Jesus der Galiläer' (1927), in *Aufsätze und kleine Schriften*, 1967, (91-108) 107f.

F. C. Baur, *Paulus, der Apostel Jesu Christi* I, ²1866, 45ff.,49ff.

J. Bihler, 'Der Stephanusbericht (Apg 6,8-15 und 7,54 – 8,2)', *BZ* NF 3, 1959, 252-70

—, *Die Stephanusgeschichte*, MTS I, 16, 1963

M. Black, *The Scrolls and Christian Origins. Studies in the Jewish Background of the New Testament*, London 1961, 75ff.

E. C. Blackman, 'The Hellenists of Acts VI.1', *ExpT* 48, 1936/37, 524f.

T. Boman, *Die Jesus-Überlieferung im Lichte der neueren Volkskunde*, 1967, 112f.

C. Burchard, *Der dreizehnte Zeuge*, FRLANT 103, 1970, 26ff.

H. J. Cadbury, 'The Hellenists', in *The Beginnings of Christianity* I, 5, ed. K. Lake and H. J. Cadbury, London 1933, 59-74

L. Cerfaux, 'La Composition de la première partie du Livre des Actes' (1936), in *Recueil Lucien Cerfaux. Etudes d'Exégèse et d'Histoire Religieuse . . .* II, Gembloux 1954, (63-91) 79ff.

P. Cousins, 'Stephen and Paul', *EQ* 33, 1961, 157-62

O. Cullmann, 'Das Rätsel des Johannesevangeliums im Lichte der neuen Handschriftenfunde', *Vorträge und Aufsätze 1925-1962*, 1966, 260-91, 273ff.

—, 'Samaria and the Beginnings of the Christian Mission', in *The Early Church*, London 1956, 185-92

—, 'Secte de Qumran, Hellénistes des Actes et Quatrième Evangile', in *Les manuscrits de la mer Morte. Colloque de Strasbourg 25-27 mai 1955*, Paris 1957, 61-74; see 135f.

—, 'The Significance of the Qumran Texts for Research into the Beginnings of Christianity'(1955), in *The Scrolls and the New Testament*, ed. K.Stendahl, New York 1957, (18-32) 21, 25ff.

S. Dockx, 'Date de la mort d'Étienne le Protomartyr', *Bibl* 55, 1974, 65-75

J. Dupont, *Les sources du Livre des Actes*, 1960, 61ff.

E. Ferguson, 'The Hellenists in the Book of Acts', *RQ* 12, 1969, 159-80, bibliography

J. A. Fitzmyer, SJ, 'Jewish Christianity in Acts in the Light of the Qumran Scrolls' (1966), in *Essays on the Semitic Background of the New Testament*, London 1971, (271-303) 277ff.

—, 'The Languages of Palestine in the First Century AD', *CBQ* 32, 1970, (501-51) 515

W. Foerster, 'Stephanus und die Urgemeinde', in *Dienst unter dem Wort. Festschrift H.Schreiner*, 1953, 9-30

G. Friedrich, 'Die Gegner des Paulus im 2.Korintherbrief', in *Abraham unser Vater. Festschrift O.Michel*, AGSU 5, 1963, (181-215) 196ff.

P. Gaechter, 'Die Sieben (Apg 6,1-6)' (1952), in *Petrus und seine Zeit. Neutestamentliche Studien*, 1958, 105-54

L. Gaston, *No Stone on Another. Studies in the Significance of the Fall of Jerusalem in the Synoptic Gospels*, NovTestSuppl 23, Leiden 1970, 154ff.

P. Géoltrain, 'Esséniens et Hellénistes', *TZ* 15,1959, 241-54

L. Goppelt, *Die apostolische und nachapostolische Zeit*, Die Kirche in ihrer Geschichte I, A, 1962, 35ff.

W. Grundmann, 'Das Problem des hellenistischen Christentums innerhalb der Jerusalemer Urgemeinde', *ZNW* 38, 1939, 45-73

F. Hahn, *Christologische Hoheitstitel. Ihre Geschichte im frühen Christentum*, FRLANT 83, ³1966, index 424 s.v. 'Judenchristentum, hellenistisches'

—, *Mission in the New Testament*, SBT 47, London 1965, 59ff.

B. B. Hall, 'La communauté chrétienne dans le livre des Actes. Actes 6,1-7 et 10,1-11.18 (15,6-11)', in *Reconnaissance à Suzanne de Diétrich, Foi et vie*, Cahiers bibliques. Paris l971, (146-56) 148ff.

A. Harnack, *Die Apostelgeschichte*, BENT III, 1908, 136ff., 169ff.

N. Hyldahl, *Udenfor og indenfor. Sociale og oøkonmiske aspekter i den aeldste kristendom*, Tekst & Tolkning 5, Copenhagen 1974, 7ff.

F. J. Foakes Jackson and K. Lake, 'The Composition and Purpose of Acts, V. The Internal Evidence of Acts', in *The Beginnings of Christianity* I,2, ed. F. J. Foakes Jackson and K. Lake, London 1922, (121-204) 147ff.

J. Jeremias, 'Untersuchungen zum Quellenproblem der Apostelgeschichte'(1937), in *Abba. Studien zur neutestamentlichen Theologie und Zeitgeschichte*, 1966, (238-55) 248ff.

S. E. Johnson, 'The Dead Sea Manual of Discipline and the Jerusalem Church of Acts' (1954), in *The Scrolls and the New Testament*, ed. K. Stendahl, New York 1957, (129-42) 138f.,141f.

H. Kasting, *Die Anfänge der urchristlichen Mission*, BEvTh 55, 1969, 99f.

H. Lietzmann, 'Der Prozess Jesu' (1931), in *Kleine Schriften* II, *Studien zum Neuen Testament*, TU 68, 1958,(251-63) 255ff.

C. S. Mann, ' "Hellenists" and "Hebrews" in Acts VI 1', in J. Munck, *The Acts of the Apostles*, rev. by W. F. Albright and C. S. Mann, AB 31, 1967, Appendix VI, 301-4

W. Manson, *The Epistle to the Hebrews. An Historical and Theological Reconsideration*, London ²1953, 25ff.

G. Mayeda, *Le langage et l'évangile*, Geneva 1948, 70ff.

E. Meyer, *Ursprung und Anfänge des Christentums* III, ¹⁻³1923, reprinted 1962, 154ff., 270ff., 303ff.

C. F. D. Moule, 'Once More, Who Were the Hellenists?', *ExpT* 70, 1958/59, 100-2

—, 'Sanctuary and Sacrifice in the Church of the New Testament', *JTS* NS 1, 1950, (29-41) 29f.

J. Munck, *Paul and the Salvation of Mankind*, London 1959, 210ff.

P. Parker, 'Three Variant Readings in Luke-Acts', *JBL* 83, 1964, (165-70) 167f.

R. Pesch, 'Der Christ als Nachahmer Christi. Der Tod des Stefanus (Apg 7) im Vergleich mit dem Tod Christi', *Bibel und Kirche* 24, 1969, 10f.

—, *Die Vision des Stephanus, Apg 7,55-56 im Rahmen der Apostelgeschichte*, SBS 12, 1966

B. Reicke, *Glaube und Leben der Urgemeinde. Bemerkungen zu Apg.1-7*, ATANT 32, 1957, 115ff.

M. Scharlemann, *Stephen. A Singular Saint*, AnBib 34, Rome 1968

G. Schille, *Anfänge der Kirche. Erwägungen zur apostolischen Frühgeschichte*, BEvTh 43, 1966, 143ff.

—, *Die urchristliche Kollegialmission*, ATANT 48, 1967, 38ff.

W. Schmithals, *Paul and James*, SBT 46, 1965, 16ff.

W. Schrage, ' "Ekklesia" und "Synagoge". Zum Ursprung des urchristlichen Kirchenbegriffs', *ZTK* 60, 1963, (178-202) 196ff.

E. Schwartz, 'Zur Chronologie des Paulus' (1907), in *Gesammelte Schriften* V, *Zum Neuen Testament und zum frühen Christentum*, 1963, (124-69) 145ff.

R. Scroggs, 'The Earliest Hellenistic Christianity', in *Religions in*

Antiquity. Essays in Memory of E. R. Goodenough, Studies in the History of Religions 14, Leiden 1968, 176-206.

J. N. Sevenster, *'Do you know Greek?'*, NovTestSuppl 19, Leiden 1968, 28ff.

M. Simon, *St Stephen and the Hellenists in the Primitive Church*, London 1958

C. Spicq, 'L'Epître aux Hebreux, Apollos, Jean-Baptiste, les Hellénistes et Qumrân', *RQ* 1, 1958/59, (365-90) 369f.

A. Spiro, 'Stephen's Samaritan Background', in J. Munck (see above under Mann), Appendix V, 285-300

F. Stagg, *The Book of Acts. The Early Struggle for an Unhindered Gospel*, Nashville 1955, 88ff., 96ff. A. Strobel, 'Armenpfleger "um des Friedens willen" (Zum Verständnis von Act 6,1-6)', *ZNW* 63, 1972, 271-6

P. Stuhlmacher, *Das paulinische Evangelium I; Vorgeschichte*, FRLANT 95, 1968, 248ff.

E. Trocmé, *Le 'livre des Actes' et l'histoire*, Paris 1957, 183ff.

B. B. Warfield, 'The Readings Ἕλληνας and Ἑλληνιστας, Acts XI.20', *JBL* 3, 1883, 113-27

J. Weiss, *Earliest Christianity*, New York 1937, 165ff.

C. Weizsäcker, *Das apostolische Zeitalter der christlichen Kirche*, ²1892, 50ff.

J. Wellhausen, *Kritische Analyse der Apostelgeschichte*, AGG phil.hist. Kl., NF 15,2, 1914, 11ff.

G. P. Wetter, 'Das älteste hellenistische Christentum nach der Apostelgeschichte', *ARW* 21, 1922, 397-429

U. Wilckens, 'Hellenistisch-christliche Missionsüberlieferung und Jesustradition', *TLZ* 89, 1964 ,(517-20) 520.

S. G. Wilson, *The Gentiles and the Gentile Mission in Luke-Acts*, SNTS Monographs 23, 1973, 129ff., 259f.

H. Windisch, Ἕλλην, *TDNT* 2, (501-14) 508f.

T. Zahn, *Einleitung in das Neue Testament* I, ³1924, 30ff., 41ff.

H. Zimmermann, 'Die Wahl der Sieben (Apg 6,1-6). Ihre Bedeutung für die Wahrung der Einheit der Kirche', in *Die Kirche und ihre Ämter und Stände, Festschrift J. Frings*, 1960, 364-78

Notes

1. Between Jesus and Paul

1. F. Hahn's particular achievement is to have stressed the significance of this early Hellenistic Jewish Christianity (see the bibliography at the end of this article, to which reference will regularly be made in subsequent notes); also id., *Der urchristliche Gottesdienst*, SBS 41, 1970, 47ff. For the assignation of the Jesus tradition to it see K. Berger, *Die Amen-Worte Jesu*, BZNW 39, 1970; id., *Die Gesetzesauslegung Jesu* I, *Markus und Parallelen*, WMANT 40, 1972; S.Schulz, *Q. Die Spruchquelle der Evangelisten*, 1972.

2. Baur, *Paulus* I (see bibliography), 48.

3. See the title of Chapter 2 of his *Paulus*, I, 49-69. Baur already stressed the special significance of Stephen in the Christmas programme of the Tübingen Theological Faculty in 1829: *Festum Christi Natalitium Anno MDCCCXXIX in Academia Tubingensi . . . interprete D. F. C. Baur, Inest commentatio De orationis habitae a Stephano Act.Cap.VII consilio . . .*

4. F. C. Baur, *Das Christenthum und die christliche Kirche der drei ersten Jahrhunderte*, [2]1860, 42.

5. See W. Schneemelcher, 'Die Apostelgeschichte des Lukas und die Acta Pauli', in *Apophoreta, Festschrift E.Haenchen*, BZNW 30, 1964, 236-50; E. Haenchen, 'Die Apostelgeschichte als Quelle für die christliche Frühgeschichte', in *Die Bibel und wir*, 1968, 312-37: 'The question of the historical reliability of Acts does not affect the main concern of the book. In that it tells the history of the apostolic age in many individual stories, it seeks above all to edify the community . . .' The question is whether historical reliability – in the ancient, not in the modern 'historical-critical' sense – and edification must be mutually exclusive opposites. The technique of narrating in 'small, easily grasped, vivid scenes' noted by Haenchen (314), which are interrupted by summaries, can also be found in Josephus, Livy and so on; cf. E. Plümacher, *Lukas als hellenistischer Schriftsteller*, SUNT 9, 1972, 80ff . . . on the 'dramatic episodic style . . . which had a long tradition especially in Hellenistic historiography' (139, see id., *TRE* 3, 1978, 510ff.). Every ancient historian wanted to entertain, even if not to edify. Luke does not descend to the level of II Macc. 15.38f. But cf. the balanced verdict of Burchard (see bibliography), 169ff.: 'a cautious and understanding historical worker, at least in the context of antiquity, and not only there' (172). Cf. also above, pp. 97ff..

6. *Ursprung und Anfänge des Christentums* I, [4, 5]1924, reprinted 1962, 2f.;

Meyer gives him 'a prominent place among the most significant historians of world history' (3). A. Ehrhardt, *The Acts of the Apostles*, Manchester 1969, 12, agrees. Cf. also Plümacher, *Schriftsteller*, passim, and *TRE* 3, 513ff., though of course he sees the connection between Luke and the salvation-historical Jewish tradition of history too one-sidedly from the perspective of an imitation of the Septuagint. Luke seeks not only to take further the Old Testament history but at the same time to go beyond it in depicting the time of fulfilment, the climax and conclusion of God's salvation history; for the community all that is now left is waiting patiently and with suffering for the parousia, which is not at an infinite distance (see Burchard. op.cit., 180ff.).

7. Tacitus, *Annals*, 1,1,3; see J. Vogt, 'Tacitus und die Unparteilichkeit des Historikers', in *Studien zu Tacitus, Festschrift C.Hosius*, Würzburger Studien 9, 1936, 1-20; A. Dihle, *'Sine ira et studio'*, *RheinMus* NF 114, 1971, 27-43. H. Wankel, 'Die Rolle der griechischen und lateinischen Epigraphik bei der Erklärung literarischer Texte', *ZPapEp* 15, 1974, (79-97) 80f., has made some apt comments: 'Every historian writes in some sense *cum ira et studio*, even if he asserts the contrary or even believes it; he is dependent on individual conceptions and political tendencies, and makes judgments; his account is governed by certain perspectives in accordance with which he arranges, evaluates, connects and stresses the facts or even leaves them out.' The exegete who has no sense for historical facts will be even less capable of judging ancient historiography. A feeling for historical realities is even more important here than the right 'theological pre-understanding'. Cf. my *Acts and the History of Earliest Christianity*, 1979, 1-68.

8. Diodorus Siculus 1, 3 – presumably following Posidonius – also sees the task of the historian as being ὑπουργοὶ τῆς θείας προνοίας. Transferred from the Stoic to the biblical picture of God that could also have been accepted by Luke. Cf. Philo on Moses as a historical writer, *Vit.Mos.* 2.48. In contrast to the completely distorted account of Luke's intentions in S.Schulz, *ZNW* 54, 1963, 104-16, Luke is not of course concerned with blind 'Tyche', with 'the working of "Ananke" or fate' (109) – all these concepts do not occur in Luke as they do in Josephus – but with God's saving will. Even Stoic πρόνοια does not appear in his work. He uses the term βουλή deliberately to point to God's saving will.

9. H. Conzelmann, *Die Apostelgeschichte*, HNT 7, ²1972, 7; cf. Plümacher (n. 5), 11.

10. Op.cit., 9.

11. 21. 18ff. The conflict with the Jewish Christians who are zealous for the law and who are to be placated by the fulfilment of the four Nazirite vows, hinted at in the speech by the presbyters of Jerusalem to Paul, leads to Paul's arrest in the Temple and ultimately to his transportation to Rome.

12. Bihler, *Stephanusgeschichte* (see bibliography), 189.

13. Op.cit., 249.

14. Harnack (see bibliography), 169.

15. The 'eleven' (Luke 24.9,33; Acts 1.26) and 'Peter and the eleven' (2.14), which differs completely from the other passages, appear in a quite different context.

16. Op.cit., 153ff., 169ff.; R. Schütz, 'Die Quellenproblem der Apg', in *Harnack-Ehrung*, 1921, 44-50; J. Jeremias (see bibliography), 247ff.; R. Bultmann, 'Zur Frage nach den Quellen der Apostelgeschichte'(1959), in *Exegetica*, 1967, 412-23 (against Haenchen); Dupont (see bibliography); W. G. Kümmel, *Introduction to the New Testament*, [2]1975, 174ff., is critical. Especially on 6.1ff. see Cerfaux (see bibliography). Conzelmann (see n. 9), 49, rightly sees here 'a piece of tradition which Luke must have already found in written form'. Strobel (see bibliography), 272, argues against an edited source, though of course without going into the striking linguistic detail.

17. Cf. already H. J. Cadbury (with F. J. Foakes Jackson and K. Lake), *The Beginnings of Christianity* I, 2, London 1922, 8ff.; H. J. Cadbury, *The Making of Luke-Acts* (1927), reprinted London 1958, 155ff., 163, on a comparison between Dionysius of Halicarnassus and Plutarch: 'A thorough examination of the two narratives in the Greek texts shows how simply the material of one writer is transferred to another without any acknowledgement and *with almost complete change of diction*' (my italics). See also J. Schniewind, *TR*, NF 2, 1930, 141. K. F. Eisen, *Polybiosinterpretationen*, 1966, 22, stresses that in using his sources Polybius has tried 'with a firm hand to bend everything to his purposes and to shape it in accordance with his views'; cf. the review by K.-E.Petzold, *Gnomon* 42, 1970, (381ff.) 389: 'The organization (which is certainly forced) of Roman history up to the *decemviri* with the help of the doctrine of 'Anakyklosis' matches the constructive thinking of Polybius, though we cannot discover whether he makes more change in the theory or the historical phenomena.' We also find similar problems in the theological historian Luke.

18. Cf. Plümacher (see n. 5), 38ff. The imitation of style related not only to the LXX but also the apocryphal Jewish literature, and there were theological reasons for it; cf. e.g. the remarkable parallels in language with the new Daniel Apocryphon in Luke 1.32f., which are pointed out by J. A. Fitzmyer, *NTS* 20, 1973/74, 394. In Acts 17.22ff. he imitates synagogue preaching with its colouring of popular philosophy, and in ch. 27 the Hellenistic account of the sea voyage. His style is amazingly adaptable. Unfortunately Plümacher's stimulating book does not do justice to Luke's theological power.

19. Cf. E. Schwartz, 'Dionysios von Halikarnassos I', *PW* V, 1905, 949: 'Only in rare instances is it possible to identify a particular author (as source).' See also 953 on the 'deliberate and intentional projection of the present on the past'. For the imitation of Thucydides see Plümacher, op.cit., 52ff.

20. Cf. already Cadbury, *Making* (see n. 17), 169ff. For the Letter of Aristeas see A. Pelletier, SJ, *Flavius Josèphe adaptateur de la Lettre d'Aristée*, Paris 1962. See now the excellent study by S. J. D. Cohen, *Josephus in Galilee and Rome*, Leiden 1979, 24ff.

21. Cf. Trocmé (see bibliography), 166, 188.

22. Wetter (see bibliography), 411f., 404f. In 2.5 Sin and an Old Latin MS (Philadelphiensis) read κατοικοῦντες ἄνδρες εὐλαβεῖς, in other manuscripts the sequence of words changes but the Ἰουδαῖοι is retained. F. Blass, *NKZ*, 1892, 826ff., had already put forward this reading. However, it is a typical simplification of the problems of Luke's text which here means to refer only

indirectly to the coming world-wide mission; cf. B. M. Metzger, *A Textual Commentary on the Greek New Testament*, London and New York 1971, 290f.

23. Cadbury (see bibliography), 68; cf. 65: 'it is a synonym of ἔθνη or Ἕλληνες'.

24. *TDNT* 2, 512 (following Wetter): 'It is not impossible that Ἑλληνισταί is an earlyChristian party name for Christians who did not live according to the Law.'

25. Schwartz (see bibliography), 146: 'Hellenistic proselytes', but cf. 147: the 'Seven', with the exception of Nicolaus, are Jews by birth.

26. Blackman (see bibliography), 524f., following Salmasius, the successor to Scaliger in Leiden, 1588-1653; see also Stephanus, etc., *Thesaurus Graecae linguae* II, 771, and the survey of scholarship in J. Lightfoot, *Horae Hebraicae et Talmudicae in Acta Apostolorum* . . ., ed. J. B. Carpzov, Leipzig 1679, 50f.: Hebraeos *fuisse, genere Judaeos, nemo negaverit: an* Hellenistae *etiam fuerint Judaei, in dubium vocant* (50). According to him, Beza already conjectured proselytes or godfearers. Like Chrystostom, he himself sees them as *Judaei inter Gentes habitantes, et non callentes omnino linguam Hebraeam* (53).

27. Reicke (see bibliography), 116f., 121. For criticism see Hyldahl (see bibliography), 28f.

28. Isho'dad of Merv, *The Commentaries of Isho'dad of Merv*, ed. M. D. Gibson, IV, Horae Semiticae 10, Cambridge 1913, already interprets the 'Greek disciples' of the Syriac text as 'aliens (proselytes = *gywr̂*) who had at one time become disciples of the law, but later received belief in Christ from the apostles'.

29. Grundmann (see bibliography). Here the tendency to repress Jewish influence in the original community is especially penetrating. With reference to the terms ἀρχηγός and σωτήρ (Acts 3.15; 5.31; cf. 4.12) he attributes a kind of Heracles christology to these supposedly Gentile-Christian Hellenists.

30. Bauer (see bibliography), 107f. (my italics).

31. Schmithals (see bibliography), 34 n. 71.

32. Op.cit., 36. Cf. id., *Das kirchliche Apostelamt*, FRLANT 79, 1961, 188ff. The hypotheses put forward by Schmithals are taken over in a toned-down way by Kasting (see bibliography), 89ff., 101ff.: see my review in *TLZ* 96, 1971, 913ff.

33. Schille, *Kollegialmission* (see bibliography), 39, my italics; cf. id., *Anfänge der Kirche* (see bibliography), 143ff. and *FF* 37, 1963, 120.

34. *Vorträge und Aufsätze* (see bibliography), 277 (my italics); cf. 274. Cf. id., *The Johannine Circle*, 1976, 39ff.

35. Op.cit., 273ff. (quotation 277, my italics); cf. 238f., 247. Cf. Geoltrain (see bibliography); Scharlemann (see bibliography), 18; Gaston (see bibliography), 155 with n. 3. M. Black (see bibliography), 75ff. conjectures that the Essenes above all stand behind the Hebrews and also behind the Hellenists (cf. also Geoltrain, op.cit., 253).

36. Spiro (see bibliography). For the Hellenists see Mann (see bibliography). Scharlemann, op.cit., 17ff., doubts whether Stephen was one of the Hellenists, but rejects Spiro's Samaritan theory. For the undoubted Samaritan influences in Stephen's speech see the survey by C. H. H. Scobie, 'The

Origins and Development of Samaritan Christianity', *NTS* 19, 1972/73. 391-
400. The only question is whether Stephen's speech really has anything to do
with the Hellenists.

37. *Homily* 21 (*PG* 60, 164), on 9.29. Chrysostom adds: καὶ τοῦτο σφόδρα
σοφῶς. Ἐκεῖνοι γὰρ οἱ ἄλλοι οὐδὲ ἰδεῖν αὐτὸν ἠθέλησαν οἱ βαθεῖς Ἑβραῖοι:
the 'Hebrews' did not want to see Paul at all. *Homily* 14 (col. 113), on 6.1 puts
it in a rather more restrained way: Ἑλληνιστὰς δὲ οἶμαι καλεῖν, τοὺς Ἑλληνιστὶ
φθεγγομένους. οὗτοι γὰρ Ἑλληνιστὶ διελέγοντο Ἑβραῖοι ὄντες. Chrystostom's
interpretation is taken over almost word for word by Oecumenicus (PG 118,
124) on 6.1: Ἑλληνιστὰς δὲ οὐ τὴν θρησκείαν, i.e. Gentiles, ἀλλὰ τοὺς
Ἑλληνιστὶ φθεγγομένους καλεῖ (cf. 173 on 9.29) and Theophylact (PG 125,600)
on 6.1.

38. Simon (see bibliography), 12f. (with reference to G. P. Wetter and W.
Bauer, 119 n. 33). Mayeda (see bibliography), 74f., arrives at a similar view:
'Nous supposons donc que ce terme est un néologisme créé par les Juifs ou
Judéo-chrétiens conservateurs remplis de mépris pour ceux qui s'adap-
taient facilement aux coutumes étrangères.'

39. Op.cit., (l6ff.) l8. In the parallel account by Hegesippus in Eusebius, *HE*
4,22,7, this mysterious group is missing. We can only guess at its significance,
see the commentary in J. C. T. von Otto, *Corpus Apologetarum Christianorum*
II, [3]1877, 291f. n. 15. Perhaps behind this we have the Hillelites mentioned by
Epiphanius, *Panarion* 30,4ff., see M. Black, *BJRL* 41, 1958/59, 289. But see M.
Simon, *Les sectes juives au temps de Jésus*, Paris 1960, 84ff., and A. Hilgenfeld,
Judentum und Judenchristentum (1868, reprinted 1966), 35: 'The Hellenians
cannot but be connected with Hellenism'. Simon, op.cit., 85, refers to the
interchangeability of the endings -ιανος and -ιστης with reference to Justin,
Dial. 35.6: Μαρκιανοί (Latinism?) and Eusebius, *HE* 4.22.5: Μαρκιανισταί.
However, we may not make Justin dependent on Acts 6.1, as is attempted in
Studia Patristica I, 1957, 535ff. Justin seems not to have known Acts.

40. Op.cit. (see n. 12), 218f., cf. 223f. He also refers to the 'Hellenianoi',
217.

41. M. Hengel, in *Abraham unser Vater. Festschrift O. Michel*, AGSU 5, 1963,
(243-56) 249ff.

42. Given the special information, Luke seems to know more about him.
As a desperate expedient one could compare his mention at the end with the
position of Judas Iscariot at the end of the catalogue of the Twelve in Mark
3.19par. Cf. Rev. 2.6,15 and N. Brox, ' Nikolaos und Nikolaiten', *VC* 19, 1965,
25-30; see already A. von Harnack, *JR* 3, 1923, 413-22, and G.Kretschmar,
RGG[3] IV, 1485f.

43. This 'xenophobia' in particular goes back to the terrifying experiences
of the 'Hellenistic reform' under Antiochus IV Epiphanes, see M.Hengel,
Judaism and Hellenism, 1974, I, 52f., 73ff., 277ff., 283ff. Between 167 and 141 BC
Gentile missionary settlers along with Jewish apostates occupied the citadel
of the Acra in Jerusalem. Herod later attempted to overcome the xenophobia
of Jerusalem and in so doing came up against the opposition of those who
were faithful to the law, see A. Schalit, *König Herodes*, 1969, 370ff.,
403ff.,412ff.: 'Through his invitation of large numbers of Gentiles to Jerusa-

lem, the citadel of fanatical Jewish segregation . . . Herod wanted to demonstrate to the whole world his intent to break through the spiritual wall with
which the Jewish people had surrounded itself . . .' (417f.). By contrast, the
Jewish rebels in AD 66 sought to drive out the foreigners and their Jewish
friends from Jerusalem as a 'purification' of the city and the Temple, see M.
Hengel, *Die Zeloten*, AGSU 1, ²1976, 211-29, 365ff. One of the weapons used
by the zealots was the forcible circumcision of Gentiles (ibid., 201ff.). Against
this background we can also shed some light on New Testament statements
like Gal. 2.3f. and Acts 21.20f., 28f. The difficulties confronting Gentiles in
Jerusalem is illustrated not only by the warning inscription in the temple (see
W. Dittenberger, *OGIS*, 1903/05, no. 598 and Hengel, *Zeloten*, 219f.) but also
the note in Pes. 3b (Billerbeck II, 551), according to which a Gentile Babylonian
was killed because he took part in a passover meal in Jerusalem. For reasons
of purity, dealings with Jews were very limited, and the same went for the
possibility of practising one's own worship. Despite the reference to the 'Gad
yawan', i.e. the Greek god of fortune, near the pool of Siloah (*Zabim* 1,5a) and
despite the conjectures by A. Duprez, *Jésus et les dieux guérisseurs*, Cahiers
Revue Biblique 12, Paris 1970, it is very questionable whether there were
pagan places of worship in Jerusalem, apart from the Roman barracks, before
AD 70. For the earlier period see M.Hengel, *Judaism and Hellenism*, I, 158. The
xenophobia in Jerusalem thus also aroused antisemitic sentiments. Thus
according to Suetonius, *Div.Aug.* 93, Augustus praised his nephew Gaius
Caesar *quod Iudaeam praetervehens apud Hierosolyma non supplicasset*. The Gentile
calumniation of the ritual murder of non-Jews in the temple in Damocritus,
Suidas, *Lex.* s.v. (cf. M. Stern, 530f.) and Apion, Josephus, *Contra Apionem*,
91-96, which goes back to earlier sources, is very abstruse.

44. A. Alt, *Kleine Schriften* II, ²1959, 436-55. Nazareth is only four miles south
of Sepphoris, which was completely destroyed by Varus in 4 BC and whose
inhabitants had been sold into slavery. Therefore the inhabitants of the city
newly founded by Antipas had no desire to join in the revolt of AD 66/67. We
may not draw conclusions from that for the Galileans as a whole. In Tiberias
the rebels gained the upper hand and destroyed the palace of Antipas because
of the pictures of animals which it contained, an act of zeal for the law
(Josephus, *Vita* 65). Among other things, 'Galilean' was a designation for
members of the resistance movement, see Hengel, *Zeloten*, 57ff. To speak of
semi-pagan or syncretistic Jewish Galilee is quite unjustified. The strict
Eleazar, who required Izates of Adiabene to be circumcised, was also a
Galilean. Cf. now S. Freyne, *Galilee from Alexander the Great to Hadrian*, 1980,
344ff., 376f.

45. W. Bauer (see bibliography), 91ff.

46. See Josephus, *BJ* 2,562ff., and the whole of book 3; *Vita* 28ff. See E.
Schürer, *The History of the Jewish People* . . ., rev. and ed. by G. Vermes and
F. Millar, I, Edinburgh 1973, 489ff.

47. Cf. J. Neusner, *Development of a Legend. Studies on the Traditions Concerning
Yohanan ben Zakkai*, Studia Post-Biblica 16, Leiden 1970, 133f. Ulla's remark is
based on the fact that during his eighteen-year stay in Arab in Galilee Johanan
ben Zakkai had presented only two instances of Sabbath halakhah (M.Shab

16.7; 22.3). The attitude of the Galileans towards the 'new' Pharisaic halakah was conservative and not weakened by Hellenistic syncretism. The same is also true of the Sadducean priests whom the Pharisees called the *'am hā-āreṣ*. In their practice of the law and justice they were in fact stricter than the Pharisees (Josephus, *Antt.* 20,199). They simply rejected the oral Torah. Furthermore, in the first century AD the influence of the Pharisees in Galilee was on the increase. That is shown by their clashes with Jesus and by the *Vita* of Josephus. For example, John of Gischala, the later leader of the Galilean rebels in Jerusalem, had excellent relationships with Simon son of Gamaliel, the head of the school of Hillelite Pharisees in Jerusalem (*Vita* 190-2). There is urgent need for a history of Galilee between Alexander and Bar Kochba, not least in order to get rid of unjustified speculations about early 'Galilean Christianity'. See now S. Freyne, above n. 44.

48. Luke mentions Galilean communities only in Acts 9.31, and Paul does not mention them at all. For Paul only Jerusalem and the communities in Judaea, in which he perhaps includes Galilee, play any role: Rom. 15.19, 25f.; Gal. 1.17f.; 2.1; I Cor. 16.3; II Cor. 1.16; Gal. 1.22; I Thess.2.14. The Gospels hardly provide any information about Galilean communities, only about the activity of Jesus in Galilee. The book by E. Lohmeyer, *Galiläa und Jerusalem*, FRLANT 52, 1936, is stimulating, but also misleading. We have a little information for the period after 70 only in rabbinic notes, Hegesippus and other reference in church fathers: only unfounded conjectures can be made about the early Galilean Christian communities.

49. Thus rightly T. Zahn, *Die Apostelgeschichte des Lucas*, [1/2] 1919/21, 226 n. 6. B. W. Bacon, 'Stephen's Speech', in *Biblical and Semitic Studies. Critical and Historical Essays . . . of Yale University*, New York and London 1902, 213-76, 219f., conjectures that the source of the passage containing 9.29 was about Stephen and not Paul.

50. For the text see now *The Greek New Testament*. The original reading of Sin was probably a Ἑλληνιστάς miswritten as εὐαγγελιστάς, Tischendorf, ad loc. *miro vitio*. For the earlier discussion see the very balanced investigation by B. B. Warfield, *JBL* 3, 1883, 113-27. The reading Ἑλληνιστάς is supported above all by Cadbury (see bibliography), 71. It has recently been defended by J. C. O'Neill, *The Theology of Acts in Its Historical Setting*, London [2]1970, 93 n. 2 and P. Parker, *JBL* 83, 1964, 167f. See also Metzger, op.cit., see n. 22, 386ff.

51.Julian, *Ep.* 84 (430d) (p. 145.Bidez) = Sozomen 5.16 (PG 67, 1264b), cf. ibid. 3.17 (1093b); 7,15 (1456a); Philostorgius 7,1 (GCS, Bidez p.77,2); 7,3 (p. 80,1); 7,14 (p. 99,23); Photius, *Bibl.*, c.105 (p.86b, Bekker). This is matched by Tischendorf in his apparatus, ad loc.: *videntur autem interpretes . . . inter* Ἑλληνάς *et* Ἑλληνιστάς *parum distinxisse*. Test. Sol. 6, 8, recension A, ed. C. C. McCown, UNT 9, 1922, 27: καλεῖται δὲ παρ ' Ἑβραίοις Πατικῆ, ὁ ἀφ᾽ ὕψους κατελθών· ἔστι δὲ τῶν Ἑλληνιστῶν Ἐμμανουήλ. The whole passage is in a magical context. The other recensions read παρὰ δὲ Ἕλληνας or παρὰ δὲ Ἕλλησιν. In my view the editor dates the writing much too early, at the beginning of the third century AD (Introduction, 40). The later recensions are said to come from the fourth or fifth century. This dating seems to me to be more realistic.

52. Op.cit., 125. Ferguson (see bibliography), 177, conjectures 'Graecizing Syrians'. For the reader of Luke this meaning would have been quite incomprehensible. Antioch was a Greek city with a tradition of which it was well aware.

53. The term does not have any negative connotations like *Graeculi* in contrast to *Graeci* or as in the distinction between *Pythagoreoi* and *Pythagoristai* in Iamblichus, *Vit.Pyth.* 18, 80, which reflects the division between the esoterics and the exoterics.

54. Cadbury (see bibliography), 60; Windisch, *TDNT* 2, 512; Schmithals (see bibliography), 27, virtually rules out the linguistic meaning, as does Wilson (see bibliography), 140f. According to R. Kühner and F. Blass, *Ausführliche Grammatik der griechischen Sprache* I/2, ³1892, 261, verbs formed from proper names which end in – ίζω denote '*the striving for similarity in customs, nature, language, disposition* with individuals or whole peoples (imitative verb)' (author's italics). The limitation of the significance of the word to the linguistic sphere is therefore all the more striking. This fact is not noted enough in the most recent investigation by Ferguson (see bibliography), 164ff., so that he arrives at the meaning 'Graecizing Jews' or 'imitating the Greeks' in the case of Jerusalem (177), and refers to Josephus, *Contra Apionem* 1,180 and II Macc. 4.9ff. However, this cultural and religious Hellenizing did not occur. These were not semi-apostates as in the reform attempt made by the Jerusalem aristocracy after 175 BC (see Hengel, *Judaism and Hellenism*, I, 70ff., 278ff.), but at least in part 'zealots for law and temple': Acts 6.9ff.; 9.29; cf. 21.27f. and Paul in Acts 22.3; Gal. 1. 14.

55. The basic study is still R. Laqueur, *Hellenismus*, Schriften der Hessischen Hochschulen, Universität Giessen 1924, Vol.1, 22ff. n. 8. Plato, *Men.* 82b: Ἕλλην μέν ἐστι καὶ Ἑλληνίζει; *Prot.* 327e: τίς διδάσκαλος τοῦ ἑλληνίζειν; *Charm.* 159a; Ps.Plato, *Alc.* I, 111a, c; Thuc. 2, 68, 5: ἡλληνίσθησαν τὴν νῦν γλῶσσαν τότε πρῶτον ἀπὸ τῶν Ἀμπρακιωτῶν ξυνοικησάντων; Aristotle, *Rhetoric* 1407a, 19; *Soph. Elench.* 182a, 34; Xenophon, *Anabasis* 7,3,25: ἑλληνίζειν γὰρ ἠπίστατο; Posidippus, *Com.fr.* 28 (p. 345, Kock, *Comicorum Atticorum Fragmenta* III), in contrast to ἀττικίζειν: οἱ δὲ Ἕλληνες ἑλληνίζομεν; Posidonius, fr. 49 (p.70, Edelstein/Kidd) = Strabo 2,3,4; Dionysius Halicarnassus, *Ep. ad Pomp.* 2.5 = Demosthenes 5; Josephus, *Antt.* 1, 129: τὰ γὰρ ὀνόματα διὰ τὸ τῆς γραφῆς εὐπρεπὲς ἡλλήνισται πρὸς ἡδονὴν τῶν ἐντευξομένων. In 1.128 Josephus uses the verb ἑλληνίζειν for the translation of the biblical *Kittim* into the Greek *Kition*, similarly Plutarch, *Num.* 13, 6. Cf. also Plutarch, *Adv.Colot.* 16 (1116E); Pausanias 9,23,6; Philostratus, *Imag.* 2, 5: Dionysius of Alexandria after Eusebius, *HE* 7, 25, 26 on the style of the Apocalypse: οὐκ ἀκριβῶς ἑλληνίζουσαν; Clement of Alexandria, *Stromateis* 2, 3, 1. Like Josephus, Dio Cassius 53, 14, 6 and 55.3.5 at times has 'translated into Greek'. In Sextus Empiricus, *Adv.math*.1, ch. 10 (περὶ Ἑλληνισμόν = about the Greek language, 176ff.); from 184ff. onwards ἑλληνίζειν appears regularly in the sense of 'speak Greek perfectly'. Telephos of Pergamum wrote a work "Ὅτι μόνος "Ὅμηρος τῶν ἀρχαιῶν ἑλληνίζει, Suidas, *Lexicon*, s.v. (IV, p. 539, Adler). A papyrus from the third century BC contains a complaint by a Palestinian agent of Zeno whose wages were constantly

withheld, 'for they knew that I am a barbarian' and 'that I do not know how to speak Greek' (ὅτι οὐκ ἐπίσταμαι ἑλληνίζειν), *Zenon papyri*, ed. W. L. Westermann and E. S. Hasenoehrl, II, New York 1940, 16ff., no. 66.18, 21; for the interpretation see C. Preaux,. *Chr d'Ég* 40, 1965, 130 n. 1 against the editor. The noun Ἑλληνισμός also usually means mastery of the Greek language, and only in Jewish texts like II Macc. 4.13 does it refer to culture and way of life; see Hengel, *Judaism and Hellenism*, I, 2; id., *Jews, Greeks and Barbarians*, London and Philadelphia 1980. Περὶ Ἑλληνισμοῦ, 'On the Greek Language', is a stereotyped title among the grammarians, see Suidas, *Lexicon*, s.v. Pakatos (IV, p. 4); Ptolemaius of Askelon (IV, p. 254); Philoxenos of Alexandria (IV, p. 729), etc. Cf. also C. J. Vooys, *Lexicon Philodemeum* I, 1934, 103f. on ἑλληνίζειν and Ἑλληνισμός. The transition to an extended meaning is indicated by Aristides, *Or*. 32 (403) (Dindorf 1, 605): ὅστις ἑλληνίζειν οἶδεν οὐ μόνον τοῖς ῥήμασιν, ἀλλὰ καὶ τῇ γνώμῃ . . ., while *Or*. 44 (571) is purely linguistic (Dindorf I, p. 843 = Keil 2, 70f.); similarly Agatharchides (second century BC; Photius, *Bibl.* ch. 250, p. 442a, 23 Bekker) on the Persian Boxus: ὃν καὶ ἑλληνίσαι γλῶσσαν καὶ γνώμην. Cf. the Jew who according Clearchus of Soli met Aristotle, Josephus, *Contra Apionem* 1,180: he was a Greek not only by language but also in his soul.

56. *De Alex. fort. virt*. I, 5 (328 C/D): θαυμάζομεν τὴν Καρνεάδου δύναμιν, εἰ Κλειτόμαχον, Ἀσδρούβαν καλούμενον πρότερον καὶ Καρχηδόνιον τὸ γένος, ἑλληνίζειν ἐποίησε: Plutarch's work can be described as the first programmatic writing of cultural Hellenization.

57. *Vit. phil*. 1,102: the Scythian Anacharsis, who had learnt Greek and had a Greek education in Athens as a friend of Solon, returned home: παραγενόμενος εἰς τὴν Σκυθίαν καὶ δοκῶν τὰ νόμιμα παραλύειν τῆς πατρίδος πολὺς ὢν ἐν τῷ ἑλληνίζειν, τοξευθεὶς ἐν κυνηγεσίῳ πρὸς τἀδελφοῦ τελευτᾷ. This statement was probably constructed by Diogenes Laertius, taking up the earlier epitaph: πάντας ἐπείθη βιοῦν ἤθεσιν Ἑλλαδικοῖς (1,103). However, this terminology is not typical, but appears only very rarely.

58. *Dem.ev*. 10,465b (GCS 23, p. 448, 9f.) on Antiochus IV Epiphanes: τοὺς Ἰουδαίους ἑλληνίζειν ἐπαναγκάζων.

59. *Orat*. 11, 103 (Foerster 1, pp. 469f.) on Seleucus I as the founder of cities: ἀλλ ἑλληνίζων διετέλεσε τὴν βάρβαρον (p. 470).

60. See *Jews, Greeks and Barbarians*, 51ff., 67ff.

61. G. W. H. Lampe, *Patristic Greek Lexicon*, Oxford 1961, 451: 'practise paganism' or 'be pagan'. There are typical instances in Eusebius, *Vit.Const.* 2,44 (GCS 7, p. 60,1); Socrates, *HE* 1, 22 (PG 67, 136f.).

62. Philo, *Leg. ad C*. 147 on Augustus: τὴν δὲ βάρβαρον ἐν τοῖς ἀναγκαιοτάτοις τμήμασιν ἀφελληνίσας; Dio Chrystostom, *Orationes* 37, 26: ὅτι Ῥωμαῖος ὢν ἀφελληνίσθη. In Pollux, *Onomasticon* 5,154 (Bethe 1, p. 302) it appears under the keyword Ἑρμηνεύς in the sense of 'translate'. Ps.Clem. *Hom*.13, 9, 3 (GCS 42, Rehm, p. 198) uses the word in the sense of 'argue out of paganism'.

63. Warfield (see n. 50), 122 already had the right idea; cf. Aeschines, *Contra Ctesiam* 172 (p. 251 Blass); τὰ δ ἀπὸ τῆς μητρὸς Σκύθης, βάρβαρος ἑλληνίζων τῇ φωνῇ (very similarly, *Chariton* 4, 5 [p. 458, Hirschig, *Erot.s-*

criptt.]: ἑλλήνιζε τῇ φωνῇ; Athenagoras 6, 231b; Sextus Empiricus, *Adv. Math.* 1,188: ἀναγκασθήσονται ἐκείνην τὴν μέθοδον κριτήριον ἑλληνισμοῦ λέγειν δι᾽ἣν καὶ οὗτος ἑλληνίζων δέδεικται. Heracleides of Miletus according to Eustathius, *Schol. in Odyss.*, p. 1759, 12: οἱ ἑλληνίζοντες δὲ ἐν Κιλικίᾳ. The verb ἐξελληνίζειν, on the other hand, again has primarily a linguistic significance, see Liddell/Scott s.v.: above all 'translate into Greek' (see n. 55 above).

64. See e.g. Bauer (see bibliography), 107. But cf. Lucian, *Philops.* 16: ὁ δαίμων δὲ ἀποκρίνεται, ἑλληνίζων ἢ βαρβαρίζων ὁπόθεν ἂν αὐτὸς ᾖ. In Sextus Empiricus, *Adv.Math.* 1,176, βαρβαρίζων, σολοικίζων is contrasted with ἑλληνίζων. Josephus, *BJ* 6, 96: ὁ Ἰώσηπος τά τε τοῦ Καίσαρος διήγγελεν ἑβραΐζων. ἑβραΐζειν otherwise appears only late (ninth century) in Achm. *Oneirocriticon* 12 (p. 8 Drexl).

65. Cf. Golgotha: Mark 15.22 par. = John 9.17; Gabbatha: *ZNW* 59, 1968 (113-22), 116ff.; John 5.2: Bethesda (cf. J. A. Fitzmyer, *CBQ* 32, 1970, 501–31). For the place names in Jerusalem and its environs see already G. Dalman, *Die Worte Jesu*, ²1930, 6f.

66. See K. G. Kuhn and W. Gutbrod, *TDNT* 3, 369ff. Josephus uses Ἰουδαῖος about 1300 times, above all in *BJ*, *Antt.* 10-20, *Vita* and *Contra Apionem*, and Ἑβραῖος about 310 times, almost only in *Antt.* 1-8. In Philo the ratio is about 720 to 60.

67. Thus in the Sibyllines, in the tragedian Ezekiel, in the accounts of martyrdoms in II Macc. 7 and IV Macc. and in the heroic book of Judith, where Ἰουδαῖος does not appear at all. For non-Jewish terminology see Gutbrod, op.cit., 374f., cf. Lucian, *Alex.* 13: φωνάς τινας . . . Ἑβραίων ἢ Φοινίκων. Chrysostom also calls Israel's Palestinian neighbours 'Hebrews', *Hom.* 25 (PG 61,569), on II Cor. 11.22: οὐ γὰρ ἦν πάντας τοὺς Ἑβραίους Ἰσραηλίτας εἶναι· ἐπεὶ καὶ Ἀμμανῖται καὶ Μωαβῖται τοῦτο ἦσαν.

68. D.Georgi, *Die Gegner des Paulus im 2.Korintherbrief*, WMANT 11, 1964, 51-60.

69. K. G. Kuhn, op.cit., 367f.; Billerbeck II, 442-53:'This new Jewish vernacular is usually called "Aramaic" in rabbinic literature . . . and more rarely "Syrian" . . . in some places also "Hebrew". In the latter connection the division of the whole Jewish world into "Hebrews" and "Greeks" is also worth noting. This formula corresponds to the juxtaposition of Ἑλληνισταί and Ἑβραῖοι in Acts 6.1' (444, cf. 447f c and d).

70. The conjecture by S. Krauss, *Monumenta Talmudica V/1, Griechen und Römer* (1914), reprinted 1972, 39, that this is Iberian in the Caucasus, is improbable.

71. *Conf.ling* 68, 129 (quotation) cf. *Congr.Er.* 44: Greek is 'our language', and *Abr.* 27: the 'beloved of God and friend of virtue, who in the language of the Hebrews is called Noah', is 'in that of the Greeks called "rest" or "the righteous" '. Cf. also 28: the day of rest 'which the Hebrews call Sabbata (Aramaic form!)', and *Somn.* 2,250. Similarly Josephus, *Antt.* 3,252: The 'Hebrews' call the Feast of Weeks ἀσαρθά (Aramaic determinative state of Hebrew *ᵃṣṣeret*).

72. *Vit. Mos.* 2,31f.; cf. Arist. 121, and Hengel, *Judaism and Hellenism* I, 59f.

For the dissemination of the Greek language in Palestinian Judaism see ibid., 58-61; Sevenster (see bibliography); Fitzmyer (see n. 65), 507ff.

73. Hengel, op.cit., 104ff.

74. Cf. Josephus, *Contra Apionem* 1,50f.; *Vita* 40; cf. *Antt.* 1,5ff.

75. For the rare occasions on which a Greek deliberately learnt a barbarian language see my *Jews, Greeks and Barbarians*, 12n.1; 76.

76. In *Vit.Mos.* 2.31 he says that the Torah had been translated from 'Chaldaean' into Greek. Here he confuses Hebrew with Aramaic (Chaldaean) square writing. For the journey to Jerusalem see *Prov.* 2, 64.

77. jSotah 7,1, p.21b, 62f., see J. Lieberman, *Greek in Jewish Palestine*, New York ²1965, 30, which contains further references to Greek in Palestine synagogues.

78. Moule, 'Once More' (see bibliography).

79. See above, p. 30–47. Cf. Scroggs (see bibliography), 198f.

80. For the meaning of the word see P. H. Menoud, 'Le sens du verbe πορτηεῖν . . .', in *Apophoreta. Festschrift E.Haenchenn*, BZNW 30, 1964, 178-86, though he wrongly waters down the word in Pauline terminology so that it becomes only a verbal contest. Inflicting the synagogue punishment of flogging could cost a delinquent his life (see n. 133 below). The catchword 'zeal' in connection with persecution in Phil. 3.6; Gal.1.14 (cf. Acts 22.3), clearly indicates the use of force, see Hengel, *Zeloten*, 151-234. Here the example of Phineas, according to Num.25, was decisive. Paul's involvement in the persecution of Stephen is now defended with good reasons by Burchard (see bibliography). 26-31, 169f., esp. 30 n. 23. For Paul's studying in Jerusalem see n. 145 below.

81. It is no longer possible to reconstruct these early experiences which led to the foundation of the community. For the problem of the connection between Acts 2 and I Cor. 15.6 see J. Kremer, *Pfingstbericht und Pfingstgeschehen*, SBS 63/64, 1973, 232ff., for the historical *datum* of Pentecost, 260f. Cf. also G. Kretschmar, 'Himmelfahrt und Pfingsten', *ZKG* 66, 1954/55, 209-53. For the connection between the event described in Acts 2.5f. and 6.1ff. see already K. L. Schmidt, *Die Pfingsterzählung und das Pfingstereignis*, Arbeiten zur Religionsgeschichte des Urchristentums I/2, 1919, 32, and following him Hyldahl (see bibliography), 33ff.

82. T. Schermann, *Propheten– und Apostellegenden nebst Jüngerkatalogen* . . ., TU 31, 3, 1907, 3-2f., 309, 315f.,319, 343-5, 347f.; for the legendary tradition about the tomb see C. Kopp, *TG* 55, 1965, 260ff.

83. M. Hengel, *Nachfolge und Charisma*, BZNW 34, 1968, 67-70, 76, 80ff., 90ff.; id.(see bibliography), 32ff. If the 'Twelve' had only established themselves in the early Jerusalem community it would be impossible to understand why there were not also several 'Hellenists' among them.

84. Josephus, *Antt.* 15, 319-22; 17, 78, 339; 18, 3; 19, 297f. A daughter of Simon son of Boethus became the wife of Herod I. The supporters of this powerful family, like the Boethuseans, made up a special group among the Sadducees: R. Meyer, *TDNT* 7, 41f., 44f.

85. *CIJ* 2, nos 1210-1414. Sevenster (see bibliography), 146, has counted 175 ossuary inscriptions the language of which can be determined. Of these, 97

(55%) are Aramaic or Hebrew, 64 (36%) Greek and 14 (8%) bilingual. See also the inscriptions of 'Dominus Flevit' in Jerusalem: P. B. Bagatti/J. T. Milik, *Gli scavi del 'Dominus Flevit'*, Part I, Jerusalem 1958. Of the 43 inscriptions 10 (about 23%) are Greek and two bilingual. The great cemetery of Beth-shearim in Galilee is illuminating for the period after AD 70: M. Schwabe and B. Lifshitz, *Beth She'arim II: The Greek Inscriptions*, Jerusalem 1967, with 218 Greek inscriptions in all. As places of origin for those recorded on the Jerusalem inscriptions we find: *CIJ* 1227, North Africa; 1233 Chalcis (in Lebanon?); 1283 Bethel (!); 1256 Alexandria; 1284 Capua in Italy; 1372-74 Scythopolis/Beth-shean (bilingual). In Beth-shearim we find places like Antioch, Berytus, Byblos, Caesarea, Palmyra, Tyre and Sidon and the region of Pamphylia, see Schwabe/Lifshitz, op.cit., 110; B. Lifshitz, *RB* 72, 1965 (520-38), 529ff.: sometimes these are whole family dynasties. For the dating of the Jewish ossuaries see E. M. Myers, *Jewish Ossuaries . . .*, Rome 1971, 39ff.

86. Rom. 11.25ff.; Acts 20.16; 21.15f.; Josephus, *BJ* 2,515: when Cestius Gallus arrived in Lydda with his army in autumn 66, 'he found the city empty, because the whole population had gone up to Jerusalem for the feast of Tabernacles'. Even for Philo, Jerusalem is the 'metropolis' of all the Jews throughout the word: *in Flacc.* 46, cf.*Leg. ad C.* 156, 203, 281: 'It is my ancestral city (πατρίς), the metropolis not only of the land of Judaea but also of most others because of the colonies which it . . . sent out . . .'; cf. H.-F. Weiss, *Klio* 43-45, 1965, (307-28) 317f. (cf. n. 145 below). For the prophetic and apocalyptic theme of the pilgrimage of the nations see D. Zeller, *BZ* NF 15,1971, 222-37; 16, 1972, 84-93. The mysterious *regnum Hierosolymorum* is attractive even to a Nero (Suetonius, *Nero* 40, 2). For the missionary significance of Jerusalem see above, 58f. For the pilgrimages to Jerusalem see S. Safrai, *hā-'aliyya lā regel bîmē hab-bayit haš-šeni*, Tel Aviv 1965, and the English summary in O. Michel, etc. *Studies on the Jewish Background of the New Testament*, Assen 1969, 12-21.

87. The widespread view, put about above all by Haenchen, that the earliest Judaism was quietistic and did not engage in mission, is untenable, see above, pp. 58f.

88. See the critical commentaries from De Wette and Overbeck, through Loisy, to Haenchen and Conzelmann.

89. See the following comparison of the Jewish-Egyptian prosopography in *CPJ* 3, 167ff.; A. Schalit, *Namenwörterbuch zu Flavius Josephus*, Leiden 1968, and J. B. Frey, *CIJ* for Europe and Palestine (I did not find any further examples in the other Jewish inscriptions):

	CPJ (Egypt)	Josephus	CIJ (Europe)	CIJ (Palestine)
Stephen	—	—	3x:404,405,642	—
Philip	2x	4x	2x:334,561	—
Prochorus	—	—	—	—
Nicanor	2x	—	—	1x: 1256
Timon	—	—	—	—
Parmenas	—	—	—	—
Nicolaus	2x	—	1x: 707	1x: 1279

The Nicanor mentioned in *CIJ* 1256 is the famous donor of a gate of the temple, who is also mentioned in the Talmud, see E. Stauffer, *ZNW* 44, 1952/ 53, 44-66, esp. 57f. For proselytes in Jerusalem see *CIJ* 1385 and Bagatti/Milik (see n. 85) no. 13a and 21ab. For Nicolaus see n. 42 above and T. Zahn, *Apostel und Apostelschüler in der Provinz Asien*, Forschungen zur Geschichte des neutestamentlichen Kanons VI/1, 1900, 221ff.

90. Thus e.g. in J. Munck, *The Acts of the Apostles*, AB 31, 1967, 57; cf. id. (see bibliography), (210ff.) 218. However, with the exception of Philip, the names were quite unusual for Palestinian Jews. Among Jews from the border between Palestine and Syria in the north east (John 1.43; Philip son of Jakim, Josephus, *BJ* 2,421; *Vita* 46f., etc.) the name was probably associated with the tetrarch Philip, son of Herod, who was popular with the people (Josephus, *Antt.* 18, 106f.).

91. Gaechter (see bibliography), 133ff.

92. See above, pp. 56ff.

93. I Cor. 14.1ff. The mockery expressed in Acts 2.13 was connected with the enthusiastic earliest Christian worship which was understood as a demonstration of the spirit. I Cor. 14.23f. shows that this of course also had an effect on the mission. Cf. now J.Hainz, *Ekklesia*, Biblische Untersuchungen 9, 1972, 88ff.

94. For the way in which gathering together constituted the 'community' see K.L.Schmidt, *TDNT* 3, 504ff. Hainz, op.cit., 230, also stresses that the συνέρχεσθαι ἐν ἐκκλησίᾳ constitutes the community. His criticism of Schmidt's view that 'any community, however small, represents the whole of the community, the church' (505), is unjustified. The ὅλη in I Cor. 14.23 is not meant to distinguish a whole community from partial communities, but simply presupposes that all the members of the community gather together in the assembly.

95. Cf. J. Weiss (see bibliography), 121 n. 2, though he regards the 'Twelve' and their leadership of the community as a later construction (34); E. Meyer (see n. 6), 296, 338; id. (see bibliography), 155 n. 1 with reference to John 12.21; W. Grundmann, *ZNW* 38, 1939, 59 n. 33; E. Bishop, 'Which Philip?', *ATR* 28, 1946, 154-9. Whereas Luke makes a neat distinction between the apostles and the evangelists (Acts 1.13; 21.8), they are connected at the latest in Papias and Polycrates of Ephesus (Eusebius, *HE* 3, 39, 9; 5, 24, 2). Given the relative frequency of the name it is no longer possible to settle the question. For Paul, Philip would presumably have been a real apostle. At a later stage we could suppose a similar transition in the case of Barnabas. Indeed, even Peter ultimately moves over from the Aramaic sphere to be a missionary in Greek-speaking areas, cf. my *Acts and the History of Earliest Christianity*, 92ff.

96. M. Hengel, 'Proseuche und Synagoge', in *Tradition und Glaube. Festschrift K. G. Kuhn*, 1971, (157-84) 158ff., 168 and n. 47. For the number ten, the *minyan*, see H. Haag in *Abraham unser Vater* (see n. 41), 235-42. In Alexandria from the Ptolemaic period onwards the Jews were more strictly organized than in Rome and in other cities of the Roman empire. They were a *politeuma* under the 'ethnarchs' dismissed by Augustus, the Jewish quarter and the

Jewish Council; cf. Tcherikover, *CPJ* (see n. 89), 1,9f., 56f. This is probably connected with the military origins of the Jewish diaspora there.

97. H. J. Leon, *The Jews of Ancient Rome*, Philadelphia 1960, 135ff.; W. Wiefel, 'Die jüdische Gemeinschaft im antiken Rom und die Anfänge des römischen Christentums', *Judaica* 26, 1970, 65-88.

98. *Leg. ad C.* 155ff. Also E. M. Smallwood, *Philonis Alexandrini Legatio ad Gaium*, Leiden ²1970, 233ff.

99. Leon, op.cit., 147ff.: *CIJ* 1, no. 291 (bilingual), 317, 510, 535. In all four inscriptions officials of the synagogue community of the 'Hebrews' are mentioned. For the inscription from Porto see H. J. Leon, *HTR* 45, 1952, 165-75: it too comes from the Monteverde catacomb.

100. Op. cit. (n.97), 154ff.: *CIJ* 1, nos. 318, 383, 398, 494. Cf. also Wiefel, op.cit., 72.

101. *Pro Flacco* 28: *scis quanta sit manus, quanta concordia, quantum valeat in contionibus.* The Jewish community in Rome goes back to the second century BC, see Valerius Maximus 1, 3, 5, and Hengel, *Judaism and Hellenism* I, 263ff.

102. In Corinth, too, we find a 'synagogue of the Hebrews' in an old inscription (*CIJ* 1, no. 718). As Corinth was refounded as a Roman colony in 44 BC by Roman freedmen, one might ask whether this synagogue community was not an offshoot of the Jewish community with the same name in Rome, see Hengel, op.cit. (n. 96), 183. Otherwise we know only of a relatively late 'synagogue of the Hebrews' in Deliler in Lydia (*CIJ* 2, no. 754). In inscriptions and papyri Ἑβραῖος appears for individuals only in the later, Christian period, see *CPJ* (see n. 89) 3, no. 511, 4; 512,2; whether it occurs in the Latin papyrus no. 463, 8 (end of the second century BC) is very questionable; for Rome see *CIJ* 1, nos. 354, 370 ('Hebrews' from Caesarea in Palestine), 379, 505; for Asia Minor, *CIJ* 2, no. 750. The late inscription no. 784 from Seleucia in Cilicia speaks of a 'cemetery of the Hebrews'.

103. Cf. E.Käsemann, *Commentary on Romans*, Grand Rapids and London 1980, 15 on Rom. 1.7: 'The absence of the term ἐκκλησία is surprising here as in the rest of Romans and admits of no plausible explanation', cf. also Phil. 4.22 in contrast to Rom. 16.1 and I Cor. 16.19. Romans 16.5 mentions a specific house community. Romans 16.1-23 is of course often thought to be a letter to Ephesus; however, the list of greetings would also be understandable if, like the whole letter, it were addressed to a community which was gradually being built up and included many people who had returned and were known to Paul. Presumably the Jewish Christians could return to Rome only after the death of Claudius in AD 54. Cf. J. Weiss (see bibliography), 357ff.; E. von Dobschütz, *Die urchristlichen Gemeinden*, 1902, 91f.; Wiefel (see n. 97), 78ff. In Rome the legal position was particularly uncertain because of the imperial prohibition against *collegia* (Suetonius, *Div.Iul.* 42,3; *Div.Aug.* 32, 1). Cf. Smallwood (see n. 98), 205, 236.

104. Ps. Clem., *Hom.* 11, 35, 4 (GCS 42, Rehm, p. 171).

105. E. Schürer, *Geschichte des jüdischen Volkes . . .*, III, ⁴1909, 76, 78, 85ff.; Leon (see n. 97), 169, 73-80, 194; S. Appelbaum, 'The Organization of the Jewish Communities in the Diaspora' (in *Compendia Rerum Judaicarum ad Novum Testamentum, Section I: The Jewish People in The First Century*, Vol.1,

1974, (464-503) 491ff.; G. Bornkamm, *TDNT* VI, 660f. A council of elders (γερουσία) and ἄρχοντες also exist side by side, in which case the ἄρχοντες were the executive. In Rome we find only ἄρχοντες and no πρεσβύτεροι.

104. Billerbeck II, 641 jMeg 3,2 p. 74a, 18: 'The three (=representatives) of a synagogue community are like the synagogue community (itself), and the seven of a city are like the city (itself)'; babMeg 26a speaks of the 'seven best of a city' (*sb'h ṭwby h'yr*); T. Meg. 3, 1 (Zuckermande, p. 224) simply of the 'overseers of that city' (*prnsy 'wth h'yr*).

107. Cf. *Antt.* 4,287; Zahn, *Apostelgeschichte*, 231; Appelbaum, op.cit., 491.

108. Rom. 8.15; Gal. 4.6; I Cor. 16.22; cf. J. Jeremias, *Abba*, 1966, 57f., 64ff.; F. Hahn, *Hoheitstitel* (see bibliography), 100 on 'Marantha': 'The only explanation of the stereotyped Aramaic form of the word of prayer is that it is a tradition from the very earliest community'; B. Sandvik, *Das Kommen des Herrn beim Abendmahl im NT*, ATANT 58, 1970, 13ff. For the linguistic form of the Maranatha cry see Rüger (n. 65), 120f.

109. *CIJ* 2, nos. 1214, 1225, 1227 b, 1234, 1236, 1237, 1273 and 1274: Verutaris; 1284: Maria, wife of Alexander, from Capua; 1293, 1302, 1324-26, 1328, 1338, 1341, 1343, 1366, 1372: Ammia from Scythopolis (bilingual); 1374b: Salome from Scythopolis (bilingual); 1376, 1378, 1382, 1387; cf. 1406; Bagatti/ Milik, op.cit. (see n. 85), nos. 2, 10, 37b, 41, 43.

110. Josephus, *Antt.* 20, 35, 49ff., 94f., 101; cf. their Aramaic epitaph, *CIJ* 2, no. 1388. no. 1230 (Greek ossuary inscription) could be an inscription by members of the family. For rabbinic accounts see B. J. Bamberger, *Proselytism in the Talmudic Period*, 1939 reprinted New York 1968, 225ff.

111. Cf. M. Hengel, *Property and Riches in the Early Church*, London 1974, 31ff. The idealistic account by Luke in Acts 2.44f.; 4.32, 34f., stylized in accordance with Greek models, should not lead us into thinking that the 'sharing of goods' in the earliest community did not have a real background; of course it was essentially different from the collective economy of the strictly organized Essenes. The whole practice is to be understood against the background of the message of Jesus and had an eschatological and enthusiastic stamp. Barnabas' gift (Acts 4.36f.) was neither an individual instance nor an exception, but was remembered because of its significance for the later Antiochene community; Luke therefore incorporated it in his historical account.

112. Against Strobel (see bibliography) and Hyldahl (see bibliography), 39ff.

113. Cf. W. Schrage, *TDNT* 7, 835f.; Conzelmann, *Apostelgeschichte*, ad loc.; cf. already Chrysostom, *Hom.* 15 (PG 60, 119f.): Διάφοροι δὲ αἱ συναγωγαὶ ἦσαν . . .

114. Schrage, *TDNT* 7, 810ff.; Hengel (see n. 96), 157-84. The earliest evidence (Philo, *quod omnis* 81) refers to the συναγωγαί of the Essenes.

115. Billerbeck II, 662ff.; jMeg 3,1 p. 73d, 39ff.; babMeg 26a. Cf. also S. Krauss, *Synagogale Altertumer*, 1922, 200f. Instead of 'metal workers' Krauss suggests the production of 'Tarsian garments' by the Alexandrians. According to a rabbinic account the Pharisaic sages in Jerusalem required that the Torah scroll of the Alexandrians, in which the tetragrammaton was inlaid in gold,

should be 'hidden', i.e. it had to be put away in a Geniza, see J. P. Spiegel, *IEJ* 22, 1972, 39ff.

116. See above n. 98; Philo, *Leg. ad C.* 155; Josephus, *Antt.* 14, 70f.; *BJ* 1, 154; *Antt.* 14, 120; *BJ* 1,180; *Antt.* 14, 275f., 304, 313: the large number of people enslaved by Cassius, the murderer of Caesar, were freed at Antony's command; Tacitus, *Annals* 2, 85, 4. Also Smallwood (see n. 98), 234ff. The LA of the Armenian translation *Libyorum* and the conjecture Λιβυστίνων of Ps. Ecumenius, Nicolaus of Lyra, Beza,etc (see Bacon [n. 49] 220 n. 1) are to be rejected. This is not a synagogue shared by the 'Africans'. Here, too, Chrysostom gives the right indication, *Hom.* 15 (PG 60, 120): οἱ Ῥωμαίων ἀπελεύθεροι οὗτο καλοῦνται. Ὥσπερ δὲ ᾤκουν ἐκεῖ πολλοὶ ξένοι, οὕτω καὶ συναγωγὰς εἶχον, ἔνθα ἔδει τὸν νόμον ἀναγινώσκεσθαι καὶ εὐχὰς γίνεσθαι.

117. N. Avigad, 'A Depository of Inscribed Ossuaries in the Kidron Valley', *IEJ* 12, 1962, 1-12. Among those names are five women, one from Ptolemais, which would fit Cyrene. Sevenster (see bibliography), 146ff., and E. Dinkler, *Signum Crucis*, 1967, 158, are more restrained about the Cyrenian origin. The interpretation of *qrnyt* to mean someone coming from Cyrene would be clear if we followed J. T. Milik in understanding the *tau* at the end as a misreading of a *he*. Such a miswriting would easily be possible; see Bagatti/Milik (see n. 85), 8l.

118. Bagatti/Milik, op.cit., no. 9. Cf. the way of writing it without an article as in Mark 15.21 in contrast to Acts 13.1.

119. *CIJ*, no. 1404. On this see L. -H. Vincent, 'Découverte de la "Synagogue des Affranchis" à Jérusalem', *RB* 30, 1921, 247-77; *Supplementum epigraphicum Graecum* 20, 1964, no. 478; Sevenster (see bibliography), 131ff.:

Θ[ε]όδοτος Οὐεττήνου, ἱερεὺς καὶ
ἀ[ρ]χισυνάγωγος, υἱὸς ἀρχισυν[αγώ]-
γ[ο]υ, υἱωνὸς ἀρχισυν[α]ώγου, ᾠκο-
-δόμησε τὴν συναγωγὴν εἰς ἀν[άγν]ω-
σ[ιν] νόμου καὶ εἰς [δ]ιδαχ[ὴ]ν ἐντολῶν, καὶ
τ[ὸ]ν ξενῶνα, κα[ὶ τὰ] δώματα καὶ τὰ χρη-
σ[τ]ήρια τῶν ὑδάτων, εἰς κατάλυμα τοῖ-
ς [χ]ρήζουσιν ἀπὸ τῆς ξέ[ν]ης, ἣν ἐθεμε-
λ[ίω]σαν οἱ πατέρες [α]ὐτοῦ καὶ οἱ πρε-
σ[β]ύτεροι καὶ Σιμων[ί]δης.

120. See M. Hengel, *ZNW* 57, 1966 (145–83) 171 n. 92.

121. Cf. H. Lietzmann, *ZNW* 20, 1921, 172; A. Deissmann, *Light from the East*, 19xx, 379 n. 1. According to Josephus, *BJ* 2, 308, even rich Jews who belonged to the Roman *equites* settled in Jerusalem. The procurator Gessius Florus had at least two of them scourged and crucified.

122. The combination of synagogue and school is typical of the Pharisees, see Billerbeck II, 662 jMeg 3, 1 p. 73d, 31ff.

123. Gal. 1.13f.; Phil. 3.5f.; Acts 22.3; 26.4f. (see n. 145 below). The motivation to return home was particularly strong among the Diaspora Jews who were close to Pharisaism, since all Gentile territory was unclean. That 'zeal for the law' could be disappointed in Jerusalem is another matter. For

the significance of the Holy Land and Jerusalem for Judaism, see now W.D.Davies, *The Gospel and the Land*, 1974, 49-74. See n. 54 above.

124. See the groups of three in Mark 5.37; 9.2; 14.33: Peter and the two sons of Zebedee; Gal. 2.9: the three 'pillars', James the brother of the Lord, Cephas-Peter and John. In Acts Luke often stresses two people: 3.1ff.; 8.14; Peter and John; 15.7ff., 13ff.; Peter and James the brother of the Lord. Individual figures kept standing out in the earliest community, despite its collective constitution. They – and not the anonymous collective – exercised a decisive influence on theological developments.

125. The connection between – eschatological – wisdom, possession of the Spirit and miraculous gifts was a mark of the whole of the earliest Christian mission in Greek alongside Paul. The theme of wisdom emerges particularly clearly in Paul's controversy in I Cor. 1 and 2, and the theme of rhetorical gifts and the ability to do wonders in II Cor., where Paul is confronted with emissaries from a Jewish-Christian/Hellenistic mission (the Cephas mission?). Friedrich (see bibliography) is not entirely wrong in connecting these emissaries with the Hellenists; that is an accurate description of the 'milieu' of this Greek-speaking Jewish-Christian/Palestinian delegation, even if we can only guess at its precise origin.

126. Among those who use the speech as a source for Stephen are Simon (see bibliography), 39-77; Scharlemann (see bibliography), 12-108, and, with more restraint, Scroggs (see bibliography), 182ff. On the other hand we cannot simply claim that it is a free composition by Luke as is done by Bihler, *Stephanusgeschichte* (see bibliography), 83-86. M. Dibelius, *Studies in the Acts of the Apostles*, ET London 1956, 167ff. already pointed in the right direction; similarly F.Hahn, *Hoheitstitel* (see bibliography), 382ff. Here Luke has incorporated material from older Hellenistic/Jewish-Christian homilies which, *inter alia*, also contained Samaritan traditions, see above, n. 36. A fundamental study is now R. Storch, *Die Stephanusrede Ag 7, 2-53*, Theol. Diss. Göttingen 1967.

127. See the old-fashioned 'servant of God' christology in Peter's speech (3.13, 26) and the community prayer (4.27, 30), the reference to justification by faith, which the law could not bring about, in Paul's first speech (13.38f.), or the proposal for the ritual 'Apostolic Decree' from James the brother of the Lord (15.19f.; cf.21.25).

128. High priests: 4.1, 6, 23; 5.24; Sadducees: 4.1; 5.17. These are basically the same groups which handed Jesus over to Pilate, see Hengel, *The Charismatic Leader and his Followers*, 1981, 38ff. Their action against the earliest community depicted in the accounts in Acts 4 and 5 is directed at the preaching of Jesus as the crucified and risen Messiah. In the case of Stephen and the Hellenists, on the other hand, the Law and the Temple were at stake, and this alarmed Pharisaic circles. However, up to the execution of James the brother of the Lord the real opponents of the Aramaic-speaking community in Jerusalem remained the Sadducaean high priests, who had control of the Sanhedrin (see also below, p. 176 n. 62).

129. Only in 23.6 does Luke make Paul give an effective account of his time as a Pharisee (cf. also 26.5). Apart from the moderate Gamaliel (5.34), in the

first half of the work only Christian Pharisees appear (15.5). Luke has his own reasons for keeping quiet about the role of the Greek-speaking Pharisees in the persecution of Stephen. It contradicts his positive attitude towards the Pharisees.

130. Cf. e.g. Wellhausen (see bibliography), 14: 'There is no verdict; Stephen is stoned without a trial. The stoning is an act of popular justice.' For the possibility of such group justice which dispenses with an orderly trial see Sanh. 9, 6b: 'A priest who officiates in an unclean condition – his brothers the priests do not bring him to the court, but the disicples of the priests take him to the forecourt and shatter his skull with wooden staves.' Cf. also Hengel, *Zeloten*, 219ff.; B. Cohen, *Jewish and Roman Law* II, New York 1966, 624-50, esp. 632ff.; A. N. Sherwin-White, *Roman Society and Roman Law in the New Testament*, Oxford 1963, 38ff., disagreeing with J. Juster, *Les Juifs dans l'Empire Romain* II, Paris 1914, 138ff., cf. 158f. Even Philo, *De spec.leg.* 1,54ff., discusses the possibility of lynch law in connection with Phineas' action in Num. 25: 'And it is lawfully permitted to all who are filled with zeal for virtue, without delay to carry out the punishment (on apostates) without taking them before a court, a council or any other authority . . .' (55). Cf. also 1.79 and III Macc. 7.10, 14. In the case of Stephen the decisive fact was probably that the 'blasphemy' blatantly went with the accusation of apostasy. Since punishment could not be expected from the Roman authorities, people spontaneously took matters into their own hands.

131. It should no longer be doubted that under both Herodian and Roman rule the Sanhedrin had no authority to carry out the death penalty. See the material in J. Blinzler, *Der Prozess Jesu*, ⁴1969, 229ff. Indeed I would differ from Blinzler in wondering whether the Sanhedrin could pronounce the death penalty at all. At any event the final decision lay with the prefect, and after Agrippa I (41-44) with the procurator. For the problem see now E. Bammel, 'Die Blutgerichtsbarkeit in der römischen Provinz Judäa . . .', *JJS* 25, 1974, 35-49. The attempt by Dockx (see bibliography) to avoid this difficulty by transferring the execution of Stephen to the time after the deposition of Pilate (between Passover 36 and Passover 37) is not convincing.

132. For the elders see the Theodotus inscription (above, p. 17) and also *CIJ* 1277: Τρύφωνος πρεσβυτέρου; for the teachers of the law see *CIJ* 1266b, 1268, 1269. Θε[ο]μν[ά]τος δε[δα]εκάλου (sic). λαός is of course a favourite word of Luke's (it appears 48 times in Acts); however, we also find it often in synagogue inscriptions, e.g. in Elche in Spain (*CIJ* 662), in Larissa in Thessaly (701-2, 704-8), in Mantinea in Arcadia (720) and in Hierapolis in Phrygia (776); for Nysa in Caria see L. Robert, *Hellenica* 11/12, 1960, 261 = B.Lifshitz, *Donateurs et fondateurs dans les synagogues juives*, Paris 1967, no. 31; cf. no. 81a Hulda and no. 64 Caesarea in Palestine. For συνέδριον with the simple meaning of 'assembly' see *CIJ* 777; Josephus, *Vita* 236,368 and E. Lohse, *TDNT* 7, 861.

133. In some instances scourging by the synagogue could result in death: Makkoth 3.14; cf. also the fatal incarceration of those who had been scourged and were still impenitent (Sanh 9.5a). Cf. Matt. 10.17; Luke 12.11 Q; 21.2.

Notes

Bacon (see n. 49), 214, already conjectures a procedure in the 'synagogue of the Alexandrians', following Hilgenfeld and Spitta.

134. Cf. e.g. the extreme reduction of the pre-Lucan tradition in Bihler, *Stephanusgeschichte* (see bibliography), 10ff. However, H.Lietzmann, *Kleine Schriften* II (TU 68), 1958, 254f., on Mark 14.58 and Acts 6.14, is positive.

135. So Schmithals (see bibliography), 26ff.

136. Cf. Acts 17.7. The term λοιμός relates to the charge made by Claudius against the Jews who had migrated to Alexandria from Syria and the Chora: καθάπερ κοινήν τεινα (sic) τῆς οἰκουμένης νόσον ἐξεγείροντα, *CPJ* (see n. 89), 2, 41 no. 153, col. 5, 99f. Here this charge is made against Paul.

137. For τὰ ἔθη cf. Acts 15.1; 16.21; 21.21; 28.17 and the numerous instances in Josephus, say in his account of the Maccabean revolt (*Antt.* 12, 255, 259, 271: εἴ τις ζηλωτής ἐστιν τῶν πατριῶν ἐθῶν . . .), 280, 324, or in the conversion of the Izates (*Antt.* 20, 17, 38f., 47, 75). For the interpretation of the Jewish Torah as ἔθη see W. C. van Unnik, *Sparsa Collecta* I, NovTestSuppl 29, Leiden 1973, 379ff., with numerous examples. This is a typically Hellenistic expression, cf. F. Hahn, *Gottesdienst* (see n. 1), 51. The restriction to 'the cultic laws of the Jews' by H. Preisker, *TDNT* 2, 371, is hardly justified. One might rather talk in terms of a Hellenizing paraphrase of the typically Jewish laws, including the first three commandments of the Decalogue. Of course this is not, as F. Hahn, op.cit., 50f., thinks, a complete abrogation of the 'validity of the law in general' (50), but a change in it on specific points. If we were to suppose that Stephen criticized the law in the same fundamental way as Paul, we would already have to attribute Paul's doctrine of justification to him. Hahn's criticism of Stuhlmacher that in the New Testament we would have 'no firm basis for the distinction between the ceremonial law and the moral law' (50 n. 18) is incorrect. In Matthew this very distinction seems to me to be present in the redactional quotations of Hos. 6.6 in 9.13; 12.7; cf. also 7.12; 22.40 and 23.23. We do not know the extent of the criticism of the law in Stephen's circle; it seems to me rather to be along the lines of the passages in Matthew mentioned above, the contrast in the antitheses in 5.21, 27, 31, 33, 38, 43, or even to follow from Mark 2.27f.; 7.15, 18ff. and 10.5. We must reckon with the possibility that in his remarks about the 'law of Christ' (Gal. 6.2; I Cor. 9.21) Paul is taking up an earlier tradition which recurs later in the Apostolic Fathers (cf. Barn. 2.6): Christ has abolished sacrifices 'so that the new law of our Lord Jesus Christ, which is no yoke of compulsion, shall contain no sacrifice, which is only the work of men.' Cf. Luke's Peter speech in Acts 15.10; Matt. 11.28ff.; Ignatius, *Magn.* 2; Hermas, *Sim.* 5, 6, 3 (59, 3); 8, 3, 2 (69, 2) and the *Kerygma Petrou* according to Clement of Alexandria, *Strom.* 1, 182, 3; 2, 68, 2. The logia source which begins with the collection of the sayings of Jesus presented in Luke's Sermon on the Plain already proclaims Jesus as the bringer of the new eschatological Torah of the kingdom of God.

138. Cf. also John 2.19, from which the χειροποίητος theme is absent. For the saying about the temple see Gaston (see bibliography), 66ff., 102ff., 152f., 154ff., 161f., and B. Gärtner, *The Temple and the Community in Qumran and the New Testament*, SNTS Monograph Series 1, Cambridge 1965, 105ff. Closer to Acts 6.14 is Gospel of Thomas 71: 'Jesus said: I will destroy this house and no

one shall build it up again.' The tearing of the temple curtain (Mark 15.38) also indicates the end of the cult, cf. M.Hengel, *Atonement*, 1981, 42, 45. The true sacrifice has taken place. The temple has lost its significance as a place of sacrifice. This may be the ultimate origin of the later rejection of temple worship by the Ebionites. The theme of the temple made with hands which appears in Mark 14.58; Acts 7.48; the Areopagus speech 17.24 and Heb. 9.11,24 is a widespread one in both Greek and Jewish criticism of the cult, cf. H.Wenschkewitz, *Die Spiritualisierung der Kultusbegriffe*, Angelos Beiheft 4, 1932; I.Heinemann, *Philons griechische und jüdische Bildung* (1932), reprinted 1962, 43-81, esp. 46ff.; for the Greek tradition see L.Ramaroson, 'Contre les "temples faits de mains d'homme" ', *RP* 3, 43, 1969, 217-38. For Judaism see I Kings 8.27; Ps. Philo, *Ant.Bibl.* 22, 5; Targ. Neofiti on Ex. 39, 43. Jewish polemic connects the concept above all with pagan idols and sanctuaries; by contrast it has a positive significance in Philo, *Vit.Mos.* 2.88; Christian usage: Sib. 14.62. This feature does not have any constitutive significance for the Stephen tradition. For the whole question see also G. Klinzing, *Die Umdeutung des Kultus in der Qumrangemeinde und im NT*, SUNT 7, 1971, 202ff.,223f., and on Philo V. Nikiprowetzky, *Semitica* 17, 1967, 97-116, who points out that the exegesis in Stephen's speech 7.48 corresponds not with Philo but with his opponents, the radical allegorists. We have a continuation in the reinterpretation of the cult in the Epistle to the Hebrews.

139. Cf. F. Hahn, *Gottesdienst* (see n. 1), 51 n. 19.

140. For 6.8 πλήρης χάριτος καὶ δυνάμεως and 6.10 . . . τῇ σοφίᾳ καὶ τῷ πνεύματι ᾧ ἐλάλει cf. the description of Joseph in Joseph and Asenath 4.9: ἀνὴρ δυνατός ἐν σοφίᾳ καὶ ἐπιστήμῃ καὶ πνεῦμα θεοῦ ἐστιν ἐπ᾽ αὐτῷ καὶ χάρις κυρίου μετ᾽ αὐτοῦ. Here we have a connection between grace, power and above all wisdom and possession of the spirit. Gen. 41.38f. in turn underlies Joseph and Asenath 4.9. However, Philonenko, ad loc., rightly goes on to point to Isa. 11.2. That in 6.15 Stephen is said to look like an angel corresponds to the appearance of Joseph, who as 'Son of God' can be confused with Michael, cf. Joseph and Asenath 14.8; 13.10f. For Joseph as a bearer of the spirit cf. also TestSim. 4.4. In LevR. 1.1, Phineas is presented as an angel: 'When the holy spirit rested on Phineas, his face glowed like torches.' See Hengel, *Zeloten*, 172 n. 1. According to Rabba b. Bar-Chana in the name of R. Johanan (third century AD), on the basis of Mal. 2.7, 'the teacher is like an angel of the Lord of hosts' (Hag. 15b).

141. See Pesch, *Vision* (see bibliography). For the Son of man standing see the discussion in Pesch, op.cit., and Conzelmann, *Apostelgeschichte*, ad loc. Cf. also Dan. 12.1 (Theodotion): καὶ ἐν τῷ καιρῷ ἐκείνῳ ἀναστήσεται Μιχαηλ ὁ ἄρχων ὁ μέγας ὁ ἑστηκὼς ἐπὶ τοὺς υἱοὺς τοῦ λαοῦ σου. Michael stands up to come to the help of his oppressed people Israel. According to *AssMos.* 10.3 God himself does this: *(sur) get enim caelestis a sede regni sui et exiet de habitatione sancta sua cum indignationem et iram (sic) propter filios eos.* In contrast to the view of Pesch, op.cit., 56, here God's wrath is not directed against Israel but against the Gentiles for oppressing his people, see 10.7: *quia exurgit summus deus aeternus solus et palam ueniet, ut unidicet gentes* (cf. Eth. Enoch 90.18). The contrast in the interpretation put forward by Pesch, op.cit., 20, that the Son

of man 'does not arise *for* Stephen but *against* Stephen's and his own opponents' is artificial. The one necessitates the other. Another possibility is to interpret the 'standing at the right hand of God' as exaltation: see *Hekhalot rabbati* in Jellinek, *Bet ha-Midrasch* 3, 83: *lh'mydw lymyn ks'kbwdw*. Besides, one should not attach too much redactional significance to the theme of the Son of man standing. Presumably Luke took over this addition, which contradicts Luke 22.69, from his source. The LA τὸν υἱὸν τοῦ θεοῦ in p[74] is secondary, contrary to G. D. Kilpatrick's theory, *TZ* 21, 1965, 209. De Wette and Overbeck in their commentary on Acts ([4]1870) already recognized the connections between the passion narrative and the martyrdom of James in Hegesippus according to Eusebius, *HE* 2, 23. Ps. Clem, *Recognitions* 1, 70f. (GCS 51, Rehm 47f.) reports a tumult against James brought about by a *homo inimicus* Saulus/ Paulus.

142. In my view the nearest parallel is the theme of the spirit in the Philip tradition, which also has strongly enthusiastic and ecstatic colouring (cf. Acts 8.6, 13, 26, 29, 39 and above all 21.9). The theme of the spirit and enthusiasm in Luke is basically an archaic feature, of course with idealistic tints. It goes against the situation of the church of his time. Matthew is polemical towards it.

143. Cf. Ascension of Isaiah 5.14: 'Isaiah did not either cry nor weep when he was sawn apart, but his mouth conversed with the holy spirit . . .' Cf. Tertullian, *De patientia* 14, CC 1, p. 315): *His patientiae uiribus secatur Esaias et de domino non tacet, lapidatur Stephanus et ueniam hostibus suis postulat*. Cf. also *Acta Carpi* 38ff., 42. According to the Latin recension Pamphilus dies with the same cry as Stephen (4 end = Acts 7.59), cf. *Passio Pionii* 21.9 and *Acta Iulii Veterani* 4.4. Thus we have to presuppose the martydom of Stephen as a model in the Christian martyrdoms. In itself it was a general view in antiquity that at the moment of death a man was open to special divine revelations, see Cicero, *De Divinatione* 1, 63: *itaque adpropinquante morte multo est diuinior*, cf. 1.47 and 64f., with reference to Posidonius; also the parallels mentioned in *Peake's Commentary*, 206. The counterpart is the Old Testament and Jewish tradition of blessings and testaments. Stephen's vision of the open heaven burst through this framework. Its nearest parallels are to be found in the visions of heaven in Rev. 4.1ff. and Jewish mysticism.

144. Luke 11.31, 32 = Matt. 12.41, 42. Also Matt. 11.9-11 = Luke 7.26-28, which certainly goes back to a saying of Jesus, implicitly puts John the Baptist, as the greatest of those born of women, who is more than a prophet, even above Moses. The antitheses in Matt. 5.21ff. are a consequence of this acknowledgment.

145. In Acts 8.1 Luke speaks of a διωγμὸς μέγας, thus over-drawing the contours of the persecution, just as he probably also exaggerates the role of Paul in it (Acts 8.3; 9.21; 22.4; 26.10f.). He is not, of course, concerned to defame Paul's past but rather wants to bring out the magnitude and unique-ness of the miracle of Paul's conversion. It is doubtful whether death sentences were involved (26.10; 22.4 ἄχρι θανάτου). Possibly, however, at the urging of the Greek-speaking synagogues the Sanhedrin in Jerusalem was also involved in the punishment of these 'despisers of the law'. Unfortunately

we do not know what kind of persecutions of the 'churches of God' in Judaea Paul is referring to in I Thess. 2.14. Still, despite Gal. 1.22, that Paul the Pharisee and scholar was involved inn this persecution (see n. 80 above) should not be doubted. It is not surprising that the Greek-speaking Diaspora Pharisee Saul of Tarsus was 'personally unknown' to the more conservative, Aramaic-speaking community in Jerusalem. However, the Hellenist community was expelled from Jerusalem; Saul had contributed to their 'destruction'. See below, p. 172 n. 39; also Hengel (n. 79), 49. The conjecture, as far as I know first put forward by T. Mommsen, *ZNW* 2, 1901, 85f., on the basis of Gal. 1.22 that Paul did not persecute the community in Jerusalem but that in Tarsus was already refuted by J.Weiss (see bibliography), 136 n. 29. This dispute should finally be put to rest and we should consider what it meant to be a Pharisee at that time: before AD 70 young, ambitious Pharisaic scholars, particularly those from the Diaspora, studied only in Jerusalem and not anywhere else, whether in Tarsus or Damascus. We have *no* evidence at all for Pharisaic scholars studying outside Palestine in the Greek-speaking Diaspora before AD 70. According to the aphorism of Abtalyon in *Ab.* 1,11, exile from Palestine led to a place of bad water, i.e. fatal, corrupting teaching. Cf. also the sharp denigration of Alexandria over against Jerusalem in the letter from Simeon ben Shetah to Yehuda ben Tabbai (jHag 2, 2 p. 77d, 35ff.) and H. F. Weiss (n. 86), 321ff. For the education of Paul in Jerusalem see also van Unnik (see n. 137), 259ff., 321ff.

146. A later parallel is the flight to Pella or migration to Asia Minor, cf. Zahn (see n. 89), 224. Cf. also Matt. 10.14f. = Luke 10.10ff. 'Guidance by the Spirit' can also be assumed behind such developments. Eusebius, *HE* 3, 5, 3 speaks of an 'oracle' given 'by revelation'.

147. Gal. 1.18ff.; 2.1. However, one should not over-interpret the very pointed account by Paul (cf. above, n. 80).

148. Hengel, *Judaism and Hellenism* I, 309f. The phenomena of 'accentuation of the Torah' and 'zeal for the Law' are expressions of this.

149. Hengel, *Zeloten*, 154ff., 211ff. For the over-reaching by Pilate see Josephus, *BJ* 2, 169ff.; *Antt.* 18, 55ff. and Philo, *Leg. ad C.* 299ff.; also P. L. Maier, *HTR* 62, 1969, 109-21. For Caligula see Philo, *Leg. ad C.*, 199ff.; Josephus, *BJ* 2, 184-203; *Antt.* 18, 261-309, and Tacitus, *Hist.* 5, 9: *sub Tiberio quies; dein iussi a C.Caesare effigiem eius in templo locare arma potius sumpsere, quem motum Caesaris mors diremit*, cf. Schürer/Vermes/Millar (see n. 46), 389ff. The remarks by Schmithals (see bibliography), 28f., on criticism of the temple show a lack of any profound knowledge of conditions in Jewish Palestine between Herod and the Jewish War. The Essenes did not reject the temple in principle – as the great Temple Scroll again shows – but *because the Second Temple was not pure enough for them*. Nevertheless, they too gave dedicatory gifts to the Temple (Josephus, *Antt.* 18.19, cf. Philo, *Quod omnis* 75) and thus were ready to compromise for the sake of peace. They threatened 'blasphemy against the lawgiver', i.e. Moses, with death (Josephus, BJ 2, 145, cf. 152). The obscene gesture by a member of the Roman guard on the roof of one of the halls of the forecourt was enough to cause an uproar (*BJ* 2, 223ff.; *Antt.* 20, 105ff.). The widespread 'spiritualization of cultic concepts' (see n. 138 above)

did not stand in the way of a positive attitude to the temple, which even for
the Diaspora was the national centre. We know absolutely nothing of any
Galilean criticism of the temple, and the Samaritans were not considered Jews
but 'enemies of the people' and had always been bitter opponents of the
Second Temple. Under the prefect Coponius (AD 6-9) they desecrated the
temple with dead men's bones shortly before the Passover (*Antt.* 18,29f.) The
murder of a Galilean pilgrim to the festival by the Samaritans provoked open
rebellion in Jerusalem (*BJ* 2, 232ff.; *Antt.* 20, 118ff.). At the time of Jesus and
of earliest Christianity the temple was not a secondary concern but a
particularly tender spot for Palestinian Judaism. Hellenistic-Jewish literature,
Jason of Cyrene, II Maccabees, III Maccabees, Ps. Aristeas, Eupolemus, Philo
the Elder, the Sibyllines, indeed even Philo of Alexandria speak of the Jewish
Temple or the Temple in Jerusalem only with the greatest respect.

150. Acts 12.17; cf. also the pride of place given to James in Gal. 2.9.
Between the persecution by Agrippa I and the Apostolic Council, i.e. between
AD 44 and AD 48/49, there seems to have been a change of leadership in the
Jerusalem community. About eight years later (AD 56/57), the situation had
become even more tense (cf. Rom. 15.30ff.; Acts 21.20): the 'myriads' of Jews
who have become believers 'are all zealous for the law'. Presumably Paul
could count on the support of the community in Caesarea, where Philip had
settled (21.8ff.), whereas in Jerusalem only outsiders like the Cypriot Jewish
Christian Mnason (21.16) took his side.

151. Cf. Hengel (n. 79), 64, on the development of earliest christology.

152. For the relationship between country and çity, of which far too little
notice is taken in the history of earliest Christianity, see E.A.Judge, *Christliche
Gruppen in nicht-christlicher Gesellschaft*, Neue Studienreihe 4, 1964. This
distinction was particularly marked in Palestine, see Hengel, *Zeloten*, 335,
371. For the Hellenistic period see M. Rostovtzeff, *The Social and Economic
History of the Hellenistic World*, Vols I-III, Oxford 1941, 1306ff. This is the
element of truth in Lohmeyer's theory (*Galiläa und Jerusalem*, see n. 48).
Contrary to Schmithals the Galilean disciples did not immediately try to
convert the Hellenistic cities of Syria – the 'religious and political connexions
of Galilee of the Gentiles' are certainly not 'at least as close to the north as to
the south' – but tried to win over one city which was all important to Jews,
namely Jerusalem. This is precisely what the Zealots attempted during the
Jewish War. In some circumstances one could speak of a 'love/hate relationship' of various country Jewish groups towards Jerusalem. This attitude
basically goes back to Jesus himself: Luke 13.3lff.; Matt. 23.37ff.: he himself
looked for a final outcome in Jerusalem.

153. K. H. Rengstorf, *TDNT* 1, 407ff., 413ff. The New Testament ἀπόστολος
can be understood only as a translation of *šalîᵃh/šalûᵃh* which is so common
throughout the Mishnah and Tosephta. The new element here is the escha-
tological motive for the sending. Cf. also J. Roloff, *Apostolat – Verkündigung
– Kirche*, 1965, 272. I Cor. 15.7, 9; 9.1-5; Gal. 1.19 support Palestinian origin.
For linguistic innovations generally in earliest Christianity see N.Turner,
NovTest 16, 1974, 149-60. Cf. already A.Deissmann, *Die Urgeschichte des
Christentums im Lichte der Sprachforschung*, 1910, 44: '. . . as Christianity put

the stamp of its creative spirit on the words *God* and *Spirit*, or the words *faith, love, hope, revelation*, so that they look like newly-minted gold coins'(author's italics).

154. Stuhlmacher (see bibliography), 209ff. and esp. 245ff. on the Hellenistic-Jewish-Christian community.

155. See now L. Hartman, ' "Into the Name of Jesus"', *NTS* 20, 1973/74, 432-40. Cf T. Hullin 2, 22 (line 503), where the Jewish Christian Jacob of Kephar Sama is said to have healed a rabbi's nephew of a snake bite 'in the name of Jeshua Son of Panter' (*mšwmm yšwᶜ bn pntr*).

156. Turner (n. 153), 154f.; W. C. van Unnik, *De semitische achtergrond van* ΠΑΡΡΗΣΙΑ *in het N.T.*, MAA, Afd. Letterkunde, NR 25, 11, Amsterdam 1962.

157. Cf. Schrage (see bibliography), esp.196ff.

158. See M. Hengel, *The Son of God*, London and Philadelphia 1976, 59ff. For the Son of God see esp. Gal. 1.16; Acts 9.20.

159. Boman (see bibliography); cf. also Goppelt (see bibliography), 36: 'Thus in all probability *the gospel will already have been translated from Aramaic into Greek* in the earliest community in Jerusalem.' I regard as unfounded the conjecture by Wilckens (see Bibliography) that 'the Hellenistic-Christian tradition of a kerygma of Christ with an exclusive christological orientation' goes back to the Hellenists. We may assume that because individual Hellenists were so near in time to Jesus, they may have come into contact personally with his preaching and activity. Possibly John 12.20ff. is a later reflection of that. It is striking there that the two disciples with Greek names, Andrew and Philip, are intermediaries in the contact with the 'Greeks'.

160. The only exception is John 5.27, υἱὸς ἀνθρώπου. For the linguistic evidence see C.Colpe, *TDNT* 8, 401ff. but see the υἱὸς ἀνθρώπου Dan. 7.13; 10.16 (Theodotion). One should not be influenced by Daniel here! For the striking manner of translation see the Tübingen dissertation (typescript) by R. Kearns, *Der Menschensohn. Morphologische und semasiologische Studien zur Vorgeschichte eines christologischen Hoheitstitels*, 1973, 1, 62f.: 'Thus it is not a newly-coined translation from the Aramaic, but a unique linguistic creation.' Cf. 1, 133f. n. 8.

161. Cf. J. Jeremias, *Abba*, 1966, 64f., 76ff.

162. Simon (see bibliography), 94ff.; see above, pp. 56ff. Cf. also A. Ehrhardt, 'Greek Proverbs in the Gospel' (1953), in *The Framework of the New Testament Stories*, Manchester 1964, (44-63) 63: 'Thus it may not be superfluous to point out the signs that not only the Evangelists but even Jesus himself was not opposed to the use of Greek thought.'

2. Christology and New Testament Chronology

1. ET London and Philadelphia ²1963.

2. F. Hahn, *Christologische Hoheitstitel*, FRLANT 83, 1963. Further literature in the survey by F. Hahn, 'Methodenprobleme einer Christologie des Neuen Testaments' *VF* 2, 1970, 3ff. Cf. also what is not a very illuminating study by W. Marxsen, *Anfangsprobleme der Christologie*, 1959; the christological sections

in H. Conzelmann, *Outline of the Theology of the New Testament*, ET 1969, 72ff., 82ff., 127ff., which unfortunately are not the strongest part of the work; K. Wengst, *Christologische Formeln und Lieder des Urchristentums*, Bonn Dissertation 1967; E. Schweizer, *Jesus*, ET 1971; W. G. Kümmel, *Theology of the New Testament*, ET 1974, 105ff., 118ff.; R. Schäfer, *Jesus und der Gottesglaube, ein christologischer Entwurf*, 1970; H. Koester, 'The Structure and Criteria of Early Christian Beliefs', in H. Koester and J. M. Robinson, *Trajectories through Early Christianity*, 1971, 205-31.

3. *The Earliest Christian Confessions*, ET 1949; further literature in the critical survey of research by M. Rese, 'Formeln und Lieder im Neuen Testament. Einige notwendige Anmerkungen', *VF* 2, 1970, 75ff. For the resurrection formula see also G. Kegel, *Auferstehung Jesu – Auferstehung der Toten*, 1970, 11ff., though his comments are quite unsatisfactory in terms of critical method.

4. Acts 18.1, 12ff. For literature on the Edict of Claudius see H. J. Leon, *The Jews in Ancient Rome*, 1960, 23ff., and R. Jewett, 'Paul's Anthropological Terms', *AGAJU* X, 1971, 13 n. 2; cf. S. Benko, 'The Edict of Claudius of AD 49 . . .', *TZ* 25, 1969, 406-18, who comes to a very improbable conclusion; also above, pp. 48f. On the Gallio inscription, A. Plassart, 'L'inscription de Delphes mentionnant le proconsul Gallion', *RÉG* 80, 1967, (372-8) 374 n. 4, cf. J. Dauvillier, *Les Temps apostoliques (Ier siècle)*, Paris 1970, 11f., 16 (lit.), 208ff. The doubts expressed by J. C. Hurd, *The Origin of I Corinthians*, London 1965, 31f., about the significance of the inscription for Pauline chronology overlook the fact that here a whole series of different historical pieces of information provide support for one another. For the reliability of Luke as a historian see also above, 97ff.

5. H. Conzelmann, *History of Primitive Christianity*, ET London 1973, 31. For Pauline chronology see J.Dauvillier (n. 4), 9-19; R. Jewett (n. 4), 11ff., who unfortunately follows the untenable theories of J. Knox; also W. G. Kümmel, *Introduction to the New Testament*, ET ²1975, 180ff.; F. Hahn, *Mission in the New Testament*, SBT 47, 1965, 86-94; D. Georgi, 'Die Geschichte der Kollekte des Paulus für Jerusalem', *TF* 38, 1965, 91-6; he is followed by G. Bornkamm, *Paul*, London and New York, 1975, xi. Given the divergences elsewhere in German scholarship, the relative consensus existing in Pauline – and therefore at the same time in New Testament chronology – up to AD 70 is amazing. The most recent investigation by G. Lüdemann, *Paulus der Heidenapostel*, Vol. 1, *Studien zur Chronologie*, FRLANT 123, 1980, is hardly convincing. See the down-to-earth criticism by A. J. M. Wedderburn, *ExpT*, 1981, 103-8.

6. Plassart, op.cit. (n. 4), 377f.: 'les dix-huit mois que saint Paul a passés à Corinthe peuvent bien être comptés de l'hiver 49/50 à l'été de 51.' Cf. the postscript on p. 166 below.

7. The decree of the Apostolic Council in AD 48 could well explain the unrest among the Jews in Rome, with their strong orientation towards Palestine (Philo, *Leg. ad C.*, 155ff.) and the reaction of the emperor which followed from it (Suetonius, *Claudius* 25.4). Leon's dating (n. 4) in AD 41 is decidedly too early.

8. A. Strobel, 'Der Termin des Todes Jesu', *ZNW* 51, 1960, 69-101; cf. J.

158   *Between Jesus and Paul*

Blinzler, *Der Prozess Jesu*, [4]1969, 101ff.; Bo Reicke, *The New Testament Era*, London 1968, 3-6 conjectures – in my view wrongly – 14 Nisan AD 33. This would make the chronological problem of earliest Christianity and its development even more difficult.

9. This problem has been seen many times by scholars, see M. Dibelius, *RGG*[2] I, 1593; W. Thüsing, *Erhöhungsvorstellung und Parusieerwartung in der ältesten nachösterlichen Christologie*, SB 42, 1969, 14f.; K. Wengst (n. 2), 6. Unfortunately too little attention is paid to the historical consequences of this 'shortage of time'.

10. In I Cor. 15.8 Paul's ἔσχατον δὲ πάντων puts him in the same chronological context as the earlier appearances: thus rightly C. K. Barrett, *The First Epistle to the Corinthians*, 1968, 344; at the same time, 'for Paul all the later visions of Christ belong in another category'; J. Weiss, *Der erste Korintherbrief*, 1910, 351. The period over which all these appearances, which alone bestowed apostolic authority, took place, cannot have been a long one. A. v. Harnack, *The Mission and Expansion of Christianity*, ET 1908 reissued 1962, conjectures on the basis of various pieces of apocryphal information that the conversion of Paul took place eighteen months after Jesus' death. However, this is only a matter of the time the Risen Christ conversed with his disciples; the connection with Paul is quite hypothetical. Cf. also W. Bauer, *Das Leben Jesu im Zeitalter der neutestamentlichen Apokryphen*, 1909 (reprinted 1967), 266, and *Epistula Jacobi Apocrypha*, ed. M. Malinine et al (1968), II, 19f., see also 40. In itself the interval of eighteen months is very short, though theoretically it would be possible.

11. See n. 3 above. Typical of this method is the attempt by H. Conzelmann to construct his *Outline of the Theology of the New Testament* from 'formula-like phrases' in which 'faith addressess itself from the beginning' (81, cf.9f.). For a basic criticism of this undertaking see M. Rese (n. 3), 93ff.

12. For Paul's letters – and at the same time his theology – as a fruit of his mission see above, pp. 49f.

13. *ZNW* 13, 1912, 320-37, reprinted in *Das Paulusbild in der neueren deutschen Forschung*, ed. K. H. Rengstorf, WF XXIV, 1964, 124-43. Page references are to the reprint.

14. Op.cit., 138, cf. 134. This view has become almost a commonplace of scholarship.

15. Above, pp. 55–9. Two disciples from the group of Twelve, Andrew and Philip, have purely Greek names. As is shown by the numerous Greek inscriptions in Jerusalem, the number of Greek-speaking Jews there must have been relatively large, see M. Hengel, *Judaism and Hellenism* I, 58ff. J. N. Sevenster, *Do You Know Greek?*, 1968, 23ff., 131ff., 143ff. The review of this valuable book by K. M. Fischer, *TLZ* 56, 1971, cols., 34ff., is a remarkable mixture of ignorance and arrogance; J. A. Fitzmyer, 'The Language of Palestine in the First Century AD', *CBQ* 32, 1970, 501-31 (507ff.). Cf. for example the inscription on the tomb of a Cyrenian Alexander son of Simon in N. Avigad, *IEJ* 12, 1962, 1-12 (9f.): this is a remarkable parallel to Mark 15.21; Acts 6.9. On the other hand I think it less probable that these 'Hellenistic influences' were already at work in the Galilean community and that the

mission to the Gentiles had already taken its starting point from there, as is conjectured by H. Kasting, *Die Anfänge der urchristlichen Mission*, BEvTh 155, 1969, 91ff. As Josephus clearly shows, the Galileans were not strongly influenced by Hellenism, but because of their frontier location were xenophobic. Furthermore we know nothing about the Galilean communities. They were not significant for Paul. See below, p. 173 n. 48.

16. W. Heitmüller (n. 13), 136, 141f. Note the dual mode of expression.

17. Heitmüller, op.cit., 139. Cf. R. Bultmann, *Faith and Understanding*, London and New York 1969, 264f.

18. Bultmann, op.cit., 283: 'But his call to decision certainly implies a christology, not as metaphysical speculation about a heavenly being nor as a characterization of his personality somehow endowed with a Messianic consciousness, but a christology which is proclamation, summons'; cf. 182. His *Theology of the New Testament*, 1951, 43 is quite similar; *Exegetica* (=SAH 1960, 3), 1967, 457; but is a 'christology' conceivable which is pure proclamation and address without the person of 'Christ'? What is the difference between the proclamation of an eschatological prophet like the Baptist and that 'implicit christology?' H. Conzelmann, *RGG*[3] III, 634: 'Jesus understands himself as the last one to call. His position is unique, as no one will "come" after him other than God himself.' This modern existentialist interpretation of Jesus rests more on a dogmatic daydream about Jesus than on 'historical-critical' exegesis. That is the explanation for the way in which – almost in a scholastic manner – it could form a school. By concealing the strangeness of the claim of Jesus determined by 'the historical gulf' separating German professors from the craftsman of Galilee', it is rooted more in the nineteenth-century picture of Jesus than it is ready to concede. Instead of an implicit christology one would do better to talk in terms of a real 'messianic secret'. Cf. O. Cullmann (n. 1), 317: 'The foundation of all christology is the life of Jesus . . . The question "Who is Jesus?" did not emerge for the first time with the early community's experience of Easter.' Cf. also n. 63.

19. Op.cit., 141; cf. W. Bousset, *Kyrios Christos*, ET 1970, 119ff. K. Wengst (n. 2), 26ff., 39ff., now adopts a similar position; without any historical evidence he affirms Paul's dependence on a 'mystery thought-pattern'(!) of the 'Hellenistic and Gentile Christian comunities before (!) and alongside Paul'.

20. Op.cit., 132; although W. Bousset, op.cit., 119 n. 2, expressly corrects his view (following Heitmüller) in the first edition, the false interpretation of Gal. 1.22 has had an astonishing influence down too the present day: cf. R. Bultmann, *Theology of the New Testament* I, 187; H. Conzelmann (n. 5), 61, 78-80; E. Haenchen, *The Acts of the Apostles*, 294f. n. 2. But see the criticism by A. Oepke in *Das Paulusbild* (n. 13), 442ff.; J. Blank, *Paulus und Jesus*, SANT XVIII, 1968, 240ff.: Paul had persecuted only the Hellenists in Jerusalem and did not come in contact with the Aramaic-speaking part of the community (246). See above, p. 13.

21. Cf. the apt criticism by Cullmann (n. 1), 206, of the basically uncritical view of history presented by 'radical criticism'. 'The manner in which some scholars distinguish between the *kerygma* of the very early Church and that of

the Hellenistic Church often rests on a really naive confidence in purely artificial and subjective assumptions and oversimplifications. In this way, for instance, some simply make the very early Church into a Jewish eschatological sect. Everything which really distinguishes Christianity from Judaism is called "Hellenistic".' But Cullmann rightly stresses (312f.) that 'certain groups from within Palestinian Christianity (the "Hellenists" in Acts, for example) could have been in contact with Hellenistic thought from the beginning'.

22. *Kyrios Christos*, 120 (my italics).

23. See above, pp. 53f., 57. In Gal. 1.21 Paul is silent about his close connection in Antioch, and in 2.1ff. about the fact that he travelled to Jerusalem under the aegis of the Antioch community. Only in 2.11 is there a direct mention of Antioch; otherwise for Paul this community just does not exist. In Rom. 15.19 we have Jerusalem, where we would really expect Damascus or Antioch. In this passage Paul proves to be relatively free with historical and geographical reality.

24. The article on 'Gentile Christianity' by H. Conzelmann, 'Heidenchristentum', *RGG*[3] III, 129f. is a typical example of the lack of clarity over this matter. It seems to me very questionable whether Paul, when he became a Christian some two or three years after the resurrection of Jesus Christ, 'already found a mixed "Hellenistic" community made up of Jewish and Gentile Christians', which had already been shaped entirely by syncretism and was thus fundamentally different from the primitive community in Jerusalem. At that time the newly-founded Jewish-Christian and Hellenistic communities at best were making their first tentative attempts at mission. F.Hahn, *VF* 2, 1970, 20f., is also unsatisfactory. The phrase used by M.Dibelius, *From Tradition to Gospel*, ET reissued 1971, 29, 'Judaism without Jewish national limits', which goes back to a characterization of I Clement by W. Bousset (n. 19), 189, is more appropriate.

25. R. Bultmann, *Theology of the New Testament* I, 167. The unfounded postulate of a developed pre-Christian gnosticism with independent communities has unduly misled German New Testament scholarship and still in some cases continues to do so even today, despite the clear refutation by C. Colpe, *Die religionsgeschichtliche Schule*, FRLANT 78, 1961. The fact that the front maintained by the defenders of a pre-Christian Gnostic redeemer myth supposed to underline Pauline christology is retreating further and further should probably be ascribed to the fact that this hypothesis has been pushed to an absurd degree by its most consistent defender, W. Schmithals.

26. Bultmann, *Theology of the New Testament* I, 298f. Bultmann has evidently taken over this remarkabe theory from R. Reitzenstein, *Die hellenistischen Mysterienreligionen*, [3]1927 (reprinted 1956), 108, 145ff. However, the links between Attis and a syncretistic Judaism are completely hypothetical, and the allusions to Attis in the gnostic Naassene sermon of Hippolytus come from a much later time. They no longer have anything to do with Judaism and primitive Christianity. See also G. Wagner (n. 57), 219-69.

27. *Faith and Understanding*, 270, 276f., 271. Bultmann endorses Bousset's historical judgment, but criticizes the mystical interpretation of Paul (274ff.); for him christology is 'proclamation, summons' (277), 'the Word of God'

(278). Here his positive connection with the dialectical theology of the Word of God breaks through. The only question is whether such an approach can be justified on these historical and exegetical presuppositions.

28. M. Hengel, 'Zum Thema "Die Religionsgeschichte und das Urchristentum" ', *TLZ* 92, 1967, cols. 801-14 (809f.); cf. *Judaism and Hellenism* I, 308, 311f. I am delighted that H. Koester (n. 2 = German edition: *Entwicklungslinien durch die Welt des frühen Christentums*, 1971, 256) has also come to recognize that 'virtually all the so-called "Hellenistic influences" adopted by early Christianity were mediated through the culture and religion of Hellenistic Judaism.' He seems to have changed his mind in the English edition), 274f., 'whatever so-called "Hellenistic" influences early Christianity accepted were mostly mediated through the *Hellenized* culture of the time'. The last sentence is a truism.

29. See F. Hahn (n. 2), 11f., and the index, 424 s.v. 'Judenchristentum, palästinisches/hellenistisches'. Alongside this, Hahn can of course also still use the old terminology (280), the contrast between 'in the Palestinian sphere' and 'in the Hellenistic sphere'. This is to overlook the fact that Palestine itself was largely a 'Hellenistic sphere'. Hahn's distinction has earlier predecessors to which he himself refers (11 n. 2). Cf. especially Cullmann, *Christology*, 321. For a continuation of the discussion see F.Hahn, *VF* 2, 1970, 20ff.

30. Hahn, *Hoheitstitel*, 120ff.

31. Cf. e.g. Hahn, op.cit., 106, 219, 221f. Perhaps Hahn's relationship to the chronological problem is so obscure because he begins from what in my view are the false premises that 'in the early commmunity . . . in view of the glow of the imminent expectation, time no longer had a function'. Above all in such intensive expectation time becomes a decisive factor. This is even more the case if one is involved in active mission on the basis of this expectation, see above, pp. 51, 58.

32. The beginnings of this conception already go back to R. Bultmann, see his review of O. Cullmann (n. 3) in *TLZ* 74, 1949, 4lf. For criticism see P. Vielhauer, *Aufsätze zum NT*, TB 31, 1965, 167ff.; H. R. Balz, *Methodische Probleme der neutestamentlichen Christologie*, WMANT 25, 1967, 31ff.; W. Thüsing, *Erhöhungvorstellung und Parusieerwartung*, SBS 42, 1969, passim. On this see Hahn, *VF* 2, 1970, 35ff.

33. Eth. Enoch 48.10; 52.4; IV Ezra 13.1-13, 25-38; also Billerbeck I, 485f., 956f., on the messianic interpretation of Dan. 7.13 by the rabbis. On the subject see also Vielhauer, op.cit., 175ff.; H. R. Balz, op.cit., 48ff. H. Koester (n. 2), 213f. Hahn's answer to Balz in *VF* 2, 1970, 15f. does not do justice to the historical position. Judaism already had a multiplicity of variable functional messianic conceptions which could be connected in different ways. Even the Qumran messianology, with such a firm chronological and sociological framework, was far from being a fixed unity: see the basic article by J. Starcky, 'Les quatres étapes du messianisme à Qumrân', *RB* 70, 1963, 481-505, which is not sufficiently taken account of, and the messianic horoscope (?) published by the same author in *Mémorial du Cinquantenaire de l'Ecole des langues orientales anciennes de l'Institut Catholique de Paris*, 1964, 51-66; cf. J. Carmignac, *RevQum* 5, 1965, 206-17. The danger of unreliable simplification

bears not only on primitive Christian christology but also on Jewish messianology.

34. Cf. F. Hahn, op.cit., 195ff., and 212 n. 3, his argument with the fundamental article by N. A. Dahl, 'Der gekreuzigte Messias', in H. Ristow and K. Matthiae, *Der historische Jesus und der kerygmatische Christus*, 1961, 149-69, which unfortunately does not do full justice to Dahl's arguments. See also M. Hengel, *The Charismatic Leader and his Followers*, 1981, 38ff.; *The Atonement*, 39ff. Cf. also above, p. 71.

35. O. Cullmann (n. 1), 321. See above, p. 64.

36. Cullmann, op.cit., 321f. The beginning of the Jewish-Christian Hellenistic community in Jerusalem comes out more strongly in Hahn, *Mission*, 59ff., and *VF* 2, 1970, 18, though here too the continuity between Jerusalem and Damascus, Caesarea, Antioch and so on would need to be stressed more strongly. See the criticism by H.Thyen (n. 55), 153 n. 2: Hahn 'does not take Palestinian and Hellenistic Jewish Christianity into account'.

37. *Christ, Lord, Son of God*, SBT 50, 70, 78.

38. Op.cit., 34ff. Similarly W. Thüsing (n. 32), 29.

39. Acts 12.17; Gal. 2.9,11ff.; I Cor. 9.5. According to the mission legend in Acts 10 from a Petrine source Peter was the founder of the Gentile mission in predominantly Gentile Caesarea. Cf. O. Cullmann, *Peter*, London [2]1962, 37ff.; see below, p. 170 n. 26. After the Apostolic Council Peter too seems to have gone over increasingly to the Gentile mission.

40. Cf. P. Vielhauer (n. 32), 144, though in his criticism of Hahn he of course overlooks the 'parallel development' when he asserts that 'Hellenistic Judaism . . . is as old as the Aramaic-speaking primitive community and is independent of it'. That is impossible simply becaus Jesus preached in Aramaic. The Greek-speaking community grew out of the original Jerusalem community very quickly as an early fruit of the primitive Christian mission, see above, p. 58. Cf. also P. Stuhlmacher, *Das Paulinische Evangelium* I, FRLANT 95, 1968, 272 n. 0 (end), and above, p. 158 n. 15.

41. Kramer (n. 37), 38ff. K.Wengst (n. 2),50ff., 65ff., is even more radical in his discussion of E.Lohse, *Märtyrer und Gottesknecht*, FRLANT 64, 1955. For the age of the conception of atoning sacrifice see P.Stuhlmacher in *Historische Beiträge zur Friedensforschung*, ed. W. Huber, 1970, 35f. n. 26 and my study, *The Atonement*, 65ff.

42. Op.cit., 37.

43. S. Schulz, 'Marantha und Kyrios Jesus', ZNW 53, 1962, 125-44 (137), cf. Kramer, op.cit., 101. *Mar(e')*, along with *ribbōn* the Aramaic equivalent of *'adōn*, had no more nor less 'religious' connotations than *'adōn* or κύριος. In Gaza in the Hellenistic period the city god Dagon was called *marnas*, in the same way as the Jews used *'adōnay* for Yahweh, see Preisendanz, *PW* 14, 1899ff. Cf. the inscription from Transjordan in S. A. Cook, *The Religion of Ancient Palestine in the Light of Archaeology* (Schweich Lectures 1925), 1930, 182f., Διὶ Μάρνᾳ τῷ κυρίῳ, and the synagogue inscription from Umm-el-'Amed in Galilee in *Bulletin for the L. M. Rabbinowitz Fund* 3, 1960, 62, with the mention of *mry šwmy*. Y. Aharoni also draws attention to an incense altar from Lachish dedicated to Yahweh, dating from the fifth or fourth century BC

with the inscription *ᵧh mr'(nn?)*, IEJ 18, 1968, 163; cf. also IQ 20,2,5 *mrh 'lm'*. Words beginning with μαρι – can be found very frequently in the magical texts, see D. Wortmann, *Neue magische Texte*, Bonner Jahrbücher 168, 1968, 74. There are numerous further religious examples in C.-F.J.-J. Hoftijzer, *Dictionnaire des Inscriptions sémitiques de l'ouest*, 1965, 166f. In the case of κύριος, as in the case of *mar(e')*, we find both religious and secular usage side by side. The Targum 11QJob, ed. J. P. M. v. d. Ploeg and A. S. v. d. Woude, Leiden 1971, has the absolute *mr'* for the designation of God in 24.7, 5(?), cf. the supplement, 26,8.

44. Kramer, op.cit., 173ff.

45. Cf. also the all too justified criticism by M. Rese (n. 3), 93ff., similarly K. Lehmann, 'Auferweckt am dritten Tag . . .', *QuaestDisp* 38, ²1969, 64f.: 'that the formulae must be regarded to a greater extent than in previous scholarship as a concentrated reflection of a more comprehensive preaching'.

46. 42, 44ff. An analogy for this transformation of a 'title' into a name can be found in the designation *marnā* for the city God in Gaza, see n. 43.

47. See Wengst, n. 19 above, on Kegel, n. 3. More significant are various Catholic works, e.g. by K. Lehmann (n. 45) and W. Thüsing (n. 32), which stand out for their balanced judgments.

48. There is a construction of this kind without any basis in the sources in S. Schulz, *Die Stunde der Botschaft*, 1967, 39f., 364 n. 51, when he wants to make a basic distinction between 'a gnosticizing Jewish Christianity of the pre-Pauline community' and a 'pre-Pauline area of the community, the Hellenistic/Jewish-Christian'. The two were then fused together in Paul. Such a separation is no more possible than one between aHellenistic 'acclamation Kyrios' and a Jewish Christian 'Mare-Kyrios', see S. Schulz, *ZNW* 53, 1962, 128, 138ff. The possibility of development as far as the absolute ὁ κύριος is indicated by Daniel's address to the angel of revelation 'like a Son of Man' (ὡς ὁμοίωσις υἱοῦ ἀνθρώπου), 10.16f. (Th); καὶ πῶς δυνήσεται ὁ παῖς σου, κύριε, λαλῆσαι μετὰ τοῦ κυρίου μου τούτου or the designation κύριοι for the angels in the Apocalypse of Zephaniah, crowned and sitting on thrones; A. M. Denis, *Fragmenta . . .* 1970, 129 = Clem.Alex, *Stromateis*, 5.11, 77, 2. If this were possible in the case of angels, how much more would it be so in the case of the exalted 'Son of Man' or 'Messiah Son of God'. Here Ps. 110.1 played a decisive role from the beginning: cf. the double usage in Joseph and Asenath 13.9. III Enoch offers further illustrative material (ed. Odeberg). Cf. *The Son of God*, 25-30, 46ff., 77ff.

49. *Christentum und Kultur*, ed. A. Bernouilli, 1919, reprinted 1963, 21.

50. W. Schmithals, *Die Gnosis in Korinth*, FRLANT 66, ³1969, 38, makes Philo not only a 'philosophical gnostic' but at the same time 'the younger contemporary of Simon (Magus)'. Philo was an old man about AD 40 (*Leg ad C.* 1.182). U. Wilckens, *ZTK* 56, 1959, 282, sees Hillel and Shammai as 'famous contemporaries' of Paul. Both were older contemporaries of Herod the Great (who died in 4 BC), but Paul was the pupil of Gamaliel, the son (or grandson) of Hillel. Still, in chronological questions one may well prefer that 'pedantry' of which R. Bultmann accused J. Dupont (*JTS* 3, 1952, 11) because in the

question of a pre-Christian gnosticism he ventured to ask about the dating of the allegedly pre-Christian gnostic sources.

51. Cf. O. Cullmann (n. 1), 3f.; on I Cor. 15.28, 268,293. Cf *The Son of God*, 1ff., 7ff.,57ff.

52. On this see C. Schneider, *Geistesgeschichte des antiken Christentums* I, 1954, 29ff.; E. Wechssler, *Hellas im Evangelium*, 1936; J. Leipoldt, *Jesu Verhältnis zu Griechen und Juden*, 1941. Of course the material iintroduced here would need critical consideration, but on the other hand it could easily be increased. An Erlangen dissertation by R. Braun, *Koheleth und die frühhellenistische Popularphilosophie*, BZAW 130, 1973, demonstrates the amazing influence of Greek gnomism and popular philosophy on Koheleth. Greece and Palestine were not as far apart as is usually assumed; see also *The Charismatic Leader and his Followers*, 33, and *Judaism and Hellenism* I, 70ff., 115ff., 146ff.

53. Cf. P. Stuhlmacher (n. 40), 280f.

54. For this widespread theory see e.g. K. Wengst (n. 2), 195ff.; H.Koester (n. 2), 114ff., 205ff.; H. Thyen, *Studien zur Sündenvergebung*, FRLANT 96, 1970, 140,150f.; cf. also H. Braun's theory of variable christology, *Gesammelte Studien zum Neuen Testament und seiner Umwelt*, [2]1967, 272, 279ff. and against this E. Käsemann, *New Testament Questions of Today*, London and Philadelphia 1969, 38, who points to 'the element of belonging to Christ' as the 'greatest constant'. In the light of this radical approach the unity of the ecclesia, which is a basic presupposition of the letters of Paul and for which the apostle fought bitterly, is quite incomprehensible.

55. Primitive Christian thinking was essentially different from our way of thinking. What seems to us to be an opposite is there sometimes regarded as quite reconcilable. That is particularly true in the case of christological titles and functions, cf. W. Thüsing (n. 32), 28f. On the 'multiplicity of modes of approximation' see H. Frankfort, *Kingship and the Gods*, Chicago 1948, VIIf.; cf. S. Schulz, *TR* 26, 1960, 222, 329, and K. Koch, *HZ* 193, 1961, 7.

56. M. Hengel, *TLZ* 92, 1967, col. 805; *Judaism and Hellenism* II, 135 n. 611. G. Wagner, *Das religionsgeschichtliche Problem von Römer 6,1-11*, ATANT 39, 1962, a work which must be challenged in many places but the basic tenor of which certainly cannot be refuted, shows that this 'influence' on the mystery religions may not be overestimated. Cf. *The Son of God*, 1976, 25ff.

57. See above, pp. 16f. I find improbable the conjecture by G. Klein, *ZKG* 68, 1957, 368, that the Hellenists in Jerusalem would already have endorsed the mission to the Gentiles apart from the law. This development went forward in stages. Turning away from the Jews and towards the Gentiles was prompted above all by the persecution of the Jewish-Christian Hellenists themselves, who must have seen in it a sign of the rejection of Israel. The situation in Jerusalem was as unsuitable as one could imagine for a mission to the Gentiles apart from the law (cf. Acts 21.29; Gal. 2.3; Pes 3b = Bill. II, 551: a Gentile Babylonian is killed because he took part in the passover meal in Jerusalem). The criticism of the Hellenists may have begun more over temple worship and the laws of sacrifice and purity, since all this had been made insignificant by the atoning death of Jesus. The temple was now only

significant as an οἶκος προσευχῆς, Mark 11.17. Cf. *The Atonement*, 57, 65ff.; see above, pp. 23f.

58. P. Stuhlmacher (n. 40), 250ff. Cf. my study *The Son of God*.

59. Acts 11.26 (see J. Dauvillier, n. 4, 692f., cf. 26.28; Tacitus, *Annals* 15.44.

60. Josephus, *BJ* 2, 184-203; *Antt.* 18, 257-309; Philo, *Leg. ad Caium* 188-337. On this see M. Hengel, *Die Zeloten*, AGSU I, 1961, 109ff., 213f., 348; E. M. Smallwood, *Philonis Alexandrini legatio ad Gaium*, 1961, 31ff., 216ff.

61. The mission to the Jews and the mission to the Gentiles could no longer be strictly separated in Diaspora mission practice. In Gal. 2.7ff., too, it could only be a matter of determining the focal point. As the Gentile mission was more successful in the long run, it is understandable that even missionaries to the Jews should turn to it. The Hellenists too had also originally begun as missionaries to the Jews. For Peter see C. K. Barrett, 'Cephas and Corinth', in *Abraham unser Vater, Festschrift O.Michel*, AGSU V, 1963, 1-12.

62. E. Käsemann, *Essays on New Testament Themes*, SBT 41, 1964, 38: 'The only category which does justice to his claim (quite independently of whether he used it himself and required it of others) is that in which his disciples themselves placed him – namely that of the Messiah.' In view of this unique claim, the question of the title Messiah is secondary, see also J. Jeremias, *New Testament Theology I. The Proclamation of Jesus*, 1971, 266. Accordingly it would be wrong to shift the question of the title to the post-Easter community on dogmatic grounds. Even during Jesus' lifetime there was a dispute over his messiahship: this is shown by his execution; furthermore use of the phrase Son of Man to a limited degree as a title also relates to the 'Messianic secret' in the proclamation of Jesus (see above, n. 18).

63. J. Jeremias, op.cit., 272ff.; C. Colpe, *TDNT* 8, 420ff., 430ff. For the questionable character of a simple 'titular' attestation of the Son of Man in pre-Christian Jewish tradition see R. Leivestad, *ASTI* 6, 1967/68, 49-105. The messianic interpretation of the resurrection of Jesus by his disciples lies quite outside the historical framework of ancient Judaism and is only comprehensible if the disciples already assumed that Jesus was a *Messias designatus* before Easter. Cf. O. Cullmann (n. 1), 157.

64. O. Cullmann, op.cit., 214.

65. For the basically functional significance of christology see already O. Cullmann, op.cit., 3: 'When it is asked in the New Testament "Who is Christ?", the question never exclusively, or even primarily, means "What is his nature?" but first of all "What is his function?"'; cf. H. R. Balz (n. 32), 118ff., 126ff. However, we may not play off 'personal' and 'functional' christology against each other, see W.Thüsing (n. 32), 32f., in his discussion with F. Hahn. Similarly J. Blank, *Krisis*, 1964, 36f.

66. O. Cullmann, op.cit., 134: 'The disciples were probably able to make their faith in Jesus understandable to the Jews of the time only by using this title.'

67. E. Käsemann, *New Testament Questions of Today*, 102, see above, pp. 60f.

68. P. Stuhlmacher, *ZTK* 67, 1970, 28ff.

Postscript

The new edition of the inscription by A. Plassart in *Ecole Française d'Athènes, Fouilles de Delphes, Tome III Epigraphie, Fascicule IV, nos. 276 à 350. Les inscriptions du temple du IVe siècle*, par André Plassart, Paris 1970, no. 286, lines 26-32 which is substantially expanded over against that in A. Deissmann, *Paul*, ET 1926, 261ff., shows in line 6 the mention of Gallio in the nominative, so that he cannot be the recipient. By contrast the latter appears in line 17 (see also the expansion of line 7); σε ἐντέλλομαι, ἵν[α, and Plassart, p. 28: 'Line 17 makes it certain that the recipient is an official representing the emperor', presumably 'the successor of Gallio in the government of Achaea'. See also the photographs of the nine fragments of the inscription in Pl.VIII and cf. B. Schwank, *BZ* NF 15, 1971, 266f. J. H. Oliver, *Hesperia* 40, 1971, 239f. corrects Plassart's interpretation and conjectures that the recipient is the community of Delphi or the council of amphictyonies, but on the whole he confirms the new reading.

3. The Origins of the Christian Mission

1.*The Mission and Expansion of Christianity in the First Three Centuries*, ET 1908, reissued 1962. Mention should also be made of the rather unsatisfactory investigation by R. Liechtenhan, *Die urchristliche Mission. Voraussetzungen, Motive und Methoden*, ATANT 9, 1946, and E. Lerle, *Proselytenwerbung und Urchristentum*, 1960, with details of earlier literature on 137-46; also O. Cullmann, 'Der eschatologische Charakter des Missionsauftrags u. des apostolischen Selbstbewusstseins bei Paulus', in *Vorträge und Aufsätze 1925-1962*, 1966, 305-36; 'Eschatologie und Mission im NT', op.cit., 348-60; 'Samaria and the Beginnings of the Christian Mission', in *The Early Church*, London 1956, 185-92; H. Schlier, 'Die Entscheidung für die Heidenmission in der Urchristenheit', in *Die Zeit der Kirche*, 1956, 90-107; G. Schille, 'Anfänge der christlichen Mission', *KuD* 15, 1969, 320-39.

2. *Mission in the New Testament*, SBT 47, 1965; D. Georgi, *Die Gegner des Paulus im 2. Korintherbrief. Studien zur religiösen Propaganda in der Spätantike*, WMANT 11, 1964; W. Bieder, *Gottes Sendung und der missionarische Auftrag der Kirche nach Mt., Lk., Pl. und Joh.*, TS (B) 82, 1965; G. Schille, *Anfänge der Kirche. Erwägungen zur apostolischen Frühgeschichte*, BEvTh 43, 1966; id., *Die urchristliche Kollegialmission*, ATANT 48, 1967; H. Kasting, *Die Anfänge der urchristlichen Mission*, BEvTh 55, 1969; M. Green, *Evangelism in the Early Church*, 1970.

3. Cf. the geographical description of the different churches in Irenaeus, *Adv.Haer.* 1, 10, 2 (Harvey 1, 92): *in Germania, in Hiberio, in Celtio, in Oriente, in Aegypto, in Lybia, in medio mundi*, i.e. all around the inhabited, civilized world.

4. Cf. H.Conzelmann, *History of Primitive Christianity*, London 19xx, and on it M. Hengel, *EvKomm* 3, 1970, 113f.

5. Cf. e.g. H. Braun, *Gesammelte Studien zum NT und seiner Umwelt*, 1962, 268ff., 275ff., 340f., and the criticism by E. Käsemann, *New Testament Questions of Today*, ET London and Philadelphia 1969, 37ff., 60f, along with the reply by H. Braun, op.cit., 349f. The fact should not be overlooked that as

well as the 'theological constant' or 'continuity' there is also a 'continuity of historical event'; this manifests itself primarily in the amazing phenomenon of the early Christian mission.

6. *Ep.* x, 96, 8-10. Despite the many who lapsed, this missionary zeal is matched by the converts' persistence in faith: *pertinaciam certe et inflexibilem obstinationem debere puniri* (10, 96, 3). For the whole question see R.Freudenberger, *Das Verhalten der römischen Behörden gegen die Christen im 2. Jh.*, Münchener Beiträge . . . 52, 1967; also E. J. Bickermann, *Rivista di Filologia* 96, 1968, 290-315, who refers to *Ep.* 10, 117 and Ulpian, *Dig.* 18, 13, and stresses: 'the Christian question (i.e. above all the active Christian mission) disturbed the quiet of the province of Asia' (301). W. Pohlmann, *TLZ* 95, 1970, 43, shows the linguistic connections with the Livy account of the Bacchanalia scandal in Rome, which arose out of the Dionysian 'mission': 39.16.6: *prava religio*; 39.9.1.: *huius mali labes . . . Romam veluti contagione morbi penetravit*.

7. *Annals* 15.44f.; also Freudenberger (n. 6), 180-4; H.Fuchs, in *Tacitus*, ed. V. Poschl, Wege der Forschung 97, 1969, 558-604. For the *multitudo ingens*, which is surely exaggerated, cf. I. Clem. 6.1: συνηθροίσθη πολὺ πλῆθος ἐκλεκτῶν . . ., the martyrs of Nero's persecution.

8. *Nero* 16.2.

9. *Claudius* 25.4; cf. Acts 18.2; Orosius, *Historia contra paganos*, 7, 6, 15f.; Dio Cassius 60, 6, 6f. Also H. J. Leon, *The Jews of Ancient Rome*, 1960, 23-6; H. Fuchs (n. 6), 566f., 594 n. 7; S. Benko, 'The Edict of Claudius', *TZ* 25, 1969, 406-18, with the most recent literature. However, his solution that Chrestus was 'an extremist ("zealot") leader' in the Jewish community in Rome is very unsatisfactory. The name Chrestus does not appear among the Jews in Egypt (see *CPJ* III, 195), in Rome (*CIJ* 1, 617), in Cyrenaica or in Josephus. The title and name ὁ Χριστός was also totally incomprehensible for Greeks and Romans (= 'the smeared', cf. p. 72); the itacistic pronunciation of η as ι gave the slave-name Χρῆστος.

10. Freudenberger (n. 6), 192f.; cf. M. Hengel, *Judaism and Hellenism* II, 173 n. 28. 'Egyptian religion' appeared above all in the successful cult of Isis. For the Roman understanding of Judaism and the Isis cult as superstitious and deceptive mission religions see Josephus, *Antt.* 18, 65-84, and H.G.Moehring, *NovTest* 3, 1959, 293-304. For the so-called Isis mission see S.Morenz, *ZDMG* 111, 1961, 432-6.

11. This dating follows from Acts 18.1-17 and the Gallio inscription, now easily accessible in E. M. Smallwood, *Documents illustrating the Principates of Gaius, Claudius and Nero*, 1967, no. 376, cf. A. Plassart, *REG* 80, 1967, 372-8.

12. Of course only if we do not follow G. Schille (nn. 1 and 2 above) and others in denying Acts any historical value at all(see n. 44 below). Without Acts the historical background of Paul's letters would also be impenetrable. The new anti-Lukan hypotheses put forward by G. Lüdemann, *Paulus der Heidenapostel*, Vol. 1, *Studien zur Chronologie*, FRLANT 213, 1980, about Pauline chronology are far from convincing. They create far more difficulties than they can solve. It is astonishing how often radical anti-Lucan criticism is linked with a wealth of fantasy.

13. Rom. 10.18, after Ps. 18.5 (LXX); cf. Acts 1.8; 13.47 (Isa. 49.6); Mark 13.10; Matt. 28.19; I Tim. 3.16; these are all post-Pauline traditions. For Paul, the subject of the quotation is not heaven, as in the Psalter, but the message of the εὐαγγελιζόμενοι ἀγαθά of v. 15 (see O. Michel, *Der Brief an die Römer*, ⁴1966, ad loc.), of whom he is the chief (n. 28 below).

14. Rom. 15.19, 23ff., 26,28f.; cf. Gal. 1.21; Rom. 16.5; I Cor. 16.5, 19; II Cor. 1.16; Phil. 4.15; I Thess. 1.7f., etc.

15. Acts 18.11; 19.10; 20.31; cf. I Cor. 16.8.

16. From Augustus to the Flavians, Syria and Cilicia campestris (along with Tarsus) formed one Roman province: *The Cambridge Ancient History* 10, 279, 621; D. Magie, *Roman Rule in Asia Minor* II, 1950, 1419f. n. 68, 1439f. n. 27. This explains Paul's terminology in Gal. 1.21. It must not be played off against Acts 9.30; 11.25f.

17. Gal. 1.21; 2.1; cf. Acts 11.25f. In Acts 13; 14, Luke has presumably made use of an itinerary coming from the Antioch source.

18. We find a typical instance of an 'uncritical criticism' in E. Haenchen's exegesis of Acts 15 (*The Acts of the Apostles*, 1971), where first on p. 464 he decrees: 'Luke's version of the Apostolic Council does not possess historical value', but then in the following pages keeps interpreting Gal. 2.1-10 in the light of presuppositions which we know only through Acts 15: 'The name of Antioch does not occur throughout the account of Gal. 2.1-10, but appears first in 2.11 in another connection. Yet there can be *no doubt* that Paul really did "go up" from Antioch to Jerusalem. This is indirectly shown by the fact that he was accompanied by Barnabas . . .' (464, italics mine) – we know both these things only from Acts 15.2. On the other hand, the account by H. Schlier (*Der Brief an die Galater*, ¹²1962, Excursus 105-17) is pleasantly to the point: 'a clear agreement in decisive elements' (115). Here on the basis of his Antiochene source Luke gives an account without knowledge of Paul's position in Gal. 2.1ff. The speeches are redactional, but as a historical nucleus they contain the positive agreement on the question of the law and circumcision. The two accounts cannot be reconciled in connection with the Apostolic Decree. Here Luke may have introduced a later, local agreement possibly connected with Gal. 2.11ff. Cf. W. G. Kümmel, *Heilsgeschehen und Geschichte*, 1965, 278-88.

19. 'Paulus und die Weisheit', *NTS* 12, 1965/66, 231-44. Cf. *First Corinthians*, Hermeneia, 1975, 45f.; like Jewish wisdom Paul 'eliminates the time factor' (45, but cf. Gal. 4.3f.; 3.19ff.; Rom. 5.20; 13.11ff., etc.). On the other hand he concedes on p. 62 that ' "wisdom" and apocalyptic pass over into each other'. I therefore fail to understand why Paul 'the wisdom teacher' as such should not at the same time have been an 'apocalyptist', of course on the basis of the ἀποκάλυψις Ἰησοῦ Χριστοῦ (Gal. 1.12), in a new way which breaks through the old Jewish patterns. On this see P. Stuhlmacher, 'Gegenwart und Zukunft in der paulinischen Theologie', *ZTK* 64, 1967, 423-50, and W. G. Kümmel, *Theology of the New Testament*, 1974, 141-50. Cf. already E. Käsemann (n. 5), 244: 'that the entire mission of Paul is determined by the expectation of the imminent end of the world'. Of course this 'imminent' must be interpreted

rather more exactly, see above, pp. 51f. For the relationship of apocalyptic and wisdom see M. Hengel (n. 10), 206.

20. *Das Geschichtsverständnis des Paulus*, BEvTh 49, 1968, 291ff., 390ff.: 'Paul does not connect the mission to the Gentiles with the parousia. Paul does not understand himself as a forerunner of the parousia and does not think that he can hasten or delay the parousia by his headlong journey with the gospel round (?) the world' (390f.) By shifting the focal point of the previous discussion to the difficult and possibly deutero-Pauline passage II Thess. 2.6f. – see O. Cullmann, n. 1 – this took a wrong turn. Conzelmann's pupil H. Kasting (n. 2), 107f., is more cautious, though of course he too rejects any connection between Paul's mission and the parousia. He fails to note that the 'fullness of the Gentiles' (Rom. 11.25) and his planned journey to Spain (Rom. 15.24, 28), i.e. to the end of the then known world, are intrinsically connected. I Clem. 5.7 quite rightly connects the journey to Spain ἐπὶ τὸ τέρμα τῆς δύσεως ἐλθών with the preceding δικαιοσύνην διδάξας ὅλον τὸν κόσμον.

21. For the interpretation of this passage in the argument over Luz's work see P. Stuhlmacher, 'Zur Interpretation von Rom. 11, 25-32', in *Probleme biblischer Theologie. G. v. Rad zum 70. Geburtstag*, 1967, 554-70, similarly stresses the link between Paul's mission and the parousia. The conjecture by C. Plag, 'Israels Wege zum Heil', *AT* 1, 40, 1969, 41, 44f., 60f., 65ff., that Rom. 11.25-27 is a secondary insertion which derives from an earlier writing of Paul's is quite mistaken, see the criticism by Stuhlmacher, op.cit., and W. Schenck, *TLZ* 95, 1970, 425f. On the subject see also J. Munck, *Paul and the Salvation of Mankind*, London 1959, 48ff.; however, his fear that πλήρωμα = full number implies 'a mechanical kind of predestination' is quite ungrounded. In addition to the parallels in O. Michel, *Der Brief an die Römer*, [12]1963, 280, see also the rabbinic ones in M. Zobel, *Gottes Gesalbter*, 1938, 115f.

22. It is improbable that Rom. 15.16 should be connected with the collection and those who are bringing it (15.26ff.; cf. Gal. 2.10), as is assumed by D. Georgi, *Die Geschichte der Kollekte des Paulus für Jerusalem*, TF 38, 1965, 85; U. Luz (n. 20), 391f., differs, though of course he misunderstands the eschatological orientation of the passage. Paul's sacrificial service as a missionary goes on until 'the fullness of the Gentiles' has been achieved. Cf. also J. Munck (n. 21), 48ff., who connects 15.16 with 11.25 and 15.18 (45). For the full number of the elect see I Clem. 59.2; cf. Rev. 6.11; 7.4; 14.1.

23. Therefore there is no justification ffor the polemical distortion of Paul's eschatologically governed mission which would claim that he 'rushed through the lands as a headlong reporter of the imminent end' – thus Conzelmann, 'Paulus und die Weisheit' (n. 19), 233. Similarly Kasting (n. 2), 107 n. 121, with reference to earlier literature. This caricature has come about not least through the non-eschatological way in which Luke describes the Pauline mission. Paul wanted to found communities which would last: only in this way would his πρόσφορα τῶν ἐθνῶν be pleasing to God (cf. I Cor. 9.2; II Cor. 3.2; 11.2; I Thess. 2.19f.). That could not happen in 'remarkable haste' (Kasting, loc. cit.). H.Schlier (n. 21), 103, 106 rightly points out that the time up to the parousia 'represents the period during which the sending of the gospel to the Gentiles takes place' (106). P. Stuhlmacher, *Das paulinische*

Evangelium 1, FRLANT 95, 1968, 252f. (esp. n. 2). Thus Mark 13.10 takes up an originally Pauline conception, see O. Cullmann (n. 1), 356: Rom. 9-11 'is virtually a commentary on Mark 13.10'. It could later also become a Petrine one, see n. 26.

24. Cf. J. Hempel, 'Die Wurzeln des Missionswillens im Glauben des AT', *ZAW* 66, 1954, 244-72, esp. 255ff. on Isa. 2.2 = Micah. 4.1ff. For the notion of the 'pilgrimage of the nations' which arises from this cf. 4QDibHam col. 4.7ff., M. Baillet, *RB* 68, 1961, 204ff., 220 = *DJD VII. Qumràn Grotte 4*, III, 1982, 144f.; also Bill.IV, 882, 908 (x); Ps. Sol. 17.31; IV Ezra 13.12f., etc. For Hellenistic Judaism see Philo, *De praem. et poen.* Cf. also Cicero, *De natura deorum* 1, 119, on Eleusis: *ubi initiantur gentes orarum ultimae.* On the subject see E. Käsemann (n. 4), 244; F. Hahn (n. 2), 91, 93. I think it questionable whether we should connect the 'pilgrimage of the nations' with the collection. For a summary see now P. Stuhlmacher (n. 23), n. 29.

25. This eschatological priority of the mission to the Gentiles must not in principle contradict the many reports in Acts that Paul first visited the synagogues. It was there that he found those 'Gentiles' with whom he had most success and whom he could therefore primarily address, i.e. the 'godfearers' (see below, n. 56); furthermore he also found temporary lodging and work as was possible through the structure of the Diaspora communities (Acts 14.16f.; 17.4f.; 18.2ff., etc.). For the Jewish synagogues as lodging places and starting points for getting work see M. Hengel, 'Die Synagogeninschrift von Stobi', *ZNW* 57, 1966, 171f. The Jewish Diaspora synagogues still had many secular functions in the first century AD.

26. Possibly Peter-Cephas himself later became more and more of a missionary to the Gentiles, despite Gal. 2.7-9, under the impact of the failure of the mission to the Jews described by Paul in Rom. 10.3,16; 11.6f., etc., a failure which is also hardly open to dispute in the non-Pauline Roman community. I Cor. 1.12; 3.10ff., 22 could also indicate this. Might Paul's opponents in II Cor. even be emissaries of Peter's mission? In that case II Cor. 11.5, which is akin to Gal. 2.6, could refer to the authorities in the background and 11.13 to the emissaries themselves. This would also be a particularly good explanation of the dispute over missionary territory in II Cor. 10.15-16, cf. Rom. 15.20, as of the fact that Paul makes his opponents anonymous. Of course it is impossible to do more than guess here. The mission legend in Acts 10.1-11.18 also shows a connection between Peter and the mission to the Gentiles; there he is made its real author, see above, p. 60 and below p. 177 n. 70. Cf. H. von Campenhausen, *Kirchliches Amt und geistliche Vollmacht*, BHT 14, 1953, 20f.

27. Therefore the argument by J. Knox, *JBL* 83, 1964, 6ff., Conzelmann (n. 19), 233 n. 8, and Luz (n. 20), 391, that Paul worked for more than a decade in a relatively small mission area, is not much use. The absolute preeminence of the mission to the Gentiles over against the mission to the Jews, related as it was to the parousia, came home only slowly to Paul. It had not been developed fully in the first decade of his activity. It is quite possible that Paul (and the Hellenists) limited themselves to this narrow area for so

long because at that stage they expected the parousia in the imminent future, so that there was no time for a planned worldwide mission.

28. I Cor. 15.10; cf. II Cor. 11.5,22ff.; Rom. 1.1,5,13; Gal. 1.15f.; Acts 9.15.

29. Rom. 15.20, 23f.; cf. II Cor. 10.13ff.

30. 'Zum Selbstverständnis des Apostels Paulus', *TLZ* 91, 1966, 321-30.

31. Op.cit., 330; the second quotation is from J. Begrich, *Studien zu Deuterojesaja* (1938), 152. Cf. E. Käsemann (n. 5), 241: 'On this tour and detour, however, Paul himself is nothing other than John the Baptist had claimed to be, namely, the forerunner of the end of the world.' To follow Kasting (n. 2), 108, in thinking that this is 'to postulate a transcendent self-awareness on the part of Paul' is to introduce modern psychology here.' Paul's 'self-awareness' has very little indeed in common with that of modern theologians. We should readily concede his otherness. Cf. already W.Bousset, *Kyrios Christos*, ET 1970, 169f., and R. Reitzenstein, *Die hellenistischen Myster-ienreligionen*, ³1927, 333-93, on 'Paul as Pneumatic'; they both recognized this otherness very clearly.

32. H. Windisch, *Paulus und Christus*, UNT 24, 1934, though he 'hellenizes' both figures too much by introducing the questionable category of the θεῖος ἄνθρωπος.

33. Acts 9.15f.; 22.15, 21, and esp. 26.16ff. For the interpretation of 'Paul's mission' in Acts see O. Betz, 'Die Vision des Paulus', in *Verborum Veritas, Festschrift G.Stählin*, 1970, 113-23. In particular 26.16ff., like Gal.1.15f., is connected with Old Testament prophetic callings, cf. already J. Munck (n. 21), 25ff.

34. J. Jeremias, 'Paulus als Hillelit', in *Neotestamentica et Semitica, Studies in Honour of Matthew Black*, 1969, 88-94.

35. See P. Stuhlmacher, ' "Das Ende des Gesetzes".'Über Ursprung und Ansatz der paulinischen Theologie', *ZTK* 67, 1970, 14-39: 'The epiphany of the crucified Jesus as the Son of God in the glory of the Risen Christ which was granted to Paul *is thus the very gospel which was given to him to pass on*' (27, my italics). See already U.Wilckens, *ZTK* 56, 1959, 274, 'that he understands the event . . . not so much as his own individual conversion to Christian faith, but rather *as his call to be apostle*' (author's italics; quoted by Stuhlmacher, 20 n. 15). Similarly W. G. Kümmel (n. 19), 150f.

36. For Paul as the 'first theologian' see G. Ebeling, *RGG³* 6, 760f.; cf. already W.Wrede, 'Paulus', *RIV* 5/6, 1904, 48: 'The religion of the apostle himself is completely theological; his theology is his religion.'

37. There is an urgent need for an account of the mission to the Jews. The summary in Kasting (n. 2), 11-32, is quite inadequate. For Hillel see n. 34 above and N. N. Glatzer, *Hillel – Repräsentant des klassischen Judentums*, 1966, esp. 75ff. For his school see M. Hengel (n. 10), 77, 82. In this particular connection we need not be concerned with the question what proportion of the Hillel tradition is historical in the strict sense. The important thing is the striking openness in many of the Hillel anecdotes. Cf. J. Neusner, *The Rabbinic Tradition about the Pharisees before 70*, I, 1971, 212-370.

38. For the Greek-speaking Diaspora synagogues in Jerusalem see Acts 6.9; Bill.II, 661ff. and the Theodotus inscription *CIJ* II, 1404. Cf. p. 17.

39. Before AD 70, to study the law in the way that Paul describes in Gal. 1.13f. and Phil. 3.5f. was possible only in Jerusalem – in particular for the 'diaspora Pharisees'. Studying outside the land of Israel was tabu, as long as it was possible to study in Palestine itself (see n. 52 below). The accounts of Paul's involvement in the persecution of Stephen in Acts 7.58; 8.3; 9.1 may be exaggerated, but they have a historical nucleus. Gal. 1.22 is certainly not to be played off against them. Paul really was unknown to the Aramaic-speaking part of the community which had not been affected by the persecution and therefore had not been driven out (cf. p. 13).

40. Gal. 2.8. While we cannot say anything about a supposed mission on the part of Paul in 'Arabia' or among the Nabataeans, especially as the duration of his stay there is unknown, at the latest he must have carried out a mission there after his return to Damascus (Gal. 1.17), since according to Gal. 1.23 the communities in Judaea – presumably in connection with his visit to Jerusalem about two or three years after his conversion – hear ὅτι ὁ διώκων ἡμᾶς ποτε νῦν εὐαγγελίζεται τὴν πίστιν ἥν ποτε ἐπόρθει. Such missionary activity would also explain the flight from Damascus reported in II Cor. 11.32f.; Acts 9.24f.

41. For the Peter source see Acts 10.1-11.18; for the 'Hellenist' or 'Antiochene' source Acts 8.5ff., 26ff.; 11.19ff. The solution of the question of sources in Haenchen, *Acts of the Apostles*, 81-90, remains unsatisfactory and the conjecture that Luke travelled round collecting reports (86f.) is too fanciful. For the problem see J. Dupont, *The Sources of Acts*, 1964.

42. Cf. Matt. 28.19ff.; Mark 16.15 (see also the second conclusion to Mark of codd. L Ψ etc.); I Clement 42 and the many later accounts in Hennecke-Schneemelcher-Wilson, *New Testament Apocrypha* II, 1965, 25ff. Luke's account of the mission goes against the usual early-catholic pattern. With it compare the account of Peter and Paul in I Clem. 5.4-7, and on this see K.Beyschlag, 'Clemens Romanus und der Frühkatholizismus', *BHT* 35, 1966, 225-99, where historical reminiscences still shine through (see n. 20 above). It is significant that Luke says nothing about missionary journeys outside Palestine by Peter, though he certainly knew of them, and has the Petrine source break off with the mysterious 12.17. He was incomparably more interested in Paul than in Peter and the Twelve, who for him above all provide the link between Jesus and Paul and according to Acts 8; 10; 11; 15 have to prepare the way for and legitimate Paul's mission to the Gentiles. G. Klein, *Die zwölf Apostel*, FRLANT 77, 1961, turns this situation upside down. For him the fact that Luke never calls Paul (and Barnabas) apostles apart from Acts 14.4,14 (source!), is from Luke's standpoint an act of 'historical criticism' of a widespread church tradition (Pastorals, I Clement). He certainly did not know the letters of Paul. This 'historical-critical' restriction of the title of apostle does not in any way alter the fact that genuine 'apostles' are involved in the preparatory work for what in Luke's view is the decisive Pauline ideal mission. The commission given by the risen Christ in Acts 1.8 is not completed by them but by the paradigmatic 'witness' (22.15; 26.16) Paul! It is rather a different matter that Luke levels down the specific features of Pauline theology. But what great theologians have not had disciples who did the

same thing? See now also C. Burchard, *Der dreizehnte Zeuge*, FRLANT 103, 1970. For the relative trustworthiness of Luke as a historian and geographer of Palestine see above, pp. 97–127.

43. Perhaps one could say that Paul drew the consequences of the eschatological 'extension of the time' which necessarily followed from the Pauline concept of mission and which is already indicated in Mark 13.10. The task of mission cannot be ignored any longer and suppresses the expectation of the end.

44. The detailed account by J. Bihler, *Die Stephanusgeschichte*, MTS 1, 16, 1963, is unsatisfactory because in principle he no longer pursues his historical investigation behind the Lucan redaction, on the grounds that the tradition – if there ever was one – has been taken up completely into the composition (249). Luke becomes basically the writer of a theological romance. If this tendency is maintained, the whole early history of Christianity vanishes into nebulous obscurity, including the historical background of the letters of Paul (see n. 12 above). However, a comparison of Acts with the apocryphal romances about the apostles shows its basic difference from later works. Furthermore, some passages can be checked historically in the light of other sources. By contrast, the most recent investigation by M. H. Scharlemann, *Stephen: A Singular Saint*, 1968, retreats behind a critical consideration of the text to the other extreme. However, it is worth noting his demonstration of some Samaritan parallels in Stephen's speech, which shows that here Luke must have used an earlier tradition. Luke's account of the dispute in the community and the motivation for the persecution of Stephen all contradict Luke's harmonizing tendency; they have a good historical nucleus. The criticism of temple and law in the proclamation of the Christian 'Hellenists' led to a violent counter-reaction on the part of their Pharisaically oriented audience from the Greek-speaking Diaspora synagogues (see n. 38 above). The view expressed by P.Vielhauer, *Aufsätze zum NT*, TB 31, 1965, 144, 'that Hellenistic Jewish Christianity . . . is as old as the Aramaic speaking primitive community and independent of it', is in these terms surely ungrounded (see below, nn. 48, 49, and for the Hellenists, pp. 54ff.).

45. See M. Hengel (n. 10), 310f., 313f.

46. Acts 8.4-24; cf. John 4.35-42 and O. Cullmann (n. 1). For the condemnation of the Samaritans see Bill. 1, 538ff.; II, 525; III, 313; IV, 333, 1183f., and M.Hengel (n. 56), 19, 38f.; cf. J. Jeremias, *Jerusalem in the Time of Jesus*, 1969, 352ff.;id, *TDNT* 7, 91ff. See also n. 59 below.

47. In Acts 8.26, 40 (cf. 21.8f.) the predominantly Gentile cities of Gaza, Ashdod and Caesarea are mentioned in connection with the mission of Philip, whereas in 9.32, 43 Peter visits the predominantly Jewish cities of Lydda and Joppa. This is no coincidence. Cf. further 8.4; 9.2; 11.19ff. 21.4,7. Cf. below.

48. G.H.Boobyer, 'Galilee and Galileans in St Mark's Gospel', *BJRL* 35, 1952/53, 334-48 already argued for a Galilean beginning to the mission to the Gentiles; W. Schmithals, *Paul and James*, SBT 46, 1965, 16-37 even conjectures that the 'Hellenists', who are critical of the law, come from Galilee. This goes completely against the fanatical zealot attitude of the Galileans depicted by Josephus. The prevalent attitude in Galilee was the typically chauvinistic

'frontier situation' with its xenophobia. See A. Alt, *Kleine Schriften* II, [3]1964, 422f., 428f., 436ff. Cf. also G. Schille, *Anfänge* (n. 2), 137ff., 149ff., 159ff.; id., *KuD* 15, 1969, 332ff.; H. Kasting (n. 2), 89ff., and K. Kertelge, *Die Wunder Jesu im Markusevangelium*, SANT 23, 1970, 185. F. Hahn, *Der urchristliche Gottesdienst*, SB 41, 1970, 47f. n. 5, and W. G. Kümmel (n. 19), 125f., rightly argue against this. The central significance of Galilee in Mark and, following that, in Matthew and Luke is not connected with the role of the later 'Galilean communities', but with the fact that the activity of Jesus was predominantly concentrated on Galilee. TThe essential role of the Lord's kindred for Galilee makes it very improbable that there should have been a particular Galilean 'mission to the Gentiles'. Mark himself does not really give any indication of this. Cf. above, p. 26.

49. For the role of Peter see above n. 26. J. Wellhausen, *Kritische Analyse der Apg.*, AGG ph. h. Klasse, NF 15, 2, 1914, 14, connects the apostle with Philip the evangelist, with a reference to John 12.20ff., cf. also E.Bishop, 'Which Philip?', *ATR* 28, 1946, 154-9. Such 'transitions' became possible because in Palestine there were a large number of bilingual 'Graeco-Palestinians', see M.Hengel (n. 10), 105f. They formed the connecting link between the two communities. Cf. below.

50. Cf. P. Stuhlmacher (n. 23), 251f. n. 2 against W. Schrage, ' "Ekklesia" und "Synagoge" ', *ZTK* 60,1963, 196ff., and F. Hahn (n. 48), 50f. Hahn overlooks the predominance of the ethical commandments and the largely ethical or spiritualistic and allegorical interpretation of the ritual commmmandments in the doctrinal writings of Diaspora Judaism such as Ps. Aristeas, IV Maccabees, Ps. Phocylides and also in Philo and Josephus (see e.g. the proselyte catechism in *C. Ap.* 184-219). Hillel's famous answer to a proselyte who approached him (Shabb. 31, Bill. I, 460) and the defence of the command about the ashes of the red cow by Johanan b. Zakkai (NumR. 19,8) show that this perspective was not unknown even to the school of Hillel in Palestine; see A. Schlatter, 'Jochanan ben Zakkai . . .', in *Synagoge und Kirche bis zum Barkochba-Aufstand*, 1966, 206, cf. 197ff. That sacrifice would cease in the messianic age was argued even by a Palestinian Tannaite (see Bill IV, 885, 936f.). Cf. below and see also M. Hengel, *The Atonement*, 34ff., 74ff.

51. For the doctrine of the two ways see G. Klein, *Der älteste christliche Katechismus und die jüdische Propaganda-Literatur*, 1909; A. Seeberg, *Der Katechismus der Urchristenheit*, 1903, reprinted TB 26, 1966, 1-44; J.-P.Audet, *La Didachè. Instructions des Apôtres*, 1958, 252-357. It is also striking that the daily recitation of the Decalogue in connection with the $š^e$*ma* prayer 'was again put on one side in the period of earliest Christianity for polemical reasons', i.e. because it played a central role in earliest Christianity, see I. Elbogen, *Der jüdische Gottesdienst in seiner geschichtlichen Entwicklung*, reprint of [3]1931, 1962, 242. For the significance of the Decalogue in earliest Christianity see P. Stuhlmacher, *EvTh* 28, 1968, 178f.

52. Cf. Barn. 2.6. Perhaps the puzzling νόμος (τῆς) ἐλευθερίας in James 1.25; 2.12 is also to be understood as the pure moral law 'free' from the ritual law, which culminates in the 'royal' commandment to love (2.8) and which must be observed as a whole.

53. For those Jews who returned see the abundant material in the tomb inscriptions of Beth-shearim (second to fourth century AD) and Jerusalem (c. 50 BC to AD 70/135), and M. Schwabe and B. Lifshitz, *Beth She'arim, Vol.II: The Greek Inscriptions*, 1967, and J. N. Sevenster, '*Do You Know Greek?*', NovTest Suppl 19, 1968, 140ff., 143ff. In the case of a considerable number of names we have to assume that those who bore them had already been settled for a long time in Palestine, e.g. with the Theodotus inscription (see above, pp. 17, 171 n. 38) in the third generation, cf. op.cit., 131ff.; further Bill. II, 662f.; for the many aspects of the meritoriousness and indeed the necessity of living in the land of Israel see J. Bonsirven, *Textes Rabbiniques*, 1955, 740, index s. v. 'La terre d'Israël', 302, 367, 536, 785, 1288, 1916, 2019, 2027f.

54. Even the school of Hillel, which was the most open in this respect (see n. 36 above), remained completely caught up in the extreme legalistic casuistry which was usually alien to the Jews of the Diaspora; however, through the Alexandrian method of interpretation of the seven Middoth, their founder had brought this to a new 'state of scholarship', see J.Jeremias (n. 33), 92ff.

55. Mark 7.15; cf. H.Merkel, *ZRGG* 20, 1968, 340-63.

56. Cf. the purification of the temple (Mark 9.15-18) and on this M.Hengel, *Was Jesus a Revolutionist?*, 15f., 33f., and also Jesus' saying, taken up in Acts 6.14, about tearing down the temple (Mark 14.58 par; John 2.19). The interpretation of Jesus' purification of the temple in Mark 11.17 by the double quotation from Isa. 56.7; Jer.7.11 could be a relic of a theologumenon of that early Jewish-Christian Hellenistic group.

57. For the 'godfearers' see now H. Bellen, *JAC* 8/9, 1965/66, 171-6; B. Lifshitz, *RB* 76, 1969, 96, and *JSJ* 1, 1970, 77-84, on the basis of new evidence from inscriptions. For the NT see K. Romaniuk, *Aegyptus* 44, 1964, 66-91. For the missionary connection see Acts 8.26ff. (according to Deut. 33.2f., the eunuch cannot be a full proselyte); 11.1ff.; 13.16, 26, 43, 50; 16.14; 17.4, 17; 18.7. Luke pays special attention to this group; one might almost assume that he himself came from it. See the fundamental study by my pupil F. Siegart, 'Gottesfürchtige und Sympathisanten', *JSJ* 4, 1973, 109-64.

58. Bill. II, 494-519 on John 7.49; cf. A. Büchler, *Der Galiläische 'Am-ha'areṣ des zweiten Jahrhunderts*, 1906, reprinted 1968, and A. Oppenheimer, *The 'Amm ha-aretz*, ALGH 27, 1977.

59. In *Antt.* 12, 346, Josephus affirms that all the Jews who transgressed the food laws and desecrated the sabbath had fled to the 'Shechemites', cf. n. 46 above.

60. W. Schrage (n. 50), 178-202; for the Palestinian origin of the term συναγωγή see my article 'Proseuche und Synagoge', in *Tradition und Glaube. Festgabe für K. G. Kuhn*, 1971, 157-84.

61. For the mission of the 'school of Hillel' (see n. 35 above), as a 'proclamation of the law' cf. Aboth 1.12b: 'Be a disciple of Aaron, loving peace and seeking peace, loving the creatures (*habbᵉriyyōt* = men) and leading them to the Torah.' For εὐαγγέλιον as a mission concept in the Hellenistic and Jewish-Christian community see P. Stuhlmacher (n. 23), 245ff.

62. *The Acts of the Apostles*, ET 1971, 189., 258; cf.264. Haenchen quotes M.

Dibelius, *Studies in the Acts of the Apostles*, ET London 1957, 124. He is followed by D. Georgi (n. 2), 24 n. 62. But see H. Conzelmann (n. 3), 32ff., who rightly refers to the contrast with the Qumran community. Similarly also H. Braun, *Qumran und das NT*, 1,1966, 153; further H. Kasting (n. 3), 46ff., 61ff., 75ff., 82ff., though he assumes that Galilee was the first centre for the mission (see n. 48 above and pp. 58f.). It is natural that this mission should soon have come up against the resistance of the Sadducees as the political leaders of Judaism. They dominated the Sanhedrin and handed Jesus over to the Romans on the charge of being a political revolutionary. Later the old enmity flared up again as a result of the persecution launched by Herod Agrippa I, who was allied less with the Pharisees than with the Sadducean nobility and by the execution of James the Lord's brother and other Christians by the Sadducean high priest Annas, the son of the Annas of the passion narrative (Josephus, *Antt.* 20, 199ff.) Luke's account of the persecution of the earliest community by the Sadducean dominated Sanhedrin is therefore no invention; see M. Hengel, *The Charismatic Leader and his Followers*, 1981, 38-42. By contrast the Pharisees responded with a violent persecution only to the criticism of temple and torah by the Hellenists, i.e. against tendencies critical of the torah. The situation only changed after 70; this is matched by the accentuation of the polemic against the Pharisees in Matthew.

63. The 'Hellenists' had their focal point in Jerusalem, where many Greek-speaking Jews lived because it was a holy place, rather than in the Galilean countryside (see above nn. 43, 47). The bridge was formed by bilingual Palestinians (above n. 48).

64. Cf. E. Lohse, *TDNT* 7, 323ff. For the appearing of the Messiah on Zion see Josephus, *BJ* 6, 285f.; *Or. Sib.* 5, 414, 420ff.; IV Ezra 13.35ff. and Bill. 1, 151; 4, 873, cf. Matt. 4.16f. and Rom. 11.26 (see p. 51 above). For the new messianic Jerusalem in place of the old see Bill. 3, 853; 4, 883ff., 919ff. For the pilgrimage of the nations see n. 23 above.

65. Here, in my view, is to be found the origin of the Pentecost tradition in Acts 2. On this festival the disciples of Jesus for the first time became missionaries in public in Jerusalem. This tradition was then later given a universalist interpretation by the 'miracle of tongues'. On the whole question see G. Kretschmar, 'Himmelfahrt und Pfingsten', *ZKG* 66, 1954/5, 209-53.

66. One basic work is still K. H. Rengstorf, *TDNT* 1, 407-45; see J. Roloff, *Apostolat-Verkündigung-Kirche*, 1965; W. G. Kümmel (n. 19), 118ff.; cf. also the critical remark at the beginning of the good account by H. Kasting (n. 2), 61: 'a field which is much disputed in scholarship and on which many hypotheses blossom out in a fantastic way'. That the consensus which was building up in the 1930s was again shattered completely in post-war Germany is at least partly the result of increasingly wild exegetical method. Cf. now K. Kertelge, *BZ*, NF 14, 1970, 161-81 (lit).

67. See the analysis of the traditions about the sending in H. Kasting (n. 3), 34-52; cf. also H. Conzelmann (n. 3), 26ff.

68. Matt. 28.19f.; Mark 16.15 (cf. also the command to the women, Mark 16.7f., which also contains a specific 'sending', though they do not obey the command because they are afraid: see M. Hengel, in *Abraham Unser Vater*,

Festschrift for O. Michel, AGSU 5, 1963, 252ff.); Luke 24.46f. (cf. 33f.); John 20.21ff.; Acts 1.8; for Paul see n. 35 above.

69. Kasting (n. 2), 86ff.; Conzelmann (n. 3), 27: Peter 'may not keep' his appearance 'to himself'; 'that is required by the very fact of the appearance'. Perhaps one could put it more clearly and say, the 'not keeping it to oneself' becomes evident from further developments after the protophany to Peter (but cf. the contradiction in the behaviour of the women between Mark 16.8 and Luke 24.9ff.; John 20.18). The tradition of the protophany to Mary Magdalene (John 20.11ff. and Matt. 28.8ff.) seems to me to be as old as that of the protophany to Peter; it caused some confusion in later tradition. Paul cannot do anything with it in I Cor. 15; it is extremely improbable that the appearances – as he describes things – were limited to males. Here we have an expression of the misogynistic tendency of the later community, which went against Jesus' own attitude. In Jewish eyes women were worthless as witnesses.

70. See the heading in Kasting, loc.cit., 'Peter the Primal Missionary', and the attempt at a reconstruction presented explicitly as a hypothesis by Conzelmann, op.cit.

71. M. Hengel (n. 62), 61, 68, 71ff., 81f.; J. Roloff (n. 66), 138ff.; W. G. Kümmel (n. 19), 25, 151. Kasting (n. 2), 124 (and bibliography) differs. The account of Jesus' betrayal by Judas, 'one of the Twelve' (Mark 14.10, 43 par.; cf. 3.19), which is rooted in tradition, is certainly not a late invention. Here the inventiveness of some modern exegetes far exceeds what is possible in primitive Christianity. That in the stereotyped, old confessional formula contained in I Cor. 15 Paul speaks of οἱ δώδεκα and – in contrast to the historicizing account in Matt. 28.16; Luke 24.9,33; Acts 1.26 – does not speak more exactly of οἱ ἕνδεκα is connected with the fact that twelve was a holy number and οἱ δώδεκα was understandable to every member of the community as a stereotyped, traditional term, whereas the unusual οἱ ἕνδεκα presupposed a historical explanation which could not be given in the confession. The rapid restoration of the 'Twelve' by the choice of Matthias (Acts 1.15ff.) corresponds to the use of οἱ δώδεκα in the formula, even if this number was not 'historically' exact. Any 'purism' here leads the interpreter astray. Nor may we attribute *a priori* unbridled historical invention to the earliest community. Just before 70, when the Gospel of Mark was written, recollection of the basic elements of what had happened around AD 30 could still partially be kept under control, just as in Germany today, thank God, enough people remember what happened between 1930 and 1945. This does not rule out the formation of legends, but we may not make this a basic principle and see nothing but unhistorical 'community formations' everywhere.

72. Op. cit. (n. 2), 126.

73. The most recent polemical discussion in Germany between W. Schmithals, *Ev. Komm.* III, 1970, 76-82, and T. Lorenzmeier, 296-8, with a reply from W.Schmithals on 416-18, only demonstrates the scholastic fixity of standpoints. Fortunately the views of H. -G. Link show that the old fronts have broken up. He rightly criticizes (486) Schmithals' assertion: 'Like any historical

entity, the historical Jesus can be replaced.' The opposite is the case. Because time and the uniqueness of every historical moment cannot be repeated, no real person, not even the lowliest, can be replaced. Of course all 'mere formulae' and 'kerygmatic formulations' can be replaced when they have lost their content. Only when the man Jesus has become a mere cipher, an empty page, because of a fixated dogmatic, uncritical and radical scepticism, does he become 'exchangeable'. This consequence is in fact drawn by J. Kahl, *Das Elend des Christentums*, 1968, 68ff. We cannot even talk of the 'Crucified Christ' and then forget that it was the man Jesus who was crucified, bringing our salvation through his death. The assertion that Paul and earliest Greek-speaking Christianity were completely uninterested in the historical Jesus and knew hardly anything of him can be refuted by the simple consideration that in antiquity it was quite impossible to proclaim as Kyrios, Son of God and Redeemer a man who had been crucified a few years before – i.e. an alleged criminal – without saying something about who this man was, what he taught and did and how and why he died. This is the origin of the Gospel tradition which grew out of the mission proclamation and the teaching of the community. Cf. W. G. Kümmel (n. 19), 'The person and proclamation of Jesus are indeed the presupposition for the confession of the risen One and for the community's preaching of God's revelation in his Son *Jesus* Christ'(25).

74. M. Hengel (n. 62), passim. For Mark 1.17 see also R. Pesch, *Der reiche Fischfang*, 1969, 72ff.; W. H. Wuellner, *The Meaning of 'Fishers of Men'*, 1967, 137ff.

75. For the tradition about the sending see F. Hahn (n. 2), 33-6; J. Roloff (n. 66), 150ff.; M. Hengel (n. 62), 73ff. The most recent position adopted by F. W. Beare, *JBL* 89, 1970, 1-3 does not present any new approaches. His objection that nothing definitive is said in the Synoptic Gospels about the purpose or success or failure of the mission (p. 12) overlooks the fact that they were in no way interested in the independent actions of the disciples but only in the activity of Jesus, in this case in the act of sending and commissioning them. In contrast to the later missionary situation, here the disciples are completely overshadowed by their Master.

76. Jesus identified himself with the coming 'Son of man' and was executed as a messianic pretender, see M.Hengel (n. 62), 38ff., 71f.; W. G. Kümmel (n. 19), 66ff., 74ff. Thus he understood his own work throughout as 'sending'. It is astonishing how quickly the post-Easter christology of the Greek-speaking community then interpreted this 'sending' of Jesus in terms of an eschatological sending of the 'Son of God' (Gal. 4.4f.; Rom. 8.3f.). This is a pre-Pauline formula, see E. Schweizer, *TDNT* 8, 374, which probably already developed in the first ten years of earliest Christian history (see Paul on himself in Gal. 1.16). Paul uses it completely as a matter of course and presupposes that it is known in the pre-Pauline community in Rome. 'The community is thus given a form of speech by which it can distinguish the sending of Jesus quite unequivocally from that of prophets and teachers and even angels' (op.cit., 375f.). Cf. also my study *The Son of God*, 1976, 10ff., 33ff. As far as I can see, had Jesus not made messianic claims, not only his actions and his fate, but also the rapid development of christology after Easter would

be completely incomprehensible. However, the 'pre-Christian gnostic myth' of the sending of the heavenly redeemer should be firmly put to rest.

77. E. Grässer, *NTS* 16, 1969/70, 22, rightly stresses: 'The Church saw in Jesus *the archetype of the missionary*. His success is the success of the disciples (Mark 6.13), his failures (6.5) are their failures (6.11). The mission of the disciples is an introduction to the fate of the Master, and therefore training for following him.' One need only add that this 'view of the church' had its ultimate ground in the conduct of the earthly Jesus himself.

78. There has been an amazingly large discussion of this problem; see the survey of literature in E. Lerle (n. 1), 142ff.; cf. J. Jeremias, *Jesus' Promise to the Nations*, SBT 24, ²1967, and the summary in F.Hahn (n. 2), 19-32.

79. Cf. Luke 4.25-28; 7.9 par.; 10.13 par.30ff.; 11.29ff. par. 17.11ff. This argument by Jesus then serves in Q as an indirect reference to the mission to the Gentiles and at the same time as a call to Israel to repent, cf. P. D. Meyer, *JBL* 89, 1970, 405-17.

80. Thus neither the form nor the content of the 'mission' in our situation is prejudiced. A concern for world mission today is as misplaced as the claim that all men and women are 'implicit Christians' and the rejection of all missionary proclamation which follows as a result. The mystery of belief and unbelief does not lie in our hands, nor can we simply deny it and replace it by an 'enlightened' faith in progress, much as all of us need real, critical 'Enlightenment' – which does not manipulate problems away, but brings them out. 'Mission', therefore, can only be realized in a church and theology under trial. Perhaps it even takes place in a provisional, deliberate silence, in the way that Dietrich Bonhoeffer described from prison on the day of his godson's baptism in May 1944: 'Our church, which has been fighting in these years only for its self-preservation, as though that were an end in itself, is incapable of taking the word of reconciliation and redemption to mankind and the world. Our earlier words are therefore bound to lose their force and cease, and our being Christians today will be limited to two things: prayer and righteous action among men. All Christian thinking, speaking, and organizing must be born anew out of this prayer and action . . . We are not yet out of the melting-pot, and any attempt to help the church prematurely to a new expansion of its organization will merely delay its conversion and purification. It is not for us to prophesy the day (though the day will come) when men will once more be called so to utter the word of God that the world will be changed and renewed by it . . .'(*Letters and Papers from Prison*, ed. Eberhard Bethge, The Enlarged Edition, London 1971, 300).

4. *'Christos' in Paul*

1. For literature, see: F. Kattenbusch, *Das apostolische Symbol* II, 1900, 541-62: cf. 491f.; E. von Dobschütz, *Die Thessalonicherbriefe*, KEK 1909 (reprinted 1974), 60f.; id., 'κύριος Ἰησοῦς', *ZNW* 30, 1931, 97-123; J. Weiss, *Earliest Christianity*, ET 1937, 133-5; W. Bousset, *Kyrios Christos*, ET 1970, 33ff.; H. Lietzmann, *An die Römer*, HNT⁴, 1933, 23; L. Cerfaux, *Le Christ dans la théologie de Saint Paul*, Paris 1951, ²1954, 361-74; V. Taylor, *The Names of Jesus*,

London 1953, 18-23; N. A. Dahl, 'The Messiahship of Jesus in Paul', in *The Crucified Messiah*, Minneapolis 1974, 37-47 (originally published in German as 'Die Messianität Jesu bei Paulus', in *Studia Paulina in honorem Johannis de Zwaan*, Haarlem 1953, 83-95: page references are to this version) ; B. Rigaux, *Saint Paul: les Epîtres aux Thessaloniciens*, Brussels 1956, 171f., 351; F. Neugebauer, *In Christus*, 1961, 44-64; F. Hahn, *Christologische Hoheitstitel*, FRLANT 83, 1962 (²1964); W. Kramer, *Christ, Lord, Son of God*, SBT 50, 1966, 19-64, 133-50, 203-14; K. Berger, 'Zum traditionsgeschichtlichen Hintergrund christologischer Hoheitstitel', *NTS* 17, 1970-71, 391-425; W. Grundmann, 'χρίω . . .', *TDNT* 9, 532-50; C. F. D. Moule, *The Origins of Christology*, London 1977, 31ff., 47ff.; also below, pp. 30-47. The studies by Dahl and Kramer are still basic.

2. K. Aland (ed.), *Vollständige Konkordanz zum griechischen Neues Testament*, 1978, 300f., 130f. With its 1318 instances, θεός is by far the most frequent noun in the New Testament.

3. Op.cit., 136f., 166; in the case of κύριος I have not excluded instances which related to God himself or have a profane sociological significance. For Paul the christological usage would come down to about 184; textual variants make the exact figure somewhat uncertain.

4. See M. Hengel, *The Son of God*, 1976, 7ff. This substantial numerical disproportion is reduced somewhat by the fact that Paul speaks of 'Son of God' at certain climaxes in his letters. Nevertheless, it has to be noted.

5. *Statistik des neutestamentlichen Wortschatzes*, 1958, 156: 266 to 529.

6. Morgenthaler, op.cit., 167, for the whole Pauline corpus; θεός, 548; Χριστός, 379; κύριος, 275; Ἰησοῦς, 213. If we leave aside the authentic letters of Paul, according to Morgenthaler the results for Eph.; Col.; II Thess. and the Pastorals are: θεός, 118; Χριστός, 113; κύριος, 91; Ἰησοῦς, 70. In Titus Χριστός appears only four times, on each occasion as a formula in the genitive: Ἰησοῦ Χριστοῦ, 1.1; 2.13; 3.6 or Χριστοῦ Ἰησοῦ, 1.4, whereas σωτήρ appears six times, three of them related to God (1.3; 2.10; 3.4) and three to Christ (1.4; 2.13; 3.6). The varied and lively terminology of Paul is here largely replaced by liturgical formulae.

7. Cf. also according to Aland's statistics (n. 2 above), κύριος, 107 (God and Jesus); Ἰησοῦς, 70; θεός, 168.

8. Cf. κύριος, 53 (only in the Gospel); Ἰησοῦς, 258; υἱός (absolute and with θεοῦ), 79; θεός, 150; πατήρ, 154.

9. Cerfaux, op.cit. (n. 1), 294.

10. Mark 12.35-37 is a didactic messianic saying which enters into critical discussion with the messianic doctrine of the 'scribes', but in which the solution of the riddle is left open. Jesus gives it only in 14.62 as a reply to the high priest's question about the Messiah, but even there he does not use the word Χριστός. None of this is at all fortuitous. In Mark the title Messiah is made a problem, although the evangelist obviously presupposes that Jesus is the 'Christ' – for whatever reasons (cf. already the introductory 1,1!). He is concerned with more than just this title. The frequency and the natural way in which Paul uses 'Christos' is therefore all the more striking.

11. See above, pp. 30ff.

12. E. von Dobschütz, *Thess* (n. 1), 60, 'Paul is remarkably varied in his

formulae'. In I Thess. there are only four formulae which connect God and 'the Lord Jesus Christ' (etc.), and fourteen different variants of Kyrios, Christos and Jesus. Accordingly the essentially more simple christological terminology in II Thess., which sounds stereotyped, is an indication that this is a secondary imitation of the first letter. Of the fifteen 'christological formulae' and terms which von Dobschütz cites from I and II Thess., six are to be found exclusively in the first letter and only one in the second.

13. I Thess. 1.1: ἐν θεῷ πατρὶ καὶ κυρίῳ Ἰησοῦ Χριστῷ. Imitated in II Thess. 1.1; 3.12; cf. 1.2, 12. For the other letters of Paul cf. Rom. 1.7; 15.6; I Cor. 1.3; 8.6; 16.23; II Cor. 1.2; 13.13; Gal. 1.3; Phil. 1.2; 2.11; 3.20; 4.23; Philemon 3; it appears above all in the salutation and the conclusion of the letter. For the form see W. Kramer, op.cit (n. 1), 151-6.

14. Cf. II Thess. 2.1, 14, 16; 3.16; Rom. 5.1, 11; 13.14; I Cor. 1.2, 8; 6.11; II Cor. 1.3; 8.9; Gal. 6.14.

15. According to F. Neugebauer, op.cit (n. 1), 48, ἐν Χριστῷ appears 25 times in the authentic letters and ἐν Χριστῷ Ἰησοῦ 27 or 28. In connection with the preposition ἐν and in conjunction with the genitive Paul tends to prefer the double name. Cf. also the statistics in W. Kramer, op.cit (n. 1), 204f.

16. Rom. 15.19; I Cor. 9.12; II Cor. 2.12; 9.13; 10.14; Gal. 1.7; Phil. 1.27; II Thess. 1.8 τῷ εὐαγγελίῳ τοῦ κυρίου ἡμῶν Ἰησοῦ by contrast is completely out of place and again shows the secondary character of II Thess. For the pre-Pauline formula see W. Kramer (op.cit.), 50ff. In the formula τὸ εὐαγγέλιον τοῦ Χριστοῦ we have an objective genitive in contrast to the *genitivus auctoris* in the parallel formula τὸ εὐαγγέλιον τοῦ θεοῦ, which in contrast to the terminology elsewhere appears more frequently in I Thess (2.2, 8, 9). Cf W. Kramer, op.cit., 50ff.; P. Stuhlmacher, *Das paulinische Evangelium*, I, *Vorgeschichte*, FRLANT 95, 1968, 258ff., 266, who rightly points out that this formal terminology is pre-Pauline. Cf. also Mark 1.1; I Peter 4.17. The comments by G. Strecker, 'Das Evangelium Jesu Christi', *Jesus Christus in Historie und Theologie: Festschrift H. Conzelmann*, 1975, 503-48, are by contrast less illuminating and helpful as they only repeat old and often questionable arguments.

17. In I Thess. 1.1 (and its imitation in II Thess. 1.1, see above n. 13), Paul puts 'God the Father' and the 'Lord Jesus Christ' together, as he is fond of doing. Presumably this is a prayer formula, cf. the greeting formulae in Rom. 1.7; I Cor. 1.3; II Cor. 1.2f. (twice); Phil. 1.2; Philemon 1.3. In Gal. 1.1, the atypical διὰ Ἰησοῦ Χριστοῦ may be caused by the subsequent καὶ θεοῦ πατρός and the liturgical custom connected with it. By contrast in the later letters the genitive form occurs, with Χριστό usually being put first: Rom. 1.1; δοῦλος Χριστοῦ Ἰησοῦ, cf. Phil. 1.1; I Cor. 1.1, ἀπόστολος Χριστοῦ Ἰησοῦ; cf. II Cor. 1.1; Philemon 1.1, δέσμιος Χριστοῦ Ἰησοῦ, see also in n. 53.

18. W. Sanday and A. C. Headlam, *The Epistle to the Romans*, ICC, 1895, 3f.; E. Kuhl, *Der Brief des Paulus an die Römer*, 1913, 7: ' "Christ" is still felt to have its real meaning (= "the Messiah")', as 'in the greeting the apostle is speaking of the "Messiah" Jesus promised in the Old Testament as the content of the gospel'; O. Kuss, *Der Römerbrief*, 1963, 3: 'the original significance of "Christ" (Messiah) as an honorific title can still be seen'. Similarly C. E. B. Cranfield, *The Epistle to the Romans*, ICC I, 1975, 51; H. Schlier, *Der Römerbrief*, HTK,

1977, 19f.; U. Wilckens, *Der Brief an die Römer*, EKK I, 1978, 61 n. 24; O. Michel, *Der Brief an die Römer*, KEK [5]1978, 66: 'Probably there is an echo of the messianic confession'. H. Lietzmann, op.cit. (n. 1), 23, quoting E. von Dobschütz, is more restrained; he also refers to the later terminology in I Clement and the letters of Ignatius, which is 'dependent on Paul'.

19. The new text of Nestle Aland[26] has changed the order of the previous text in several places, e.g. in II Cor. 1.19; 4.5; Gal. 2.16; 3.14; Phil. 2.21. In all these passages a final verdict is extraordinarily difficult. According to W. Kramer, op.cit. (n. 1), 204, of the 60 instances with a double name in Paul, only 42 are really certain. For the problem of transposition see also S. V. McCasland, 'Christ Jesus', *JBL* 65, 1946, 377-83: 'I am unable to say why 48 of the 91 examples of "Christ Jesus" are in the dative and why 102 of the 127 instances of "Jesus Christ" are in the genitive. It is difficult, if not impossible, to explain how or why idiomatic expressions in any language arise and survive' (383). The figures given relate to the whole of the NT.

20. O. Cullmann, *Christology of the New Testament*, [2]1963, 134, argues that Paul's 'occasional practice of putting "Christ" before Jesus shows that he was still clearly aware that the title is not a proper name'. G. Bornkamm, *Das Ende des Gesetzes. Paulusstudien*, 1952 (= *Gesammelte Aufsätze* I, [2]1958), 40, puts forward a similar view: 'The fact that Paul can occasionally use the name Christ as a proper name has led to the widespread notion that the title Christ has become almost insignificant for him and has been replaced by the title *kyrios*. However, that is by no means the case. In Paul both names have primarily the significance of titles and have quite different functions.' Cf. also F. Hahn, op.cit. (n. 1), 213f., who refers to Bornkamm.

21. E. von Dobschütz, op.cit. (n. 1), 61. Cf. the investigation by W.Kramer, op.cit., 199ff., 203ff., which confirms von Dobschütz's theory: 'The designations "Jesus" , "Christ" and "Jesus Christ" have exactly the same meaning in the Paulines' (202). Only if we recognize this presupposition can we go on to ask whether we cannot sometimes find linguistic reminiscences of the usage as a title and why Paul is so fond of using the name Christ.

22. Op.cit (n. 1), 83f.

23. The absolute use of Χριστός -*māšīᵃḥ* without a genitival attribute is extraordinarily rare in pre-Christian Jewish texts: Dan. 9.25 *'ad māšīᵃ·ḥ nāgīd* = Theodotion ἕως Χριστοῦ ἡγουμένου, presumably to be referred to Cyrus, Zerubbabel or the high priest Joshua. 9.26: *yikkaret māšīᵃḥ*, a reference to the murder of the high priest Onias III. The form with the determinative, *hammāšīᵃḥ* possibly occurs in 1QSa 2.12, see A. S. van der Woude, *TDNT* 9, 509f.

24. See M. Hengel, *Son of God*, 59ff.; U. Wilckens (n. 18), I, 56ff.; J. D. G. Dunn, *Christology in the Making*, 1980, 33-5; 138f.

25. E. von Dobschütz, op.cit. (n. 1), 61.

26. Translation and interpretation following H. Lietzmann and W. G. Kümmel, *An die Korinther*, I/II, HNT [4]1949, 120f.

27. Luke 4.18; Acts 4.27; 10.38; Heb. 1.9; cf. IIQMelch 3 II, line 18: *hw("h) mšyḥ hrw(ḥ)m* and Isa. 61.1; also J. T. Milik, *JJS* 23, 1972, 98, 107f.

28.*Paulus der Bote Jesu*, 1934, 482; cf. W. Grundmann, op.cit. (n. 1), 549f., who understands the 'anointing' in terms of incorporation into the body of Christ.

29. E. von Dobschütz, loc.cit.; N. A. Dahl, op.cit (n. 1), 86.

30. Loc.cit. However, in n. 2 Dahl expressly stresses: 'In no passage in Paul may one translate Χριστός with "Messiah".'

31. Op. cit., 84; W. Kramer, op.cit. (n. 1), 209f., would only accept an interpretation as a title in Rom. 9.5; I Cor. 11.3, and even there only as a possibility.

32. Cf. e.g. the imperial edicts in Cyrene in V. Ehrenberg and A. H. M. Jones, *Documents illustrating the reigns of Augustus and Tiberius*, ²1955, no. 311, 139, which have a stereotyped introduction with this formula. Often a *divi filius* (θεοῦ υἱός) is inserted between Caesar and Augustus or added after Augustus. Augustus-Sebastos was then transferred to all successors to imperial office. In other words, what was originally a surname gradually took on almost the significance of a title.

33. Cf. OGIS 19.1; 25.1; 249.1; 250.1. Here too expansions were possible, e.g. Σωτὴρ καὶ Θεός, 16.2.3; Θεὸς ἐπιφανής, 246.10; 253.5.

34. W. Grundmann, op.cit. (n. 1), 534f. on Augustus, see the reference to Risch in n. 324.

35. κύριος Ἰησοῦς; Rom. 10.9; 14.14; I Cor. 12.3; II Cor. 4.14; 11.31; Phil. 2.19. For I Thess. see nn. 12,13 above. κύριος ἡμῶν Ἰησοῦς (or Ἰησοῦς ὁ κύριος ἡμῶν); Rom. 4.24; 16.20; I Cor. 5.4; 9.1; II Cor. 1.14; κύριος Ἰησοῦς Χριστός, Phil. 2.11; cf. n. 13 above.

36. W. Kramer, op.cit., (n. 1), 214 n. 744 wants to regard this as an 'inexplicable exception', but see N. A. Dahl, op.cit. (n. 1), 84, who also points to the Deutero-Pauline Col. 3.24, τῷ κυρίῳ Χριστῷ δουλεύετε. It should be noted that in Rom. 16.16 a τοῦ Χριστοῦ comes first and in vv. 7-12 ἐν Χριστῷ and ἐν κυρίῳ, appear with the same meaning. In Rom. 14.18 Paul speaks of a δουλεύειν τῷ Χριστῷ, and in 12.11 he has the imperative τῷ κυρίῳ δουλεύετε. This regular change between κύριος and Χριστός and the theme of lordship and service may have brought about the unusual mode of expression in which the genitive pronoun ἡμῶν toned down the gulf between τῷ κυρίῳ and Χριστῷ.

37. Cf. Rom. 6.23; 8.39; I Cor. 15.31; Phil. 3.8.

38. See W. Kramer, op.cit. (n. 1), 26ff.; K. Wengst, *Christologische Formeln und Lieder des Urchristentums*, 1972, 78ff.; M. Hengel, *The Atonement*, London 1981, 34ff.

39. In *Theologie als Schriftauslegung: Aufsätze zum Neuen Testament*, 1974, 110 (= 'Was glaubte die frühe Christenheit?', *STU* 25, 1955, 65): ' "Christ" has the significance of a title, where there is a definite article, and also where "Christ" (without the name "Jesus") is the subject of a sentence.'

40. See n. 16 above.

41. As in the case of ἐν κυρίῳ. The exceptions are : I Cor. 15.22, dependent on ἐν τῷ Ἀδάμ; II Cor. 2.14; F. Neugebauer, op.cit. (n. 1), 47; W. Kramer, op.cit. (n. 1), 208f.

42. II Cor. 5.20; 12.10; Phil. 1.29.

43. Rom. 16.5; I Cor. 8.12; II Cor. 1.21; Gal. 3.27; Philemon 6; in II Cor. 11.3

the text is uncertain. Nestle Aland[26] has inserted the article, in contrast to Nestle Aland[25].

44. διὰ τοῦ Χριστοῦ, II Cor. 1.5; 3.4; διὰ Χριστοῦ, II Cor. 5.18; διὰ Χριστὸν, I Cor. 4.10; διὰ τὸν Χριστόν, Phil. 3.7.

45. W. Kramer, op.cit., 209; cf. N. A. Dahl, op.cit., 85.

46. Cf. W. Kramer's basic comment, op.cit., 211: 'These conclusions show that it is not permissible to confuse the question of the article with the question of titles.'

47. 39 times used absolutely, and 8 times as a composite. By contrast, κύριος occurs only 29 times, 21 of which are in the absolute; Ἰησοῦς only 19 times, 7 of them in the absolute. In the other letters, the relationship between the absolute use of 'Christos' and that in the composite formulae is as follows: Rom. 36 : 30; I Cor. 40 : 24; Gal. 20 : 18; Phil. 17 : 20; Philemon 3 :5.

48. Against W. Kramer, op.cit., 148.

49. See the highly detailed analyses by W. Kramer, op.cit., 19-64, 133ff. For the sending of the Son see M. Hengel, *The Son of God*, 66ff. For ἐν Χριστῷ see F. Neugebauer, op.cit. (n. 1), 65ff.; W. Kramer, op.cit., 141ff.

50. Kramer, op.cit., 143ff.

51. Dahl, op.cit., 92.

52. Rom. 9.3-5; 15.8; I Cor. 5.7; 10.4, 9; 15.3f.; Gal. 3.13f., 16, 22, 24. Cf. W. Kramer, op.cit., 148.

53. Op.cit., 41-60; above n. 17.

54. We can hardly follow P. Vielhauer, *Aufsätze zum NT*, TB 31, 1965, 183f., in explaining this from the fact that Philippians is Paul's 'latest' letter. It could very well have been written from Ephesus on the 'Third Journey', before Romans, II Corinthians and Philemon. Cf. also I Thess. 5.24; I Cor. 1.7f., with a combined formula, and also I Cor. 15.22f.; II Cor. 5.10. Vielhauer's conclusion, loc.cit., that 'the term "Christ" is not originally native to eschatology but to soteriology' produces a false contrast: the two cannot be separated. What else could Χριστός mean for Paul but 'eschatological redeemer', even if he uses the title Kyrios particularly often in the parousia tradition? Granted, the title Kyrios has a role in connection with the parousia tradition. As the Maranttha prayer indicates, this may be connected with the fact that the expectation of the exalted Lord (cf. Ps. 110.1) had taken the place of hope in the Son of Man. However, this sphere too was by no means closed to Christ as a title or a name. It was only as bearer of the name or title 'Christ' that Jesus was at the same time the Kyrios. There was no Kyrios christology in earliest Christianity independent of the messiahship of Jesus.

55. The tired cliché of the delay of the parousia should also no longer be used in this connection; it is too simple to explain the complicated process of the development of the earliest christology, even in part. Moreover, there is nothing specifically Christian about it: see A. Strobel, *Untersuchungen zum eschatologischen Verzögerungsproblem*, NTSuppl 2, 1961.

56. I Cor. 1.17; Phil 3.l8; cf. Gal. 6.12, 14.

57. I Cor 1.23; 2.2; Gal. 3.1.

58. The harsh verb πορθεῖν (Gal. 1.13, 23; Acts 9.21: 'annihilate, ravage, destroy, blot out, exterminate', see Arndt-Gingrich-Bauer, ad loc.) is to be

taken seriously and should not be toned down. This suggests a persecution in Jerusalem ,where the possibilities of both legal and extra-judicial proceedings against the new messianic doctrine were at their most favourable. Paul's Phariseeism and his study of the Torah, too, can only be explained meaningfully if we begin from the fact that he was active as a persecutor in Jerusalem before he became a Christian (Phil 3.5; Gal. 1.14). In Pharisaism before AD 70, specialist study of the Torah in connection with training as a scribe was concentrated on Jerusalem for religious reasons. The Holy City was the unique centre of scribal learning. In speaking of the 'scribes from Jerusalem', Mark (3.22, cf.7.1) is reflecting the historical situation accurately. Cf. also above.

59. See M. Hengel, *The Atonement*, 1981, 44ff.

60. See *The Son of God*, 42f.

61. Rom. 1.2; 3.21, 31; 4.14ff.; 9.4f.; 15.8; II Cor. 1.20f.; Gal. 3.14-29.

62. Cf. W. Grundmann, TDNT 9, 533.

63. O. Cullmann, *Christology of the New Testament*, 133, 'becoming fixed as a proper name'; F. Hahn, op.cit (n. 1), 39, 'Christ is merely a proper name without colouring or a structural scheme of its own'.

64. J. Weiss, *Earliest Christianity*, p. 175.

65. Op.cit., 176.

66. *Claudius* 25.4. See Arndt-Gingrich-Bauer s.v. χρηστός and K. Weiss, *TDNT* 9, 473 n. 1. For the proper name χρηστός see W. Pape and G. E. Benseler, *Wörterbuch der griechischen Eigennamen*, ³1911, 1690; F. Preisigke, *Namenbuch*, 1922, 478.

67. See Harald Fuchs, *VC* 4, 1950, 65-93, and the additions to his article in *MusHelv* 20, 1963, 221ff. P. Keresztes, *The Imperial Roman Government and the Christian Church I, From Nero to the Severi*, ANRW II.23,1, 1979, 247-57 (250 n. 12), gives a survey of research. See also A. Wlosok, *Rom und die Christen*, 1970, 8f. Following H. Hommel, she points out that Tacitus uses the phrase *quos per flagitia invisos vulgus Chrestianos appellabat* as an ironic play on words: 'Who called the people the "righteous" although they were hated because of their shameful deeds'(p.10).

68. W. Grundmann, *TDNT* 9, 485; C. F. D. Moule, *The Origin of Christology*, 197, 32 n. 37.

69. W.Kramer, op.cit. (n. 1), 39f.x: 'His eschatological status can no longer be inferred from the designation "Christ", but depends solely on the acts of which the statements in the pistis formula speak' (p. 44). Against this it should be pointed out that for Paul the name Χριστός – like his gospel – *ipso facto* had eschatological significance. This name, which was applied uniquely and exclusively to Jesus, gave his person an eschatological character.

70. See above, pp. 38f.

71. See the apt argument by W. Schmithals in his otherwise over-imaginative book *Der Römerbrief als historisches Problem*, 1975, 76: 'We must venture to suppose that the early Gentile-Christian communities were essentially composed of former godfearers, and that only as numbers slowly grew, above all in the post-apostolic period, were there Gentiles in the community who had had no previous connections with the synagogue.' One might add

that these real 'pagan Christians' at first had little theological influence since they were barely acquainted with the scriptures – the LXX. For the godfearers see the study by my pupil F. Siegert, 'Gottesfürchtige und Sympathisanten', *JSJ* 4, 1973, 109-64; cf. also G. Delling, 'Die Altarinschrift eines Gottesfürchtigen im Pergamon', *NovTest* 7, 1964, 73-80 = *Studien zum NT und zum hellenistischen Judentum*, 1970, 32-8.

72. Of course we cannot at this point presuppose any criticism of the law which has been completely thought through theologically, as is the case with Paul, see pp. 25ff.

73. This is difficult solely for chronological reasons. According to Gal.1.15f., Paul began his mission to the Gentiles soon after his conversion, between two and five years after the event which gave rise to the earliest community, though at that stage not exclusively nor with a world-wide scope. G.Lüdemann, *Paulus der Heidenapostel*, I, *Studien zur Christologie*, 1980, 23 n. 14, distorts what I say in *Acts and the History of Earliest Christianity* by his quotation. There is no question that in Paul's view the 'apostolic council' and the events in Antioch which led to the separation from Barnabas had a decisive significance for his strategy of worldwide mission. There is nothing in Gal. 1.12-21 to suggest that Paul had already moved on to Macedonia and Greece at this time – independently of Barnabas. It is remarkable that those radical critics who accuse Luke of having written a kind of novel about Paul find it difficult themselves to resist a romantic transformation of what the sources say.

74. Cf. the catalogue of the Seven (Acts 6.5f.), the five 'prophets' (Acts 13.1) in Antioch, the names which are listed in Corinth (Acts 18.2, 7f.), the list of names in Rom. 16.3ff. and also Col. 4.10ff.

75. Mark 8.29; 12.35; 14.61; 15.36; Luke 2.11, 26 etc.; Matt. 1.17; 11.2; 16.16; I John 2.22; 5.1; John 1.25, 41; 3.28; 4.25, 29; 7.26f. etc.; Rev. 1.5; 12.10; as Justin shows, this knowledge appears above all in dialogue with Jews. This does not exclude the possibility that 'Christ' is not the only nor the most important honorific title of Jesus. Mark, Matthew and John attach more importance to Son of God. Luke makes at least Kyrios as significant as 'Christos'; cf. Luke 2.11; Acts 2.36. For the early Christian use of 'Christos' in the second century see F. Kattenbusch, op.cit. (n. 1), 553-60. Even in the Roman Creed, πιστεύω . . . καὶ εἰς Χριστὸν Ἰησοῦν τὸν υἱὸν αὐτοῦ τὸν μονογενῆ τὸν κύριον ἡμῶν, according to Kattenbusch 'Christos' still has connotations of an honorific designation. 'The community which created R (i.e. the Roman creed) still thinks in messianic terms and is important in that it has understood that the messiah is a given factor which has appeared in Jesus' (541).

76. Acts 9.22; cf. 20; 17.3; 18.5; cf. 26.23 and Apollos, 18.26. Luke's schematic account still does not mean that it has abandoned historical reality. For the use of 'Christos' in Luke see F. Bovon, *Luc le théologien*, 1978, 201, 207ff.

77. For the old argument over 'Christos' without the article in I Cor. 15.3, see finally J. Jeremias, *ZNW* 57, 1966, 211-15; 60, 1969, 214-19, and the criticism by I. Plein, *EvTh* 29, 1969, 222f. of E. Guttgemanns, *EvTh* 28, 1968, 533-54.

78. W. Grundmann, *TDNT* 9, 533.

79. A. Schalit, *Namenwörterbuch zu Flavius Josephus*, 1968, 60f. counts 19 people with the name, Tcherikover-Fuks, *CPJ* III, 1964, 180, another 10. J.B.Frey, *CIJ* II, 1952, from Palestine Y*ᵉhošuᵃᶜ*, no. 897, 1196; Y*ᵉšuᵃᶜ*, no. 1317; 1345; 1365; Ἰησοῦς, no. 1231; 1327. B. Lifshitz, *Donateurs et fondateurs dans les synagogues juives*, 1967, no. 73a, Ἰσουος. It is all the more striking that soon after 70 the short form *yešũᵃᶜ* disappears almost completely from Jewish sources as a proper name. *Yešũᵃᶜ han-nōṣrī* had made it impossible for Jews.

80. F. Blass and A. Debrunner, *Grammatik des neutestamentlichen Griechisch*, ¹¹1961, 254, 158.

81. *Die Worte Jesu*, ²1930 (reprinted 1965), 239ff., with reference to F. Delitzsch.

82. *Die Auferstehung Jesu*, ⁵1967, 129ff.

83. *ZNW* 60, 1969, 214-19.

84. CD 20.1. Cf. K. H. Rengstorf, op.cit. (n. 80), 131; J. Jeremias, op.cit. (n. 83), 219.

85. Without a determinative in I Chron. 21.1; cf. I. Plein, op.cit. (n. 72), 223.

86. The boundaries between title and proper name are fluctuating, see W. Foerster, *TDNT* 7, 153f.

87. See Preisendanz, *PW*, 14, 2, 1930, 1899.

88. See M. Hengel, *Judaism and Hellenism* 1, 297f.

89. For the background of christological titles see *NTS* 17, 1970/71, 391-425 (391f.). Of course 'Christ' and 'Peter' should not simply be put on the same level as 'eschatological proper names'.

90. For a basic study see J. A. Fitzmyer, 'Der semitische Hintergrund des neutestamentlichen Kyriostitels', in *Jesus Christus in Historie und Theologie: Festschrift H. Conzelmann*, 1975 , 267-98.

91. But note Fitzmyer's remark, op.cit., 297: 'Nevertheless, we cannot simply rule out the idea that the title Kyrios, when used of Jesus, implies a transcendence which puts Jesus on a level with Yahweh, in a kind of "equality", even if this does not amount to an identification, for he is not *'abbā'*, "Father".' I would prefer to speak of an 'assimilation' of the exalted one to God encouraged by Ps. 110.1.

92. See W. Kramer (n. 1), 19-44, on the 'pistis' formula and the qualifications made in criticism by K.Wengst, *Christologische Formeln und Lieder des Urchristentums*, 1972, 78ff., 92ff.; M. Hengel, *The Atonement*, 1981, 33ff.

93. *The Atonement*, 57ff.

94. Gal. 1.12 and on this P. Stuhlmacher, op.cit. (n. 16), 71.

95. See N. A. Dahl, 'The Crucified Messiah', in *The Crucified Messiah and other Essays*, Minneapolis 1974, 10-36, 161ff., 167-9.

96. But see the so-called *Testimonium Flavianum*, the Christian interpolation, *Antt.* XVIII, 63: ὁ Χριστός οὗτος ἦν. For the tradition history of the various attempts at reconstruction see A. -M. Dubarlé, 'Le témoignage de Josèphe sur Jésus', *RB* 80, 1973, 481-513. He follows the version of Jerome and of Michael Syrus (495-511): *credebatur esse Christus*. For the bibliography see A. Schalit, *Zur Josephus-Forschung*, Darmstadt 1973, 417-19; there is a summary

account by P. Winter in E. Schürer, *The Jewish People in the Age of Jesus Christ* I, Edinburgh 1973, 428-41.

5. Hymns and Christology

1. H. Lietzmann, *A History of the Early Church*, I, *The Beginnings of the Christian Church*, ET ²1949, 147.

2. Ibid.

3. A. Schlatter, *Paulus, der Bote Jesu*, Stuttgart ⁴1969, 383.

4. Cf. I Cor. 14.15: ψαλῶ τῷ πνεύματι, ψαλῶ δὲ καὶ τῷ νῷ. For this see also Test.Job chs. 48-52.

5. In addition to this the Septuagint only has the relatively rare term ἄσμα, which does not appear in the earliest Christian literature.

6. O.Hofius, *Der Christushymnus Phil. 2, 6-11*, WUNT 17, 1976, 8f., 54f., 65f., has convincingly demonstrated that the closing doxology Phil. 2.11 is a quite essential and original element of the hymn.

7. The preceding admonition καὶ μὴ μεθύσκεσθε οἴνῳ, ἐν ᾧ ἐστιν ἀσωτία, may be connected with a defence against the festive practices of Dionysian thiasoi and the drinking customs of pagan cultic associations.

8. R. Deichgräber, *Gotteshymnus und Christushymnus in der frühen Christenheit*, SUNT 5, 1967, 60f., 207f., etc.

9. See K. -P. Jörns, *Das hymnische Evangelium*, SNT 5, 1971, 178ff.

10. Hofius, *Christushymnus*, 80.

11. Ps. 2.7; Deut. 32.43; Ps. 104.4; 45.7f.; 102.26ff.; 110.1, in each case in the Septuagint version.

12. The christological interpretation of Ps. 8 is, of course, connected with the υἱὸς ἀνθρώπου in v.5b. The statement by E. Grässer, 'Beobachtungen zum Menschensohn in Heb 2,6', in *Jesus und der Menschensohn, Festschrift Anton Vögtle*, ed. R. Pesch and R. Schnackenburg, Freiburg 1975, 412f., that 'the writer to the Hebrews did not read and interpret Ps. 8, seldom (?!) given a christological interpretation in earliest Christianity, in a messianic perspective but in an eschatological one', is as misleading as his conjecture that here the author is arguing 'by means of the (gnostic) anthropos and συγγένεια doctrines' (411). As though Messiah and heavenly Son of Man were opposites! Chronologically 'pre-Christian' Gnosticism should be left on one side. It is a figment of the imagination of some exegetes and historians of religion.

13. The theme of the connection of enthronement at the right hand of God from Ps. 110.1 with the subjection of all things according to Ps. 8.7 also recurs in a credal hymnic form in Polycarp 2.1f.:

> Believing in him who raised our Lord Jesus Christ from the dead
> and giving him glory and a throne at his right hand,
> to whom he subjected all things in heaven and on earth,
> to whom all that breathes pays homage,
> who is coming as a judge of living and dead.

For the influence of Ps. 8.7 cf. also Phil. 3.21; Justin, *Apology* 40,1, and in a different form, Athenagoras, *Suppl.* 18, 2.

14. We also find the high priest Christ as intercessor and helper in I Clement 36 in a text with a liturgical shape. There is also a quotation from Ps. 110.1 at the end. Contrary to the interpretation by G. L. Cockerill, 'Heb. 1.1-4, I Clem. 36.1-6 and the High Priest Title', *JBL* 97, 1978, 437-40, I Clement is not simply dependent on Heb. 7. Behind it is an earlier high priestly tradition which both have in common.

15. Mark 12.36 = Matt. 22.44; I Cor. 15.25-27.

16. For the connection between the 'Son of Man' and 'sitting at the right hand of God', see Mark 14.62 = Matt. 26.64; Luke 22.69; cf. Acts 7.55f.; Barn. 12.10f. (where the designation as 'son of a man' is rejected); Hegesippus (Eusebius, *HE* 2, 23, 13). See D. M. Hay, *Glory at the Right Hand. Psalm 110 in Early Christianity*, *JBL* MS 18, Nashville 1973, 108f.

17. Cf. Heb. 4.16; Rom. 5.2; Eph. 2.18; 3.12; Heb. 10.19, 22. Cf. *The Son of God*, 77ff.

18. I Cor. 16.22; Rev. 22.20; Didache 10.6.

19. The investigation by G. Schille, *Frühchristliche Hymnen*, Berlin 1965, is a deterrent example of an early Christian 'panhymnology'.

20. *Agnostos Theos*, [4]1956, 177ff., 201ff., 240ff., 250ff. Cf. J. Kroll, *Die christliche Hymnodik bis zu Klemens von Alexandreia*, Darmstadt [2]1968, 8ff.

21. For the hymns of the 'heretics' see J. Kroll, *Hymnodik*, 82ff. The Muratorian Canon, lines 82ff., reports that the Marcionites used a *novus psalmorum liber*. Cf. A. v. Harnack, *Marcion*, Darmstadt 1960, 175. Cf. also J. Kroll, op.cit., 38: 'The orthodox circles regarded this hymnody (viz., of the heretics) as too modern and too secular and wanted to stop the people once and for all from being poisoned by the heretical spirit, by prohibiting in principle all non-biblical hymns from their circles.'

22. Cf. e.g. CH 1, 31; 5, 10ff.; 13, 17-21, etc. For the last hymn see the brilliant analysis by G. Zuntz, *Opuscula selecta*, Manchester 1972, 150-177, who refers to the Septuagint parallels (167ff.).

23. I. Elbogen, *Der jüdische Gottesdienst in seiner geschichtlichen Entwicklung*, Hildesheim [4]1962, 502ff., on the song and 208ff. on the *piyyut*. It should be noted here that the reading from scripture and prayer were also presented in exalted, cantillated form. For further details see J. Heinemann, *Prayer in the Talmud*, SJ 9, 1977, 139ff.

24. W. Bauer, 'Der Wortgottesdienst der ältesten Christen', in id., *Aufsätze und kleine Schriften*, Tübingen 1977, 155-209, esp. 171ff.

25. See E. Werner, 'Musical Aspects of the Dead Sea Scrolls', *The Musical Quarterly* 43, 1957, 21-37; H. Haag, 'Das liturgische Leben der Qumrangemeinde', *ALW* 10, 1967, 78-109; S. Talmon, 'The Emergence of Institutionalized Prayer in Israel in the Light of the Qumran Literature', in *Qumrân. Sa piété, sa théologie et son milieu*, BETL 46, 1978, 265-84, 274ff.

26. Ps. 51.1; cf. Ps. 40.4; 1QH 9.10f.; 11.4: 'Thou gavest hymns of praise into my mouth and songs of praise to my tongue.'

27. J. A. Sanders, 'The Psalms Scroll of Qumran Cave 11', in *DJDJ* IV, 1965, 91f.: 11QPs[a]DavComp.

28. J. Wellhausen, *Einleitung in die drei ersten Evangelien*, [2]1911, 150.

29. Cf. O. Betz, *Offenbarung und Schriftforschung in der Qumransekte*, WUNT 6, 1960, 76f.

30. Eusebius, *HE*, 2, 23, 14.

31. R. Bultmann, ἀγαλλιάομαι etc., in *TDNT* 1, 1964, 19.

32. See H. Gese, 'Psalm 22 und das Neue Testament. Der älteste Bericht vom Tode Jesu und die Entstehung des Herrenmahles', in id., *Von Sinai zum Zion. Alttestamentliche Beiträge zur biblischen Theologie*, BEvTh 64, 74, 180-201.

33. See above, n. 4.

34. See *The Son of God*, ET 1976, 66ff.

35. See my outline, 'Jesus als messianischer Lehrer der Weisheit und die Anfänge der Christologie', in *Sagesse et Religion. Colloque de Strasbourg (Oct.1976)*, Paris 1979, 147-88.

36. Pliny the Younger, *Ep.*, 10, 96, 7.

37. G. von Rad, *Wisdom in Israel*, ET London and Nashville 1972, 48f.

6. *Luke the Historian and the Geography of Palestine*

1. *Petrus* (Typescript dissertation, Heidelberg l966), 48, referring to H.Conzelmann, *The Theology of St Luke*, ET London 1960, '18ff. passim'. Similarly, most recently, G. Lüdemann, *Paulus der Heidenapostel I: Studien zur Christologie*, FRLANT 125, Göttingen 1980, 3l n. 38: 'There are substantial doubts as to whether Luke is a reliable historian given his ignorance of the geography of Palestine, the main scene for his church history.' In his often unqualified attacks on Luke the author only shows his inability to pass a reliable historical judgment on ancient texts.

2. Op.cit., 18-94: 'Part One: Geographical Elements in the Composition of Luke's Gospel'; 13: 'His acquaintance with Palestine is . . . in many respects imperfect.' More sharply 18 n.: 'At all events the variations in information about the Jordan in Luke arise from the fact that Luke has no personal knowledge of the country.' On Luke 17.11, 'The expression indicates that Luke imagines that Judaea and Galilee are immediately adjacent and that Samaria lies alongside them' (69). I find improbable the hypothesis that there is a fixed christological scheme behind Luke's inaccurate geography. This can only be read into the text with a degree of imagination. The picture sketched out by W. Marxsen, *Introduction to the New Testament*, Philadelphia 1970, 160, 'According to Luke's geographical conceptions Judaea (alongside the Mediterranean) and Galilee (to the East) are immediate neighbours . . . Samaria is thought of as being north of the two territories', turns into a caricature. For criticism of Conzelmann see H.- M. Schenke and K. M. Fischer, *Einleitung in die Schriften des NT* II, Gütersloh 1979, 132, and I. H. Marshall, *The Gospel of Luke*, Exeter 1978, 198f., on Luke 4.44; 650 on Luke 17.11. See also below, nn. 5, 28, 123: wrong combinations of names of places and provinces occur relatively frequently in ancient historians.

3. 'Gospel Geography, Fiction, Fact and Central Section', *JBL* 57, l938, 51-66.

4. *Theology of St Luke*, 19 n. 1.

5. Strabo, *Geography* 16, 2, 16-46, pp. 754-65. M. Stern, *Greek and Latin*

Authors on Jesus and Judaism I, Jerusalem 1974, 288-311, nos. 112-15 gives a selection relating to Jewish territory. Strabo 16, 2, 16 = 754 makes the Antilebanon begin at Sidon and has the inhabitants of Arados travelling on the Lycus and the Jordan in ships, presumably confusing the Jordan with the Orontes (Stern, *Authors*, 289). According to Strabo, Phoenicia is a narrow coastal strip extending from Orthosia to Pelusium (!), 'the interior lying behind this as far as the Arabians, between Gaza and the Antilebanon, is called Judaea' (16, 2, 21 = 756). At Joppa the coastline coming from Egypt, which has previously run in an easterly direction, takes a turn to the north; the city is said to be situated at such a height that one can see Jerusalem from it. Gadara in Transjordan is confused with Gadaris (= Gezer) captured by the Jews (16, 2, 28f., cf.41f., 45 = 758f., 764) as is the Dead Sea with the Sirbonian Sea east of Pelusium. Jerusalem is said to lie close to the sea. The main places (or territories), 'Galilee, Jericho, Philadelphia and Samaria' (note the sequence) are inhabited by a mixed population of Egyptians, Arabians and Phoenicians (16, 2, 34 = 760, 763).

6. *Hist.nat.* 5.66-73; Stern, *Authors* I, 468ff. no. 204.

7. *Annals* 12, 54, 2; Stern, *Authors* II, Jerusalem 1980, 76ff., no. 288. Cf. *Hist.* 5, 6, 1; Stern, *Authors* II, 19 no. 280: Judaea is bounded on the south by Egypt, on the east by the Arabians, on the west by the Phoenicians and the sea. The miraculous river Belius (5, 7, 2), which is said to flow into the Jewish (Dead?) Sea, is in fact outside Judaea near Acco-Ptolemais, cf. Pliny, *Hist.nat.* 5.75; 36, 190f., and Josephus, *BJ* 2, 189ff.; see Stern, *Authors*, II, 45f.

8. *Geographia* 5, 15, 1-7 (Müller) = 5, 16, 1-10 (Nobbe); see Stern, *Authors* II, 166ff., no. 137a, also 163 and M. Linke, 'Syrien und Palästina in der Karte des Ptolemäus', WZ Halle-Wittenberg 14, 1964, 473-77.

9. Judaea: *Ep. Arist.* 115-18; the Temple and Jerusalem, 83-91, 100-7.

10. In Josephus, *Contra Apionem* 1, 196f.: the Temple is said to be in the middle of the city; similarly Tacitus, *Hist.* 5, 8, 1. Cf. also the imaginary description of the water supplies of Jerusalem in the earlier Philo, according to Eusebius, *Praeparatio evangelica* 9, 37, 1-3 (GCS 43, 1, pp. 546f.) = A. -M. Denis, 'Fragmenta pseudepigraphorum quae supersunt Graeca ', in M.Black (ed.), *Apocalypsis Henochi Graece*, A. -M. Denis, *Fragmenta pseudepigraphorum quae supersunt Graeca*, Leiden 1970, 204.

11. *De prov.* 2, 107, = Eusebius, *Praeparatio evangelica* 8, 14, 64 (GCS 43, 1, p. 477): 'There is a city of Syria by the sea called Ashkelon; when I came into this city on the occasion of a journey to my ancestral sanctuary, to pray and to sacrifice there . . .' For knowledge of this temple see I. Heinemann, 'Philo von Alexandrien', *PW* XX, 1, 1941, col. 3: '. . . that his description is only correct in so far as it refers to the peribolos of marble and the cedar table and the inner enclosures. Everything else is wrong, false, derived from the description of the tent of meeting in the Old Testament or by transference from the building and arrangement of Greek temples to Jewish ones.' Cf. id., *Philons griechische und jüdische Bildung* (reprinted Hildesheim 1973), 17: 'Doctrinaire people – and Philo is one of these – are taught by life only what they already know from books or talk.' I would not condemn Luke as severely

as this, but certainly he is a 'tendentious historian' who deals selectively with reality.

12. There is urgent need for an assessment of Josephus as a geographer of Palestine. For individual details see now C. Möller and G. Schmitt, *Siedlungen Palästinas nach Flavius Josephus*, TAVOB 14, Wiesbaden 1976. Among other points see the description of Galilee, Peraea, Samaria and Judaea: 3.35-58; Lake Gennesaret: 3.506-521; the Dead Sea: 4, 477f; Jerusalem and the temple: 5, 136-257. Cf. also *Antt.* 5.80-87: the division of the land among the twelve tribes. In all probability, for the *Bellum Judaicum* Josephus could refer to Roman military commentaries, cf. A. Schlatter, *Zur Topographie und Geschichte Palästinas*, Stuttgart 1893, 348ff. (I am indebted to G. Schmitt for this reference.) See above all his concluding verdict, 360: 'It is strange that he is accurate where he was not present and inaccurate where he was.'

13. Cf. F. -M. Abel, 'Topographie des campagnes Maccabéennes', *RB* 32, 1923, 495-521; 33, 1924, 201-17, 371-87; 34, 1925, 194-216; 35, 1926, 296-222, 510-533. Cf. also B. Bar-Kochva, *The Battles of the Hasmonaeans. The Times of Judas Maccabaeus*, Jerusalem 1980, 139ff., 353ff. (in Hebrew).

14. 5.61.3-62.6; 66.1-72.12; the quotation of Josephus (*Antt.* 12, 135f.) from the lost account of the Fifth Syrian War and the victory over Scopas is not very accurate, see p. 206, n. 125 below.

15. O. Cuntz (ed.), *Itineraria Romana*, Leipzig 1929, 149, 5-150, 4; 169, 2-5; 199, 1-4, 11-200, 3 (p. 21, 23, 27) = Stern, *Authors* (n. 5), nos. 470a-471b, 488ff. For the *Itinerarium Burdigalense* see Stern *Authors*, no. 488, on 150, 2.

16. See now R. K. Sherk, 'Roman Geographical Exploration', *ANRW* 11, 1, Berlin and New York 1974, 534-61. Military maps: 558-61: 'Although maps and itineraries may not have been readily available to the general public even by the age of Augustus, at least they become more common by the Late Empire' (560). Note 83: 'Knowing that maps exist is not the same thing as being able to acquire them.' Cf. *Anth.Pal.* 9, 55f. On the subject see also F. Lasserre, 'Geographie', in *KP* 2, Munich 1975, cols.751ff.; 'Karten', *KP* 3, cols.131ff., and Kubitschek, 'Karten', in *PW* X. 2, 1919, col.2100, though he overestimates the significance of maps for schools in antiquity. Such maps are found only in a later time and are primarily maps of the world (col.2133). It is no coincidence that so few maps on papyrus have come down to us. Apart from the fact that the large-scale maps were very inaccurate in detail (see the illustration of Cyprus on the Peutinger Tafel, col.2116), they were above all of military importance.

17. Konrad Miller, *Die Peutinger'sche Tafel*, Stuttgart 1887, reprinted 1962; id., *Itineraria Romana*, Stuttgart ²1929, reprinted 1963; on Palestine, 810ff.; F.Gizinger, 'Peutingeriana', *PW* XIX, 2, 1938, cols. 1405ff. They go back to the famous but inaccurate map of the world by Vipsanius Agrippa, the friend and son-in-law of Augustus, see what is probably the ironical verdict by Strabo (2, 5, 17) and his remarks on the making of maps (2, 5, 10).

18. Cf. M. Avi Yonah, *The Madaba Mosaic Map*, Jerusalem 1954, and H.Fischer, 'Geschichte der Kartographie von Palästina', *ZDPV* 62, 1938, 169-89. For the historical map as the starting point for the *Onomasticon* see Eusebius, *Onomasticon*, GCS (ed. Klostermann), Leipzig 1904, p. 2, 7f.:

ἔπειτα τῆς πάλαι Ἰουδαίας ἀπὸ πάσης βίβλου καταγραφὴν πεποιημένος, καὶ τὰς ἐν αὐτῇ τῶν δώδεκα πυλῶν διαιρῶν κληρου(χία)ς.

19. The verdict by P. Vielhauer, *Geschichte der urchristlichen Literatur*, Berlin and New York 1975, 346f., 'But the incorrect geographical views which can often be noted exclude a Palestinian, and therefore John Mark', expresses a widespread view which for its part displays a certain naivety over geographical knowledge in antiquity. From Jerusalem to Capernaum is about 66 miles as the crow flies; only in exceptional circumstances will someone living in Jerusalem have travelled to the distant province of Galilee, as the *Life* of Josephus shows. With the best will in the world one could not expect exact knowledge here about the borders between the city territories of Tyre and Sidon and Galilee or the Decapolis (cf. Mark 7.31). R. Pesch, *Das Markusevangelium*, Part 1, HTK 1976, 10, begins from quite incorrect historical presuppositions: 'Mark has . . . no personal knowledge of Galilean geography around the Sea of Galilee, as might have been expected from a (travelled) inhabitant of Jerusalem. 'A journey to Rome – from metropolis to metropolis – would be more likely for a better-class Jerusalem dweller – than one to provincial Galilee, which was the back of beyond.' The command to go on pilgrimage to the temple naturally made journeys from Galilee to Jerusalem a matter of course, but travelling the other way round was an exception. The people of Judaea despised the uneducated Galileans and were not particularly interested in this remote province, cf. (H. L. Strack-) P. Billerbeck, *Kommentar zum Neuen Testament aus Talmud und Midrasch*, I, Munich ²1956, 156-9. The geographical question is kept well back in the sadly neglected study by F.G.Lang, ' "Über Sidon mitten ins Gebiet der Dekapolis". Geographie und Theologie in Markus 7, 31', *ZDPV* 94, 1978, 145-60, which shows that Mark was not as naive as all that. Still less, of course, should one follow W.Marxsen, *Introduction* (n. 2), 143, in putting the origins of the Second Gospel in Galilee or the Decapolis; S.Freyne, *Galilee from Alexander the Great to Hadrian 323 B.C.E. to 135 C.E.*, Wilmington 1980, 357ff., is correct here.

20. See the unfortunately rather one-sided account by M. Bachmann, *Jerusalem und der Tempel*, BWANT 9, Stuttgart-Berlin-Köln-Mainz 1980, 67-131.

21. Cf. Luke 3.1 and 23.6.

22. Luke 1.5; 7.17; 23.5; Acts 10.37.

23. Luke 4.44; 5.17; Acts 1.8; 9.31; 11.29; 12.19; 15.1; 20.10; 26.20; 28.21. In Luke 1.65; 2.4; 21.21; the old hill country of Judah is meant. For Caesarea see n. 99 below.

24. Luke 6.17; Acts 1.8; 8.1.

25. Cf. Luke 1.39.

26. See now M. Bachmann, *Jerusalem* (n. 20), 274ff., etc.

27. Luke 9.52; 17.ll, l6.

28. E. Schweizer, *Das Evangelium nach Lukas*, NTD 3, Göttingen 1982, 177. For the conclusions of Conzelmann and his followers, which go much too far, see n. 2 above. I. H. Marshall, *The Gospel of Luke* (n. 2), 650, considers various other possibilities. For the problem of the sequence see below p. 206 n. 125.

29. Still the best is the brief but full survey in A. v. Harnack, *Beiträge zur*

Einleitung in das N.T., III, *Die Apostelgeschichte*, Leipzig 1908, 69-80. The large but somewhat laborious work by M. Bachmann, *Jerusalem* (n. 20), is unfortunately limited to the temple, Jerusalem and the term Judaea.

30. M. Bachmann (n. 20), 132ff., 171ff.

31. See pp. 61f.

32. It is only mentioned in 9.31, to some degree *en passant* (see the note below). It is striking that Paul, too, speaks only of Jerusalem (Rom. 15.19, 20f., 30; I Cor. 16.3; Gal. 1.17f.; 2.1) or Judaea (Rom. 15.31; II Cor. 1.16; Gal. 1.22; I Thess. 2.14). The communities in Galilee no longer seem to have been significant, so we know nothing more about them.

33. Cf. Mark 13.10; 14.9; 16.15; Matt. 28.19; Luke 24.47; cf. also I Clem. 42.3f.; Hermas 69.2 (*Sim.* 8, 3, 2); Aristides, *Apology* 15.2 (Goodspeed 19); Justin, *Apol.* 31.7; 39.1ff. following the quotation of Isa. 2.3f.; 45.5; 50.12; *Dial.* 53.5; 109.1. There are further partly apocryphal traditions in E. Hennecke-W. Schneemelcher -R. McL. Wilson, *New Testament Apocrypha* II, London 1965, 25ff. This 'world-wide' universal programme of mission primarily based on Isaianic texts may in the last resort go back to Paul, see above, p. 52. The other early Christian missionaries – in my view including Peter – took it over from him, cf. M.Hengel, *Acts and the History of Earliest Christianity*, London and Philadelphia 1979, 93f., 97f. By contrast, the deutero-Pauline tradition, like Luke, can stress the universal influence of Pauline preaching: Col. 1.23; I Tim. 4.17; cf. also I Clement 5.7. Cf. O. Bauernfeind, *Kommentar und Studien zur Apostelgeschichte*, ed. V. Metelmann, Tübingen 1980, 337ff.

34. Against E. Haenchen, *The Acts of the Apostles*, 144, and H. Conzelmann, *Die Apostelgeschichte*, HNT 7, Tübingen ²1972, 27.

35. See C. Burchard, *Der dreizehnte Zeuge. Traditions- und kompositionsgeschichtliche Untersuchung zu Lukas' Darstellung der Frühzeit des Paulus*, FRLANT 103, Göttingen 1970, 174: 'Paul is the only witness who travels around and the only one who appears in person before all the audience mentioned in Acts 1.8.' Luke may very well have been familiar with 'the theme of the spread of the apostles throughout the world, which has become determinative of the historical view of the early church.' If he 'interprets the farewell tradition . . . as a promise of their being witnesses to the ends of the earth' (Acts 1.8), but not as a sending out, and if he has the apostles remaining in Jerusalem and subsequently makes them fade out of the picture, this must be a deliberate restriction of their role' (175).

36. Isa. 8.9; 48.20; 49.6; 62.11; I Macc. 3.9; cf. Acts 13.47, where Paul refers Isa. 49.6 to himself and Barnabas.

37. Against H. Conzelmann, *Apostelgeschichte* (n. 34), loc. cit.; see J. Roloff, *Die Apostelgeschichte*, NTD 5, Göttingen 1981, 23. Similarly already W. M. L. De Wette and F. Overbeck, *Kurze Erklärung der Apostelgeschichte*, Leipzig ⁴1870, 6.

38. W. C. van Unnik, *Sparsa Collecta* I, Leiden 1973, 400. He points out that Pompey 'had fought against Sertorius in Spain for many years before he came to the East in 66 BC and captured Jerusalem in 63 BC'. Ps. Sol. 8.15 could be a specific reference to this. Cf. now also G. Schneider, *Die Apostelgeschichte* I, HTK 5, Freiburg-Basle-Vienna 1980, 203 n. 41.

39. See above, pp. 1ff. Also A. Lindemann, *Paulus in ältesten Christentum*, BHT 58, Tübingen 1979, 68 n. 117.

40. Cf. Luke 19.47; 20.1; 21.5, 37f. Conzelmann, *Theology* (n. 1), 78, sees the Cleansing of the Temple as a 'means of taking possession' which in contrast to the original in Mark of itself no longer has any eschatological significance.

41. Cf. Luke 24.52; Acts 2.46; 3.1ff.; 5.20ff.; 5.42, and M. Bachmann, *Jerusalem* (n. 20), 160ff. (167 n. 99), 279f. Following B. Reicke and T. Zahn, among others, he sees the οἶκος in Acts 2.2 as a place in the sanctuary. Cf. Isa. 6.1 LXX καὶ πλήρης ὁ οἶκος τῆς δόξας αὐτοῦ, and 6.4 καὶ ὁ οἶκος ἐπλήσθη καπνοῦ with Acts 2.2 . . . καὶ ἐπλήρωσεν ὅλον τὸν οἶκον. However, the addition οὗ ἦσαν καθήμενοι tells against the Temple. Possibly the original had this in mind, whereas Luke related the whole event to the 'upper room' (1.13). The subsequent assembly of festival pilgrims from all over the world for the Feast of Weeks can only be imagined as in the outer court of the Temple, which of course in Luke's view was not part of the ἱερόν, see above, p. 105. As elsewhere in Luke, the account does not give us a really clear idea.

42. *Antt.* 20, 221; cf. *BJ* 5, 185; cf. T. A. Busink, *Der Tempel von Jerusalem* II, Leiden 1980. 1198f. A. Schlatter, *Zur Topographie* (n. 12), 197ff., wanted to put it on the east side of the inner sanctuary, in order to avoid the difficulty with the 'beautiful gate'.

43. Cf. the plural αἱ θύραι, Acts 21.30; Josephus, *BJ* 5.201ff., *Antt.* 15.410f.; Middot 1.3f.

44. M. Middot 2.3, cf. *Antt.* 15, 410f.; Middot 1.3f. Also Middot 1.4; 2.6; M. Yoma 3.10; M. Shekalim 6.3.; M.Sota 1.5; M. Negaim 14.8. See also P. Billerbeck, *Kommentar* (n. 19) II, 623, and the literature in G. Schneider, *Apostelgeschichte* (n. 38), 300 nn. 30,31. Also the surveys by A. Schalit, *König Herodes*, Berlin 1969, 387ff.; T. A. Busink, *Tempel* II (n. 42), 1079ff. For Nicanor see also *OGIS* 599 and J. B. Frey, *CIJ* II, 1256.

45. Zuckermandel (ed.), reprinted Jerusalem 1962/63, 183. Cf. the heightening of detail in jYoma 2,8,41a line 40: *hyh mshyb wywtr yph mšl zhb*, 'it shone and was finer than gold'. In both cases, of course, gold is used only as a comparison.

46. *BJ* 2, 411; 6, 293: it was made of bronze and was particularly heavy, needing twenty men to open it.

47. *BJ* 5, 204; cf. 201: more valuable than the other silvered and gilded gates of the Temple. R.'J. Forbes, *Studies in Ancient Technology*, VIII, Leiden ²1971, 275 conjectured that the door was made of more valuable brass. See also M.Hengel, *Achilleus in Jerusalem*, SAH 1982, 1 n. 106.

48. 'Die ΘΥΡΑ oder ΠΥΛΗ ΩΡΑΙΑ Act. 3, 2 u. 10', ZNW 7, 1906, 51-68; P. Billerbeck, *Kommentar* II (n. 19), 620-5, and G. Dalman, *Orte und Wege Jesu*, Gütersloh ³1924, 315, agree.

49. *Herodes* (n. 44), 393ff.; cf. also T. Busink, *Tempel* II (n. 42), 1080ff.

50. O. Holtzmann, 'Tore und Terrassen des herodianischen Tempels', ZNW 9, 1908, 71-4; id., 'Middot', in *Die Mischna*, V, 10, Berlin- New York 1913, 15, 26ff., 29f.; E. Stauffer, 'Das Tor des Nikanor', ZNW 44, 1952, 44-66; J. Jeremias, πύλη, TDNT 6, 921 n. 3; id., *Jerusalem in the Time of Jesus*, ET London 1969, 23f., 128f. C. Kopp, *Die heiligen Stätten der Evangelien*, Regens-

burg 1959, 345, suggested that the 'beautiful gate' was at the east of the Court of the Women and distinguished it from the Nicanor Gate, between the Courtyard of the Women and that of the Men; similarly now B. Mazar, *Der Berg des Herrn*, Bergisch Gladbach 1979, 110ff. For discussion see also M. Bachmann, *Jerusalem* (n. 20), 292ff. n. 345.

51. For the dating see E. Stauffer, ZNW 44, 1952, 58. The Nicanor ossuary is dated by Sukenik towards the end of the forties on the basis of a coin of Agrippa I and points of style. U. Rappaport, *EJ* 12, 1971, 1133f. suggests a post-Herodian origin 'about the middle of the first century, a generation before the destruction'. We therefore do not know whether the gate was already in existence between AD 30 and 40.

52. For the problem see J. Jeremias, *Jerusalem* (n. 50), 128f., and T. A. Busink, *Tempel* (n. 42), 186, who also refers to 1QSa 2,5-7 and II Sam.5.8 LXX; cf. also 1QM 7,4f. and 11QTemple 45,12, where not only the unclean but even the blind are prohibited from staying in Jerusalem. We know nothing of any prohibition against the lame and the crippled stopping in the inner sanctuary, see G. Dalman, *Orte* (n. 48), 406. Lev. 21.21ff. refers to the Temple service of the priests, but if there were always crippled beggars by the main gate of the inner sanctuary this must have caused considerable disruption to the ordering of the Temple. Certainly we should not suppose that Luke had such concerns; they will have been part of the original Jerusalem legend about Peter. M.Bachmann, *Jerusalem* (n. 20), 295f. n. 345, points to the possibility of outer gates. He connects the adjective ὡραῖος as applied to the temple gate with the first-fruits, because he supposes the word to have a chronological and not an aesthetic significance, referring to the same usage in Philo, *De spec.leg.* 2, 220, and Josephus, *Antt.* 4, 241. Stephanus-Dindorf, *Thesaurus Graecae Linguae* VIII, Paris 1829, 2057ff. says on the use of ὡραῖος in connection with sacrificial terminology: 'idemque ὡραῖα accipi etiam ἐπὶ τὸν καθ᾽ὥραν τελουμένων ἱερόν, et ὡραῖον vocari τό θῦμα τὸ καθ ὥραν . . .' He also refers to the later instances of ὡραῖαι πύλαι as a designation for the church doors between the narthex and the nave proper (col. 2060). They might be dependent on Acts 3.2,11. I cannot discover any pre-Christian instances of the use of ὡραῖος for buildings.

53. *Tempel* II (n. 42), 1185ff., cf. 984f., 1178ff. For a description of the gate see also O. Holtzmann, *Middot* (n. 50), 50f. T. A. Busink further complicates the matter by wanting to extend the enclosed area of the ἱερόν proper as far as the east gate of the outer wall.

54. Ch. 17, see H. Donner, *Pilgerfahrt ins Heilige Land*, Stuttgart 1979, 276 n. 83; C. Kopp, *Stätten* (n. 50), 362f.; T. A. Busink, *Tempel* II (n. 49), 984-9.

55. *Antt.*15, 410; *Middot* 1.3. Cf. T. A. Busink, *Tempel* II (n. 49), 968ff., 1178ff.; B. Mazar, *Berg* (n. 50), 119ff.

56. B. Mazar, *Berg* (n. 50), 121, 126; *Jerusalem Revealed. Archaeology in the Holy City 1968-1974*, Jerusalem 1975, 26ff. According to Sanh. 11.2 even legal sessions took place in one of the gigantic gates giving on to the temple mount.

57. See above, p. 105. Cf. G. Schrenk, τὸ ἱερόν, *TDNT* 3, 234ff. The New Testament texts do not know of the distinction between outer and inner sanctuary which Josephus takes for granted. Which part of the sanctuary is

meant can only be discovered from the context. On the other hand there is usually a distinction between ναός and τὸ ἱερόν.

58. T. Zahn, *Die Apostelgeschichte des Lukas* I, KNT 5, Leipzig-Erlangen ³1922, 147ff.,150; id., *Forschungen zur Geschichte des ntl. Kanons* IX, Leipzig 1916, 251; A. C. Clark, *The Acts of the Apostles*, Oxford 1933, 17, on Acts 3,8-11; K. Lake – H. J. Cadbury, *The Acts of the Apostles* V (*Beginnings* IV, V, London 1933), (479-850) 484; J. Duplacy, *REAug* 2, 1956, 231-42. But see B. M. Metzger, *A Textual Commentary on the Greek NT*, London and New York 1971, 308f., and G. Schneider, *Apostelgeschichte* (n. 38), 303f.: there is a discussion of the various reasons for change.

59. *Apostelgeschichte* (n. 34), 38; similarly E. Haenchen, *The Acts of the Apostles* (n. 34), 189n.12, 204.

60. Cf. G. Schneider, *Apostelgeschichte*(n.38), 300, 303, conjectures that in the pre-Lucan narrative the 'beautiful gate' was identical with the Nicanor Gate and that Luke understood it as a gate which led into the whole Temple area. He was also the first to connect the Hall of Solomon with the miracle story. Cf. already O. Bauernfeind, *Kommentar* (n. 33), 62 on 3.11: 'the whole verse is typical of the carefree way in which Luke often works.'

61. For the offering of the evening *tamid* sacrifice see Pes.5.1: between half-past the eighth and half-past the ninth hour. See also Josephus, *Antt.* 14.65; περὶ ἐνάτην ὥραν ἱερουργούντων ἐπὶ τοῦ βωμοῦ. For the evening sacrifice as a time of prayer see already Dan. 9.21 and Judith 9.1. Cf. M. Bachmann, *Jerusalem* (n. 20), 346ff., 357ff., on the primitive community's prayer in the Temple.

62. Cf. Sir. 50.11ff. and P. Billerbeck, *Kommentar* II (n. 19), 57ff.

63. Yoma 2, 1-4; Tamid 1, 2; 2, 5; 3, 1; T. Yoma 1, 10, 12f. (Zuckermandel [n. 45] 181); P. Billerbeck, *Kommentar* II (n. 19), 57f.

64. P. Billerbeck, *Kommentar* II (n. 19), 696ff.

65. M. Hengel, *The Atonement*, London 1981, 55,57; see above, pp. 23f.

66. P. Billerbeck, *Kommentar* II (n. 19), 761f.; M. Hengel, *Die Zeloten*, Leiden ²1976, 219ff.: E. Schürer, G. Vermes, F. Millar and M. Black, *The History of the Jewish People in the Age of Jesus Christ* II, Edinburgh 1979, 222. E. Bickerman, *Studies in Jewish and Christian History* II, AGAJU 9, Leiden 1980, 210-24.

67. Cf. Matt. 23.35 and P. Billerbeck, *Kommentar* I (n. 19), 942; and also Josephus, *Antt.* 18.30; M. Hengel, *Zeloten* (n. 66), 189f.

68. *BJ* 5, 242-5. Cf. T. A. Busink, *Tempel* II (n. 49), 1233ff., 1195ff.

69. For Luke and Hellenistic historiography see E. Plümacher, *Lukas als hellenistischer Schriftsteller*, SUNT 9, Göttingen 1972, 80ff.; id., 'Lukas', *PWSuppl* 14, 1974, 255ff. In my view Plümacher's works are the most important contributions to the study of Acts in the German language since Dibelius, because they take research out of the cul-de-sac into which it has been led by the development of Haenchen's theory that Luke was only an edifying writer of devotional theology, more bad than right, with a one-sided redaction-historical perspective. For II Maccabees as the 'Old Testament' parallel to the two-volume work see E.Meyer, *Ursprung und Anfänge des Christentums*, I, Stuttgart-Berlin 1921, 1 n. 1; cf. also H. Cancik, *Mythische und*

historische Wahrheit, SBS 48, Stuttgart 1970, 108ff.: on Hellenistic historiography in the Old Testament.

70. For historiography and rhetoric see E. Norden, *Die antike Kunstprosa* I, Darmstadt [3]1979, 79ff.; H. Strassburger, *Die Wesensbestimmung der Geschichte durch die antike Geschichtsschreibung*, Sitzungsberichte der wissenschaftliche Gesellschaft and der J. W. Goethe Universität Frankfurt/Main 5, no. 3, [3]1975, 78ff.: 'that history can have its complete content of reality and be fruitful only as *experience*' (78). On the definition of *mimesis*: 'the potential living truth of images which allows the reader to be grasped by events as in the theatre. The idea of mimesis is . . . an appropriate means of historical realization in some circumstances even when faithfulness to the facts is replaced by fictitious or potential reality, given that the writer is working only with an authentic experience of life.' See E. Plümacher, 'Die Apostelgeschichte als historische Monographie', in J. Kremer (ed.) *Les Actes des Apôtres*, BETL 48, Gembloux-Lyons 1979, 457-66, and his reference to Cicero's letter to Lucceius, *Epp. ad fam. 5.12*, with its invitation to write a special historical study on Cicero's activity as a politician *quasi fabulam rerum eventorumque nostrorum*(6). 'My career will also give you abundant variety, not completely without charm, and could entrance people who read it in your account. Nothing is better suited to captivate the reader than the changing tides of events and fortunes': *multam etiam casus nostri varietatem tibi in scribendo suppeditabunt plenam cuiusdam voluptatis, quae vehementer animos hominum legendo te scriptore tenere possit. Nihil est enim aptius ad delectationem lectoris quam temporum varietatis fortunaeque vicissitudines* (*Epp.ad fam.* 5,12,4). Luke writes about Paul in a comparable way.

71. Critical scholarship has long and rightly demonstrated that it is historically unlikely that Paul, mistreated (Acts 21.31f.) and in fetters (Acts 21.33), guarded by soldiers, could have quietened the raging crowd (Acts 21.34; 22.22) with one of those gestures of the hand so beloved of Luke and by his speech 'in Hebrew' (Acts 21.40; 22.2). For Luke's story, Paul's account of himself before the people at this dramatic climax is absolutely necessary as testimony by the one called by Christ to the people of Jerusalem and the pilgrims to the festival (Acts 22.15, 21).

72. *Nat. hist.* 5.70, see M. Stern, *Authors* I (n. 5), 469f., nos. 477f. Cf. id., in *Jerusalem in the Second Temple Period, A. Schalit Memorial Volume*, Jerusalem 1980, 257-70 (in Hebrew); H. Heubner and W. Fauth, *Kommentar zu P. Cornelius Tacitus: Die Historien*, Bd V, Heidelberg 1982, 109.

73. Luke 19.37, 41ff.; 21.24. Cf. also David's lament in Josephus, *Antt.* 7, 203 and II Kings 15.30.

74. Luke 19.45. According to the Mishnah, Ber. 9.5, the Temple mount, i.e. the forecourt, was not to be trodden by people dressed for travelling with staff, sandals and purse, and the dust of travel on their feet. However, Luke, the Greek author, need not have troubled himself over this at all.

75. Cf. G. Schneider, *Apostelgeschichte* (n. 38), 71f.

76. G. Lohfink, *Die Himmelfahrt Jesus. Untersuchungen zu den Himmelfahrts- und Erhöhungstexten bei Lukas*, SANT 26, Munich 1971, 207. G. Schneider, *Apostelgeschichte* (n. 38), 205, agrees.

77. *'Amwās* and *Mōṣā/Qalūniya*. For the two places see C.Möller and G.Schmitt, *Siedlungen* (n. 12), 15ff. (and the bibliography). The reasons given there for identifying it with the second place are illuminating: 'should be added that the distances of thirty (Josephus) and sixty (Luke 24.13) stadia are both round numbers which are used frequently and stand for one and two hours' travelling: *Qalūniya* is only four miles from Jerusalem (the Jaffa gate). For the distance between Jerusalem and Αμμαους 1 one would have to take 150 stadia (as a round - and also more accurate – number) rather than 160 stadia (Origen's text), and it would be remarkable if the traditional round number had arisen by the accidental omission of 100.' E. Schürer, G. Vermes, etc., 1 (n. 66), 512f. n. 142 arrive at a similar solution: 'Thus, our Emmaus is most probably identical with that mentioned in the NT (Luke 24.13), even though the distances in both cases . . . are only roughly correct.' On the other hand we cannot completely rule out an error on the part of Luke or his original. Details of distance are often questionable in the ancient geographers.

78. J. B. Frey, *CIJ* 2, no. 1404; see below, p. 17.

79. See J. Jeremias, *Heiligengräber in Jesu Umwelt*, Göttingen 1958, 56-60. For Acts 2.29 see also 129. See also ARN vs.A. c.35, ed. Schechter, p. 104: there was no tomb in Jerusalem 'apart from the tombs of the House of David and the prophetess Huldah'(= Vs. B c.39 p.107 also adds the tomb of Isaiah).

80. The description of the tomb in Luke 23.53b also appears in John 19.4b. By contrast the Fourth Gospel in 19.20, 41, presupposes further knowledge of the place of the crucifixion and the tomb which could rest on earlier tradition.

81. Presumably identical with Ramathaim. For the somewhat uncertain identification with *Rentîs* about fourteen kilometres north-east of Lydda see C. Möller and G. Schmitt, *Siedlungen* (n. 12), 158f.

82. E. Haenchen, *Acts* (n. 34), 243, remarks on the Lucan phrase τῶν πέριξ πόλεων, 'there are of course no real πόλεις in the vicinity' and in n. 4 goes on to conclude: 'Luke had no exact ideas of the geography of Palestine.' The problem is how we understand the term πέριξ, which appears only here in the New Testament. In *BJ* 4, 241, Josephus speaks similarly of the 'filth and offscouring of the whole land' which, after it has vented its madness first of all ἐν ταῖς πέριξ κώμαις τε καὶ πόλεσι 'in the end secretly streamed into the holy city'. As A. Loisy, *Les Actes des Apôtres*, Paris 1920, reprinted Frankfurt 1973, 27, already observes, the author is thinking 'sans doute . . . aux villes de Judée'. Cf. also *Vita* 81: Josephus conquered the Syrians, who inhabited τὰς πέριξ πόλεις (around Galilee) and took plunder from them. For the stereotyped experession see *BJ* 2, 505, 514, 528; 3, 134, 430; 4, 438, 443, 488 etc.: αἱ πέριξ κῶμαι is a phrase from later *koine*, see Liddell and Scott, s.v., which means that the villages are under political control. Luke uses πόλεις instead of the more frequent κῶμαι in Acts 5.16 because this is more appropriate to the status of Jerusalem as the capital of Judaea; moreover in Hebrew 'city' and 'village' (*'îr* and *qiryā*) are largely interchangeable. Cf. A.Schlatter, *Der Evangelist Matthäus*, Stuttgart 1948, 48, on Josephus, rabbinic texts and the NT. For the formula see also Dio Chrysostom 34, 27, of cities with equal rights and indeed hostile cities. On the subject see also Tacitus,

Hist. 5.8.1: *magna pars Iudaeae vicis dispergitur; habent et oppida*, also H. Heubner and W. Fauth (n. 72), 106.

83. See above, p. 42; *Acts and the History . . .*, 78f.

84. O. Bauernfeind, *Kommentar* (n. 33), 122.

85. These facts were known to any Greek with some degree of education. The Greek reader must therefore already have seen here an indirect reference to the fulfilment of Acts 1.8:
Homer, *Odyssey*, 1.22ff.:

ἀλλ᾽ ὁ μὲν Αἰθίοπας μετεκίαθε τηλόθ᾽ ἐόντας,
Αἰθίοπας, τοὶ διχθὰ δεδαίαται, ἔσχατοι ἀνδρῶν,
οἱ μὲν δυσομένου Ὑπερίονος οἱ δ᾽ ἀνιόντος.

'Now he went away to the distant Ethiopians – they are the people at the edge (of the earth); their people is divided: among some Hyperion rises and among others he sets.' See Herodotus 3, 25, 114; Ephoros, *FGrHist* 70F 30 a/b = Strabo 1, 2, 28 and Cosmas Indicopleustes, *Top. Christ.* II, p. 117. At the same time the Ethiopians were idealized, see Nicolaus of Damascus, *FGrHist* 90 F 103m = J. Stob., *Anth.* 4, 2, 142 (ed. Hense IV, 157): ἀσκοῦσι δὲ εὐσέβειαν καὶ δικαιοσύνην.

86. *Adv.haer.* 3, 12, 8; 4, 22, 2.

87. See W. C. van Unnik, 'Der Befehl an Philippus', in *Sparsa Collecta* I, NTSuppl 29, Leiden 1973, 328-39.

88. Strabo 16, 2, 30, ἔνδοξός ποτε γενομένη (sc. ἡ πόλις = Gaza) κατεσπασμένη δ᾽ ὑπὸ Ἀλεξάνδρου καὶ μένουσα ἐρημῶς. Here the Greek reader thought of Alexander the Great. In reality the city which he destroyed in 332 BC was quickly rebuilt. So the note refers to the destruction of the place by Alexander Jannaeus in 96 BC after a one-year siege. After the capture of Jerusalem in 63 BC, Gaza was liberated and restored under Gabinius, see M. Stern, *Authors* I (n. 5), 291, 293f., and E. Schürer, G. Vermes et al., II (n. 66), 98ff. (101). The reason for the note by Strabo, who wrote his *Geography* between 7 BC and his death (after AD 23) is that when it was rebuilt under Gabinius the city was constructed rather further south. However, Strabo knows nothing of this new city.

89. For the later legendary 'Philip spring' see H. Donner, *Pilgerfahrt* (n. 54), 63 n. 111; 158f. n. 68; 205, 295 n. 146.

90. The theme of transportation associates Philip with the Old Testament prophets, cf. I Kings 18.12; II Kings 2.16; Ezek. 3.14; 8.3; Bel and the Dragon 36. It continues to have an influence in early Christian prophecy: Hermas 1.3 (*Vis.* 1.1); Eusebius,*HE* 5, 16, 14; the Montanist Theodotus, Mani: the Codex Manichaeus Coloniensis, *ZPapEp* 19, 1975, 51,6ff.; 52.2f.; 55.16ff. etc. Cf. also *Hebr.ev.fragm.* 3 (Origen, *Comm. in Joh.* 2, 12, 87) in Hennecke-Schneemelcher-Wilson, *NT Apocrypha* I (n. 33), 158f.

91. Josephus, *BJ* 2, 266ff.: The Jews 'made the claim that the city belonged to them as its founder was a Jew'; the Greeks pointed out that the statues and temples showed that the city was not Jewish. In the argument the Jews proved to be 'superior in riches and physical strength, the Greeks in the support of the soldiers' (268). L. J. Levine, *Caesarea under Roman Rule*, Leiden

1975, 22, conjectures a numerical superiority of Jews, but this is not justified by the information given by Josephus. According to Josephus, *BJ* 2,457, at the outbreak of the war, 'in a single hour more than 20,000 were killed, so that the whole of Caesarea was without a Jewish population.' Cf. also *Antt.* 20, 355ff., 361: the behaviour of the citizens of Caesarea and Sebaste on the death of Agrippa I.

92. *Vit.proph.*, see T. Schermann, *Propheten- und Apostellegende*, TU 31,3, Leipzig 1907, 55 lines 4f. (I am grateful to my colleague Götz Schmitt for this reference). M. Avi-Yonah, *The Holy Land*, Grand Rapids 1966, referring to Josephus, *BJ* 4, 130, conjectures that at that time Azotus was a Jewish city. However, see n. 97 below. The sources in no way indicate that it was a centre for one of the 24 lay divisions responsible for serving in the temple. Herr Gottfried Reeg of the Tübingen Atlas project has pointed out to me its absence from Talmudic literature.

93. H. Conzelmann, *Apostelgeschichte* (n. 34), 64 ad loc.

94. M. Avi-Yonah, *Land* (n. 91), 149, see Georgii Cyprii, *Descriptio orbis Romani*, ed. H. Gelzer, BT: Leipzig 1890, 52 line 1021; A. H. M. Jones, *The Cities of the Eastern Roman Provinces*, Oxford ²1971. 273, 275.

95. *Leg. ad C.* 200. Cf. 197-206. On this see E. M. Smallwood, *Philonis Alexandrini Legatio ad Caium*, 262ff.; id., *The Jews under Roman Rule*, Leiden 1976, 175. According to Josephus, *BJ* 1, 166, 'the inhabitants readily returned to each (rebuilt) city'; cf. *Antt.* 14, 88. As Azotus was nearer to Gentile Ashkelon, the influence of the non-Jews will have been stronger there than in Jamnia.

96. Cf. Philo, *Leg. ad Caium* 205: the hate of the neighbouring Ashkelonites towards the Jews.

97. Josephus, *BJ* 4,130. Azotus and Jamnia should not be regarded as Jewish places in the same way. It is no coincidence that Josephus mentions Jamnia, with its stronger Jewish stamp, much more frequently above all in the contemporary *BJ* and in the last books of the *Antiquitates*, see C. Möller and G. Schmitt, *Siedlungen* (n. 12), 7f., 97. According to *BJ* 4, 444 Vespasian settled 'pacified' Jews in the Jewish towns of Jamnia and Lydda but evidently not in the more markedly Gentile Azotus. For the history of the two places see E. Schürer, G.Vermes et al., *History* (n. 66), 108ff. For the city territory see M. Avi-Yonah, *Land* (n. 91), 149. It was divided into two at a later period.

98. E. Schürer, G. Vermes et al., *History* II (n. 66), 145ff.; L. J. Levine, *Caesarea* (n. 91), 6-32. Cf. also I. Heinemann, 'Antisemitismus', in *PWSuppl* 5, 1931, 16ff.; U. Rappaport, 'The Jewish Relations and the Revolt against Rome in 66-70 CE', in *The Jerusalem Cathedra* I, 1981, 81-95. For Caesarea as a 'Hellenistic' *polis* see also B. Lifshitz, 'Césaré de Palestine, son histoire et ses institutions', *ANRW* II, 8, 490-518.

99. A. von Harnack, *Beiträge zur Einleitung in das NT*, III, *Die Apostelgeschichte*, Leipzig 1908, 71: 'It is worth noting that Luke is aware that Caesarea is not part of Judaea in the strict sense.' Tacitus, *Hist.* 2, 78, 4, gives the Roman perspective, as seen from Italy. Mucanius goes to Antioch, Vespasian to Caesarea: *illa Suria, hoc Iudaeae caput est*. Cf. also Josephus, *Antt.* 19, 351, quoted below, n. 115.

100. Acts 1.11; 2.7: Γαλιλαῖοι; 4.13: Peter and John: ἄνθρωποι ἀγράμματοι. For the contrast between city and country see M. Hengel, *Zeloten* (n. 66), 335; id., *Judaism and Hellenism* I, 53f.; G. Theissen, *Studien zur Soziologie des Urchristentums*, Tübingen 1979, 142-59.

101. Pliny, *Hist.Nat.* 5.68: *regio per oram Samaria*, see M. Stern, *Authors*, I (n. 5), no. 204 p. 473: 'Samaria seems to have included the coast from somewhere north of Jaffa up to and including Caesarea; see *Antt.* XIX, 351. This was possibly part of the new Roman ordering of the country after Pompey and Gabinius and before Herod. For the Samaritans in Caesarea see L. J. Levine, *Caesarea* (n. 90)., 107ff. Although we have no accounts of Samaritans in Caesarea from the first century, we must assume that there was a Samaritan element in the population from the start. According to the later Pseudo-Clementines the clash between Peter and Simon Magus took place in Caesarea, 'the largest city in Palestine'. *Recogn.* 1, 12, 1ff.; 1.72: Peter is called from Jericho to Caesarea to meet Simon; cf. *Hom.* 1,15,1. See below, p. 209 nn. 140-2. Samaritan elements in the population were to be found scattered throughout the coastal plain, see M. Avi-Yonah, in M. Safrai and M. Stern (eds.), *The Jewish People in the First Century* I, Assen 1974, 107; cf. also H. G. Kippenberg, *Garizim und Synagoge*, RVV XXX, Berlin and New York 1971, 80, 142, 155f., 160.

102. Papias in Eusebius, *HE* 3, 39, 9, cf. the fragment of Philippus Sidetes in F. X v. Funk – K. Bihlmeyer, *Die apostolischen Väter*, Tübingen and Leipzig 1924, 138f. Polycrates of Smyrna, Eusebius, *HE* 3, 31, 2-5; 5, 24, 2; cf. the defence against the Montanist reference to Philip's daughters, *HE* 5,17,3. See T. Zahn, *Forschungen* VI (n. 102), 158-75: 'Philip in Hierapolis'.

103. R. A. Lipsius – M. Bonnet, *Acta Apostolorum Apocrypha* II, Leipzig 1898, 1-90; R. A. Lipsius, *Die apokryphen Apostelgeschichten und Legenden*, Brunswick 1884, II, 2, 5f., 36ff., 40f.; also O. Bardenhewer, *Geschichte der altkirchlichen Literatur* I, Freiburg ²1913, 584; A. Kurfess, 'Zu den Philippusakten', *ZNW* 44, 1952/53, 145-51. For the apocryphal Philip tradition see especially also T. Zahn, *Forschungen zur Geschichte des neutestamentlichen Kanons* VI, Leipzig 1900, 18-27.

104. See already the vivid description by A. Schlatter, *Topographie* (n. 12), 1-43.

105. See F. -M. Abel, *Géographie de la Palestine* I, Paris ³1967, 414f. (415 n. 1).

106. A. Schlatter, *Topographie* (n. 12), 29: 'In the Persian period Lydda had vigorously asserted its Jewish character.' For the history see G. Hölscher, 'Lydda', in *PW* XIII, 2, cols.2120ff. and M. Avi-Yonah, *Land* (n. 91), 226f., index s.v. Lod, Lydda and Diospolis. For the mention in Josephus see C. Möller and G. Schmitt, *Siedlungen* (n. 12), 131f. (and literature there).

107. For the toparchies see A. Schalit, *Herodes* (n. 44), 205-19; Pliny the Elder, *Nat.Hist.* 5, 14, 70 also mentions a toparchy of Jopica whose existence A. Schalit questions, as under Herod Joppa was not legally incorporated in Judaea (209f.). But see Josephus, *BJ* 2, 567: John the Essene as governor of the toparchies of Thamna, Joppa and Emmaus. It is significant that as mixed areas Azotus and Jamnia are not mentioned here (see n. 96 above). For the whole question see also M. Stern, *Authors*, I (n. 2), 476f.

108. For the history of Joppa, see G. Beer, 'Joppe', in *PW* IX, 2, cols.1901f. E. Schürer, G. Vermes et al., *History* II (n. 66), 110ff.; M. Avi-Yonah, *Land* (n. 91), 227, index s. v. Joppe. For Josephus see C. Möller and G. Schmitt, *Siedlungen* (n. 12), 105; A. Schalit, *Herodes* (n. 44), 198ff., 206ff.; *EJ* 9, 1250f.

109. The predominant interpretation of this as a tour of inspection has been challenged by W. Dietrich, *Das Petrusbild der lukanischen Schriften*, BWANT, Stuttgart 1972, 262ff. However, as the spokesman for the community in Jerusalem Peter also had responsibility for the communities in Judaea most closely connected with Jerusalem. For Luke, however, according to 9.31 these together form the one 'church throughout Judaea' (9.31; cf. 11.1, 29; 21.10; 26.20; cf. Luke's Paul in Acts 28.21; cf. II Cor. 1.16; Gal. 1.22; I Thess. 2.14). Further, Peter has to travel alone because the subsequent Cornelius episode, to which the account as a whole is leading up, is connected only with him. Possibly Luke shaped the whole passage on analogy with the activity of the individual 'travelling charismatic' Philip. It is quite unjustified to see as the reason for the journey 'certain happenings in the Jerusalem community' (W. Dietrich, *Petrusbild*, 264). We can hardly say anything about the historical situation of the community in Jerusalem and Judaea before the persecution by Agrippa I. It simply follows from Gal. 1.18f. that James the brother of the Lord already played an important role – as second-in-command (cf. Acts 12.17) – but that Peter's authority was unshaken. For Luke it is only the baptism of the first godfearing Gentile which leads to conflict(Acts 11.1f.).

110. For the 'plain of Sharon', from the Hebrew *šārōn*, flat land, see K. Elliger, *BHHW* III, cols.1673f.; cf. already Josh 12.18, but see also n. 105 above.

111. The old dispute over the 'historicity' of this information is pointless. It may be an anachronism but need not necessarily be so. Auxiliary cohorts could be posted anywhere in the Roman empire according to need, cf. Josephus, *Antt.* 19, 364-6: the problem of posting the Sebaste cohorts. For the 'Italian cohort' and on the occupation of Judaea see T. R. S. Broughton in *Beginnings* V (n. 58), 427-45 (441f.); E. Schürer, G. Vermes et al., *History* I (n. 66), 361ff. (365). The epitaph (loc.cit., n. 54 = *CIL* 13483a) of an *optio* (centurion's auxiliary) Proculus Rabili filius, who came from Philadelphia in Palestine, had served in a *cohors secunda civium Romanorum . . . exercitus Syriaci* and presumably had died on the march of the Syrian army to Italy towards the end of AD 69, indicates the presence of such a cohort in Syria *before* 69. The Philadelphian Proculus son of 'Rabel' (at any rate a Semitic, and presumably a Nabataean name), will probably have begun his service in his homeland, like the people of Sebaste. Finally, a centurion could also be appointed for administrative or other political or police duties, and not just for army service (cf.Acts 27.1). This certainly does not prove the historicity of the information. 'Proofs' in the strict sense are impossible, since our knowledge of Roman troops in Syria and Palestine is simply too small. But those who challenge the detail should not make it too easy for themselves. In mentioning the 'Italian' cohort Luke presumably wanted to portray Cornelius as a Roman and not a Jew. He will be right in the fact that the 'historical' centurion Cornelius, whose existence should not be disputed, had virtually nothing to do with the

severely anti-Jewish people of Sebastene, who stood out among the Gentile population of the country (particularly in Sebaste). For the social position of the centurion see A.N.Sherwin-White, *Roman Society and Roman Law in the New Testament*, Oxford 1963, 154ff., and now B. Dobson, 'The Significance of the Centurion and Primipilaris in the Roman Army and Administration', *ANRW* II, 1, 1974, 392-434. The rank of a centurion was relatively high. To reach it a capable soldier had to have served in the legions and auxiliaries for between twelve and twenty years (see D. J. Breeze, *ANRW* II, 1, 1974, 438-51), for the auxiliary troops in general see D. B. Saddington, 'The Development of the Roman Auxiliary Forces from Augustus to Trajan', *ANRW* II, 3, 1975, 175-201 (and the literature there); id., 'The Roman Auxilia in Tacitus, Josephus and Other Early Imperial Writers', *Acta Classica* 13, 1970, 89-124 and 121f. on Acts 10.1; 27.1. A. N. Sherwin-White, op.cit., 156, 160f., sees Cornelius as 'a provincial, living with his kinsmen' (156). At a later stage the *cohors Italicae* also recruited from *peregrini*, as did the other auxiliary cohorts. All in all we know far too little about military conditions in Palestine to be able to draw any clear conclusions.

112. See the basic study by F. Siegert, 'Gottesfürchtige und Sympathis-anten', *JSJ* 4, 1973, 109-64. Neither the eunuch nor the centurion could become full Jews, above all because of their political and social status.

113. For the forced march of Roman troops with full baggage see J.Kroh-mayer and G. Veith, *Heerwesen und Kriegführung der Griechen und Römer*, HAW, 1928, 423: '45 miles in twenty-eight hours with three hours' rest at night' (Caesar, *De bello gallico*, 7, 40f.). According to Plutarch, *Mark Antony*, 47, 2, on the return from Media, in adverse conditions, the Roman army covered 240 stadia, i.e. about 27 miles, in a night. Josephus bears witness to similar figures for Palestine. According to *Antt.* 15, 293, Sebaste, which was about 42 miles from Jerusalem, could be reached from there in a day. From Sogane (Sichnin) in the northern part of Lower Galilee a large group of travellers could reach Jerusalem itself in just three days. The distance was about 90 miles. Cf. *Vita* 266-70 and C. Möller/G. Schmitt, *Siedlungen* (n. 12), 180f. By contrast we need to be sceptical about the indications of distance in Herodotus, according to which Sinope on the Black Sea, about 360 miles away as the crow flies, could be reached from the hill-country of Cilicia by 'an able-bodied man in five day's journeys'. In 4, 101 he assumes more realistically that a day's march would cover a distance of 200 stadia = about 24 miles (I am grateful to Dr Lichtenberger for these reference to Herodotus).

114. The conjecture by E. Haenchen, *Acts* (n. 34), 346ff., (following F. C. Baur and J. Wellhausen, *Kritische Analyse der Apostelgeschichte*, AAG 15, 2, Berlin 1914, 10: 'unhistorical fudging') that this is a free, didactic composition by Luke misunderstands his way of working, see F. Bovon, *De vocatione Gentium*, Tübingen 1967, 304ff.; id., 'Tradition et redaction en Actes 10, 1-11, 18', *TZ* 26, 1970, 22-45; K. Haacker, 'Dibelius und Cornelius', *BZ* 24, 1980, 234-51; J. Roloff, *Apostelgeschichte* (n. 37), 165f., though he underestimates the distances of marches in antiquity (169).

115. See above, n. 99. Cf. Josephus, *Antt.* 19, 351 on Agrippa I: ἐβασίλευσεν καὶ τὴν Ἰουδαίαν προσέλαβεν Σαμαρείαν τε καὶ Καισάρειαν.

116. For its situation and history see E. Schürer, G. Vermes et al., *History* II (n. 66), 107f.; M. Avi-Yonah, *Land* (n. 91), 100, 106, 111, 144-7, where there is also a description of the city territory. The cities founded by Herod, Caesarea, Sebaste, Gaba Heshbon, all also had a strategic character. There are instances from the Mishnah in B. Z. Segal, *hag-gēʾ'ografya bam-mišnā*, Jerusalem 5739 = 1979, 13f. (in Hebrew): *'yr gbwl*. The strategic significance of the place emerges from *BJ* 2, 513, 554, 443: Vespasian begins the expedition against Judaea in early 68 with a march from Caesarea to Antipatris, where he lets the troops rest for two days. Cf. also C. Möller and G. Schmitt, *Siedlungen* (n. 12), 20 (lit.).

117. M. Hengel, *Zeloten* (n. 66), 211-29. E. Haenchen, *Acts*, 650, as usual mocks the inaccurate ideas Luke has of the geography of Palestine. He fails to understand that Luke wants to use the forced march by this substantial unit to stress Paul's importance. For the marching capacity of Roman armies see n. 113 above.

118. M. Hengel, *Zeloten* (n. 66), 349-61. For the procuratorship of Felix see also E. Schürer, G. Vermes et al., *History* I (n. 66), 460-6. Cf. the reference to the Egyptian (Acts 22.38) and his 4000 sicarii. Apart from Luke, the term σικάριος appears in Greek literature only in Josephus, in his description of conditions in Judaea from Felix to the Jewish War (Masada). This Latin loanword is unknown to all other Greek texts. See M. Hengel, *Zeloten* (n. 67), index of subjects s.v. His usage was evidently connected with the particular situation in Palestine. Therefore we also find it as a rabbinic loanword.

119. M. Hengel, *Zeloten* (n. 66), 289–91, 375f. or the defeat of Cestius see E. Schürer, G. Vermes et al., *History* (n. 66), 487f.; M. Smallwood, *Jews* (n. 94), 297f. For upper and lower Beth-horon see C Möller and G. Schmitt, *Siedlungen* (n. 12), 32f.

120. Justin mentions Simon Magus six times (*Apol.* 26.2 [twice]; 26.4; 56.1, 2; *Dial.* 120.6) and his disciple Menander twice (*Dial.* 100, 4; 106.3). K Beyschlag, *Simon Magus und die christliche Gnosis*, WUNT 16, Tübingen 1974, has clearly demonstrated that one may not simply read later Simonian Gnosticism into Luke's Simon Magus. See also the balanced judgment of R. McL. Wilson, 'Simon and Gnostic Origins', in J. Kremer (ed.), *Les Actes des Apôtres*, BETL 48, Gembloux-Lyons 1979, 485-91.

121. For the Jews and Samaritans as ἔθνος see M. Hengel, *Judaism and Hellenism* I, 20, 24f. (II, 18 n. 156), 28. This designation introduced in the early Hellenistic period lasted on into the Roman period.

122. For the sharp disputes between Jews and Samaritans under the prefects or procurators see Josephus, *Antt.* 18, 30; 20, 118-30 = *BJ* 2, 232-45. Cf. also H. G. Kippenberg, *Garizim* (n. 100), 85-93.

123. Cf. Acts 4.1; 5.17; 23.6ff. For the comparison between Sadducees and Samaritans see Ps. Clem., *Recog.* 1, 54 (ed. Rehm, GCS 51, p. 39); Hippolytus, *Refutatio* 9, 29, 4 (ed. Wendland, GCS 26, p. 262) etc.; see H.G. Kippenberg, *Garizim* (n. 102), 130f., 135.

124. In Acts 26.20, where he makes the Pauline mission follow a scheme similar to Acts 1.8, Samaria can be left out, but not the plerophorous πᾶσάν τε

τὴν χώραν τῆς Ἰουδαίας. According to Paul's biography he puts Damascus at the beginning.

125. Lists of territories in an apparently misleading order are not infrequent, cf. Josephus, *BJ* 1, 302: Idumaea, Galilee, Samaria; 2, 247: Judaea, Samaria, Galilee, Peraea and Trachonitis, Batanaea, Gaulanitis; Polybius 16, 39,1, 3f. = Josephus, *Antt.* 12, 136: Batanaea, Samaria, Abila, Gadara, the Jews in Jerusalem. Eupolemos in Eusebius, *Prep. Ev.* 9, 39, 5 (4F) on Nebuchadnezzar's campaign: and Scythopolis and the Jews settled in Galaditis . . .', similarly 9.30, 5 (2F) the sequence of David's campaigns: the Syrians on the Euphrates, the Commagenes, the Assyrians and the Phoenicians (?) in the Galadene (Gilead), Idumaeans, Ammonites and Moabites, Ituraeans and Nabataeans. Like Josephus, Eupolemus was a member of the Jerusalem priestly aristocracy, see N. Walter, *Fragmente jüdisch-hellenistischer Historiker*, JSHRZ 1, 2, Gütersloh 1976, 95f. These results of random reading could easily be increased, see also above, p. 190 n. 5.

126. Cf., already correctly J. Boehmer, 'Studien zur Geographie Palästinas . . . Samaria Stadt oder Landschaft', ZNW 9, 1908, 216-8. Cf. also B. M. Metzger (ed.), *Commentary* (n. 58), 355 and G. Schneider, *Apostelgeschichte* (n. 38), 482 n. 6.

127. For Sebaste see E. Schürer, G. Vermes et al., *History* (n. 66), 160-4; G. Beer, 'Samaria', in *PW* 2.R., I,2, cols.2102ff.; A. Schalit, *Herodes* (n. 44), 358-65; A. H. M. Jones, *Cities*, 271ff., 274f., 279ff.; M. Avi-Yonah, *Land* (n. 91), 36, 48, 90, 102, 106, 151-3; cf. 153: the map of the city territory in the late Roman period. It will hardly have changed since its foundation. Only the north-west part of the Samaritan area (hardly more than 20%) was part of it.

128. *BJ* 4,449; Pliny the Elder, *Natural History* 5, 14, 69 = M. Stern, *Authors* I (n. 5), 469, 474 no. 204: *intus autem Samariae oppida Neapolis, quod antea Mamortha* (Josephus, *BJ* 4, 449 Μαβαρθά from *ma'bartā*, crossing, ford, pass = the col between Gerizim and Ebal) *dicebatur Sebaste in monte, in altiore Gamala* The last mentioned is a clear mistake: Gamala is to be located in the Gaulanitis, *BJ* 4, 4ff. For Neapolis see E. Schürer, G. Vermes et al., *History* I, (n. 66), 520f.; G. Hölscher, 'Neapolis 19', *PW* XVI, 2, cols.2128ff.

129. M. Avi-Yonah, *Land* (n. 91), 112, 115, 152-154: 'This city obtained the whole area to the Samaritans, as well as the toparchy of Acraba, detached from Judaea by Vespasian. Its northern boundary corresponded to the southern one of Sebaste.'

130. C. Möller-G. Schmitt, *Siedlungen* (n. 12), 164f., count Σαμάρεια as the name of a town even where the territory of Samaria is clearly meant. Josephus has no firm terminology and can use Σαμαρεῖτις (vl. Σαμαρίς) and Σαμάρεια interchangeably. Above all in the late mentions after the founding of Sebaste only the province is meant: thus *BJ* 1, 213, 302, 303, 314; 2, 234, 247; *Vita*, 269; *Antt.* 15, 246: ἐν Σαμαρείᾳ τῇ κληθείσῃ Σεβαστῇ; 292: τρίτον παντὶ τῷ λαῷ τὴν Σαμάρειαν ἐπενόησεν ἐπὶ τείχισμα, καλέσας μὲν αὐτὴν Σεβαστήν; cf.296; 19, 274, 351 see n. 100 above); 20, 118, 129: here Σαμάρεια is confused with Καισαρεία, cf. *BJ* 2, 241. The exception which proves the rule could be *BJ* 2, 69 = *Antt.* 17, 289 on the invasion of Varus in 4 BC: in my view this means the

territory of Samaria *and* the city. Evidently Josephus' source, Nicolaus of Damascus, still follows the old terminology here.

131. Any connection between the cult of Persephone-Kore in Sebaste and the Helen of the Simonians (Justin, *Apol.* 26, 3) is conjured up completely out of thin air. The tradition connects the latter only with Tyre (Irenaeus, *Adv.Haer.* 1, 23, 2). The hypotheses which seek to associate with Helen the statue of Kore found in Samaria, with its torch and the inscription, Εἷς θεὸς ὁ πάντων δεσπότης μεγάλη κόρη ἡ ἀνείκητος (J. W. Crowfoot et al., *Samaria-Sebaste* II, London 1957, 37 no. 12), rest on sheer speculation: thus L. H. Vincent, 'Le culte d'Hélène à Samarie', *RB* 45, 1936, 221-32; D. Flusser, *IEJ* 25, 1975, 13-20; G. Lüdemann, *Untersuchungen zur Simonianischen Gnosis*, Göttingen 1975, 20, is more restrained. The syncretistic cult of Zeus on Mount Gerizim between the time of Antiochus IV, 167 BC, and the erection of a temple to Zeus-Jupiter there under Hadrian, postulated by G. Lüdemann (52ff.), following H. G. Kippenberg, *Garizim* (n. 101), 80ff., 98ff., 345ff., is another figment of the imagination. At that time Neapolis already existed as a Gentile city, and the building of the temple is to be seen as running parallel to Hadrian's religious policy towards the Jews and the founding of Aelia Capitolina; see the judgment of K. Rudolph, *TR* 42, 1977, 350: 'The return to seeing a syncretistic cult as the earliest foundation of Simonianism does not take us any further, but entangles us even more in the jungle of assumptions and hypotheses which already surrounds the prehistory of this sect.'

132. In addition to the investigation by K. Beyschlag, *Simon Magus* (n. 116), see R. Bergmeier, 'Quellen vorchristlicher Gnosis', in *Tradition und Glaube, Festschrift K. G. Kuhn*, Göttingen 1971, 200-20, esp.205ff.

133. 8.5-8, 12 and 13-18 give an excellent context. I regard the remark by the former Gentile Justin from Neapolis, *Apol.* 26.3, that 'almost all Samaritans confess Simon as that God' as excessive exaggeration; possibly Justin confused Simon with the Samaritan eschatological prophet Dositheus, who was also active in the first century, probably before Simon, and for a long time won considerably more support in Samaria. See what is now the basic study by S. J. Isser, *The Dositheans. A Samaritan Sect in Late Antiquity*, Leiden 1976. For Caesarea as the location of the dispute with Simon see already E. Preuschen, *Die Apostelgeschichte*, Tübingen 1912, with reference to the Pseudo-Clementines, '. . . that the source meant the city of Caesarea Pal., with which both Simon and Philip had contacts'.

134. J. Wellhausen, *Apostelgeschichte* (n. 114), 14; cf. J. Boehmer, *Studien* (n. 126), 218; E. Meyer, *Ursprung* III (n. 69), 277; T. Zahn, *Forschungen* (n. 58), 273; A. Wikenhauser, *Die Apostelgeschichte*, RNT 5, Regensburg ⁴1961; with some hesitation G. Stählin, *Die Apostelgeschichte*, NTD 5, Göttingen ¹⁰1962, 252. Against this H. H. Wendt, *Die Apostelgeschichte*, KEK III, Göttingen ⁵1913, 154: 'This can only be the capital of the country, old Samaria, which Herod called Sebaste'; similarly H. Conzelmann, *Apostelgeschichte*, n. 34, 60, on v.5: 'Luke thinks that the district of Samaria has only one polis (of the same name).' However, in connection with v.8 he adds: Luke of course thinks of Samaritans in the ethnic and religious sense . . .; he also makes Simon one, hardly rightly. There is no trace of the Hellenistic character of the capital

Samaria/Sebaste.' One can fully agree with the latter, but that also makes this interpretation of v.5 questionable. In the two most recent commentaries, J. Roloff, *Apostelgeschichte* (n. 37), 133, leans towards Shechem; G. Schneider, *Apostelgeschichte* I (n. 38), 487, leaves the problem open: 'It is impossible to decide with any certainty whether Luke here is thinking of Shechem or (rather) of the Hellenistic city Samaria/Sebaste.' See now also R. J. Coggins, 'The Samaritans in Acts', *NTS* 28, 1982, (423-33) 429f. The historical dubiety of these false alternatives has so far not been recognized.

135. Josephus mentions Shechem (Σικιμα) only up to the Hasmonaean period, see C. Möller and G. Schmitt, *Siedlungen* (n. 12), 173; cf. *BJ* 1, 63, 92; *Antt* 13, 255f., 377. Cf. G. E. Wright, *Shechem. The Biography of a City*, London 1965, 172, 183f.; H. G. Kippenberg, *Garizim* (n. 101), 85ff. Possibly the place was only finally destroyed after the subjection of the Samaritans in connection with the conquest of the Macedonian colony of Samaria in 109 BC. The mention of the place as an assembly point for rebel Jews and Demetrius Eukairos who was allied with them in the fight against Alexander Jannaeus in *BJ* 1, 63; *Antt.* 13, 377 does not tell against the fact of the destruction. The ruins could be meant here. The col was a highly significant strategic position. At the latest towards the end of the second century BC Shechem disappears from history as an inhabited place. Eusebius, *Onomastikon* (ed. E.Klostermann, GCS 11, 1, p. 150,1) describes it as: Συχὲμ ἡ καὶ Σίκιμα . . . πόλις Ἰακὼβ νῦν ἔρημος.

136. Apart from John 4.5, the pilgrim of Bordeaux, H. Donner, *Pilger* (n. 54), 52f.; Sechar = P. Geyer, *Itinera Hierosolymitana Saec. 4-8*, CSEL 39, Vienna 1898, 20; Eusebius, *Onomastikon* (n. 135), 164,1: πρὸ τῆς Νέας πόλεως πλησίον τοῦ χωρίου οὗ ἔδωκεν Ἰακὼβ τῷ υἱῷ αὐτοῦ. For the rabbinic mentions see P. Billerbeck, *Kommentar* II (n. 19), 431; B. Z. Segal, *hag-gēʾōgrafyā*, (n. 114), 138f. I am grateful to my colleague G. Schmitt for further references: M. Menahot 10, 2: *mibbiqʿat ʿēn sōker*, the omer sheaf 'from the plain of 'ἐν σōκερ', and jSheq 5, 148d, 25; Men 64b; Sota 49b. In the context of the haggadah on Jacob's struggles with the Shechemites the place appears in Yalq. Shim.Bereshit. para. 135, line 4, ed. J. Schiloni, II, Jerusalem 1973, 693: *mahanē šehīr*; cf. also para 134 lines 76f. (p.692): *šehīr mēlēk mahānē*, and in addition already Jubilees 34.4: the king of Maanisakir. On this see K. Berger, *Das Buch der Jubiläen*, JSHRZ II, 3, Gütersloh 1981, 492 n. 12. Thus the tradition of the place goes back to pre-Christian times. For the Samaritan accounts see H. G. Kippenberg, *Garizim* (n. 101), 164 from the *Tolida*: (the district of) Sychar up to Tiberias. According to the Chronicles of Abul Fath (ed. E. Vilmar, Gotha 1865, 151ff.), translated in S. J. Isser, *Dositheans* (n. 133), 77, Dusis (Dositheos) came to a wise teacher in Askar (Sychar). Cf. also G. Dalman, *Orte* (n. 48), 226f.; C. Kopp, *Stätten* (n. 50), 197-211; H. M. Schenke, 'Jakobsbrunnen–Josefsgrab–Sychar. Topographische Untersuchungen und Erwägungen in der Perspektive von Joh. 4.5, 6', *ZDPV* 84, 1968, 159-84: 'Sychar/Askar must have been quite a large and significant place in Roman times, . . . before the foundation of Neapolis in AD 72: unfortified and therefore laid out on broad lines, in size presumably greater than Shechem, which had been a fortified town' (182).

137. Report by E. Damati, *IEJ* 22, 1972, 174, plates 35B/36, a mausoleum

with a Greek inscription in Askar: 'It appears that this mausoleum belonged to a wealthy Samaritan family residing in Neapolis at the end of the 2nd or the beginning of the 3rd century A.D.' The question is whether the owners of the tomb really lived in Neapolis, about two miles away, and are not rather to be located in Sychar/Askar itself. Neapolis, which was at first Gentile, only appears later as a religious centre of the Samaritans, see the Samaritan synagogue in Thessalonica: B. Lifshitz and J. Schiby, 'Une synagogue samaritaine à Thessalonique',*RB* 75, 1968, 368-78, with the wish: Αὔξι Νεάπολις μετὰ τῶν φιλούντων [αὐτούς or αὐτήν . . .].

138. See the Samaritan eschatological prophet in AD 36, *Antt.* 18, 85-89, who invites the Samaritans to go with him to Gerizim.

139. K. Lake and H. J. Cadbury, *The Beginnings of Christianity* IV, London 1933, 89, ad loc.: '. . . it is tempting to guess that it was Gitta'; I.H.Marshall, *The Acts of the Apostles*, Leicester 1980, 154 n. 1, lists the three possibilities: 'Sebaste . . . Shechem or possibly Gitta'.

140. Justin, *Apol.* 26. 2: ἀπὸ κώμης λεγομένης Γίτθων; Ps. Clem. Hom. 2, 22, 2 (GCS 42, ed. Rehm, p. 44) Σαμαρεὺς τὸ ἔθνος ἀπὸ Γετθῶν κώμης, τῆς πόλεως (Caesarea) ἀεχούσης σχοίνους ἕξ (= about 36 miles, though the detail about distance is useless); cf. Ps. Clem. Rec. (GCS, ed. Rehm, p. 55): *ex vico Getthonum*.

141. *Kleine Schriften* II, Munich ²1959, 200 n. 2 = *BHHW* IV, 207: Ġett (map D 6); T. Zahn, *Apostelgeschichte* I (n. 58), 273, on the other hand conjectures the *Qaryet Ġīt* six miles west of Nablus = *BHHW* IV, 207 Gitta? (map D 7). According to A. Alt, Kappareitaia, according to Justin, *Apol.* 26.2, *the home* of Simon's disciple Menander should be located in the coastal plain = *Ḥirbet Kafr Ḥatta*, about two miles north-east of Antipatris, *BHHW* IV, 231 (map C 7).

142. O. Bauernfeind, *Kommentar* (n. 33), 122, assumes that the pre-Lucan tradition already abandoned geographical accuracy because of the 'resonance of the words' in Matt. 10.5, and that Luke 'did not obliterate what was probably a well established peculiarity' (125).

143. II Kings 17.24, 26; 23.19. But cf. Isa. 36.19. I cannot find any corresponding formulation even in Josephus.

144. J. Jeremias, Σαμάρεια, *TDNT* 7, 92 n. 29.

145. H. Conzelmann, *Theology of St Luke* (n. 2), 70.

146. Cf. A von Harnack, *Beiträge* (n. 98), 70: 'We may therefore assume that while Luke trod the soil of Palestine and Jerusalem with the apostle, he left it very soon afterwards. Accordingly we expect that he will certainly show himself familiar with the country and the city to the degree that a traveller might be after a short stay. This is confirmed by his account.' Cf. above n. 11 and Philo's one visit to Jerusalem.

147. Josephus, *Antt.* 20, 199-203. For the community in Jerusalem this must have been the most serious catastrophe in their history so far. Jewish Christianity never recovered from the blow.

148. A comparison with other ancient accounts of sea voyages and the geographical and nautical details shows that despite all the miraculous features this is no romantic fiction. The dedication to Theophilus and the use of the first person singular and plural in Luke 1.1-4; Acts 1.1; 16.10ff. and

from Acts 20.6 onwards give the two volume work its literary consistency, i.e. its framework. Theophilus was certainly a historical personality and not a fictitious figure, though his name could be a pseudonym. He must have known the author, who sometimes writes in the first person. If he published the work, he might in the last resort be responsible for the κατὰ Λουκᾶν of the Gospel. Thus the work was in all probability written by an 'eyewitness' of the second, 'post-apostolic' generation and a companion of Paul's on his later journeys. All attempts to explain the traditional name of the author, Luke, as a secondary addition, remain incredible speculation.

Index of Biblical References

Made in the USA
Middletown, DE
03 December 2015